Further praise for *Darkness Was My Candle*

"As a sexual abuse survivor, I long for authentic tales of the human experience to help me reassemble the pieces of my life in a way that creates meaning for it. Lora's story, *Darkness Was My Candle*, encompasses the disturbing and haunting reality of our humanity along with astonishing moments of beauty and exquisite tenderness that buoy our capacity to heal. She illuminates a spiritual path forward beyond traditional therapy that eases my soul-shaking traumas and offers an invitation for all of us to examine one of the greatest struggles of our lives: Will we and our collective energies remain incomplete or courageously step into wholeness, for ourselves and one another?"
Sheila Bauer, M.Ed., Parent & Family Educator, Faculty with The Center for Mind-Body Medicine

"To read *Darkness Was My Candle* is to experience a deep and profound healing. Lora DeVore's memoir has a revolutionary premise: spirituality and compassion may blossom from the basest of soils, may arise from abuse and trauma. As Lora takes us on an intimate journey from trauma to transcendence, the impact of her story has the power to evolve us. Her life experience encompasses post-traumatic stress from sexual abuse and medical torture, as well as the tortuous withdrawal from enforced medication within a psychiatric hospital. This book also explores our collective systems and their history through the personal lens of one who has endured horrendous systemic abuse – from psychiatric and medical, to military, as well as religious violation. Lora DeVore skillfully weaves together her memoir – a healing journey that embraces dreamwork, visionary experience, and a Kundalini energetic awakening. Trace the development of spiritual embodiment through the process of healing fractured and dissociated selves. This author is someone who truly embodies the soul of the world."
Janet Elizabeth Colli, author of *The Dark Face of Heaven*

"*Darkness Was My Candle* is a must-read for anyone that is interested in transforming hardship into personal growth. The life story of Lora Devore, a gifted mind/body/spirit guide, is both heartbreaking and inspirational. The lessons learned through her suffering easily apply to all that want to add meaning and purpose to their lives."
Joel M. Evans, M.D., Director, The Center for Functional Medicine

"Struck by Lora's deep empathy, I once remarked to her, 'you must have had a mother who loved you a great deal'. Little did I know that Lora had been birthed to a mother incapable of parenting but had found mothering and mentoring throughout her life in ways that reflect both grace and self-efficacy.

Lora's story is one of almost unimaginable trauma, abiding memory, and the triumph of the human spirit. It is a true 'hero's journey'. Told with intelligence and with the intent to teach, it shows us how hope can be kept alive by simple acts of kindness by ordinary people, how easy it is to fail the most vulnerable young people in our midst, and how presence and compassion can change the course of a life. *Darkness Was My Candle* deserves to become a classic in the literature of trauma and healing. It should be required reading for all students and practitioners of the healing arts as well as for educators, who have more power to transform young lives than they may realize."
Penny George, PsyD, Chair of the Board, George Family Foundation

"*Darkness Was My Candle* is a story of horror and hope, a searing indictment of individual and institutional cruelty, and a soaring celebration of our human capacity to find light in the darkest places and saving grace in small kindnesses. Lora DeVore shows us how a terribly exploited, fearfully isolated, wounded child can learn to trust her own inner wisdom and grow into a deeply compassionate woman who brings hard-won understanding and skilful healing to others. She inspires each of us to look within the darkness of our own life's traumas for the warmth and light of transformation. Lora DeVore is a wonder, and so is *Darkness Was My Candle*."

James S. Gordon, M.D., author of *Transforming Trauma: The Path to Hope and Healing* and founder of The Center For Mind-Body Medicine

"The integrative and multi-disciplinary approach to the inner psycho-spiritual work that Lora describes in *Darkness Was My Candle* is a blueprint for a new humanity that comes about through the pioneers on the frontiers of consciousness suffering deeply, and daring to brave new inner vistas and possibilities for the human race.

This book is a testimony to the grace, devotion, hard work and vision she has had to share her process with the rest of humanity. She describes the labor and birthing of this new Self out of the degradation and misery of suffering, in a way that inspires us all to continue to search and devote our lives to the inner path. The great turning and transition from an externally focused life, to an inner life of integration of all aspects of our being is described. It is the great turning and shift that is required of us all if the planet is to heal, and humanity is to redeem itself so that true and lasting change can happen on this planet. The failure of every system in her life is well documented, and impeccably researched. Her capacity to find a way through the horrors of the systems in place to 'help,' is the map we all need to aspire to.

She introduces us to a community/communion of 'saints' in her life, angels in situations of hell – but they could not do anything unless she had wanted to become one herself. By her account she used every scrap of care that came her way, from every walk of life, every discipline, every opportunity, to learn to relate to herself in a loving, reverential, dignified, and integrated way. And so, through this inspiring account, we are all called to the inner path as well."

Lyndall Johnson M.A., L.P., President, Aslan Institute, Executive Director, Sacred Service at Aslan Institute

"From the first shocking pages to the last inspiring ones, Lora shares the unvarnished truth of her life that began with betrayals, first by a deeply disturbed mother, followed by a cruel and sick therapist and later by the courts and a state hospital. She shares her inner responses to all that happened and we feel her helplessness and vulnerability.

This is also a story of the longing for life that was kept alive like a sacred flame inside her that flickered, but never went out, even in the most devastating circumstances. She tells of the light that can appear for a day, or a few weeks, in the deepest darkness as she weaves into her story the synchronistic appearances of 'human angels' that appeared, sometimes as a neighbor, a nun and even a woman on a snowy street corner who turned out to be a famous artist.

Readers also have the benefit of a skilled writer and natural storyteller who has the perspective and insights of the wise woman who is now a skilled psychotherapist and teacher to others. Even though every aspect of this page-turner is a true saga, it reads like the best of a fictional page-turner. She shows us how the heroine – herself – not only survives multiple terrors of darkness, but conquers them through the alchemy of spiritual and psychological transformation. This is a timely book, a cautionary tale. In this era of secrets and abuses, systemic injustices are surfacing. Through Lora's courageous testimony, she invites us to look with clear eyes and awareness at what can happen in any system, including those designed to help, if we look away, refuse to listen or require accountability.

This book belongs in the libraries and teaching labs for all people who desire to live and serve consciously. It certainly should be required reading for doctors, therapists, ministers, lawyers , judges, social workers, prison personnel, teachers and volunteers in human service. I will be proudly and gratefully recommending this book to clients, workshop attendees and friends."
Gloria D. Karpinski, holistic counselor, spiritual director, teacher and author of *Barefoot on Holy Ground* **and** *Where Two Worlds Touch*

"*Darkness Was My Candle: An Odyssey of Survival and Grace* is a work of the divine which guides us through the tenacity of the human spirit to endure the unspeakable, the untenable and emerge with the light that had fallen and has now been resurrected and restored back to its original brilliance. In this expedition of the heart and spirit, Lora gives voice to the many dark hallways of the soul, the raw honesty of experiences that left her reeling from betrayal and abuse in all its unforgiving forms. We watch the metamorphosis take place that will transform her from the inside out and the powerful recognition of being 'beloved' when she discovers that she was never alone and her sharing that neither are we. Her journey to becoming an unwitting Sage has come full circle and as a result of this work, she has created a reverberation of hope for all those who sit in hopelessness and despair, those who have lost their voice and those who think there is no way to heal from the damage done to them over their lifetime. Those who read this work, will truly be forever changed."
Dr. Rita Anita Linger, PhD, CPC, CMBP

"In captivating and lyrical prose, this is a story of one individual's fortitude and determination, showing the luminosity of the human spirit to survive, and ultimately to prevail. *Darkness Was My Candle: An Odyssey of Survival and Grace* depicts the challenges in the life of an unloved and profoundly abused child. It reveals how hope and healing can be ignited through the caring acts of others as we traverse the depths of life's pain and disillusionment, to discover the power of love to ignite, evolve, and transform us. Lora DeVore speaks for those with no voice and illuminates the shortcomings of some of our medical systems today. She invites us to envision a more loving way of bringing healing to the world. The time is ripe for this message. We are called to become conscious of a deeper, more awakened version of ourselves, and in an unprecedented way, express ourselves as profoundly and soulfully empowered."
Dr. Sue Morter, author of the National Bestseller *The Energy Codes: The 7-Step System to Awaken Your Spirit, Heal Your Body and Live Your Best Life*

"This book is an exquisitely authentic account of Lora's life journey filled with powerful stories of trauma, healing, and transformation. Lora's writing mirrors her courage to not just survive, but to embody a wise, creative and empowered voice. In a humble yet captivating way, Lora models the potential that each of us carries to heal. As a fellow

trauma survivor and psychiatrist with a focus on integrative approaches to mental health, I recommend this memoir to both mental health professionals and anyone searching for hope, healing, and meaning."
Noshene Ranjibar, M.D., Medical Director, Integrative Psychiatry Clinic, University of Arizona College of Medicine

"*Darkness Was My Candle: An Odyssey of Survival and Grace* tells the captivating story of how one woman, despite a devastating and exploitive childhood, used her tenacity and brilliance to not only survive, but to thrive. At times searing and raw, Lora DeVore's story reveals the transformative power of others' care and love, as well as the capacity of the human spirit to endure the unspeakable and to emerge whole. Lora calls into account the institutions that fail us and offers us a vision of a more conscious way to bring healing to the world. This is a perfect book for these challenging times, as it encourages us to move beyond old boundaries and see ourselves and all of life in a fresh, new way."
Marci Shimoff, New York Times #1 bestselling author of *Happy for No Reason* and *Chicken Soup for the Woman's Soul*

"*Darkness Was My Candle* by Lora Devore is a riveting, can't-put-down read, sensitively detailing the author's harrowing and dark life experiences, starting at birth and extending well into adulthood. Unlike many individuals who suffer these intolerable, shaming, and life-threatening circumstances, Lora managed, over and over, to grasp the slender lifelines offered her. She learned and searched and, eventually, turned her knowledge and understanding into a vocation of healing and helping others. From the bleak cauldron of her life emerged a magnificent therapist and healer, who shines a brilliant beacon of hope to the literally thousands of lives she lifts up. Don't miss this rare, astounding book."
Jan Thatcher Adams, M.D.

"If you want to explore the darkest realms of human suffering and the potential of survival of unimaginable atrocities, this breathtaking journey into the abyss of trauma is a must-read. The author takes us on an excruciating process of excavation to retrieve her wounded soul from the hell of familial, systemic, and institutional violence. Illuminated most poetically with quotes from the wisdom traditions, is a healing path through a threatening perilous world of utter darkness to love, spiritual awakening, luminosity, and transcendence. Far from narrating only her personal history of abuse and exploitation, she reveals also the shocking collective shadow in psychiatric institutions, pharmaceutical companies and the therapeutic profession. I highly recommend this memoir of a transformative individuation process of dying and becoming."
Ursula Wirtz, Ph.D., author of *Trauma and Beyond: The Mystery of Transformation*

DARKNESS WAS MY CANDLE

David
Ava, Sophia
Gabriel and Morgan
You inspire me and light up my world.
And may you discover that:

Only full, overhead sun
diminishes your shadow.

But that shadow has been serving you.
What hurts you blesses you.
Darkness is your candle.
Your boundaries are your quest.

DARKNESS WAS MY CANDLE

AN ODYSSEY OF
SURVIVAL AND GRACE

Lora DeVore

First published in the United States of America, 2022
by CONFER US LLC, 1934 Hennepin Av, Ste. 201, Minneapolis, MN 66416, USA

Subsequently published in the United Kingdom and rest of world by Confer Ltd
Registered office: Brody House, Strype Street, London E1 7LQ, UK
www.confer.uk.com

A catalogue record for this book is available from the Library of Congress.

ISBN: 978-1-913494-49-0 (Paperback)
ISBN: 978-1-913494-50-6 (eBook)

Typeset by Bespoke Publishing Ltd, UK.
Printed and bound in the United States of America

CONFER US LLC is committed to using paper from a sustainable source

To find out more about our authors, speakers, books and events visit www.confer.uk.com
To find out more about Lora DeVore visit www.loradevore.com

Contents

Contents

Acknowledgments

The birth of this book is owed to a wide community of individuals. Had it not been for Deena Metzger's keen insight and understanding of dreams and patterns, and her persistence and belief in me, this book would not be what you hold in your hands today. Deena has been midwife and godmother, gently pushing and prodding me when I thought my skills insufficient to the task of this labor. Always calm but insistent that I could write this, gentle, yet firm – exactly what I've needed. Much gratitude to the women and men from the Topanga Writing Intensives and ReVisioning Medicine, for your encouragement and support.

Next, a very special thank-you to Anne Marie Wirth Cauchon for her tireless help at every step of the way and for helping me to deepen my understanding of the craft and art of writing: gratitude especially for being there and gently nudging me along to finish what I had started while recovering from Covid-19.

I am profoundly grateful to Dr. Stephen Setterberg, for his faith and support in the birthing of this book. His insights, feedback, and belief that the book would be valuable and have the potential to be of service to both professionals and the general public have been invaluable. I'm also very thankful for the support of the CEO, Todd Archbold, and the staff of PrairieCare: your interest and encouragement have been amazing.

Deep gratitude goes to the staff at Confer Books: Christina Wipf Perry, Publishing Director, Jane Ryan, Founder and Creative Director, Stephen Setterberg, Director & Publisher, Liz Wilson, Managing Editor, Emily Wootton, Publishing Assistant, Viv Church, Line Editor – and a very special thanks to Stephen Taylor of Heat Design for the cover. A special thank-you to Orlando Vincent Truter, graphic designer, for his amazing logo design and collaboration on the book cover. Also, a very special thank-you to Sandra Julian, one of my dearest friends, a woman of many talents, for the time, energy, and amazing professional photos, and other sources of help too numerous to mention.

In addition, it is important that I express my sincere gratitude to Dr. Sydney Krampitz for her truthfulness and help with research, and our visit to Elgin State Hospital in the spring of 2017. A very special thank-you to William (Bill) Briska for meeting with us, for his kindness, showing us around, and taking us to Elgin's cemetery.

Much love and gratitude to so many of you who I know through workshops, training, small groups, leadership development, and keynote talks. And to Dr. James Gordon and fellow colleagues through the Center for Mind–Body Medicine, who again and again, after hearing just a small snippet of my history, said: "You have to write a book." Your encouragement over these many years has been invaluable and created a tidal wave – I could no longer refuse.

Also, huge appreciation for each of you who is named in this book for all of your care and support through the years and allowing me to write about you. And for those human angels, such as Dale, Diane, Sister Sebastian, Dr. Callahan, Lee Godie, and so many more who have passed away, I hope their spirit knows, in the great beyond, that they not only helped me along the way, but also changed the course of my life. Gratitude to Kapra Fleming, filmmaker, who supported and validated my recollections of Lee Godie, and asked to film so that I could make a small contribution to Lee's legacy.

I would particularly like to express my love and sincere gratitude to my son, David, who provided enormous encouragement and support for this book. Much love and gratitude to my many friends who have supported me over the years. You know who you are and how grateful I am for each and every one of you. You each bring a richness and color to my life that is extraordinary. For those of you who have been beta-readers, your commitment to this book and feedback has been invaluable! Thank-you from the bottom of my heart. For each of you who showed up so fully to care for me, bring me food, take me to appointments and so much more when I came home from the hospital after Covid, you've taught me what it's really like to feel a part of a community and to be loved and cared for so fully – I could burst.

Special gratitude goes to Suzanne K. and the Catalyst Initiative, Dr. D. Jan, and all the young people they touch every single day through the Irreducible Grace Foundation, oh my – I know you learned from me – but I have equally learned and grown every single time that I have been with you. You've called out the best, bravest and most authentic in me – I will never be the same. You give me hope for the world as you take your own courage, grit, and grace out into the world to pay it forward. I'm so proud to have played a small part in your growth and evolution.

Much love and gratitude to my coach AlexSandra Leslie for all that you are, for fully seeing me, and all the ways in which you have inspired me – I will never be the same. Also, love and gratitude to Dr. Lorri Beaver-Mandekic. You have believed in me, helped to clear what was no longer needed, and made room for me to shine. And to Suzanne Lawlor, thank-you for your support, presence, and words of encouragement, and the many ways in which you have shown your support.

Lora DeVore, November 2021

EPIGRAPH CREDITS AND ACKNOWLEDGMENTS

The epigraph for Chapter 2, is reprinted by the permission of Russell & Volkening as agents for The Welty LLC. Copyright © 1971 by Eudora Welty.

The epigraph at the beginning of Chapter 3 is from 'Perspectives' by Nikita Gill © Nikita Gill.

The epigraph at the beginning of Chapter 5 is printed with permission from Many Rivers Press, www.davidwhyte.com. David Whyte, No One Told Me, *Fire in the Earth*, © Many Rivers Press, Langley, WA, USA.

The epigraph for Chapter 10 is reprinted by permission © Hay House, Inc., Carlsbad, CA for Agapi Stassinopoulos, *Unbinding the Heart* (2013).

The epigraph for Chapter 14: Reprinted by permission of HarperCollins Publishers Ltd © 1954, J. R. R. Tolkien.

In the UK, the epigraphs for Chapter 19 and Chapter 22 are reproduced from *Four Quartets* by T.S. Eliot, with permission from Faber and Faber Ltd. In the USA, the excerpts from "Little Gidding" from FOUR QUARTETS by T.S. Eliot. Copyright © 1942 by T.S. Eliot, renewed 1970 by Esme Valerie Eliot. Reprinted by permission of Mariner Books, an imprint of HarperCollins Publishers.

The epigraph at the beginning of Chapter 28 is reproduced with permission from the Foundation of Pablo Neruda. "Si cada dia cae", EL MARY LAS CAMPANAS © Pablo Neruda, 1973 and Fundación Pablo Neruda. Pablo Neruda, "If each day falls" from *The Sea and the Bells*, translated by William O'Daly. Copyright © 1973 by Pablo Neruda and the Heirs of Pablo Neruda. English translation copyright © 1988, 2002 by William O'Daly. Reprinted with the permission of The Permissions Company, LLC on behalf of Copper Canyon Press.

Forgetting our pivotal experiences of the numinous that mark our lives or worse, perjuring them by acting as if they make no difference, exposes us to the risk of insanity. Encounters with the Holy are like flames. They must be shared, to keep the light alive, or they will burn us up or burn us out. The spiritual life is one of increased alertness, of keen watchfulness of what goes on between this mysterious Thee and me. Sharing with the community the secret numinous experience helps us to digest whatever the experience represents, gives us the meaning of the fire that inflames life itself.

Dr. Ann Belford Ulanov, *Spirit in Jung*
Einsiedeln: Daimon Verlag

Introduction

War is the father of all things

Heraclitus, On the Universe, Fragments 44

War never occurs in just one place, one life, one family. It moves through the chambers of the heart, the underground trenches of the belly, the rivers of blood. It slowly and invisibly whittles away at the immune system and memory, impacting every aspect of a society and all we hold dear. The loss of human life, the loss of the land itself, including the plants and animals that inhabit it, each of the multitude of visible and invisible wounds turns out to be catastrophic. Sexual violence, trafficking, and prostitution increase during and following war due to the breakdown of values and the long-held belief that men need to be sexually serviced during times of war. This belief goes back to the Civil War in the United States and perhaps even further back in history.

I witnessed this breakdown first-hand as I was forced to watch my mother as she worked the strip, picking up men in uniform. Night after endless night. As a child, I observed bar-room brawls, the exchange of drugs, and the lure of scantily dressed women, colored in neon lights, outside the gates of local military bases. My mother appeared to be fighting her own war, using the art of seduction as a weapon, weakening men in order to conquer them.

Those who witness and participate in death, destruction, and torture return home with hyper-aroused nervous systems set on high alert, often resulting in an increase in suicide, domestic violence, alcohol use, and drug abuse. The effects of war are then passed down to subsequent generations, as they were in my family.

There are many forms of war. We have become a society that has

1

embedded war thinking and trauma so deeply within our culture that we don't recognize that it impacts our daily lives. As a mental health professional, I have daily encountered the effects of violence, fear, power, greed; I witness the exploitation of individuals alone and within families, neighborhoods, institutions, and across invisible lines of color, culture, religion, gender, and socio-economic status.

Another form of war is that which traumatized individuals declare on themselves. Not only did my dysregulated nervous system war with other parts of my brain for dominance but for years this form of warfare showed up in my life as constant self-criticism. I became the enemy, throwing words of self-contempt into my already battered psyche— like hand grenades—as I repeated the hateful and shaming, degrading messages that were being hurled at me. Adding to my arsenal of poor self-esteem were the secrets, too heavy for any child to carry. Shame became debilitating, creating invisible walls of separation between me and others. Isolation followed me into young adulthood.

We have implanted war thinking and language into the systems that claim to promote healing. We declare war on cancer, drugs, immigration, poverty, obesity, mental illness, terrorism, crime, and more. We are constantly engaged in the war of words, such as in politics with winning battleground states. The language of war is exciting for many and seems to create a desire for more war. There are endless wars we don't even begin to understand.

In a shameful and dark time in US history, this country declared war on its people, by subscribing to eugenics, judging who was valuable and who was not, and seeking to eliminate the latter. The eugenics movement took root in the United States in the early 1900s. Eugenics is "the science of improving a human population by controlled breeding to increase the occurrence of desirable traits." The US eugenics movement focused on what came to be known as "degeneracy" and the continuing decline of the "human stock." Eugenics thinking extended its reach to psychiatric care and impacted me and so many others who were made research subjects without consent on behalf of the government and pharmaceutical companies during the cold war.

Several years ago, while conducting research for my writing mentor, Deena Metzger—I was preparing for a trip I would accompany her on to conduct interviews and research for a book she was writing—I stumbled upon references to experimentation in Illinois, a place that had once held great pain for me. It reflected a time I hadn't ever intended to revisit. Seeing the words Elgin State Hospital on a computer screen in front of me awakened unbearable memories. It was not that I had ever repressed those memories, but my life had changed so much I believed they were no longer of influence or importance. Until that moment, I was unaware that I still carried the stigma of having been committed to a state hospital. Although I had begun to write this book, this portion of my life was not anything I ever intended to write about.

Few people knew anything about that time in my life. Although I had worked through those memories, psychologically, I was not aware of these larger aspects of my own and our national history. State hospital patients throughout the United States were easily available as research subjects, routinely and strategically abused and neglected, often resulting in premature death. I had my own painful memories of abuse and being given a great number of drugs, and suffering procedures against my will. Now, I reluctantly wondered whether I had been one of those patients experimented on in the 1960s.

Since then, I've come to understand that mental patients, prisoners, institutionalized children, African–Americans, Native Americans, newborn healthy infants, our own military, and cities at large were all used as unsuspecting research subjects. In reviewing declassified records, I discovered that those who were used in this way were labeled as "less desirables." I eventually came to learn that I was one of these subjects. The influence of the eugenics movement can be seen in the history of that research and is embedded in the history of psychiatric care. Declassified documents reveal that the United States, in the guise of national security, justified conducting research without informed consent on me and thousands of others because we were seen as less important, albeit American citizens.

A legacy of fear, poverty, and war was woven into my DNA, moving through my bloodstream while still in my mother's womb. My family's history followed me with toxic tentacles of ruin and destruction for years, into every interaction with my shell-shocked uncle who brought the Second World War home with him, my ravaged mother and her subsequent life of prostitution—leaving us both extremely vulnerable. Emotionally and physically malnourished, I was an easy prey to other children's taunts, predatory individuals, and eventually corrupt practices of medical research conducted on me, just one member of many defenseless populations.

Throughout elementary school in the 1950s, I joined classmates in air-raid drills, hiding under our desks, instructed to "duck and cover" as an imaginary enemy dropped bombs. Our developing nervous systems ramped up in terror as we were schooled in hate and fear.

We cannot deny the history of our country. All of it, even the lesser-known parts, is woven into our country's DNA and nervous system, lingering in our lakes, rivers, and streams poisoned from the toxic waste dumped by pharmaceutical companies that benefit from such research, in our dying wildlife, and in the changing weather patterns. Ongoing news tells us of continuing ethical violations by psychology, medicine, pharmaceutical companies, corporations, and politicians. Everything hidden and criminal in our common lives is rising to the surface to be looked at on the collective level and the personal.

Discovering the social, political, and historic factors that had tormented me as a child forced me to yet another review of my personal life. Just as the dark was such a revelation, so it turned out was the constant coexistence of light. The life I finally created, the life I am living, did not come out of the blue. Potential seeds of transformation were buried deep within me from birth perhaps, as visible and invisible as were the unimaginable horrors. While surviving the impossible, I also drank from the wellspring of dreams and visions, where soul survival and thriving is watered. I've come to understand my life as a weaving of dark and light. For years, I searched to make meaning of my life and reached out to a transcendent God. In reviewing my life, I find signs everywhere. In addition to that transcendent presence, I discovered the immanent indwelling nature of the creator within myself where deep and sustained healing could take place.

This felt sense of luminosity and transcendence has come to me intermittently since childhood. This mystery has appeared throughout my life in synchronistic events. It has shown up in unexpected ways I identify as angels wearing flesh and a human face, carrying the medicinal quality of compassion and love. By their unexpected presence, they assisted in my survival and ultimate healing.

Somehow, I was sustained always through music, beautiful churches, sacred scriptures, and poetry. The rituals and ceremonies of many religious traditions and forms of meditation and prayer have fed my soul. The natural world, in the voices of trees, animals, birds, insects, and the beauty of flowers, has been a source of inspiration and peace.

Spirit has come to me over the years, in a quiet but undeniable inner voice of guidance, and consistently in the language of dreams. Luminous Presence continues to offer moments of reflection as it moves behind all things, which it did as I was writing this book—some of these unexpected moments are found in the sections titled The Web of Life.

Fifty years later, with an advanced degree in clinical psychology, a long history as a successful mental health professional, recognized as a national leader in training others in the field, and a sought-after public speaker, I was compelled to return to Illinois to revisit the site of where I was once kept in inhumane, degrading, and life-threatening circumstances. In this book, I trace my life backward and forward, seeking a resolution to unanswered questions. Having experienced such horrifying and traumatic events, how did I survive? And to what purpose?

As I've written this book and revisited my history, examined archival documents, and conducted other research, I've come to understand my past as a reflection of a much larger story. History reveals what needs to be known so that we learn even from the grievous mistakes of the past, even those we don't want to acknowledge. It is my hope that as you read this book, you will learn from my story and discover insight into your own stories, and learn some lesser-known facts about our collective history. Change begins with awareness. This is not the only time that humanity has been at a crossroads. We must each ask ourselves what is ours to do during this time. This book is my offering of radical honesty as I faced my past and learned about our collective history. It is also an offering of hope and transformation.

1.

The Smell of Suffering

Patients in the 10 psychiatric hospitals run by the State of Illinois encounter conditions so filthy, harsh, and unsafe that they sometimes lie in their own excrement, are tied down for hours at a time, or become victims of physical assault, a court-ordered study of the system has found.

Court-Ordered Study Condemns Illinois Psychiatric Hospitals,
New York Times, December 22, 1995

I hadn't slept all night and still wore the clothes I had on the day before. As the sun rose, a nurse silently walked me to the front lobby and handed me over to a man in a white coat. He checked my name off on a clipboard and ordered me to find a seat in the back of the bus. There were a few others already seated, still and somber, avoiding eye contact. The bus drove from one hospital to another in the Chicago area, picking up other patients—it was half full as we left the city. We were all subdued and appeared to range in age; I seemed to be the youngest. The only people talking were the bus driver and the two men dressed in white, sitting in the front seats. Their laughter drifted to the back of the bus and seemed so normal. But nothing was normal, or was ever likely to be again.

April had brought an early spring. The world was waking up with the green growth of grass, tulips, and birdsong. In shock and grief, my world was dying. I cried silently with longing to be outdoors, wondering if I would ever again have that freedom.

My mind filled with the memory of the courtroom the day before, and the judge's stern voice as he issued my commitment. "By the power of this court and the State of Illinois, I hereby order the patient to be committed and removed to Elgin State Hospital."

With the loud bam of the gavel ringing in my ears, I knew my life was over. For the rest of the ride, my mind returned again and again to the judge's voice and the sound of that gavel, going round and round in concert with the gears of the bus and the heavy tires moving me closer and closer to the end of my life.

One of the old entryways to Elgin State Hospital

Hours later, we arrived at the entrance gate to Elgin State Hospital. An ancient sign on the gate read "Northern Illinois Hospital and Asylum for the Insane." My body jerked to attention, startled, as the bus came to a grinding stop at the gate. We waited as the men in the front of the bus talked and joked with the guards who then waved us through. The bus continued its slow drive through a deceptively peaceful, winding, park-like setting of trees and spring flower beds of tiny green shoots. Standing in stark contrast, the buildings were large, gloomy structures with windows covered by wire mesh and bars.

We stopped in front of the largest building. It rose up like a nightmare—an ancient, gothic structure. The man with the clipboard called out names one by one as I stared, aghast, at the ominous, dark building. I was both relieved to be getting off the bus and filled with trepidation. Panic broke through my apathy as my body began to shake in terror.

Directed to "hurry it up and get off the bus," I hesitated at the bottom of the stairs and was pushed from behind. I stumbled down the final step and looked around, searching for a way of escape, and took my place in the line. We slowly shuffled forward. My turn to enter the building came

Elgin State Hospital

far too quickly as an attendant shoved me across the threshold. I caught my elbow against something sharp hanging from the heavy, metal door; I didn't notice the long bleeding welt until much later, as I watched one woman after another pushed or dragged by the men into a large area that I later learned was women's admissions. Two male hands reached out, directing me forward. One by one, we were each checked for jewelry, money, and legal documents. Everything was confiscated.

The smells and sounds of suffering nearly brought me to my knees. I was assaulted by the sharp stench of urine, loosened bowels, and over one hundred years of accumulated filth. From somewhere in the large, dark building, I heard unintelligible moans and terrified screams, and I began to sob with wracking grief and terror. The nurse in uniform leaned toward my face and looked at me, hissing between clenched jaws: "Stop that! Stop it right now. Stop feeling sorry for yourself. You wanted to be crazy, well you came to the right place. You'll be as crazy as the rest of these loonies soon and won't even know where you are."

She stared at me with disgust. "I'm in charge here and will not put up with any crap, including self-indulgent crying."

I hung my head in shame and terror.

"Look at me when I'm talking to you. Do you understand me? I'm in charge. What's your name? Legal, last name first, no nicknames here."

She checked something on her clipboard. "Set your suitcase over there with the others, then move on and get your clothes off and leave them in the pile you see. Do what you're told. Now!"

9

The woman in line just ahead of me, older than me, and younger than many of the others, had a thick red scar that encircled her throat from ear to ear. Her hair was cut short like a boy's. She stood unmoving, like someone paralyzed, clutching her arms around her chest, eyes vacant, staring off into space. A male attendant addressed her in a low, threatening tone.

"You better get them damn clothes off, or we'll be getting them off for you."

There was no response, her entire body still.

"Miss P, what do you want us to do with the sister here?" the nearby attendant yelled.

The nurse looked up. The entire room fell still as she slammed her clipboard down with a violent whack on the nearby table. Fear reverberated throughout the room and bounced off the walls. "She's no damn nun in here and don't refer to her as one. You're Maryanne here if we call you anything."

Her voice grew louder as if she was talking to the whole room. "This isn't a nunnery—those days are forever over. Got it, the convent is O-V-E-R," she spelled out with biting sarcasm. "Get those damn clothes off, or I will rip them off of you myself."

The room was silent, tense, and alert. Minutes ticked by. Maryanne didn't move or respond. I watched, horrified, with blinding panic, aware I had to get my clothes off when it was my turn or the same thing could happen. Extremely modest, I wasn't sure I could do it. My breath grew shallow and rapid as I watched the nurse pull a pair of scissors from her pocket. She cut and tore the clothes off of the trembling nun, then tossed everything she had been wearing in pieces onto the floor. In seconds, Maryanne stood naked in the same spot, unmoving and unresponsive to the violent slap across the face that followed her naked exposure—before being shoved forward.

My turn came. Terror replaced self-consciousness and my aversion to nudity. I held my breath as I scrambled out of my clothes, leaving them in a pile with the others. Another attendant kept up a chorus of "Hurry it up, I don't have all damn day, get a move on it," as he shoved me through a door. I was ordered to stand still as searching hands, designed to humiliate me, did just that. Rough, calloused fingers ran up and down and across my naked flesh, touching and searching inside my ears, under the back of my hair, inside my mouth, under my arms.

I bit my lip bloody trying not to scream out as this stranger's hands bent me over and searched my buttocks and anus, then turned me around and probed my vagina and under my breasts until not an inch of skin on my trembling body lay untouched. I glanced up when I heard a snicker and saw that the man searching me was smiling. He saw me looking at him and the smile turned to a sneer as he pushed me away to the next man waiting in line. This attendant handed me a bar of soap and ordered me into the shower to scrub everywhere, including my hair.

The shower was one large room, with no privacy and a dozen shower heads spread around it. As I moved towards one of the free showers, my feet slipped out from under me on the wet, soapy floor. I went down hard, the fall knocking the breath out of me.

"Get off the damn floor and stop fooling around or we'll send you to lock-up," the shower attendant threatened. "I said, get your sorry ass up!"

Struggling to stand, I slipped and fell again. Somehow, by crawling over to the shower wall, I pulled myself into a standing position. Savoring the feel of the hot water washing away the touch of intrusive, rough hands, I stayed in the shower as long as I dared. A short while later I emerged with soaking wet hair and a sore hip and arm. The attendant threw a state-issued, loose grey dress and slipper socks at me. Noticing Maryanne huddled inside herself, holding clothing in her arms, I pulled mine on and moved over to help her, watching all the time to make sure this wouldn't get either of us in trouble. She didn't respond, continuing to stare off into space as I quickly pulled the dress over her head and placed the slipper socks in her hand. Days later she walked around still clutching them. I wondered if she knew what they were.

The remainder of that day, and those that followed, became a blur of sickening smells, sensations, and the frightening sounds of women mumbling to themselves, others screaming. Heavy metal doors slammed and echoed up and down the narrow, poorly lit hallways—they reverberated with the sound of threat, as did the jangling keys on massive key rings carried by the attendants. Dark and dingy, the unit was worn with age and filth. Its windows were covered on the outside by thick mesh and metal bars that let in little light.

There weren't enough chairs or benches, and those patients not fortunate enough to have a place to sit shuffled up and down the halls, or wandered the overcrowded dayroom in circles. Many were incontinent and naked. Most seemed out of touch with reality and were unresponsive. Here and there, curled-up bodies slept in drug-induced hazes on the cold linoleum floor for as long as they could get away with it. It was impossible to understand the rules as they were arbitrary and changed throughout the day, depending on the attendants working and the mood they were in.

The nurse came onto the ward only once a day, if that. The attendants ran the unit and spent most of their time locked behind a barred, heavy glass-enclosed office. Without notice, they often flew out, enraged at those sleeping on the floor. They kicked or slapped the sleeping person awake, yanking them off of the floor with violence, throwing them against the wall or hitting them—often with their keys or closed fists. I watched in horror as this happened time and again. Sometimes this was followed by putting the patient into a straitjacket or restraints and leaving them shackled to a chair, or removing them to one of many small restrain/seclusion rooms.

My body and mind slowly grew numb with shock. I was assaulted by the harsh, hateful voices of the attendants, the ongoing terror of screaming patients, and the rancid mixture of smells. It was inescapable.

The unit was either cold and damp or hot and steamy. Privacy was non-existent. Like the shower room, the bathroom had no outer door, exposing it to the entire ward, the inside lined up with toilets on one wall and sinks on the other.

My life became determined by the daily routine. Awakened at 6:00 a.m. we were herded out of the dormitories. An hour later, we were pushed into line to go to the dining room, where watery oatmeal or tasteless eggs were served. Three times a day, when the word "medications" was called over a microphone, we were required to line up immediately. This was often a time the attendants watched for someone to pick on. There was little talk, the only noise coming from the TV blasting from high on the wall, unless an attendant dragged a resistant patient in or out of the line, swearing and hitting them in the face with fists or their ring of keys.

A return trip to the dining room for an unappetizing lunch at noon, and then again for watery soup for dinner between 5:30 and 6:00 p.m. The wait for the 9:00 p.m. bedtime stretched into an agitated eternity of building tensions in the understaffed unit as the attendants grew even more unpredictable and violent, some reeking of alcohol as the evening shift moved toward bedtime. There were about one hundred and fifty patients on the unit. At night we were divided between different dormitories and locked in for the night. The dorm was crowded with row upon row of metal beds, each with a three-inch plastic mattress and a threadbare thin blanket. Sleep was difficult; most nights were filled with the sounds of anguish and patients often screaming out in confusion or nightmares. Some were shackled to their beds.

The day after I was admitted, a female psychiatrist saw me for about five to ten minutes. She never once looked up from her desk. I asked her how long I would be a patient.

"The rest of your life as far as I know. People don't leave here. It's the end of the line. You might as well accept that you're here to stay."

Her indifferent words merged in my head with those of the judge—who with the sound of a gavel had committed me. Words tumbled around, growing into a giant, numbing snowball of self-recrimination. Life sentence. Life over. Failure. You caused it. You brought this on. The rest of your life.

After several days, it became clear that certain staff were out for blood and appeared to take great pleasure from dispensing punishment. The air became charged and amplified with agitation during their shifts. Those patients who seemed out of touch with reality also appeared more sensitive and tense, as if a storm was about to break.

After morning medications, my days revolved around hoping to get to a chair, but if I got one, I felt compelled to give it up to someone who seemed to need it more. One day moved into another as I walked the hallway and dayroom, attempting to stay awake, discarding pieces of myself as I went. The drugs they gave me three times a day affected me to such a degree that sometimes I could no longer stand up. Dazed, I slid to the waiting floor like the others, promising myself it would be brief and for just a little rest. The drug-induced urge to lie down was just too strong and overrode my determination to stay on my feet to avoid the wrath of the attendants. The drugs muddled and slowed down my thinking. Walking became difficult. I shuffled. My mouth was always dry. Extreme thirst was an ongoing challenge as water was not readily available. Cups weren't allowed, so I had to use my hands to drink out of the bathroom sink, but it was never enough and the thirst persisted. My stomach grew painfully distended from constipation. Years later, I realized the gravity of these symptoms when I learned through a report that there had been many deaths in state hospitals due to bowel impactions, a result of the overuse of Thorazine. I bounced back and forth between feelings of extreme agitation, anxiety, and a racing, irregular heartbeat to numbness and extreme fatigue.

One day I kept the medication cup, hoping to use it for water, rather than placing it in the waste basket. Without warning, an attendant grabbed me. He wrestled me into the restraint room and left me in tight, leather cuffs shackled to the metal bed by my wrists and legs. As I protested that I only wanted a drink of water, he replied, "You will do a lot more wanting in here. This will teach you a lesson about following the rules."

After the first time I was put in restraints, there were too many incidents to keep track of, one bleeding into another. I was put in restraints in the seclusion room for sitting or sleeping on the floor, for refusing to take medication, pretending I had swallowed the pills, holding them in my cheek, or when I was caught spitting them out. I was put in restraints when I intervened and tried to help others. Once, I was placed in restraints for trying to run out the opened door as someone was being brought in.

Some days, I couldn't bear the sounds and smells of human misery. Witnessing others beaten and humiliated, or the smells of hopeless flesh deprived of decent food and sunlight, and of urine and feces, nearly undid me. I couldn't think in the constant, jarring noise of the overcrowded ward. The restraint/seclusion room became a welcome relief from the chaos and abuse. Still, the attendants were brutal and punitive, hitting and punching me even when I didn't resist being taken there.

In the restraint room, the universe contracted to the limits of the small room with its locked metal door, the dirty walls, and cracked, peeling paint. The bare hanging light bulb could be flipped on from the outside with no warning—jarring my senses and activating fear. If sleep came, it was fitful, moving me from one nightmare to another. Awake, I counted the tiles and tried to flee the cold, barren room and the reality of hopelessness. Sometimes I conjured the memories and images of those who had cared about me—if only briefly—until blessed relief came and I found my mind and awareness somewhere else, outside those hurtful walls.

Sometimes I would find a sense of solace in remembering the experience of once being loved. I listened from far away—outside time and place—to the muffling white noise of my breath as I discovered ways to escape the agony of the too-tight restraints by counting the cracks in the wall. Once, I watched entranced as a spider in the corner of the room wove her web, silently begging her to teach me how to spin my mind out of this horror.

Thirst was problematic enough on the unit. In restraints, it became unbearable. I was thirsty for hours and days on end when in restraints.

I begged for water when the attendants came in to give me bitter liquid medication—or shots. My pleading fell on deaf ears. The four-point restraints, tightened beyond endurance, cut off my circulation, creating sores on my wrists and ankles, an aching back, joints and muscles stretched too tight.

Shame grew in me daily along with the toxicity growing in my body from the pills. Refusal was not an option. I had no control over the drugs they forced on me, how my body was abused, or the fondling that occurred by the angry and bitter attendants whenever they checked on me in the restraint room. Their fingers chafed me raw, leading to burning urination. I wet myself and developed sores on my buttocks from lying on the urine-soaked mattress pad for days and weeks at a time. This reinforced all my entrenched beliefs, carried from childhood, that my life had no value. Humiliated and disgraced by my abandonment—by the medical system and the state—I grew indifferent.

Weeks passed, followed by months.

One day another younger patient arrived. At first, Melinda helped with the boredom—she was someone my age to talk to and provided a distraction. Before long, she set up a business having sex with attendants after meals under the oilcloth-covered dining-room tables in exchange for cigarettes or other favors. I had flashbacks of life with my mother and I begged her to stop. She laughed at me, shrugging, indifferent to my concerns, and told me that the attendants would treat me better if I had sex with them. I declined. She shrugged and told me she couldn't care less if I didn't want to look out for myself.

Melinda's rebelliousness and refusal to let Elgin get her down were admirable. She connived and lied daily to gain privileges that no one else had. She never ended up in the restraint room or drugged like the rest of us, but I couldn't imagine ever engaging in the same kind of behavior. As I worried about Melinda, my mind would inevitably turn toward my mother. I wondered what using her body had ever gotten her. Before long, I was surprised to hear about Melinda's upcoming discharge. At the time, I didn't believe that patients ever left Elgin.

"My wacko, so-called parents are the ones who put me here, not the state, and I guess they figured out it hasn't made any difference." She shrugged in dismissal.

It was both a relief and a loss the day that she left.

One evening, I returned from the dining room a little earlier than the others. The ward was quiet, nearly empty. Finding a chair by the window for the first time since my admission was a rare gift. As I sat looking outside, I gazed at a tree illuminated by the late afternoon sunlight. The Thorazine-drugged, rusty, and worn hinges in my brain opened to the wonder of this tree. Despite the cruelty and suffering around me, there in the gentle wind and the dappled leaves was a magnificent old tree illuminated by the filtering light of sunset. The beautiful, low-arching branches reached out to me like extended arms, much like those of another tree had long ago.

The tree that nourished my spirit was seen through this window

Through the haze of drugs—like a half-dead thing—the memory of that childhood tree surfaced. It was a very large, expansive tree that provided me with a source of nourishment and sustenance at a crucial time in my life. Sitting slouched, imprisoned in Elgin, I could almost see my childhood self climbing up into that other tree's branches, as high as possible. Nestling against her bark, held above the taunts and bullying of neighborhood kids, I'd sit reading for hours.

It didn't matter if my mother was drunk at home with some guy she'd picked up or home at all when I was curled around those warm dark branches. Returning to her often as a child, I learned her language and seasons, the texture of her dark skin and her earthy smells. The life lines in her leaves became more familiar than my own heartbeat. I studied the small critters she housed in her curved limbs, the birds that stopped to visit if I sat very still. I loved the variations of light and shadow in her leaves and weathered skin. I came to know her as my mothering tree and talked to her about everything.

One night, home alone, tired of the loneliness of the empty, silent apartment, the smell of stale cigarettes, beer, and sex, I went to that tree, intending to spend the night. Nestled in her upper branches, enveloped by the smell of fresh-cut grass from a nearby yard, I gazed upward. The stars and the curve of a crescent moon blinked back at me. The canopy of the heavens opened, giving me a small look into infinity. Sighing in contentment, I was home—the only home I had ever known.

Elgin's barred, dirty window framing the sight of living, growing life in the tree outside brought me back to where I was. Overcome with reverence, my chest ached in connection and longing—it felt as though the tree's energy reached back toward me, meeting me. The filtered light streaming through her branches lulled me. Closing my eyes for a moment in the wonder of this tree and the return of peaceful childhood memories, the tree outside those grimy windows and the tree of my childhood merged and became one and the same.

I stood, leaning toward the window, mesmerized. I felt alive for the first time in many months. My forehead and the palms of my hands touched the barred window as a deep longing to be on the other side arose, pushing me against the barrier of separation from the beauty and smell of outdoors. The pain of months and months of isolation from growing things— juxtaposed against the inside of the ward's stagnant, long, drawn-out daily dying—nearly shattered me. My hunger for connection with life pushed me further, and I leaned as hard as possible against the barred windows.

I was suddenly grabbed violently from behind by arms pulling me away from the window. Desperate to escape from the attendant as he wrenched me away from the hope of living things—my life seemed to depend on this small miracle—I kicked and screamed, fighting the arms imprisoning me, keeping me from life itself. Another set of hands joined the first and dragged me toward the middle of the room as I screamed and attempted to fight them off. The two attendants picked me up, carried me into a dark solitary confinement room, and threw me down.

I lay pinned to the metal bed with leather restraints and fought them for hours, my hands and ankles turning chafed and bloody. I stared at the artificial light of the naked dirty bulb above the bed. Enraged that it was dead in contrast to the living light I had seen outside the windows, I screamed "You're dead. Dead. Dead" until my throat grew raw and swollen with grief, no strength or sound left in me to protest. But I'd had that glimpse of the tree outside the window. Seeing it gave me a tiny dose of hope in living things.

Days or weeks later, one late afternoon, an attendant told me his shift was ending and he had to take me to another building for an appointment on his way home. Through my drug-induced daze, I asked why. "You ask too many questions—just shut up."

He placed my arms into a straitjacket; the elongated white sleeves pulled my arms and shoulders painfully tight across my chest, and secured them behind me. We exited through a back door. I had not left the building—except once—since being admitted many months before. For a few moments I savored the warmth of sunshine and fresh air as he walked me briskly to our destination.

Two other attendants met us in the doorway of a small building with boarded-up windows. I didn't recognize them. An inner alarm went off when I caught the whiff of alcohol and heard their slurred voices. They ushered me into a vacant, garage-like building, with tires and tools strewn around and several piles of beer cans and liquor bottles on the floor. I backed away toward the door, but insistent hands grabbed me and threw me down. My body met the cold of concrete. The attendant who had brought me began to laugh. "Ready for your appointment?"

He held me down with his foot in the middle of my chest. My body screamed in pain. One of the men licked his lips and gyrated his pelvis toward me, gesturing what he intended to do. "Time for a party. We've been waiting for your sweet young ass since you first arrived."

One straddled me, pulled off the straitjacket, and tore off the state dress and underwear. Frozen as though in a dream, I tried to scream but nothing came out of my mouth as one of them put tape across it. I kicked at the hands holding down my legs. The huge, overweight man who escorted me to the garage fell on me, crushing my body into the floor, grinding himself into me. They took turns filling every orifice, filling my psyche with their degrading words and wet hate.

I stared at the unusual rosette tiles of pressed tin above my head and was intermittently able to direct my energy and awareness to the ceiling. I watched from a great distance the girl on the floor, lying in mute, frozen surrender. The men became even more intoxicated from bottles of whiskey and the cans of beer I had noticed when I was first shoved into the garage. As their drunkenness and cruelty escalated, I slipped in and out of consciousness.

A bucket of ice-cold water revived me. One of the men hit me hard across the side of the head, demanding that I wake up and listen. "You know what happens to crazies around here who make up stories? This was a figment of your imagination, you fucking loony. We've got eyes everywhere."

Late afternoon had given way to night; I could hear my abusers stumbling around but could barely see them. Two of them carried me outside, laughing as my teeth chattered uncontrollably. Already cold from the water, the cool night air was intolerable. They lifted my body above their heads and heaved me over the top of something high. My body slammed into unforgiving, cold metal, every bone and muscle screaming in agony. Then followed the sound of metal hitting metal from above, leaving me in total darkness.

I tried to stand up but dizziness fell like fog, bringing me to my knees in excruciating pain. Something was wrong with my left hip. I tried again to stand, but couldn't. Bile and vomit rose in my throat from the pain and smells of human garbage. I panicked; the tape was still covering my mouth. Choking and coughing, I realized my hands were free and I was able to tear off the tape to vomit—until nothing life-giving remained in me.

I woke up days later at the on-grounds medical building. A nurse told me I was found in a garbage bin with my hip dislocated, covered with vomit, and surrounded by beer cans and trash. My terror was all-encompassing. I couldn't fit it into my body. Words sounded muffled and far away. Words and images slowly surfaced, shattered like broken glass. If I had a soul left, it had been flung to the outer edges of eternity—with no conception of where I ended or began.

I don't recall ever being asked how I had gotten into the dumpster. I'm not sure I could have told them anything coherent anyway. Outside myself—disconnected and dissociated from any sense of physicality or body—there was little to communicate. But in a shard of memory, a man in a white coat is talking as though from under water—even though he was standing next to the bed, his voice foreign and garbled to my ears. He lectured me about the stupidity of trying to run away and hide in a dumpster. Without warning, memories from that day emerged in shards and splinters—flashes of shattered, puzzle-piece images and smells. Kept in the medical building for a short while, my body healed—but not my psyche. I was returned to the same unit.

My memories were fragmented and colored with hopelessness, reduced to less than an animal in a human-made trap. I had previously witnessed women on the unit beaten, suffering all forms of abuse and humiliation when they tried to report something an attendant had done. Taunted and called "crazy," "cuckoo," or "nut job," they were abused further. There was no one I could tell. To make matters worse, the attendant who had taken me out the back door was a constant threat—looking for any opportunity to further abuse me.

That incident in the garage became a threshold for me, marking the place where I lost all hope or care of what was done to me. Beyond the reach of emotions most of the time, it occurred to me that I wasn't drugged enough to survive this place—its daily terror, the unpredictability, and my constant worry about the next assault. The grinding boredom and bearing witness to the daily forms of abuse, degradation, and humiliation hurled at other residents were beyond my capacity to survive anymore. A drugged zombie-like state actually became preferable to any form of awareness. I barricaded myself deep inside with the help of the handful of pills I was given three times a day until any semblance of the girl I had once been ceased to exist.

Days and weeks appeared to go by in a blur. I was numb to everything, both within and without. Deadened and empty, my will and sense of self or soul had fled—leaving my body an empty shell. It seemed as though nothing could touch me, hurt me enough, or surprise me anymore. I continued to be put in and out of restraints for no reason—now not caring. My muddled brain was making it difficult to make sense of anything. From a great distance I felt the burns on my buttocks and vagina from lying in feces and urine after developing a bad infection. Seeping sores on my wrists and ankles became infected.

I developed a raging infection from unnecessary and puzzling tooth extractions and was sent to the University of Illinois for surgery to remove the roots that were left in my mouth, causing blood poisoning and a raging infection. After security returned me to Elgin, I was again placed on the medical unit for IV antibiotics and recovery before being sent back to the ward. I wondered why they bothered to waste antibiotics on me. I wondered why they bothered to keep me alive. I was disconnected, uninterested in what was happening to the empty shell of a body I once inhabited.

2.

In the Beginning—War on the Home Front

My wish, indeed my continuing passion, would be not to point the finger in judgment but to part a curtain, that invisible shadow that falls between people, the veil of indifference to each other's presence, each other's wonder, each other's human plight.

Eudora Welty, *One Time, One Place*

Eighteen years later, in another hospital, in a city I had never been to before, in a different state, I was recovering from unexpected emergency surgery and a vague, ghost-like feeling of familiarity hovered around me as I sat staring out the hospital window at the back of the Minnesota State Capitol. I had the persistent feeling that I had known this place, been here before, and needed to pay attention. Earlier that morning I'd written in my journal, "I wonder if I was born here? Poor baby, born premature and sick because her mother was drunk."

An idea came to me, perhaps a way to settle this déjà vu feeling that hovered in the air with each breath I took. I picked up the phone, deciding to settle this once and for all, and called my mother's oldest sister to see if she had any idea where I had been born. Aunt Ethel picked up on the third ring. By the end of the call, she had confirmed that I had indeed been born in St. Paul, Minnesota, in a hospital close to the state capitol. I was staring out the window at the gilded, gold leaf ball at the top of the dome of that very building as she told me this. The sun reflecting off the dome seemed to blink in my direction. Before we hung up, the name of the hospital came to her.

"It was Bethesda Hospital," she said with conviction.

I was enchanted. I couldn't believe I was sitting on a bed in Bethesda Hospital where I was born. I think, *Wow, I really have been here before, but how could I possibly remember that?*

23

At this time in my life, I lived in South Dakota, but while attending a professional training I was rushed to the hospital and required the surgery from which I was recovering. Later that day, I learned from the medical records department that the surgical floor had been the maternity ward in October 1947 when I was born. It was October of 1985, the month of my birth. Records also revealed that my mother was a patient throughout her long and complicated labor in the room right next to the one I was inhabiting as a patient. The nurses' station had once been the nursery for premature and medically compromised newborns. My mother was discharged a week after delivery but I stayed on in an incubator and on life support in that very room.

I had always felt a deep melancholy during the fall season. This year was no exception. I found myself watching the silent trees letting go of their leaves as I gazed out the window of my hospital room. My mind drifted off as I thought about the strange coincidences of how I had come to learn that I was in the place of my birth. Perhaps my discomfort through the fall was related to my birth. I didn't know the season itself was a portent of things to come and that, before long, my life would dramatically change once again. The changes would each require letting go. Trees eventually revealed to me that in order to create space for new growth, I would frequently need to go inward and learn lessons about the dark dormancy of winter. The kaleidoscope of fall colors taught me of the nuances and varieties of the constantly changing self.

Several months after release from the hospital, armed with a tape recorder, I visited Aunt Ethel at her home in Wisconsin. When I learned from her what had occurred before my birth, I began to see the influences that conspired against me in my early years and eventually led to my unjust commitment to a state institution while a college student. It wasn't just one thing, but an accumulation of events. As I looked closely, many silken threads emerged, weaving my life into a much larger tapestry. It tells a story that is not only mine, but a much larger story: a story of ancestors, the influence of history and culture, and the power held by systems and institutions.

The feeling of déjà vu in the hospital that day called me to fully explore my place of birth, the history of my mother, and to visit my aunt, Ethel. She was the oldest of seven siblings and became the keeper of family history, as well as the secrets and fears the others found too unbearable to talk about. She grew up into a caring, no-nonsense woman, the most stable of her siblings.

Edna, who would eventually become my mother, was barely three when she lost her father, Hans, to a winter blizzard. Hans, also known as John, came to the United States as a young boy from Denmark. He was a hard worker, occasionally drank too much, and by Ethel's report he loved his large, noisy group of young-uns. Hans was the solid foundation of what kept his family running smoothly on their struggling farm in northern Wisconsin.

Well into the first years of the Great Depression, between crop failures from poor weather and a bug infestation, the family of nine was in real trouble. Luckily, however, Hans was able to get a job with the Bell Telephone Company selling stocks, walking from one small town and farm to another. One day while Hans was out working, the snow grew heavy and the wind came up. He stopped at a neighbor's farm to sit before the fire and have a drink to help warm him before continuing to walk the remaining miles home. Several days later, his body was found frozen in a four-foot wall of snow. His death certificate recorded the reason for death as "heart attack and frozen to death." There were no available death benefits given to the already-impoverished family.

What Hans had referred to as "real trouble" in their lives now became catastrophic. Maude and their seven children had little food stored in the root cellar, and no way to bring in money or grow food until after the next spring thaw. When Hans died, Eleanor was just still a brand-new baby. Edna was three, Eunice seven, followed by nine-year-old Myrtle, then the older three: twelve-year-old Clinton, fifteen-year-old Dean, and seventeen-year-old Ethel.

As Ethel recalled, her mother Maude looked haggard and sickly after Eleanor's birth. Maude was small in stature, shy and retiring. She had always been seen as having a "poor constitution and fragile." After Hans died, she seemed to get smaller still, disappearing into herself as she descended quietly into a "catatonic state." Ethel described this as a "madness" which had her so lost to an inner numbness that not even the needs of baby Eleanor or the other children could reach her.

The family was isolated, with no relatives nearby. As the oldest, Ethel and Dean made the decision not to tell anyone about Maude's condition—they'd both heard terrifying stories and feared the children would be farmed out to an orphanage if their mother was taken away to an institution. They were able to avoid the outcome they feared only by keeping their true poverty and extreme living conditions a secret.

This instinct to protect Maude did not appear to apply to subsequent generations. My aunts who lived nearby were not able or willing to protect me from my mother's abuse or my subsequent institutional commitment. Although they knew what our life was like, they looked the other way. And so, during the harshest years of the Depression, the seven children suddenly had to look out for themselves. Ethel bathed, dressed, and fed her inanimate, mute mother and the new baby, while Clinton, Dean, Myrtle, and Eunice were left to fend for themselves. Edna was caught in the middle of all that hardship as each day, work-worn, resentful siblings' hands dressed her. During that first harsh winter the children moved from room to room, seeking warmth in any way they could get it.

Fear, loss, and resentment colored Edna's days. There was little to eat, hunger driving everyone to irritability and easy anger. None of the older kids talked much or helped her make sense of what was happening to them all. Day after day, Edna played by herself at the feet of her silent, unmoving mother. With no one to guide her, she grew in months and eventually years, but not in maturity.

Edna was prone to tantrums from early on, demanding her way and seldom getting it. The older kids thought of her as a pest and said she got meaner by the day. They were resentful that she didn't have to work like the rest of them, and they didn't want to be bothered with her. Her brown eyes grew dull and cold as she looked out on such a miserable world, all the time wondering what had happened to her papa. She must have also wondered where her mama was: she couldn't find the mother she had known inside this mute, frozen shell of a woman. This woman seemed to look straight through her without seeing anything—not even Edna's brown curls, dull and unkempt, caught her attention. Ethel told me that Edna frequently brought brushes to her mother's lap as she begged for a brushing and a mother's loving touch. It never came.

Ethel tried to manage it all, but after vagrants broke into the root cellar and stole the remainder of the small stash of vegetables, the family literally had nothing left to eat. So, Ethel got a job in town to keep the family from starving. She hated to leave her mother and younger sisters with the two boys in charge. They had always been wild, somewhat unruly boys, and pa used his belt on them now and then. Now they could hardly take care of themselves, and they were mean. Managing chores, the baby girl, the three in the middle, and a "better off dead mother" made them meaner yet.

There just wasn't any way around it, Ethel told me. "We would have all starved, and nearly did anyway. I tried to manage it all the best I could by working in town during the week and walking to the farm, then working all weekend catching up with the laundry, cooking for the upcoming week, and bathing ma, the baby, and other younger kids. I grew more and more concerned about what went on in my absence, but I dared not look too closely at what worried me." She paused in thought. "It might have become that last straw that broke my already breaking back. It could have been my undoing, just like pa's death was my mother's. I did worry about Edna, though." She sighed. "The four older kids were almost big enough to look after themselves. The baby was a baby after all, everyone felt so sorry for her because ma never mothered her at all. Baby Eleanor got plenty of holding and attention by the rest of us. The little girls, Myrtle and Eunice, dragged her along with them like a pretty baby doll," she said with a smile and deep in memory.

"Edna was a different story; she pretty much raised herself from then on. The older kids ignored her. They had no patience for her daily tantrums and neediness. The boys were just plain mean, teasing her endlessly. They spanked her poor bottom so red, it sometimes blistered and bled."

Dean was the withdrawn, silent type, but boy you didn't want to mess with him because he had some awful temper. Although the oldest at home during the week, he pretty much kept to himself and worked outside to get away. At age twelve, Clinton really became the man of the house, responsible during the week for inside chores and looking after the little ones when Ethel was in town. Too young to be in charge and easily overwhelmed, he took his frustration and unhappiness out on the younger children by beating them and withholding what little food there was. Ethel told me her fear grew when she came home one weekend to find that the three youngest had been locked in the shed for days.

"Another time, walking down the road to the farm, I noticed something peculiar about the plow moving up and down the rows. We had finally gotten some rain so the earth was moist and turning up the earth shouldn't have been too difficult. Then I saw it: the little ones, not the horse, were pulling the plow. My heart started beating furiously as I ran screaming into the field, yelling for all I was worth: 'My God, Clint, you're going to kill them!' I screamed so loud they might've been able to hear me in the next county. 'They're just little girls, you're going to kill them!' I was bawling so hard I could hardly see as I unbuckled and pulled at the leather that harnessed Edna and Eunice to the plow. I couldn't believe what he said to me. He said, 'So, what's wrong with giving the horse a day off? He's getting skinny and these two brats should be good for something. All they do is eat, while the rest of us work our fool heads off.'"

Yes, Ethel grew concerned, but she didn't dare look too closely with the Depression still going. The line between starvation and survival was dangerously thin. Soon after, on top of it all, Ethel became pregnant. The father was a married man from the nearby town.

"There were already too many mouths to feed. I was scared, really scared, and barely holding myself together and working to take care of everyone besides. I was afraid it might just break me."

Ethel looked away, embarrassed, as she told me how she thought that what had begun as Edna seeking comfort through sexual interaction with the brothers when she was young had turned into a habit of sexual promiscuity as she got older. "But I knew it wasn't her fault, and I'm sure Clinton started on her young, and maybe Dean, too.

"Mind you, I was no angel myself, but as Edna grew older, the boys fancied her for sexual favors—and she really learned to work it to her advantage. She learned how to keep them running, just like a cow in heat. She flaunted her looks and sex like a fool waving a red kerchief at a bull, flirting and seducing about anyone in pants. She once told me she thought it was the only thing she was any good at. I don't blame her, at least she got some attention and a present now and then, and they stopped being so harsh with her. It's a miracle that any of us survived at all." She studied me quietly, seeming to assess how I was taking in what she shared. "You ok?"

I nodded and encouraged her to continue. "Your mom was considered by everyone, especially the boys, to be a real beauty."

Tall and thin. Soft, chestnut, natural curls, and big brown eyes featured in a heart-shaped face. She knew how to work it to her advantage.

Eventually, Dean and then Clinton had enough with raising kids and enlisted in the army to go off to fight in the Second World War. Clinton became a war hero—"if you can imagine that," Ethel proclaimed. "He returned home a wreck, with jungle fever and a whole lot more than a Bronze Star. He wasn't the boy who left, determined to send his check home so I could quit working and care for my mother and sisters. By that time, I had a baby of my own to take care of."

Mother, a "real beauty"

It was too little, too late for Edna: she learned to bicker and bargain her way through life but had difficulty mastering the ABCs. At twelve, she climbed out of a window to have sex with a farm hand and got her first pair of shoes. This began a pattern of selling herself to fund her needs and desires. I never knew if I should blame those damn boys or Edna for continuing on with something they had started. Ethel said things were different back then.

"Edna went off on her own for a while at seventeen, moving to the big city of St. Paul, Minnesota, where she worked in a factory, lived in a boarding house, and picked up men as often as she could for an extra buck. But she always seemed to find her way back to Clinton after he returned from serving Uncle Sam. He followed her to the city for a while. But he quickly grew overwhelmed, proclaiming city life was not for him—it made him nervous. So, he traveled back and forth to home in the country. At just around twenty, Edna got herself pregnant with you by some married guy or some other Tom, Dick, or Harry, for all the family knew." But Ethel confessed in a whisper that their brother Clinton wondered if the bastard was his.

"Your mother liked to believe your father was that bartender, Bud.

She thought of Bud as sophisticated, and the best thing that had ever come along in her pitiful life. She was sure he was taken with her looks and always bragged that she was his 'beautiful, extra good-looking gal.'"

Bud was older by seven years and had been around the world compliments of the Navy. He had a high school diploma, unlike Edna or anyone else she knew. He was married and had a couple of kids, but he kept promising Edna that he was trying to get a divorce. His wife supposedly just wasn't ready to give him one. Edna still thought Bud would be good marriage material. She didn't take into account the fact that since leaving his first wife, Bud didn't financially support the two kids he had and seldom saw them. Months into her pregnancy, she convinced herself that the baby's father really was Bud. Bud had a steady job and liked her well enough—this alone made him pretty stable compared with some of her other one-night stands.

Edna gave birth to me in the fall of 1947. Most children grow up with birth stories. Mine was colored with my mother's bitter disappointment. She swore that it was the worst day of her life, that she hadn't wanted a kid anyway. When I was older, one of my aunts told me that my mother had been "shit-faced drunk" throughout her labor and delivery. I was born about ten weeks premature, in convulsions, and I was kept in the hospital for several months. At the time, Edna was convinced it wouldn't be long before Bud would get divorced and marry her. Aiming to please, she named me after his only sister, a decision she said she regretted for the rest of her life. Although they weren't married, she had his last name illegally put on my birth certificate, though later she was prone to calling me a "bastard" because I was "born out of wedlock."

Ethel believed that Edna couldn't really handle being a mother and thought of the baby as marriage bait. But a baby turned out to be more of a turnoff than anything for Bud, who resented having another mouth to feed. Over the years, Edna was frequently overheard telling others she never bonded with me because she couldn't nurse me or take me home like a normal baby. She blamed me for having ruined her life and the fun she'd had before my birth. My outer life lacked any semblance of bonding, belonging, or connection to family or place. My mother's inability to parent, her abusiveness, poverty, and the crush of her own violent history combined to make my childhood hard to bear.

The resentments and anger between my mother and Bud escalated, gradually growing violent. Edna soon believed Bud had no intention of

Me at two before my mother disappeared from my life

ever marrying her. Sometime between my first and second birthdays, my mother decided to give up on Bud and move back to rural Wisconsin to live with Clinton. Along the way, she changed her story, working to convince him that I really was his child.

Clinton alternated between being glad she was back in his life to taking out his mistrust and anger on her. He was bad-tempered about everything. He was also jealous, unpredictable, irrational, and often confused about where he was. Sometimes, he grew confused and thought he was still in the jungle, in the middle of combat, where everyone was the enemy—especially Edna and this bastard she had brought home.

According to Ethel's memory of this time, my mother tried her best to appease and calm Clinton, but to no avail. "Edna appeared to grow increasingly frightened for herself, but abandoned you to his rages. I wonder now if she was reminded of Clinton's violence towards her as a child as she walked around with a busted lip and blackened eyes, watching him use your small body as a punching bag." Ethel sighed, got up to move around before returning to the table where we sat. "I hope you know I regret so much. I just didn't know how to stop it all," she said.

Clinton wore his face like a fist. His hair was unkempt and face unshaved. Ethel told me that she noticed during this time that he began to deteriorate, seldom taking a shower or brushing his teeth. I remember that I could smell his sour breath and alcohol-soaked sweat from two rooms away. Instinctively, I became quiet and vigilant in his presence—my survival depended on it. As I neared my third birthday, Clinton had taught me to run at the sound of footsteps, duck at the sight of hands, and find clever hiding places.

"Get that damn thumb out of your mouth before I break it off," he'd threaten.

His rough hands and harsh sandpaper voice sent me into hiding under the slipcovers behind the living room couch. Holding my breath became nearly as easy as breathing. I learned early not to hide behind doors since once when he found me there, Clinton hit the door into my screaming body over and over again, teaching me a lesson I'd never forget. By my third birthday, my mother and Clinton were in a full-out war. They struggled for control over each other, their relationship ambivalent and volatile, with me caught in the crossfire of their insane passions.

One day, Aunt Ethel came visiting, bringing birthday presents. I remember my excitement at the dollhouse complete with small furniture and tiny people that she helped me unwrap. It filled me with wonder as Clinton berated Ethel for bringing the "damn brat" anything. He saw no reason to clutter his house with junk. He insisted that she take it to her house, he wasn't about to keep it in his. She held her own and refused. I stood in a nearby corner, trying to make myself small. He shouted with fury that she was just "spoiling me." He glanced at me with pure hatred. My mere presence was the kindling for his fiery rage as he turned it on my mother for having given birth to me in the first place. Then, the torrent of his anger reached out toward me. Clinton grabbed me with his big, rough hands as he shouted at my mother and Aunt Ethel that he was going to get rid of the shit that Edna had dragged home once and for all.

Out to the outhouse he flew with me under his arm. He held me by my ankles down the smelly hole as he threatened to drop me, calling me a piece of shit as he pulled me up and down, more violent and threatening with each gesture, letting go of one ankle, laughingly counting to three, and vowing to drop me as Ethel stood by helpless, begging him to stop. I don't remember if my mother followed us to the outhouse or tried to stop him. It was Aunt Ethel I remember screaming, the one who eventually intervened.

As fall crept toward winter, Clinton grew confused, erratic, paranoid, and violent. He was unpredictable and increasingly pulled his gun out of the closet, wild eyed, yelling for anyone around him to "get in the trenches." My mother begged Aunt Ethel and her husband, Jack, to do something before he killed someone. They had tried to intervene and begged him to get help, but to no avail. Day by day, Clinton became more unpredictable and fragmented—an explosion waiting to happen. People would later say that Clinton had left his humanity and peace of mind back in the trenches. Maybe he had "jungle fever," they'd guessed when he returned from combat, a walking time bomb that could go off at any moment. The events that transpired on Thanksgiving Day 1950 came neither suddenly nor unexpectedly, but arrived with more violence than anyone could have predicted.

On that fateful cold and snowy morning, the bomb exploded. The deafening sound of gunfire shattered my world. My uncle-father's brains were everywhere, splattering me and catching me in flight as I slipped on the blood and torn tissue slowly spreading over the linoleum floor. Clinton's agony and rage had finally been silenced, by his own hand, with the roar of the gun. My crazed mother's anger exploded tenfold, roaring out of her and through the house as she hurtled blame for Clinton killing himself on me. She beat me with her fists, then carried me upstairs and threw me in my bed. I silently watched and listened, frozen in terror as she put clothes in a suitcase, muttering to herself from across the room. The sound of her running down the stairs, followed by the deafening slam of the kitchen door, was terrifying. Then an eternity of snow-muffled silence filled the house.

I have vague memories of calling out again and again. Long periods of hunger, fear, and longing were followed by fitful sleep. Time was non-existent for the next three days, drifting like the snow accumulating outside the windows. I perceived everything from a great distance, including the pain in my shoulder and arm. I remember once waking, enveloped in hunger, in the cold, quiet house, but I managed to crawl out of the crib and scoot on my bottom down the stairs, too weak to stand. In the kitchen I was greeted by a puddle of sticky blood and gore covering everything—but Clinton's body was gone. The house was empty.

I have a distinct memory of climbing on a chair to get some bread left out on the table, then slipping in the blood while trying to escape the kitchen. I made it to the living room and frantically tried to get outside but could only open the door part way. Blizzard snow blew in, jamming it open. Screaming for my mother, I struggled to open the door further. Eventually I grew tired and curled into a ball on the living room floor, sucking my thumb, terrified by the silent, lonely house and longing for something I couldn't name.

As I remember it, suddenly, there was a sound. I turned toward it, expecting my mother or my aunt. It was neither. What I saw was an ethereal presence showing up against the reality of absence—like hot against cold. A warmth emanated from this female specter, casting radiant light near the blowing of the curtains. Mesmerized, I watched the loving lady in her dust-dappled shaft of light, warming me with flowing words as she talked to me in a soft, soothing voice. She told me to move away from the door and carefully go back up the stairs and climb into my bed and cover up.

Obediently, I scooted away from the mounting drift of snow, the bone-chilling wind whistling through the house, the dark of early evening beginning to set in. Hesitantly, led by her voice, I crawled up the stairs, backwards on my bottom as she instructed. Upstairs, the new dollhouse Aunt Ethel had given me sat, inviting me to play. Momentarily forgetting everything else and ignoring my painful shoulder and arm, I escaped into childhood's blessed make-believe land, moving the tiny furniture around with my one good arm. Perhaps I was attempting to find relief in the play.

Soon the lady told me to get in my bed and cover up—she promised to watch over me.

Years later Ethel told me that she had phoned when we didn't come to Thanksgiving dinner—no one answered. She was so mad; she got in the car and drove over to give my mom and Clinton a piece of her mind. She discovered Clinton's body in the kitchen and my mother nowhere to be found. She said she had started halfway up the stairwell, calling out my mother's name. When no one answered, she assumed my mother had taken me and left. She breathed a silent thank you that the phone still worked as she frantically called the sheriff.

It was a holiday; the blizzard conditions were getting worse by the minute. Assuming the house was empty and that my mother had left with me, Ethel told the coroner and sheriff that she had searched the house. They didn't bother to search upstairs either, eager to get home before the roads became impassable. The sheriff thought the gun he found held in Clinton's tightly-clenched fist told the whole story. He had no idea of the untold story lying asleep in a crib upstairs.

Me with my mother in St. Paul

Three days later my mother wandered drunk into the middle of Clinton's small funeral. She was disoriented and had no idea where I was. Aunt Ethel and others frantically rushed to the house. They found me unconscious, covered in dried blood, with a broken arm and collarbone. I have vague memories of being bathed in warm water, needles and tubes, my body burning hot, then cold, until my entire tiny frame shook. My mother was not part of this picture.

These were followed by memories of a very long car ride, wrapped in warm, soft blankets and the whispered voices of my Aunt Eunice and Uncle Mike driving me to their home in Illinois. I lived with my aunt and uncle and Grandma Maude for the next year. My mother had simply vanished from my life and no one talked about her. I don't remember missing her.

Aunt Ethel told me they all thought I might be deaf from being in such close proximity to the gun when it went off. Retreating deeply into myself, I had stopped talking and regressed to wearing diapers again. I found solace in my thumb and the silk edging around blankets. There wasn't much that interested me. Sometimes, I found distraction and was mildly engaged in watching the activity of my cousins, who played around me with trucks, blocks, and such. I never joined in. Although they had brought the dollhouse and my few other toys from Clinton's house, I never touched them again. I watched everything around me, mute and alert to the slightest possibility of threat. My mother was not around to recognize that her three-year-old daughter had emerged from that Thanksgiving Day into a mute stillness, much like the one her own mother had been in when Edna herself was three.

I was terrified of large, quick-moving male hands and easily startled into crying silent tears. Although my grandma never called me or my cousins by our correct names, always using the names of her grown children, I sometimes relaxed sitting on her lap, enfolded into her soft stillness. I took pleasure in gazing at a small potted Easter lily that I was given when Aunt Eunice took me to church with her on Easter. It was a quiet time. I was comforted and distracted myself by rocking as I sucked my thumb, sitting on the living room couch watching *Howdy Doody* on the black and white TV in the late afternoons.[1]

My mother returned a year later on one of those *Howdy Doody* afternoons to take me away with her. I was watching TV when she suddenly blew in like a tornado, immediately starting a fight with my aunt about the thumb in my mouth as she yanked it out and yelled at me about the nastiness of sucking my thumb. She demanded that I look at her when she talked to me and pronounced that she was taking me far away to a "brand-new life" with my "real daddy."

A flash of memory—her high, nervous voice, the smell of liquored breath, my trembling body. I scooted off the couch and attempted to run away, but she quickly grabbed me, smacked me on the legs, yanked me back to where I had been sitting, and told me to stay put. Aunt Eunice grabbed her hands, screamed at her as they fought, and begged her not to take me. She finally succumbed to my mother's insistence that she had no right to keep me since I was not hers. Eunice solemnly left the room to gather my things as my mother had ordered.

There are no words that can sufficiently describe my terror as I was torn from my aunt's arms after being instructed to kiss everybody goodbye. Scrunched into the corner of the back seat of an unfamiliar car, we drunkenly wove our way to "our new life."

3.

Tornado Alley

Some people are born with tornadoes in their lives, but constellations in their eyes. Other people are born with stars at their feet, but their souls are lost at sea.

Nikita Gill, *Perspectives*

After returning to my mother, I quickly learned that if we were to survive, my job was to take care of her—for both our sakes. She barely functioned. Her hopes that I would cement the bond between her and Bud blew up in her face months, just months after my arrival. He had no more time or patience for me than he had when I was a newborn. Annoyed by my presence, he mostly ignored me, but when hung over he raged at me to get the hell out of his sight, pushing, pinching, or shoving me aside, and sometimes using his belt until my legs and backside were blood raw.

Like Clinton, Bud frequently erupted in violence. My mother often started it and seemed to enjoy his increased frustration with her and the loss of his self-control. Bud hurtled degrading words like bombs at my mother, saying, "You're a disgusting waste of my time, you're not even a good lay." He called her a stupid, ugly, worthless bitch, a poor excuse as a lay, dumb as an ox, and just lazy. She fought back with her own words. When she called him a "sonofabitch," this always further enraged him. He continued to tear what little self-esteem she had into shreds as he threw words at her—like fists—until her face grew still and slack, her eyes focused far away. Although I didn't understand the meaning of many of the words, the sound of his angry voice and the energy that accompanied them told me they were truly awful—perhaps enough to kill her.

When not in a drunken stupor, she was remote and appeared to be trapped in a never-ending nightmare. When she emerged for small amounts of time, she launched her frustration and disappointment at me. Locking herself in the bedroom, she screamed, "Get out of my sight, I'm sick of looking at you." Her looks of disgust branded me with self-loathing. "You ruined my life once—now you're ruining it again." It wouldn't be until several years later in moments like these that I would scream back at her, "I never asked to be born and never wanted to come live with you, so don't blame me."

As though the destructive anger of my mother and Bud wasn't enough, within a month of living in St. Louis I experienced my first weather-made tornado. Late one hot, muggy morning, my mother left me with June, a neighbor who lived across the street. Sitting on the sidelines, I watched the other children running in and out of a wading pool and through the sprinkler. The sky changed colors to a murky greenish hue and the wind stilled to a heavy foreboding. Suddenly, the deafening tornado sirens went off. June rushed a half-dozen children playing in her yard into the storm cellar. Catching sight of me sitting in the grass, she waved her hands. "Come on, come on, you too," she hollered.

The large, dark, swirling funnel cloud of the tornado dominated the sky a few blocks away. The force of the wind made it difficult to walk. June grabbed my hand, pulling hard as she and the wind fought over my small body.

We descended the steps into the dark storm cellar where several other adult hands reached out for me and to help June pull the heavy doors closed as the wind raged and fought them. A small lantern cast eerie shadows over the walls. The entire basement shook. A frightening roaring sound began at the same time June noticed her own child missing. She raced back to the steps, sobbing, screaming for Molly as she tried to push the heavy doors open. Two other mothers held her back, pulling her away from the doors as June continued screaming her daughter's name. She finally collapsed into the arms of one of them, sobbing. I chewed my fingernails, wondering if my mother was worried about me, and anxious about where she was. The all-clear sirens eventually went off. The wind quieted as we emerged from the basement to sunlight, soft rain, broken trees, and downed power lines. June immediately found her daughter, who emerged from another neighbor's house, unscathed. I watched in fascination the holding and tears between them.

My mother returned with Bud from wherever she had been, without comment or question. We walked around the neighborhood looking at one block of devastation after another. In the block next to ours, we saw that every house had been flattened. Emergency vehicles loaded the injured. My entire body felt weak and shaky. Bud muttered something I couldn't hear, and my mother's face turned white as she stiffened.

"I don't have the stomach for this. I'm going back to the apartment."

Bud looked at her, nodding, and said, "I couldn't agree more. I'll go back with you."

Turning back toward the way we had just come, Bud reached for my mother's hand. They didn't notice my thumb in my mouth or that I was having trouble keeping up. It wasn't the first time my mother forgot me, and it wouldn't be the last.

During those early months in St. Louis, my mother lost me five times—once for an entire day at a state park. I quickly realized I needed to keep track of her instead of the other way around.

Whatever nightmares my mother might have had would become my own. I wet the bed and often my pants during the day, and frequently woke screaming from night terrors. Obsessed about burning cigarettes, I made sure that they were put out—she once fell asleep in an overstuffed chair that caught fire late one evening when Bud was gone. A constant

Me drinking something surrounded by beer bottles

source of frustration to the two of them was the thumb I often had in my mouth—a sure way to get a spanking. I tried to suck it out of sight, but sometimes the need for this small comfort outweighed my vigilance.

Bud spent less and less time with us. The fights grew more physical, leaving my mother black and blue for days. My life revolved around her as I ran errands, fetching her cigarettes, a can of beer, ice for her blackened face, or closed the shades when the light was too bright.

One day, in a flurry of making up and forgetting the last fight, they got legally married at the courthouse. A few days later they took me to be baptized in the local Catholic church. Bud was insistent it would be the only possible way his mother would ever accept me. He decided we needed a fresh start and he wanted to move to a Chicago suburb near where his mother lived. We left the threat of weather-induced tornadoes behind us. But it was impossible for the two of them to leave behind the unpredictable violence of their relationship.

✳✳✳

After the long drive to Highwood, Illinois, we arrived mid-afternoon at Bud's mother's, where we would spend the night. A big, sturdy, serious, and stern woman answered the door. She was neither welcoming nor kind when Bud introduced my mother. It wasn't until Grandma Margaret turned and looked at me. "And who is this pretty little girl?"

Bud realized he hadn't introduced me. Grandma made it perfectly clear to my mother and to Bud that smoking had never been tolerated in her house. When my mother went outside for a smoke, I overheard Grandma tell Bud that she hoped he knew that I wasn't his blood and looked nothing like him. Bud was subdued and non-committal around his mother and answered that she was probably right. But maybe not, I just might be his kid. I hoped that I wasn't.

The next day they left me with Grandma while they went in search of an apartment. Bud told me to be quiet and entertain myself or he'd give me a good spanking when he got back. After giving me a deck of playing cards and a box of dominoes, Grandma Margaret showed me how to make small houses out of the cards and use the dominoes for fences. I spent the afternoon patiently creating one small world after another. She told me I had good hand–eye coordination and that she was pleasantly surprised that I was very obedient. Bud glowed at her praise of me when they returned. My mother sulked.

I started kindergarten at St. James Catholic School. Grandma Margaret had taught in the Catholic schools since Bud was a boy, so she was able to secure a scholarship for me. This was my second year of kindergarten. I hadn't done well in St. Louis because of my "issues" of not talking, and sometimes having accidents in my pants. Through kindergarten at St. James Catholic School, I mostly sat in frozen fear and shyness, hoping no one would notice me. In first grade, although I had trouble learning and remembering things, I was obedient and polite. I loved the routine and structure school provided. By the second grade, it was clear I was falling behind academically but I had made a friend and talked more when spoken to. It still didn't take much for me to be overtaken with shy self-consciousness.

Even though we had moved to several different apartments in Highwood, I continued at St. James for two years. The familiarity nurtured me. I loved everything about the school and church. The colors and pictures on the bulletin boards cheered me up, no matter what was happening at home. I loved the smell and feel of the books that I desperately wanted to learn to read. But each month I found it more difficult and quickly fell further behind.

On the home front, Bud regularly disappeared from our lives. He was often gone for days and weeks at a time, leaving us with empty cupboards and no money. Some relief came when my mom started to go out, looking for money, looking to get "lucky." Nearly every late afternoon, she spent hours getting ready: applying makeup and changing from one dress to another. I remember watching her, mesmerized as her face slowly changed. As though she was performing a ritual, she lined up jars of makeup, beginning to quietly hum as her whole body softened, leaning toward something or someone, yet indescribable to me. Watching, entranced, the physical transformation from her drunken stupor or dangerous anger into a primping, excited beauty was fascinating. Sometimes, she caught my face in the mirror and would wink at me. Turning, she'd ask, "Am I pretty?"

I'd nod and manage to whisper in a small voice, frightened of breaking the spell, "Oh, yes!"

She was more than pretty, she was beautiful, soft, and captivating. She had transformed herself into someone I desperately wanted as my mother.

"Are the fellas going to fall in love with me tonight? Will I get lucky?" I somehow knew to say "yes," not understanding the implications of what she meant, or the potential cost.

Music seemed to wake her up, taking her into another dreamscape, or sometimes into a deep, sobbing grief that curled and rocked her whole body. When I changed the channel on the radio, she didn't seem to notice. Once, I wrapped my small arms around her shaking frame. She came out of the tears in a fury of anger, knocking me to the floor. "Don't ever touch me like that again," she shrieked.

In the evenings, she would drag me with her to the bars. I watched her, spellbound, as she emerged as though from a deep sleep, the embodiment of Sleeping Beauty. On good nights, she'd sweep over to the booth she had planted me in and would throw me a candy bar, a bag of chips, or set a Coke in front of me. "I think I'm getting lucky," she'd laughingly whisper.

The music seemed to bring her alive. Hope and possibility lit up her eyes, making her look beautiful to me. I'd watch, mesmerized, as she swayed in the arms of one strange soldier after another to the rhythm and blues music that changed her, softening the contours of her face, animating her entire body, and magically whisking away the tension and hard lines of disappointment. The stories told in the lyrics of the songs filled with longing love, disappointment, and regret seemed written just for her. Her entire body unwound, transforming her into movie-star beautiful in my eyes. Sometimes, she sashayed over to the booth, giggling, and feeling open and generous gave me money for a soda or candy bar.

A song about a moon and river always made her cry and beg someone to buy her another drink after it ended. As I listened to the words, I'd wonder: if she followed the moon and river, would she take me with her or leave me behind? Would she really find the end of the rainbow? Then I'd start to cry, too, or fall asleep in the hard, smelly booth from thinking about how big and hard the world is, and even if you're a drifter like my mom and the guy in the song, perhaps nothing ever got better no matter how hard you dreamed it would.

While my mother found inspiration and release in military men and music, I began to find it in church. I fell in love with the music, incense, ritual, and slow predictability of the Latin-sung mass. Enchanted with the back-and-forth rhythm of the Latin words, I quickly memorized them by listening closely to the others in church.

The priest would first sing "Dominus Vobiscum." "Et cum Spiritu tuo," I would sing in response, with the rest of the congregation. In those moments, I felt part of something larger than my small world of chaos. After hearing stories of some of the saints, I fell in love with the statues of several in the church. I would have long, fervent conversations with the Blessed Virgin, St. Christopher, and St. Therese, the little flower. St. Jude was one of my favorites because he was a patron of desperate cases and lost causes.

Second grade was challenging as I struggled with what seemed impossible tasks. My anxiety grew daily with my feeling of shame that I had been required to go to kindergarten for two years and had just gotten by in first grade. My second-grade teacher, Sister Richard Anne, was kind and patient, but seemed to have given up hope of teaching me how to read. Despite this, I began to learn by memorizing whatever I could on the good days, when I had gotten enough to eat and enough sleep the night before. Yet, I could tell some days she seemed just as discouraged by my lack of progress in reading as I was.

I had always been sensitive to the nuances of the world around me, to the moods of others, and to an unseen world. I was a dreamy child as well as a dreamer. I don't remember many of my early dreams, but one in particular has stayed with me—perhaps because the theme of tornadoes in my dreams has recurred throughout my life.

A tornado gently but firmly picks me up, and I'm holding the hand of a very old woman with lots of wrinkles. I don't know who she is, but I know I am safe with her as she whispers, "We're in the center of it, stay calm. It's calm in the center." At the outer edges of the funnel cloud, furniture, trees, my mother, and other adults are being tossed about. I calmly stand alert, holding the hand of the old woman, whispering to me, "It is always calm in your center."

I didn't really understand the dream as a child or how to find my center, but shortly after this dream I moved into a time of being calmer and more centered in my turbulent life.

I distinctly remember developing a new skill in second grade. Every afternoon, a half hour before the final bell rang and announcements were made, I would focus on casting the net of my imagination out toward home, scanning my mother and the apartment. Before leaving school, I would know if my mother would be sober or drunk. Checking to see if Bud was home, I would try to pick up whether the environment was calm or tense. If I felt signals of danger in my casting net, I would stop by the church, light a vigil candle, and pray in front of St. Jude, asking him to help me find and stay calm in the calm place if the situation at home was hopeless.

Second grade also brought preparations for the mysterious First Confession and First Communion. As a prerequisite to making Holy Communion, we prepared for an examination of conscience by memorizing the Act of Contrition, and the outlined steps of making your First Confession. This seemed to bring fear into the hearts of my classmates but relief into mine. I longed for *confession* and felt the burden of imagined sins and carried the hope for my burden of inner being lightened by the magic of the confessional. I had a good memory and quickly memorized the words. Sister Richard Ann just needed to read them to me a whole lot of times. I knelt in the darkened confession booth and began. "Bless me Father for I have sinned; this is my first confession."

I confessed anger at my mother. Bud. The multiple men who were in and out of my mother's bed. Sinful thoughts. I carefully counted up the times when I stole change from Bud's pockets. I wondered if it was my sin or my mother's if she had told me to do the stealing from the men who visited her. Her face and words threatened my hungry belly as she hissed at my hesitation with, "Do it right now if you want anything to eat next week." I apologized to God for letting my belly make the decision instead of obeying the commandment of "Thou shalt not steal."

One day after school, Sister held me back. She asked me if I had a dress yet—every girl was required to wear a special white dress—and I hung my head in shame. My mother had ignored the notes that were sent home. Sister handed me a piece of paper. "It's OK. Give this to your mother. It's a special paper to take to the store, written on the top—here," her finger pointed to a place on the paper. "You can pick out a pretty First Communion dress," Sister said with a smile on her face. As though reading my mind about the problem of money, she continued, "Your mother won't need any money; it's all been taken care of."

My mother succumbed and took me to the store. She handed the voucher to the manager. As she argued with him to give me the least expensive dress they had in the store, and then give her whatever money was left over, I grew anxious. He patiently explained that vouchers didn't work that way, as I grew self-conscious and embarrassed. Shopping for the dress no longer felt very special.

First Communion came and went. No one from my family attended, not even Grandma Margaret, who said she was too lame with the gout. Sister Richard Ann hugged me and handed me a beautiful card of St. Therese before I left the church. Bud was at the apartment when I returned from the communion mass, and he told me to walk to Grandma Margaret's before I changed so she could see my dress. It was a simple white dress with a crinoline underneath, beautiful white shoes, and anklets. And, of course, the required veil and white gloves.

Grandma Margaret surprised me when she gave me a beautiful light blue rosary made of smooth, polished beads and a prayer book. I held the little silk bag that contained the rosary and the beautiful ivory-covered book close to my heart as I thanked her, and I really meant it. It was the most beautiful thing I'd ever been given. I guess she didn't know I couldn't read yet. I also didn't think she knew Bud came and went, or that my mother sinned, breaking her marriage vows. Since learning the Ten Commandments, I now had concepts and words to better understand what was happening in my life and the funny feelings I had each time my mother took a new man to her bed or disappeared into parked cars or back rooms, leaving me to fend for myself. When I learned the ten commandments, a feeling of rules and order that made sense was created for me in contrast to my disorganized world. At the same time, the memorizing of the "holy laws of God" contributed to my mounting fear and shame about my mother.

The summer after my First Communion, simmering tensions between my mother and Bud grew more pronounced. I walked on eggshells all of the time. We moved several times that year because of unpaid rent, or because Bud's fist broke through the wall. Neighbors complained about all of the yelling and screaming. Eventually, Bud said we had run out of options. I wasn't sure what that meant.

That hot, muggy summer, filled with the sounds of locusts, found us living above a bar on Highwood's Main Street in a shabby one-room. Bud worked in another bar down the street. The simmering between them grew to a boiling point one afternoon, leaving my mother resentful and careless. Throwing caution to the wind, she dressed carefully. She was going out.

"Bud can go screw himself, I could care less. You stay in the room and go to bed," she ordered.

What had been simmering between Bud and my mother materialized when I was startled awake by the sound of loud explosions and the entire building shaking. Someone in the hallway yelled, "Fire, Get Out!" The wail of sirens and banging doors, yelling voices, and bright lights was jarring.

I wondered if the yelling to "get out" included me. My mom had told me to stay in the room. Hot and sweaty, I crept to the window and saw flames shooting from the ground floor upward—firefighters were putting up ladders on either side of our room. The neon sign was in front of our window, making it difficult to see out and impossible for anyone to see me inside. Trying with all my might to open the window left me gasping for breath and exhausted, with no results.

The room was becoming smoky. Running to the door to the hallway, I grasped the solid metal doorknob with both hands. Heat and pain raced from my hands up my arms. The door wouldn't budge—it was impossible to hold on to the knob. My hands came away bright red and blistered while my terror mounted and my heart pounded. Panicky, I tried the door again, to no avail, only more pain in my burned hands. Back at the window, I screamed until I had no voice. Then I sought the corner of the room farthest away from the door and curled into a small, still ball.

Firefighters eventually rescued me through the window. I was taken down a ladder, wrapped in something warm and slick, and held in the arms of a man with a soothing voice and blue eyes who carried me to a waiting ambulance. Bud was impatiently waiting nearby. Soothing, cool ointment was applied to my hands, followed by bandages. Bud kept asking me where my mother was. I didn't know and grew tired of telling him that she just said she was going out. I knew there would be hell to pay when he found her as his anger and impatience mounted, a thunderstorm ready to break free.

After sitting with an oxygen mask on for a while, they released me to him. He roughly grabbed my arm and dragged me up the street in my nightgown and bare feet, in and out of bars, searching for my mom. We found her sitting on the lap of a soldier from Fort Sheridan. Bud pulled her off the man's lap and dragged her outside as I begged him not to hurt her. He was deaf to my pleas, his rage out of control as he beat her senseless—and left her lying unconscious on the sidewalk in a pool of blood.

Sobbing, I went inside and begged the bartender for help. He called us a taxi after getting my mother sitting up and told me to take her away. At first confused, I protested that there was nowhere to go, our rooming house had burned down. He looked at me with sad, tired eyes. "Kid, there has to be somewhere, a relative, friend, or someone to help," he said.

I had an excellent memory for directions, a life skill developed by how essential it was to always know where we were—since my mother so frequently didn't. Somehow, by watching for visual clues, I was able to direct the cab driver, step by step, to another suburb where my Aunt Myrtle lived. We had only been there a few times. I hoped and prayed that she would let us in.

Weeks later, we were still with Myrtle and my mother had promised not to go back to "that worthless son of a bitch." Aunt Myrtle had three daughters. Donna was a lot older and living in Wisconsin with Aunt Ethel, cause she "got too wild." Sharon was thirteen and Linda eight, a year older than me. Linda was willing to share her toys and Sharon lavished me with the attention her younger sister didn't seem to welcome. But for the first time, I felt jealous. Linda seemed to have everything a little girl could want but I had nothing. Since the fire even the clothes I wore were Linda's hand-me-downs.

Every week Linda went to a ballet class. The day I got to sit on the side and watch, I was sure my jealousy would kill me. Linda was possessive, but once she let me try on her ballet slippers, and sometimes she'd let me open and close her jewelry box, which was filled with trinkets and a tiny ballerina who danced to tinny, soft music. I prayed silently at night that God would forgive me for breaking the commandment "Thou shalt not covet thy neighbor's goods." Grateful for three filling meals a day, a playmate, attention from Sharon, and some daily structure, I quickly began to feel like an ordinary kid, and would have been content living with them forever.

All too soon, Aunt Myrtle had a fight with my mother. She quickly helped us find a small apartment in a two-family house. Though I missed Aunt Myrtle's home, I loved this new place. I learned to climb the apple tree in the backyard and swing like a monkey from the clothesline pole. Best of all, I taught myself to roller skate on the sidewalk and on the smooth, concrete basement floor with the second-hand clip-on skates Linda had outgrown. Life seemed better for a few weeks, until my mom resumed drinking and going out at night. The bad news was I was in a new school. I don't recall friends; what I remember most is that we lived close to a factory that made medicine. Several days a week, my teacher handed out white-squared fabric to cover our noses as we walked home from school. Horrid, smelly fumes and smoke came out of big, long smoke stacks, coloring the sky gray and our clothes with soot.

One morning, many months later, Bud showed up. "Go play in the traffic," he told me and gave me a quarter to buy something at the corner store. They kept the door locked all afternoon. When I returned home from the store, I snuck into the screened-in back porch. I busied myself, creating a parallel world from my imagination, another life from my cousin's cast-off paper dolls. The door to the apartment had not been opened the rest of the day or evening. I was sure my mother had forgotten me, again. That night, my guardian angel tucked me into the old rollaway bed on the back porch and curled herself around me as I fell sound asleep.

4.

Love's Awakening

... deep inside,
in that silent place
where a child's fears crouch ...

Lillian Smith, *The Journey*

My ninth year found me tiptoeing into local churches to sit in the back of funeral services one Saturday after another. Fascinated by death, not only did I have flashes of my uncle Clinton's death, I found myself fixated on my own demise. My mind churned round and round, trying to solve a problem that I didn't fully understand. In my mind, I wondered, *if people died and went to heaven, then how come their body was left behind?* The more funerals I observed, the more confused I became.

My obsession grew when after a week of spying into the windows of a local funeral home, I snuck inside, having seen a dead body though the window. I needed to get closer and touch the woman I'd seen. My risk was rewarded as I found my way to the large room filled with flowers. The body was laid out in a bed like the one Snow White laid on after she ate the poisoned apple. I slowly crept up to her. Looking down in awe at the woman in the coffin, I gently touched her arm, then her face.

In a flash, I *knew* that nothing was there, except the empty shell that the woman had once lived in. It reminded me of the loud cicadas that had been everywhere the summer before. Walking down the street had been frightening because you never knew if you were stepping on an empty shell, or a live one that would startle you by taking flight.

I'd seen what I wanted to do and was ready to leave my own shell of a body behind. I took two bottles of aspirin and some red pills in the medicine cupboard and lay down waiting to go to sleep and die. I waited, and waited, and waited, growing confused and concerned that I hadn't just slipped out of my shell. Minutes lengthened, drawing out the day as I felt sicker and sicker, filled with ringing in my ears. My mother came home drunk and disheveled. Frightened, I stumbled into the living room and told her what I had done.

"You wanted to die, go ahead and die, just get the hell out of my sight," she slurred.

Fear of the physical sensations moving through my body overtook fear of my mother. "Please, please, help me," I begged.

"You heard me, get out of my sight, you disgust me," she said through gritted teeth. "I've put up with you for nine miserable years and I'm through."

I had believed you just laid down and went to sleep and died. But before long a loud ringing in my ears accompanied my disquieting, galloping heartbeat and burning stomach pain. The bed became a giant merry-go-round, spinning faster and faster with no way to stop. I hadn't counted on the terrifying ways my body would be screaming for help, regardless of my desire to be dead. My mother passed out, and I was able to crawl to the neighbors for help. They called the police, who took me to the local emergency room where I was given black charcoal to drink until I threw up.

When the emergency room discharged me, the policeman took me to his office. For the next hour, he showed me horrible pictures of dirty rooms with garbage everywhere, mattresses on the floor with rats nearby. Rooms with broken windows and falling plaster. He pointed his finger at me and then at the picture. "If you don't live in a place that looks this bad, you should be ashamed of yourself." I was. The ache in my stomach and burning throat reminding me of the stupid thing I had done. The policeman took me back to my mother. She had fallen asleep in the chair before I left and was still there. I remember that he shook her awake and told her she had to take better care of me and asked if there was a father in the picture. My mother roused for the first time. Narrowing her eyes, she told him that "the worthless sonofabitch could go fuck himself." I worried she was now in trouble for talking to him like that, but he told her that when Bud came, he should call, and he left a card on the table. My mother lifted her white-knuckled, clenched fist in my direction. "Get out of my sight—before I kill you myself. Bud's going to give you the beating of your life when he comes back."

He didn't come back for months. She'd forgotten her threats by then, and the officer's card had long since disappeared.

On hot, muggy summer nights when my mom was out with her men, I waited to hear her returning footsteps, my emotions swinging from rage to terror. When angry, I fantasized about finally shouting my nearly nine years worth of anger at her. I sometimes pictured my frustration and anger spilling everywhere. My pent-up words became a boiling liquid eating the linoleum floor, the crappy furniture, my mother herself. I'd pretend to hurl wounding words like arrows: "I hate you. You don't take care of me. I'm scared all the time—all the time."

Deep inside, I didn't want to be like her or Bud in their destructive rage. I made a vow and buried the feelings until the boiling and churning lay pent up inside, leaching the life out of me. When frightened, I saw myself clinging to her legs as she tried to kick me away, or wandering alone forever in the narrow confines of our apartment. Loneliness descended, snuffing out the candle of hope and replacing it with exhaustion and despair. These nightly terrors were fueled by my mother's uncontrollable mood swings during the day when she'd threaten to disappear.

Ongoing isolation and loneliness threatened to devour me, as I was often targeted by other kids in school and the neighborhood. I couldn't name one friend. Myrtle had been mad at me when she found my paper dolls having sex and wouldn't let me play with Linda anymore. My aunts had washed their hands of my mother and me completely when she let Bud back into our lives. The last time we saw Myrtle, she screamed at my mother, "Edna, you've made your own bed, now you can damn well lie in it." Turning my head to look at my aunt, I silently wondered why my Aunt Myrtle made me lie in it too.

One day in my ninth summer, I came home and found a strange man sitting in our living room with my drunk mother. Pausing in the doorway, I studied the two of them. He was older than the men she usually picked up. He looked unkempt and the white of his sailor uniform accented his rolls of fat. He was disgusting—radiating danger through the sweaty and hungry way he looked at me.

"Say hello to my new friend, Oscar," my mother slurred. "Thanks to him being such a gentleman, we don't have to move this month. You act really nice to him now." She pulled a wad of money from her bra, her look signaling a warning as she demanded that I say hello.

Cautiously moving into the living room, I muttered a greeting.

Although I didn't know what was to come, my body hummed with fear and a warning of danger. I dropped my school bag in the corner, mumbling that I had to go to the library and do homework, and quickly left.

Oscar began to be a daily presence. They sometimes went out together but more often drank at home. The two of them took up so much space in our small one-bedroom apartment that I had trouble breathing. He seemed to enjoy my discomfort when I would wander in and find them naked. He announced one day that I'd soon have a friend to play with because his seven-year-old niece was coming to stay for the rest of the summer. Lucy and I played paper dolls, climbed trees, and built a tent. She whispered secrets in the darkened tent about how sometimes Oscar made her make-believe she was his girlfriend because her sister, his wife, was too sick all of the time to be a wife to him. At first it was fun, but she really hated it. She made me promise not to tell.

My excitement at having a summer playmate was short-lived. On a muggy summer night, Oscar took us out for ice cream, then to a vacant parking lot, the site of a closed plant near Lake Michigan, and then he sexually abused me. Lucy, who I thought was my friend, knelt on my arms, pressing them into the pavement, "You be good to him for me, since I'm too little to do what he needs to do," she begged. My back screamed with pain from the cinders biting into my flesh. My heart broke from her betrayal.

As I gazed into the eyes of the little girl I'd known as a friend, holding my arms to the ground as Oscar beat his body into me, I whispered "Why?" over and over. I had difficulty making sense of how she could help him hurt me after she'd spent so much time complaining about what he was doing to her. We'd planned to run away together. Now, I blamed myself for being such a fool to have ever trusted. "Your mama says, you better be nice to me," Oscar threatened.

From that night on, I avoided all overtures of friendship. Fear engulfed me each time I ran into either Oscar or Lucy. Sick with humiliation, I spent as much time as possible out of the house, often sneaking in long after dark, in terror of being cornered by Oscar.

Lucy eventually left, returning to wherever she was from.

There was a brief respite from Oscar for a couple of weeks while he was on duty at the base. I lit vigil candles in church daily and prayed he would never come back. I couldn't bring myself to tell the priest in confession anything about Lucy or Oscar. In early September, I was home from school recovering from chickenpox—red, hot, and covered in itching scabs—when Oscar returned. He and my mother spent the day drinking. Around the time I normally would be coming home from school, Oscar left to go to the liquor store to get my mother some beer and cigarettes. "I'll be back for the kid in a little while," he said as the screen door slammed behind him.

Staggering into the bedroom, my mother instructed me to get up and get dressed—Oscar wanted to take me to the movies. I cried and begged that I was too sick, but to no avail. She warned me to shut my mouth, reminding me that she expected me to be nice to her friends who wanted to be nice to me. Growing increasingly desperate for protection, I blurted out what Oscar had done to me the night he took his niece and me out for ice-cream. At first, she looked at me incredulously. Then her face grew distorted with a mixture of hatred, hurt, and determination. I hadn't ever seen her look like that before. Caught in her studied gaze, I was chilled to the core and suddenly felt in fear for my life. She turned and walked out of the room, muttering under her breath. Curling into a small ball under the covers, I shook in terror, trying to get smaller—to disappear.

A short while later, the door slammed and I heard voices. My mother yelled that I was to get my ass into the living room or I'd get a beating I'd never forget. She stumbled into the room and pulled me from the bed, hitting me anywhere within reach as she dragged me into the living room. "Sit," she ordered.

"Why isn't she dressed? We'll miss the movie."

"The brat just told me what you did to her this summer. You stole from me and now you're going to pay me back." Her voice was threatening and measured. She walked behind the chair she had sat me in and held my shoulders, squeezing hard as she worked herself up to the next level of threat.

"The only show anyone is going to see is the one that you are going to give me. Show me exactly what you did to her, you, sonofabitch," she hissed, smacking me in the side of the head as I attempted to pull away from her. "Do it! Or else, I'm calling the cops."

Understanding what was about to happen, I scrambled to get away. She immediately pushed harder on my shoulders, pinching tender flesh with her sharp fingernails.

"Now! Do it, you fucking bastard."

Oscar, angry at her threats, grabbed me, threw me down, and did what she commanded as I stared into the empty eyes of my mother. Her fixed, glazed-over expression would haunt me for years, at times matching my own.

"Is that what you wanted, Edna?" Oscar asked sarcastically as he put his pants on.

"Now, I expect you to pay double for both times. Or by god, I will call the cops and maybe the commander at your base, too," she snarled.

Oscar pulled a roll of bills from his pocket and threw it down.

Before leaving he asked her if they were still friends. My mother told him that as long as he paid her, he was welcome to come around. A giant fissure of grief cracked open in me that day, soon replaced by a deep, abiding numbness. I lived swaddled in the confusion of incomprehension. I simply could not understand how my mother could sell me—and then watch my terror and humiliation. I had no idea how to live—or why.

As I think back on this event, my mother's face and empty eyes are what I see. At the time, I felt at first she watched what she'd insisted Oscar do to me, but her face slowly morphed and changed into a vacant and still emptiness. Now that I better understand her history and that of abused children, I can't help but wonder if she hadn't seen me because she was seeing herself in that place of frozen surrender, the first time one of her older brothers broke her open. The moments when she could do nothing, but then vowed to never, ever let a man touch her again unless she made him pay for it. I also realize another thing we shared was resentment and the feeling of being unwanted. My mother had passed down the indifference and resentment she received from her siblings, as well as a core truth of being unwanted, to me.

This event seemed to turn on a compulsion in my mom and there was no turning it off. Now my mother not only went out and picked up men, but she frequently brought them home and like some coy game show host, she made them choose between herself and me. Holding my breath with anxiety each time a man was around, waiting for him to tell her the right answer, was exhausting. I quickly learned that there was never a right answer. If they chose her, she was angry, seething at a missed opportunity for extra money and perhaps the thrill of watching me being humiliated and raped. If they chose me, she was demeaning and cruel: ignoring me and acting as though I was invisible for days afterwards. Nonetheless, she always watched as I gazed into those empty eyes. I remember this period of time as one of constant knots of anxiety and terror balled up like tight springs in my belly.

It wasn't until years later that I began to understand the concept of a double bind. There simply was no good resolution—a right decision— any man could make, or any way this could turn out right or that I could feel safe. I imagine my mother felt double bound by Clinton—perhaps he didn't treat her as badly as her siblings if she came to his bed, and she hated herself by acquiescing. Perhaps it was my vulnerability, like her own, that she really hated.

Living in a near-constant state of anxiety when she was out for the night, I'd walk around the apartment in circles, caught between wanting my mom to come home and terrified that she would—along with some new boyfriend, uncle, or whatever she told me to call him that time.

One Saturday morning, after one of those anxiety-ridden nights, I wandered outside to sit on the front steps and watch for her to return. I was hungry and she'd been gone for several days. A stirring in the air, a shift in my body temperature, and an increase in adrenaline alerted me to be careful. Neighborhood kids—three boys and two girls—stopped in front of me. They had teased and taunted me before.

A girl named Barbara asked friendly-like, "Hey, what are you doing out here?"

I shrugged my shoulders and looked away.

"We're trying to be nice. We thought you would want to play with us," a red-headed, freckle-faced boy said. Loneliness—longing for company and friendship—made me drop my guard. "I'm waiting for my mother."

One of the boys stuck out his tongue and grimaced. "I bet she's out being a slut," he taunted.

I'd momentarily mistaken their attention for friendship, but I knew enough to get away. As I jumped up to move inside, they ran past me into the apartment and slammed the door in my face. I wasn't allowed to have kids in the apartment and panicked. Worse were the images of what I knew they'd see and spread around the neighborhood: ashtrays overflowed with cigarette butts, bags of empty beer cans cluttering the small kitchen, the sink full of weeks-old dirty dishes. Ketchup colored the wall like blood from where my mother had thrown it at Bud several weeks before during one of his unpredictable visits. Filth was everywhere, including the bathroom with a clogged toilet. The small apartment was filled with the rancid smell of beer, whiskey, and sex.

Blindly, frantically, I pushed to get in. Five of them held the door closed from inside, whispering to each other and laughing at my ineffective effort to push the door open. Suddenly, the energy of fear and anger coalesced, giving me the strength to push harder. My hands and arms broke through the upper glass in the door. Only the sudden explosion of broken glass and blood stopped me.

The kids scattered, except for one—Barbara, who dragged me up the block to a weekend emergency room on the first floor of the small mental health center. "I'm sorry, I'm sorry," she pleaded, as though she was praying the rosary.

"It wasn't your fault," I mumbled. I was just happy she was going with me to the ER.

Several hundred stitches closed torn flesh, while my anxiety mounted about my mother returning. Barbara said she had to say goodbye or her mom would be mad, and ran off toward her own house. I wondered if she had a mother who had made lunch for her. Overwhelming dread and misery engulfed me as, step by step, I neared the apartment. With bandaged arms and hands, a beating seemed certain for the mess, the broken window, and the bill from the emergency room stuffed in my pocket.

Pausing as I approached the entryway because I had seen movement inside, I stiffened, anticipating the blows my mother would rain down upon me. To my surprise, the kind face of the upstairs neighbor greeted me. The hall was cleaned up and he'd almost finished installing a new window. "Hi, are you okay? My wife, Dale, came down and looked for you after we heard the glass break and all the commotion. She cleaned things up a bit and sent me to the hardware store. I'll be finished here in a little while," he said with a smile.

Speechless, I stared at him.

"Your mother doesn't seem to be home yet. Dale's making lunch and said to send you up when you got back. Why don't you go on upstairs now?" The door at the top of the steps stood open and inviting.

Dale tenderly touched my bandaged arms and hands and asked me if they hurt. I shrugged as I shyly looked around her apartment. Although the floor plan was the exact same layout as the one I lived in, it could have been in a different world. It was orderly, neat, and clean, with beautiful potted plants everywhere. It smelled like sunshine and the chocolate-chip cookies Dale had just pulled from the oven.

My mother didn't return that night. Dale and her husband invited me to sleep on their couch. I shook my head no, but smiled as I clutched the "just in case you change your mind" key tight in my closed fist. Dale told me to keep the key just in case there was another time. I was both intrigued and frightened by their kindness, they didn't seem to want anything in return.

Several days later my mother still hadn't returned. Dale sought me out, bringing food and friendship. She always asked if I wanted to change my mind and sleep on the couch. I knew I'd be in trouble with my mother if I did, so each time I said no, letting her care and the key be more than enough.

Dale was stunningly beautiful, with the raven hair and porcelain skin that made Elizabeth Taylor a star. And she was kind to me. I was enchanted. For the next several months, Dale warmed me with grown-up attention. She noticed my feelings. One morning I sat on the porch trying to comb snarls out of my long, wavy hair. She watched me quietly.

"You've just had a shower and look so pretty." She reached out for the brush. "Here, let me help you get the knots out of your hair. I promise to be gentle." She smiled. She took her time as she combed through the tangles, soothing me with her quiet reassurance. I wished inside that she would never stop. She finished the task by braiding my hair.

She often made cookies to share, and I'd pretend she'd made them just for me. I found myself pretending that she was my mother, or that she

Our neighbor, Dale, who taught me how to love

was going to offer to adopt me, or buy me from my mom straight out, for money. After hearing so often that money was one of our main problems, I just knew my mom would say yes, for money.

Oscar had started coming back around regularly again—paying double for me and for my mother. It was impossible for me to understand how she would both threaten Oscar and then manipulate him, winding him around her little finger like she did.

Dale and her husband only lived upstairs for a couple of months. Her husband had just been discharged from the Navy so they were moving "back home," to a place way south of Chicago, "almost in Indiana," Dale explained to me one day. I had lived in a realm of shadows and dead expectations for so long that until the day when Dale and her husband were to move away, I hadn't realized how I had come to cherish and depend on her. Dale's presence had become the only thing keeping me alive, as important as oxygen. Frantic at the thought of her leaving, I was sure I would die—I would drown in my longing.

As I made the slow and painful climb up the stairs to say goodbye, I hoped she wouldn't see my legs and arms. They were bruised by Oscar, who had been there the night before pounding me into the bed, down to the springs. He'd given my mom enough money for beer and cigarettes for weeks, as well as the rent money.

I tried to focus on the flowers I'd picked from the courthouse lawn as a surprise. But the grief and terror of Dale's departure overtook me. I choked back tears, my panic of losing her mounting with each step. As I limped into her apartment and saw the stacked boxes, I took one look at her soft, beautiful face and fell apart—my body shook with sobs. Dale reached for me, pulling me to her, and held me close.

"I love you. I love you, shush now, there, there. I love you," she murmured.

The gap between the life I knew and this holding and murmuring was wide enough for me to fall through. My hand crept up, touching her neck in wonder. The warmth of her skin filled me and plummeted me further into infant-like, racking sobs.

"I know, I know," she crooned. "I want you to know I love you," her voice soothed.

Dale held me, rocking me close for what seemed like hours. I wanted to melt into her body and never leave its soft, warm contours. As she cradled my head, gently patting my matted hair, I begged her not to leave me, at the same time knowing that I had been indelibly imprinted with something important—and yet intangible.

"This is very important, look at me as I tell you this. I want you to remember every word." She sat me up, lifting my chin gently, taking my face in her hands as she looked deeply into my eyes. "I love you. I wish you were my little girl so that I could take you with me, but I can't because you're not mine. You must learn to take better care of yourself, because your mother is too sick and can't take care of you," she continued. "Do you understand that?"

I nodded and whispered, "Yes."

"I love you and I'll always keep you in my heart." She pointed to her heart. "Right here. You have to reach out and trust others like me."

"I guess," I replied, uncertain.

"Do it for me. Promise you won't forget and will try for me."

I promised, as tears coursed down both our faces. I felt something alive and tingly rippling through me. I looked at her in wonder. "You love me," I whispered, tasting the sweet mystery of the words.

"Yes, I really love you." Dale's smile was wide open, lighting up her face and blue eyes with love.

I saw the truth of it radiating from her face. In that moment, Dale, and this living thing she called love, moved fully into me and took up residence. It filled me inside as I had never been filled before, reaching the empty, aching spaces of longing. "I love you, Dale. I'll always keep you here too," I whispered, tasting the newness of these words, as I pointed to my own heart.

Something life-giving, like air, but not air. Something like what I often felt in church, in the music, lifted me, enfolded me, and I suddenly became part of everything. My heart and body continued to open to something intangible and as essential as food and water. For the first time in my life, I felt like I not only deserved to be alive but knew *why* I was alive. For this: to accept, feel, and learn to receive and give this thing called love.

That night as I lay in bed looking out the window at the rising full moon, I noticed for the first time how beautiful it was. As the moon wrapped me in its mantle of light, I fell into a deep, peaceful sleep, snug in the embrace of love. My days had been defined by thousands of ways a child can be hurt, disconnected, and unmoored from everyone and everything. I now felt connected to everything and everyone—to the earth itself. Throughout the days to come, I repeated Dale's message to take better care of myself because my mother was too sick to take care of me. I warmed myself with the memory of her touch, her voice, and the energy of being wrapped in love.

I worked hard to be kind, carrying groceries home for people who needed help. I went to church even more often than I had before. Continuing to seek out choir music, I became acquainted with every church in town. Church music held me in a place of love and connection. The courthouse lawn became my personal gardens where I weekly collected flowers to put in front of the Mary, Queen of Heaven statue. Talking to her endlessly, I believed she listened.

I also brought home flowers for my mother, who was either angry or didn't notice. Ignoring her responses, I was driven in my mission to be the love I had received. I noticed how tired and confused she often was. An average day for her consisted of five to ten men, at least four six-packs, shots of whiskey when it was available, a Lucky Strike or Camel continuously burning in the ashtray, and some feel-good music from the radio. I felt the smallness of her life—as mine expanded. And I felt sad for her.

Dale's love had created its own longing, a hunger which I did not know how to meet. I was starving. One day as I watched a daytime TV game show called *Queen for a Day*, an idea came to me.[1] I decided to create my own "Queen for a Day" show. I listened to Jack Bailey and practiced the words, "Would YOU like to be Queen for a Day?" I got the magical sound of YOU just right. The girl Barbara who had taken me to the emergency room when I cut my arms had become my one friend. I compiled a list of ideas and talked her into playing the game with me. We spent hours constructing criteria and tests to determine the perfect queen. She had to be young, pretty, patient, gentle, smile a lot, speak in a soft voice, like kids, and not have any of her own. I assumed anyone that had their own wouldn't like kids anymore. Our Queen, like the contestants on the show, had to have had a recent tragedy and risen above it. Our list of requirements was nearly endless. No smoking, drinking, or excessive makeup: she must smell nice and be willing to talk to us and answer our questions. I prayed to the Queen of Heaven statue for assistance and wisdom in knowing who would be the "right" one.

We set out on our search, in and out of local stores, being cute and questioning, obnoxious and testy. Block after block: Sears, Walgreens, Ace Hardware, Fine Jewelry, and the A&P. We were purposeful in our quest.

We tested for patience by "accidentally" knocking items off shelves. We coyly looked clerks over and approached only the real possibilities with our list of questions. JCPenney, Wards, the corner bakery, First Bank. Some flunked immediately. Others, we weren't sure. Our Queen had to be perfect. Running from each store, we carefully used the cardboard meter I'd constructed to score the questionnaire we'd written up ahead of time. I thought that even host of the show, Jack Bailey,would have been proud of our organization and persistence.[2]

It was a warm day when we found her, after searching for two weeks. We ran from that store ecstatic, giggling and shouting in nine-year-old delight. Our Queen was twenty-one years old and worked as the cosmetic clerk at Osco Drug. She'd passed the tests one hundred percent, including her reaction to the "accidentally" broken perfume bottle. Her name was Diane. She had a heart-shaped face that seemed to smile all of the time and the kind of hair I'd always wished for. It was like Shirley Temple's—golden blond and just-right curly.

The day of the coronation arrived. We marched solemnly and slowly into Osco Drug, singing. I ceremoniously took the crown from the pillow and placed it on top of her curls. We solemnly read off the list of her deserving attributes. Patient, kind, honest, beautiful, calm, non-smoker, without children—and she really liked us. If she was embarrassed or thought us silly, it never showed. She said she was "touched" and, as her hand patted her heart, her eyes glistened with unspent tears. A real sign

Diane, the "queen" Barbara and I chose

of nobility, I thought with a deep, satisfied sigh. She gently kissed each of us on the cheeks.

Life with my mother continued—with men coming and going. In the meantime, I survived through the memory of Dale, and with Diane's continued kindness and attention. During the next months, Diane encouraged me in small, supportive ways and helped me with my homework during her breaks. A third-grade substitute teacher helped me learn to read. She helped me gain the confidence I needed to finally stick with it. Diane helped me sign up for a library card and then, I discovered magic as I checked out unlimited books from the library. Diane had faith in my ability to learn and was always encouraging. Dale had told me to reach out to the world, and in doing so I found that I could begin to trust others and that others saw me differently than my mother did.

5.

Dismemberment

No one told me
it would lead to this.
No one said
there would be secrets
I would not want to know.

No one told me about seeing,
seeing brought me
loss and a darkness I could not hold.

No one told me about writing
or speaking.
Speaking and writing poetry
I unsheathed the sharp edge
of experience that led me here.

No one told me
it could not be put away.

...

David Whyte, No One Told Me, from *Fire in the Earth*

My mother's moods grew bizarre and unpredictable throughout 1957. Her habit of making men choose between us had become a compulsion she couldn't control. She used my body as if it were her own. Oscar continued to be the most terrifying visitor, as he seemed to enjoy hurting me as much as possible, and she seemed to like nothing better than watching him.

One night, Oscar showed up, bringing beer and cigarettes and a bottle of hard liquor. In desperation, I called the police. Two officers came to the house and after talking to my mom and Oscar like they were old friends said I was wasting their time, they saw no emergency, and told me to listen to my "mom and dad."

"You're the parents and it's your job to take care of your kid and make her behave. We don't want any more phone calls," the officer warned.

"Yes, sir, we'll take care of her alright," Oscar said with a low chuckle.

Goosebumps climbed up my flesh as I tiptoed into the kitchen, snuck out the back door, and walked the two blocks to the Waukegan Police Department and begged them to help me.

Every time they tried to get me to leave, I held on to the arms of the chair as though it were my only lifeline, screaming and begging to be locked up. They eventually moved me into the room where the police dispatcher sat answering calls and drinking coffee. Her name was June. She talked to me much of the night between calls about the sickness of alcoholism and drug addiction. I wasn't certain if she was trying to offer support or excuses for my mother's behavior.

The next day, after repeatedly being asked if I had any relatives they could call, I gave them my Aunt Eunice's number. Too scared to tell them what my mom was letting men do to me or what I often was subjected to watch them do to her, Uncle Mike and Aunt Eunice drove me to my mother's as I begged them not to make me go back.

Years later, I asked Aunt Eunice if she remembered taking me from the police station back to my mom. She did.

"Why did you take me back?" I asked.

"You weren't my kid, I had no rights to you, what was I supposed to do?" Eunice said.

"Did you know my mom was picking up guys and selling herself and me to them?"

"Edna was Edna, you were her kid, there was nothing we could do."

I realize now that this was a different time in history. But when I asked her, I felt disappointed at the answer. I couldn't imagine that kind of thinking then, nor can I now. The other thing is, neither Aunt Eunice nor any of my relatives stepped forward and offered to provide a home for me when the court searched for placements several years later. I'd eventually come to understand just how dysfunctional each one of my mother's sisters was. The eldest, Ethel, always seemed the healthiest, perhaps because she was parented the longest while the others grew up without a father and an incapacitated mother.

My mother grew increasingly violent, beating me with one of Bud's old belts, with a hairbrush, a coat hanger, the broken handle of an old broom, and her closed fist. Unknown to us, as I grew increasingly absent or showed up at school with bruises, a file of reports was growing. One day, a man from the courthouse came with a subpoena for us to appear in court. My mother's face turned red as she read it. As soon as he left, she started in on me.

"You fucking brat. I hope you're satisfied." She glared at me as her shaking hands tried to light a cigarette. "We are ordered to *go to court*. I hope they put you away where I never have to see you again." Her words were biting, brittle with accusation. "You're nothing but an ungrateful little bitch," she raged.

My built-up anger gave way as I whispered back at her, "I wish I was dead. I hate myself and everything because of you."

She slapped me. "I could care less. You disgust me."

I was no stranger to my mother's anger, but that day it was a fire that simmered and flared off and on into the night as she screamed and swore at me. For days I was left shaking, terrified of what going to court would mean and what would happen to me. I also worried about what would happen to her.

When our day of court arrived, my mother's anger was still a boiling cauldron that could have burned down the whole town. The courtroom was intimidating with its somber, wood-paneled walls, dark benches, and the large, austere judge's bench that sat on an elevated platform in the front of the room. The juvenile judge looked down and studied me for several minutes. Then he began to ask my mother a series of questions.

She made me sound like the worst kid in the world, and told the judge she didn't care if I was "removed and put away." Looking down, I wanted to protest but was intimidated by the judge, the room, and what my mother was saying. I believed that adults would always take each other's word over anything a kid might have to say—so I said nothing.

A woman sat taking notes on a tiny machine off to the side of the judge's bench. Before we left the courtroom, Judge Hulse ordered my mom and me to begin seeing a psychiatrist at the nearby mental health center and assigned a woman from the Juvenile Department to oversee our case. "I'll see you back in this courtroom in three months and at that time, determine how things are going." With the bang of his gavel, the court was adjourned.

By the time we left, another court date had been scheduled and an appointment with an unknown doctor. Innocent as the court's order seemed, it marked a grave shift in my life—where I had been the victim of my desperate mother's broken psyche, we were now both catapulted into an even more dangerous and vicious realm of men and drugs that even my mother couldn't control.

My mother neither looked at me nor talked to me during the week we waited for our first doctor's appointment. Feeling invisible was worse than getting beaten and screamed at. Around my mother I was numb and frightened. I desperately wanted to believe the doctor would help us.

The first time my mother and I met with Dr. L, he greeted each of us with a smile and took us to an office, indicating the chair he wanted my mother to sit in. "Here, Edna, you should sit in this comfortable chair. It's just right for a lady like you."

He gestured to another one for me. My feet couldn't touch the floor. Hope and anxiety competed in my body, making it nearly impossible to sit still.

He was handsome and tall with sandy blond hair. His lyrical, warm voice made me think of the golden syrup and pancakes I once had at Grandma Margaret's. It eased my anxiety and discomfort and my mother's anger. Dr. L said he wanted to listen to both of us—he was there to help. He invited my mother to start first. She talked about what a "pain in the ass" I was and that she never wanted me. "I can understand that," he said.

When he looked at me, I felt studied and uncomfortable. I had to remind myself that since the judge sent us here, he would know how to help us. My mother droned on and on about my failures and her chronic disappointment since my birth. He looked at me and winked. She didn't miss it—her face slammed shut as she slipped back to her earlier anger.

He turned to her, smiling. "Just giving her a little honey, Edna. You and I are going to have some alone time real soon—I see you and hear you loud and clear."

My legs started to shake up and down as I nervously bit my fingernail, doing everything I could to not stick my thumb in my mouth. As though my mother could read my mind, she complained about my thumb sucking. "She sucks her thumb like a stupid baby. I'm sick and tired of it. She thinks I don't know that she tries to sneak the damn thing in her mouth when I'm not looking. I'm not stupid."

The doctor's head moved back and forth in agreement. "No, of course you're not," he said.

Caught in a frozen state of humiliation, I felt trapped as he looked over at me, his eyebrows slightly raised in a question. I desperately wanted to say something and couldn't get one word out. I looked down.

"It's a pain in the ass, Edna, sure enough, but sometimes kids her age still do that. You've most likely done the same thing as all good parents do with the hot sauce and the drug store stuff. You might just let it go for now—it's not hurting anybody."

"That's another thing, when she decides to stop talking, there is not one fucking thing anyone can do about it," she ranted.

"Now that's something important we need to work on."

His quiet, hypnotic voice seemed to calm her. She moved into the self that I remembered watching in the mirror when I was little. She turned into someone beautiful as she got ready to go out—her hard edges relaxed into a pretty face, open with expectation. My mind slipped away from the room, disappointed that, like most adults, he was just believing her.

I startled to attention when he said my name and stood motioning for me to come with him, telling my mother he would be back in a few minutes—he was going to give me an assessment and would return to talk with her.

"I'm going to have you wait here so the grown-ups can talk by themselves," he said, gesturing to a table that he wanted me to sit at in the next room.

Dr. L wrote "1, 2, 3" on the top of three pieces of paper. On the first, he instructed me to draw a house, on the second, a tree, and on the third, a person. "I better get back and talk to your mom." He gently patted my shoulder, instructing me to finish the assessment, and to wait until he came back. "You're going to have to be a little patient with me, it will take time to get to know what your needs are."

I nodded as he put a small bag of candy in front of me and smiled as he left the room. When he returned and took me back to the room with my mother, I should have known something was up—my mother wore her "I think I'm getting lucky" expression. I thought she was stupid; he was a doctor and I believed that helpers helped. It was only later that I began to realize that I misread the situation through the desperate hope that he would help us.

I was to come back and see him three days later, alone. Dr. L never met in that office with my mother and me together again. We saw him for nearly four years, but it was only in retrospect that I realized that the seduction that would eventually break us both had started in this very first session.

I have no idea what he did with my mother those first few months when she had her own appointments separate from mine. My mother's moods swung from sulky to secretive. She seldom said much to me, but the hitting and yelling had stopped. Still, I was confused and jealous. I wanted him to like me. I wanted him to think I was special and to treat me like I was the only special one. I was afraid my mom would convince him that I was a bad and stupid kid.

The mental health center was in a small two-story house, a couple of blocks from where we lived. There were seldom others working in the building when I saw him around 5:00 or 6:00 p.m. In the early weeks of seeing me, I was eager to talk to him. I was hungry for grown-up attention and he lavished me with praise, filling the gaping hole of need. He had me bring schoolwork so he could look at it. He complimented me on my drawings and talked about them at length. He was interested in ME, and I soaked it up.

He teased me and called me "hon" and "sweet girl." We played tic-tac-toe and checkers. He bought paper dolls and had me show him different things from my life. I blossomed under his careful manipulations. I told him and showed him everything. My memories and confusion of being three and living with Daddy-Uncle Clinton. My memories of the day he shot himself. As I dissolved into tears after showing him with the paper dolls where I was standing, where my mother was, and recounted the smattering of blood, he pulled me into his arms and wiped my tears with a large white handkerchief. "There, there, what an awful thing to see."

He had me recount it several times, each time with more detail as I tunneled through layers of memory before floating outside my body and out of the room, watching as he consoled the little girl in his arms, her chest heaving, and scalding sobs burned her eyes and wet the front of his shirt until she grew still and distant.

He asked me how often that happened to me. I wasn't sure what he was talking about—it was as natural to me as breathing. I shrugged and looked down. "Your ability to float away and disconnect from pain." He made it sound like a good thing. I shrugged again, frightened, but I didn't know why. "You are very good at leaving your body."

I looked up. He looked at me encouragingly. "Yes, very good. Not everyone can do that, you know. I want you to begin to tell me all the times you remember floating away."

Eager to please, I told him the little I remembered. I was confused because it had been called daydreaming at school and been labeled a bad thing. I told him everything about Oscar and the other men, about the beatings from my mom, and other things. I told him about all the trouble in school remembering and feeling as though I'd die when people looked at me, or when my teacher would expect an answer and I would freeze and float out the window to climb a tree—in my imagination. One teacher got mad and smacked my fingers with a ruler and yelled at me to quit daydreaming. I even told him about the make-believe worlds that I created, whole fantasy worlds to hide in. Escaping this way was easier than being present in most places of my life: school, the playground, alone at home. It also happened suddenly when really scary things began to happen—like Oscar.

I didn't know then that by trusting Dr. L I had stepped into a trap that he would eventually tighten around me—imprisoning me within myself. By telling him all the intimate details of our life, I made both my mother and myself putty in his hands.

One day, Dr. L said he had a special present for me, but I needed to leave it in the office, so it would keep its special qualities. "It is a magic box and has hidden compartments, just like you," he teased.

"Really?" I was intrigued.

"It can make things disappear, just like you, but I don't think you fully understand how you do that yet, do you?" He winked and smiled in a teasing way.

Looking back on it later in my life, I saw he seized on my ability to easily dissociate, due to my ongoing trauma from age three. He used that knowledge to further exploit me, eventually accelerating my dissociative tendencies with the use of hypnosis.

At first, we practiced making coins and other small articles disappear into the secret compartments of the box. Next, he taught me how to imagine parts of myself disappearing into the box along with uncomfortable feelings. Then we practiced making my innermost fears and secrets disappear. We built on and rehearsed these same "skills" in different ways over the next several years. As I watched the pendant he held between his fingers swing back and forth in front of my eyes, his soft, hypnotic voice soothed me, and made me disappear to a place where there was nothing, just the nothingness of a blank, white paper. I would emerge from those sessions relaxed, having no memory of the story he had told me or where I had disappeared to—my mind empty of all thoughts and somewhat disoriented.

My hope and idolization of this man grew, seeming to have no bounds. I told him everything about our life. I just knew he would either help my mother and me or save me by finding me another place to live. By the time he began to remove my clothes and photograph me, I didn't have a clue that this wasn't what a good psychiatrist did. By then he knew about my mother's prostitution and her selling of me to Oscar and other men. "You are so beautiful and sweet, such a little sexy thing," he said. "Of course, those men would want to do those things to you."

He was kind and gentle with his words as he went on in his sing-song hypnotic voice. "Those men should have treated you like a delicate treasure and been gentle and tender to you, like I would. You are so special."

One day turned into another and another as he began taking pictures of me in different poses. At first, I felt pretty and special as he instructed me into different positions. Over time, I grew troubled and afraid. "A little more sassy, darling girl. Little more. Good, you've got it. I love you—love this."

Tears of fear and joy coursed down my cheeks. I couldn't have stopped them if my life depended on it.

"What's wrong? Are you being a baby now?" He teased.

"You said you—love me?" I stammered, hesitantly.

"Of course, I do." He laughed as though it were the best joke and started to sing Elvis Presley's "Wooden Heart."

I had no language for the feeling of dissonance I felt in those moments. Hope and confusion warred inside me. This was the same word Dale had first spoken to me—*love*—coming out of Dr. L's mouth. It somehow set off a small warning that I had no understanding of, or that I chose in my desperation for help and love to ignore, but inside I knew this love was way different than the kind I'd felt in Dale's presence.

"I bet you don't know that song is from a movie called *GI Blues* and Elvis Presley sings it." Snap, snap. He moved around excitedly—he said to get just the right shots.

"You've got what it takes to be a model or a movie star—you take my breath away." He made it sound like a good thing. He stooped down near me again. My body had started to shiver. He dropped to the floor, wrapped his arms around me, and pulled my trembling body into his lap. "What's wrong, hon? You're not scared, are you?"

I shook my head. I had no idea why I was crying or my body had started to shake. He reminded me that we were doing this so I would feel better about my body and what the other men had done to it. He held me close, like a real dad, as he sang to me in his hypnotic voice.

I would eventually come to know and to hate each and every word of the wooden heart song—but this day I felt loved and cared for. I never saw the danger of the wolf, masked as a doctor. He lurked nearby, getting ready to tiptoe into the inside of me as well as take over my outer life.

In time, he systematically and intentionally took control of nearly every aspect of my mind as well as my body. As he stroked my hair, tears continued to course down my cheeks. It wasn't until a few weeks later—after he took more "therapy pictures," this time making me laugh and pretend I was a beautiful movie star—that he went further, and I began to feel a funny feeling in my stomach and wondered if what he was doing was wrong. But even this bit of awareness, conscience, and inner fear was silenced by his reassurances and my huge need to believe in him. I still believed he would either help me or get me away from my mother and her life. He led me to believe that I was special.

Not long after, my life became dissected into parts. There was "special time" with him in his office—the him I still idolized and saw as a father figure—and there were times he enlisted me as his special secret agent, promising, "You will be just like your favorite heroine, just like Nancy Drew."

Weekend parties were held in North Chicago at the military base we were living near. My mother and other women, myself, and, occasionally, another child or two were used as prostitutes at these events. At first, my job was to watch and listen and tell Dr. L what I heard, but it wasn't long before I was also on the list of options for the night.

Because of an annual holiday party at the base, I still have difficulty listening to holiday music. This was the night I learned that as much as I had felt special to Dr. L, he could as easily humiliate me. At that point, he was the most important person in my life.

Dressed up as a ballerina—ballet slippers, tights, tutu—I had been trained by Dr. L to act shy as I came into the room when the clock struck 8:00 p.m. I was to dance to music I came to hate in a room full of strangers. That alone was terrifying to the introverted, self-conscious kid that I was. I was about to learn about real terror at the hands of the doctor I had seen as my rescuer.

Although Dr. L had prepared me for a "magical evening," my nervous system detected upcoming danger. I remember the feeling of fear in my body, amped up to terror, creating a feeling of disconnection and disorientation woven into the brightly lit, holiday-decorated ballroom, filled with men and women. I nearly ran screaming from the room in panic, but Dr. L grabbed me by the shoulder and squeezed so tight that tears poured from my eyes. He hissed into my ear, "Stop it, take those damn feelings to the magic box if you have to. Don't you dare embarrass me."

The scratchy ballet dress was covered with a beautiful soft velvet cape. My hands were sweaty and ice cold as Dr. L stood my robotic body on a table and whispered in my ear that I better make him proud and not make even one mistake.

Shivering more in fear than from cold, I watched myself from a distant corner as I as Maria moved stiffly around—danced, if you can call it that. Then she slowly took off one garment at a time to hoots and cheers of drunken men dressed in green uniforms, white, and blue. The women in the crowd, including my mother, were just as bad as they laughed and pointed at me. My face grew hot and tears coursed down my cheeks as I curtsied, yawned, and rubbed my sleepy eyes like I'd been instructed.

Dr. L's betrayal and violence psychologically broke me into splintered bits. Later that evening he raped me in front of a smaller group of men before handing me over to them. As he left me with them, he smirked, "She's a special one." In those moments I realized I wasn't special at all and I no longer wanted to be—it was too much. My previous adoration turned to hatred; a hatred that I was sure would send me straight to hell. I wanted to scream, yell, and destroy everything in the room, including his smiling face and most of all myself —for trusting him.

My rage quickly knotted up in the bottom of my stomach, calcified, and stayed there—for decades. But by then I knew my life depended on obedience and always doing exactly what Dr. L instructed. This was essential for my survival and for that of my mother, who I felt responsible for, because it had been my behavior that had led us to him and my disclosures that had alerted him to our vulnerability and availability in the first place. I knew we were in grave danger and it was all my fault.

It would take many years, well into adulthood and my professional life, to begin to recognize that this occurred on many military bases throughout the country, that I was not the only child subjected to such treatment, nor was my mother the only woman recruited into such behavior. The US military has a long and known history of using prostitutes overseas, as described in the *Washington Post* article by Dan Lamothe: "It's an uncomfortable part of the US military's long history with prostitution. The world's oldest profession has long catered to U.S. troops, whether at home or abroad."[1]

In addition, prostitution has been an issue in the United States, as detailed in *The New York Times* article titled "Navy is cracking down at biggest training base," about Great Lakes Naval Station and the area known as the strip of my childhood where my mother frequently hung out picking up enlisted men.[2] A *Chicago Tribune* article titled "Prostitutes are blamed for N Chicago's woes" by Jerry Thomas describes the ongoing and pervasive problem at Great Lakes Naval Station, which the local police claim they have tried to clean up for years.[3]

My everyday world became more challenging to navigate. With no ability to stay present in my body because of the ongoing abuse, it was nearly impossible to focus in school, complete homework assignments, or remember to bring them back the next day. I had increasing and random challenges with memory. Once, I nearly went into a full panic attack in the cloakroom as I stood helplessly overwhelmed—unable to recognize my own coat.

In sixth grade, all the girls were taken on a field trip to St. Therese, the local hospital, for "sex education." I was mortified, embarrassed, and certain everyone could see through me, could see what was being done to me. In my own estimation, I was a shameful thing, my body sold to men just like my mother. I shivered in the darkened room as we watched a movie, followed by a talk on "periods" given by the head of the maternity unit, Sister Sebastian. She was an older nun with deep-set, nearly black eyes, bushy eyebrows, and a long angular face, full of expression. Her face could quickly move from complete seriousness to pure joy, like when she moved from talking about the act of procreation to showing us pictures of the results. As she showed us slides of newborn babies, her tenderness and joy at gazing at new life were unmistakable—making her look beautiful in my eyes. There was something about Sister Sebastian that spoke to me. I had never heard anyone talk about the body, or the sexual act, like that before. I wanted to know her and hear her talk more. Little did I know that when things got even worse, Sister Sebastian would become the most important person in my life.

We toured the hospital and were told about their adolescent volunteer program, known as "the candy striper program" because of the white and red striped uniforms that adolescents wore when volunteering in the hospital. I immediately signed up. From then on, the hospital became a refuge for me, providing me with at least one good meal a week, a sense of purpose, and a relationship with the formidable and loving Sister Sebastian. The nurses referred to her affectionately as "one tough old broad." She had served in the Women's Army Corps before entering the convent later in life. Over time, she took me under her wing.

The days I volunteered at the hospital were rewarding. I also felt more peaceful than anywhere else in my life. Gazing at Sister Sebastian's thin face and dark, soulful eyes, framed by her white wimple and veil, deeply comforted me. She often invited me for a tea break with her during the afternoon or evening shift. Some days, before I left for home, we would sit together, shoulder to shoulder in the small chapel, praying. On warmer days, we would walk in the sisters' meditation garden. Frequently, I found myself asking her questions and she would casually teach me about what she referred to as "God's ordained purpose of sexual activity." She made it sound beautiful, nothing like my experiences or what I had seen my mother and the line-up of men in her life do. It was a world away from the one I knew, but made me feel hopeful that there was such a place. Thriving under Sister Sebastian's tutelage provided me an oasis of calm and safety in the desert of my impossible life.

Outside of these times, Dr. L controlled nearly every aspect of my life. After learning about my volunteer job, he tried to talk me into quitting. He argued that I didn't have enough time to be doing it, reminding me that the court expected me to see him twice a week. I suspected his saying no was a way to keep tight control of my life. Angry at me for signing up before telling him, he seemed to be weighing the safest options of allowing me to continue or insisting that I inform the hospital that I wasn't available. To my great relief, he eventually agreed for me to continue, saying, "It will look good in court."

He showed an interest in what I did each time I volunteered. One day, he ordered me to bring my red and white pinafore uniform and hat to his office. More pictures were taken, with me in and out of the uniform. I nearly quit candy striping after that—fearful that he had desecrated something that to me was sacred. I begged the Sister who was the volunteer coordinator for a different uniform.

"This is a perfectly good uniform; I see nothing at all wrong with it."

I had no answer, but she must have felt some sympathy for me when the tears sprang to my eyes. "I just had a really uncomfortable thing happen when I was wearing it one day and every time, I put it on, I think of that day. Maybe a brand new one would help me get over it," I muttered.

She looked at me, thoughtfully, then smiled as she handed me a new uniform. "I hope this helps," she said kindly.

I grew terrified that Dr. L would find out about Sister Sebastian in the sessions where he used his funny voice. I somehow knew it was essential that my growing connection with her stay a secret or he'd find a way to put an end to my ability to be a candy striper or to see her. In the meantime, the dissonance of my life grew into a huge gulf that was increasingly difficult to navigate. I was living two vastly different realities.

Sister Sebastian, a crucial figure in my life

My increasing awareness of the difference between the sacred and the profane was pulling me apart. My islands of nourishment and serenity spent with Sister Sebastian were worlds apart from my increasing life as a child prostitute. The horrific abuse and violence I was subjected to at Dr. L's hands stood in harsh contrast to the gentle guidance and direction I received from Sister Sebastian. I knew with a fierce certainty I didn't want to grow up living the lifestyle and legacy of my mother.

Dr. L was systematically escalating his threats and violence, keeping me trapped in secrecy and manipulating me with shame. It grew more difficult to go to his office. I'd slowly make my way up the stairs. If I "dawdled," he was punishing. His office door had a skeleton key he used to lock the door from the inside—then he'd put the key in his pocket. Over time, my anxiety of being trapped for an hour or two with the click of the door mounted.

On the shelf behind his chair sat a large, very thick dictionary. Sometimes, I'd find myself staring at it, wondering how to steal the contents. The book was not what it seemed. Inside, the center was cut out, creating a compartment filled with copies of nude pictures of me. There were several taken at the holiday party that he used to humiliate me, even threatening to show them to my classmates and the nuns at my school. In the pictures of myself that Dr. L forced me to look at, I saw a naked girl with terrified eyes. Some showed her sitting, others standing, while others showed her lying on her belly with knees bent behind her. Her hair was arranged this way and that to suit him and to "get the right look." I remembered that Dr. L had never seemed to look directly at the shy, self-conscious, skinny girl that was me in the pictures. The camera he held had done most of the looking, while the child-me in the pictures frequently stared vacantly into space. If smiling, the smile was guarded and tentative—my body seeming to know more than my mind could allow in.

There were increasing trips to a room—somewhere, I think on the base. I remember it as the metal room, perhaps some sort of lab, where I was given drugs through an IV, or injections that caused confusion, making me see strange colors, bugs, snakes, and terrifying faces that changed like melting crayons. The bright metal cabinets and counters provided a mirror I'd often stare into, sometimes seeing multiple images of myself, at times using my image to hold onto reality and silently promising my terrified, pale face to never forget what he did. And, sometimes, begging the reflection to completely disappear and die.

The first time I was given the drug curare, Dr. L told me it was a drug that would cure something. I rolled the interesting word around like a marble, cure … are … a … and never found the end of it. The repeated use of the dreaded drug completely suppressed my will and eradicated any desire in me to live. Years later, after talking about it for the first time in therapy, my therapist looked up information about the drug, whose name I had never forgotten, and found out that "the poison produces muscle paralysis by interfering with the transmission of nerve impulses at the receptor sites of all skeletal muscles and competes with acetylcholine. This prevents acetylcholine from activating muscle cells—something known to South American Indians of the Amazon River Basin, who used curare as an arrow poison for hunting."

What took much longer to discover were the probable reasons why it was being used. A devious, "scientific" purpose seemed to be aligned with Dr. L's now clear perversion.

The drug initially made me dizzy and warm, followed by weakness, then the impossibility of moving any part of my body. With my mind alert, terror, physical sensations, pain, and sexual stimulation were amplified to unbearable heights. Sometimes, Dr. L strangled me into unconsciousness while in this state. My psyche torn apart, scattered, and nearly dying, I'd then be yanked back. It was a torment to be unable to move, and worse to be brought back.

By this time, Dr. L threatened often enough that he would kill my mother and I if I ever told anyone. I never knew if I would survive to see another day. Sometimes he terrified me with his service revolver, leaving me a shaking, begging puddle of misery as he activated the traumatic memories of Uncle Clinton's suicide. He threatened that the next time I would be splattered with blood, it would be my mother's, and I wouldn't know until then if she shot the gun or I did.

I knew for certain that my safety was precarious at best. Eventually, I came to know that there was nothing and nowhere that was safe. Having been taken so repeatedly to the edge of mortality, I no longer cared if I lived or died, and mostly just wanted to die, but I didn't want to kill my mother or anyone else. One day in a meeting with Miss F, the appointed court worker, I blurted in a rush to get the words out that Dr. L was selling my mother to men for money and hurting me. She didn't believe me and said I should be ashamed of myself for making up stories like that about such a wonderful doctor. She insisted that I apologize and admit I had made it up for attention, and threatened to tell the judge that I was a liar.

By the time I saw Dr. L the next day, she had called him. I can't remember what he did to me—in my mind, everything had begun to run together like a river of blood. I do know that the next day I came home to a nearly dead, drugged mother. It was a warning. I knew he had done something to her, and a few days later he confirmed the truth of it.

Dr. L took me to a place where there was an enclosed water tank in which I was put for hours or perhaps days. When I was eventually taken out, a headset was placed on my head. His voice whispered words and phrases I can no longer remember. Sometimes the wooden heart song played repeatedly to the girl who no longer lived in a body. With the precision of a surgeon, Dr. L extracted information from me about who he had ordered me to spy on at military parties. He said I was just like the popular adolescent heroine in the series "Nancy Drew." I was also to report information to him about my mother, about every aspect of my daily life, and any other information he demanded that I tell him. But he never discovered the new secret I carried deep inside me.

The secret was that I liked the tank after the first time. It created a respite, a time of being able to float out and away from my body—most important to me, a time of communing with the god or spirits from my childhood, a time to go with my imagination, wherever I wanted. This fortified me so that the words coming through the headset never fully penetrated.

There were times Dr. L shocked various parts of my body, through wired cables connected to a device with dials inside a small suitcase. The pain eventually caused me to lose consciousness.

Dr. L continued to whittle away at my will through the use of hypnosis and games; even tic-tac-toe and checkers became hypnotic devices. So many triggers were implanted in me, my psyche became a minefield. Years later I would learn that what he was doing to me was a form of torture. As the physical torture grew increasingly vicious, I sensed he was breaking my will and somehow my brain. The emotional brutality of knowing he was stealing something from me grew unbearable. I grew terrified that he was stealing my soul, what made me *ME*.

Obsessed with finding a way to hold on or to buy back what he was taking, I lit vigil lights in the church, prayed, said the rosary, and went to confession repeatedly, magically believing if I could just pray hard enough, it would end. I was certain that I had to atone for my sins. The sin of wanting more than my mother could provide, the sin of telling him everything that made us vulnerable to him, the sin of being drawn in and seduced by his attention, the sin of my body responding to him, and the sin of lighting the vigil lights without having the money to pay for them. These were all sins I couldn't take to the priest in the confessional, which added another huge sin—the sin of failing to make an honest and true confession.

When I talked with Sister Sebastian about my growing obsession about feeling impure and declared that no amount of confession or penance would ever be able to remove it, she was patient and told me she was worried about me. She begged me to tell her what specifically I was talking about. I bit my bottom lip to keep from blurting it out—all of it was too heavy for me to hide anymore. Yet, I was terrified that I had already said too much and was frightened that I might have put her, as well as my mother, in danger.

In the meantime, my mother was disappearing. Not literally—she seldom went out on her own anymore—she seemed to be evaporating before my eyes. I wondered if I looked the same to her, or if she had the capacity to see me or anything else during this time. Where before she reminded me that I repulsed her with my presence, now she seemed to depend on it—cloying and near desperate to have me around. "Where the hell were you? I'm your mother and should know."

She was nervous, clingy, and insecure when she wasn't staring off for hours into space. She wanted me to sleep in the same bed with her because of her nightmares.

We had always moved. Once, we moved five times in less than a year. In the "therapy" years with Dr. L, there was more outer stability than I had ever known—we stayed in the same apartment. Previously, there had been little money for food. During this time we had money, but my vacant, drugged mother couldn't be motivated to leave the house and shop for groceries. Bud occasionally came. He yelled at her about the drugs "that damn psychiatrist is giving you." The changes in her were obvious. Where before she would fight back, now, zombie-like, she would nod off or wave him away like a pesky fly. I once begged him not to leave us, to help us, but I was too afraid to tell him what was really happening.

I was growing toward adolescence during eighth grade. This was a time of careful words. I often fell into near muteness again, like I was after the death of Uncle Clinton. Life flat and devoid of color and texture,

I was in and out of awareness of the split-off parts of myself—the ones I once hid away in compartments in that magic box. Bud came back one late afternoon for the first time in over a year. By this time, the full weight of Dr. L's betrayal and the danger we were in had become completely debilitating, paralyzing, coloring every day in dread. Missing school had become a matter of course, the same with my time volunteering at the hospital. Afraid of blurting everything out to Sister Sebastian, I avoided her.

Defiance and despair had lain coiled in the bottom of my gut until they erupted as full-blown rage, with nowhere to turn—other than on myself that day toward the end of eighth grade. The apartment had never had a bathroom door that locked. Bud walked in on me the morning after he had come back and commented on my changing figure as he reached toward me—or maybe the sink, where he had set down his razor. In a flash I came to life, grabbed the razor, pulled out the blade, and started to slash myself. I was wild, with an unstoppable intent to destroy my body—assuming he was reaching to touch my newly budding breasts, I screamed in hatred as I cut myself over and over. "You nor any other asshole will ever touch me again."

Blood started to squirt across the room. Bud quickly tore his shirt off, ripping it into strips, and applied a tourniquet. I immediately tore it off, laughing in hysteria. "Too late, you're way too late," I screamed, continuing to slash at myself.

He tried to apply pressure, then another tourniquet. I just as quickly tore it off—mounting in hysterical glee at releasing all that had been tamped down and suppressed. He grabbed my shoulders, trying to shake sense into me until I slowly lost consciousness and slid down the bloody bathroom wall in relief—I was finally dying.

Waking from a coma in the hospital, I found Dr. L standing, threatening, at the end of the bed as he held some of the tubing entering my body and slowly twisted and bent it in his hands. I turned my head away. When a nurse came in sometime later, I didn't realize or didn't care that he hadn't done anything, or that he had left the room.

Sister Sebastian told me that Judge Hulse ordered that I wouldn't be returning to my mother. It didn't matter, nothing did as I recovered from the disappointment of finding myself not dead. The one thing that helped me begin to rally—to find the will to begin again—was Sister Sebastian. She visited me nearly every day. What willpower I lacked, she made up for, tenfold. One day, I begged her to leave me alone. "I just want to die, don't you understand, just let me die."

She looked at me with her deep-set, warm, chocolate eyes and shook her head sadly. "It's not as easy as you might think. If God wanted you dead, you wouldn't have survived what you already have." She looked at me thoughtfully. "I too once begged to die," she quietly confessed as she reached for my hand.

Incredulous, tears sprang to my eyes as I whispered, "You?"

She nodded as she reached into her pocket for a handkerchief and began to wipe the tears that ran down my face as well as her own. "It was a long time ago, right after the war, the senselessness of war, the violence and killing, broke my heart and will to live. But I want to know what is breaking your heart and will to live, my dear."

"I'm dirty and impure, men have made me do horrible things," I blurted out between wondering if even now I might have put her in danger by saying this much.

"I think I'm beginning to understand some things about you, some of our talks and questions you've asked me," she said, deep in thought. "My body has also been violated," Sister Sebastian confessed. "I've healed and I believe you can as well. That time in my life eventually created my future and my vocation as a nun."

Sister Sebastian prayed for me before she left my room and continued to come every day until I was discharged.

The day after I was released from the hospital, I felt nothing as the new foster mother drove me to see Dr. L for the last time. As I walked into his office, the fear that normally hounded me had been replaced with a dark heaviness. I felt leaden and far removed from myself within a vacuum of emptiness where colors and words were muted. And then, suddenly without warning, I started to violently throw up and couldn't stop. He phoned the foster mother and asked her to immediately come and get me and walked me outside to wait on the steps. He was in a hurry to be rid of me. He told me the military was transferring him, he would never see me again. There was no immediate relief because I'd become so numb, I couldn't feel anything.

Every inch of me was covered in the scars of his "therapy," leaving me in the land of the living dead for a long time. My ravaged body seemed to be all that was left. The depth of the most inhumane pain had been targeted at my sense of self—a child/adolescent's growing identity. The desire for connection or relatedness had nearly been completely killed. In the aftermath, I had little will to be, to exist. My deepest struggles, for years to come, would be the challenge in recovering even a small semblance of my normal instincts toward life, relationships, and the feeling of safety that I had lost. Over the years this resulted in using the default of suicide as an escape hatch whenever I felt unsafe or overwhelmed. I believed this would take me to another place, a better one. It had become an instinctual and automatic form of escape, conditioned into me at the hands of a man the court had ordered me to see, a man whose job was to help me.

6.

Ward of the Court, 1962

"For all these years, you've lived under the illusion that, somehow, you made it because you were tough enough to overpower the abuse, the hatred, the hard knocks of life. But really you made it because love is so powerful that tiny little doses of it are enough to overcome the pain of the worst thing life can dish out."

Rachel Reiland, *Get Me Out of Here*

Used with permission of Hazelden Publishing from *Get Me Out of Here* by Rachel Reiland, (2004) permission conveyed through *Copyright Clearance Center, Inc.*

I quickly settled into the routine of the "placement" home, made up of a young couple and four children under the age of four, with another baby on the way. Home became a too small, crowded bungalow. Quickly days became filled with the busyness of caring for young ones. I always had a baby on my hip and another in my arms. I functioned for some time in a robotic, disconnected daze, helping with the little ones. It became clear that this was why they had taken me in. They needed a "mother's helper" and I needed them to need me.

I was assigned to another psychiatrist, a wise older woman. Dr. Mary Rootes was practical and encouraging. She and Sister Sebastian were two of the few constants in my life over the next several years.

When I began therapy in earnest about thirty years later, I called and asked Dr. Rootes if she knew that Dr. L had sexually abused me. She grew quiet on the other end of the phone, then replied as I quickly took notes on what she said. "I suspected as much, but I never knew for sure."

I asked if we had talked about him or worked in therapy on anything related to him. "You were very fragile. I felt like I was working with someone on a balance beam who could fall off at any minute. My job was to help keep you balanced, give you time to gain some ego strength and help get you through high school," she replied thoughtfully. Disappointed that she didn't have more to offer, it was also clear that her decision had been the wisest way of helping me at that time in my life.

One early spring day of my second year of high school, I sat in the assembly hall riveted, listening to a woman named Shirley Tometz speak passionately about equality and the work of the NAACP. She had created a summer pilot program for impoverished inner-city preschoolers, in the hope of helping close the gap in their readiness to enter the school system. She explained that a handful of high school students would be chosen for the program to be launched that summer. Something came alive in me as I listened to her. More excited about this than I had been about anything in a long time, I remember checking with Dr. Rootes to see if she thought it was a good idea for me to apply. Both excited and hesitant, I wondered if I really had anything to offer. She was very encouraging and supportive, and pushed me to promise to at least give it a try. I quickly filled out the application and wrote the required essay. Following an interview, I was thrilled to learn that I was one of the few sophomores selected, along with a classmate whom I had come to really like, Carole Robbins. This success motivated me to do better in school and paid off, with all my grades coming up. I grew excited at having something special to look forward to.

As soon as school was out, we were taken to Evanston, Illinois to the National College of Education to learn how to write lesson plans, the basics of child development, and effective ways to teach preschoolers. Each of us was then paired up with another student who would be our teaching partner.

Carole and I were paired as teaching partners, to my delight. Every morning, Carole and I would meet up and walk house to house collecting our small students. The little ones thrived in the program and we each thrived with them. I came alive that summer. I loved working with the children and came to love their families.

The program culminated with an open house. Every classroom worked on a song or two to perform on the stage in the assembly hall of the school. The children were adorable and confident. We all felt gratified and proud, along with the parents. The entire program had proven to be an enormous success. Children had become an important part of my life. I realized that caring for the little ones in my foster home had given me experience and prepared me for this role. Feeling anchored in a sense of belonging and purpose, my self-esteem grew. For the first time, I saw myself as capable of contributing to the world, and encouraged by Carole's ongoing friendship began to think about the possibility of college.

That fall, as I started my junior year, my foster mother decided to start working the evening shift at the hospital as she'd earn more money than on the day shift. Her husband also worked evenings. I was now expected to immediately come home from school, cook supper, do several loads of diapers, feed the babies, and get them to bed in a timely manner. I took it in my stride. I was a little disappointed I had to give up all extra-curricular activities and come straight home from school, but I liked caring for the babies and it helped me feel a sense of belonging and security.

The week before the change in schedule, I let Sister Sebastian know that I could no longer be a candy striper and would be turning in my uniform that evening before leaving. She asked me why. I answered her question honestly. She didn't say anything other than "That's too bad."

A few days later my foster care placement unexpectedly fell apart. I came home from school on a Friday and saw to my amazement several boxes and bags sitting on the front lawn. The foster mother came out screaming to put my things in the car and to get in—they were done with me. I was flabbergasted and confused. To my knowledge, I had not done anything wrong. Apparently, she felt differently as she raged about how embarrassed she was because of what I had done. I truly had no idea what she was talking about. Apparently, Sister Sebastian had tracked down the foster mother at the hospital and confronted her about expecting me to babysit so much.

"This was a real slap in the face after all we've done for you. I can't believe you went complaining to that nun about babysitting," she yelled.

"I wasn't complaining about babysitting. You know I love to take care of the kids. I just answered Sister's question about why I had to stop being a volunteer. You never asked me to keep it a secret, I don't understand why you think I should have lied when she asked me."

There was no reasoning with her. "It was none of her business. My business stays in my home. I've never been so embarrassed. We're done with you after this. We never should have taken you in the first place and this is what we get for it." She fumed, throwing more of my stuff in the car as fast as she could.

It was a Friday and because she couldn't get hold of my court-appointed worker, Miss F, she took me to my mother's apartment. She went upstairs to talk to my mom, instructing me to unpack the car. I ran away. The first thing I did when I arrived at the train station was to call my friend Carole and told her what had happened.

Shortly after, Carole and her father picked me up at the train station. Carole's family was willing to let me stay at their home, but her dad felt he had to let the authorities know where I was. Soon the police arrived and insisted that they needed to take me to the local youth home. Carole and her family felt awful but it was clear—there was nothing they could do. I was put in Lake County Youth Home, a jail-like, cinder-block facility for delinquents.

One day while in the youth home, the bedroom doors had just unlocked and we were called to breakfast. My roommate, a girl with epilepsy, started to have a full seizure. I ran out yelling for the staff to help her and was told it was none of my business and to get myself to the cafeteria. As I looked behind me, I noticed that the staff member walked over to the bedroom door and re-locked it.

"You need to help her!" I yelled.

"Don't you order me what to do and talk to me in that tone of voice. She'll be fine, you're not an expert here, now get yourself to breakfast, I don't want to tell you one more time or I'll write you up."

After breakfast, I watched horrified as they removed my roommate from the room we'd shared, on a stretcher, her body covered in a white sheet.

More days passed in the youth home. One morning I was told to get my things—I was going to court. I sat on a bench for quite a while waiting to be called into the judge's chambers. I was surprised to see Shirley Tometz sitting in the room already, along with Miss F and Judge Hulse. The judge invited me to sit down. He looked at me directly, studying me. "Mrs. Tometz has been telling me about how dedicated and effective you were last summer in the pilot program she ran. She has an important question to ask you," he said.

Shirley asked me if I would like to live with her and her husband and young sons. She also told me that when she brought up the possibility of applying to take me as a foster child in a family meeting, each of her three little boys had immediately voted yes. They would very much like to provide me with a home. I was speechless and nodded my head. When we arrived at her house, she showed me to my room. On the door was a drawing made by her young son with the words "Welcome Home New Sister."

Unfortunately, my time with the Tometz family was short-lived. Shirley was diagnosed with cancer and shingles several months after I arrived, but she saw to it I was placed in the neighborhood with another family she knew. I worked that first summer and then a second one in the program she had started. In addition to Carole's influence, volunteering in the program was the most important motivating factor for me to go to college. Within several years, Shirley eventually recovered and continued to be an active change agent in the community.

As senior graduation approached, I became a walking time bomb of stress. Senior prom turned out to be a disaster. I had only agreed to go because of being pushed into it by the foster parents who had friends whose son had no date. Vulnerable and triggered by his aggressive sexual behaviors toward me, the bomb went off the day after prom, leading to a failed suicide attempt. It had been four years since the last time I'd visited that threshold. I woke in the hospital to the disappointment and anger of the foster parents.

The foster father was furious. "You're an embarrassment to us and we're here to tell you, you're not welcome back in our home." His wife sat quietly and nodded in agreement.

"I thought we could help you amount to something. I was obviously wrong or you wouldn't have done a damn fool thing like this, We're done with you." They walked out, leaving me stunned. They never asked me why I tried to kill myself. I couldn't have told them anyway.

Next the court worker, Miss F, raged through the door, disgust and fury written all over her face. "How dare you screw up another placement. You're just going to have to go back to live with your mother. You're looking just as crazy as she is, so you belong together," she seethed.

The hospital discharged me and Miss F drove me to the current hovel my mother resided in. She left quickly, seemingly not remembering that I hadn't seen my mother in four years, and not acknowledging that my mother was already drunk, with a man sitting at the table in his boxer shorts in the very small kitchenette apartment. My mother looked at me with squinty, calculating eyes. At first, she didn't say a word.

"Guess no one else wanted you either, huh?" Numb, I ignored her. My mother left with the guy for a few hours and I fell into a fitful sleep across the one bed squeezed into the corner of the small living room. I was awoken when they stumbled in arguing about how much money he'd give her. I was exhausted and had trouble getting up.

An exchange of money briefly caught my attention out of the corner of my eyes, but I was too tired to register exactly what had transpired. I'd missed the opportunity to run. The drunken stranger was suddenly all over me. More natural than breathing, I fled out the top of my head and watched from a corner of the room the body of the slight, pale teenage girl being raped by the stranger. A stranger who had just paid the mother for the body of her daughter. He rolled off and fell asleep in a drunken stupor. The girl—me—sat up and saw my mother, sitting at the table with a satisfied smirk.

"I always told you men are only out for one thing, it doesn't matter if it's a hole in the wall. Just get paid for it, make them pay good, and you can get along ok like I do," she slurred. This litany had been recited to me for as long as I could understand language.

A wave of fury overtook me, moving from my belly upward, out my arms and hands. I grabbed the hard metal object wrapped in leather that the man had dropped on the floor as he'd removed his pants, picked it up, and lifted my hands, gripping the firmness of the hard club over my head, my entire body shaking as I looked down on his snoring body. I would kill him. This man had become every man who had ever touched me, every bastard who had ever hit me and forced himself on me. The

Carole and I with the preschoolers in the summer pilot project
directed by Shirley Tometz

suppressed rage and revulsion that I'd carried in my body unraveled, moving me backward between time and place to the first man that my mother had sold me to at nine years old, my mind screamed—Oscar.

In a flash of clarity, I knew that if I started hitting this man, I wouldn't be able to stop. I would also kill my mother. Turning my fear and hatred on her for the first and last time in my life, my body unknotted its repressed rage at her. "I hate you, you sick, twisted bitch. I wish you were dead, the air you breathe is wasted on you! You are such a sorry excuse for a mother."

With what little control I had left in me, I threw the truncheon down, grabbed my clothes and a handful of the cash laying on the table, and fled. I not only fled from my mother's apartment, but from the intensity of feelings that had come up. I had vowed to never feel or act on the kind of anger my mother and those around me had exhibited my whole life. In those moments I was more terrified of my near loss of control than of any pain anyone could ever inflict on me.

Walking the streets until the sun rose, I turned my unspent rage on myself. I entered the drug store and left with three bottles of over-the-counter sleeping pills held tightly to my chest. I regained consciousness three days later in a bed at Lake County Hospital after being found unresponsive in the park.

Jerking awake late in the afternoon, I was filled with frustration and anger at finding myself alive. Miss F, "guardian" of the courts, stood at the end of my bed. "You're going right back to your mother! You won't manipulate me, young lady. I can't wait until I can wash my hands of you."

Several minutes after she left the room, I blindly tore out the IV and catheter and tried to strangle myself with the tubing. The nurse, Connie, cried as she and several others held me down and put me in restraints.

Days passed as I lay restrained to the bed. One afternoon, Dr. Callahan, the medical director of the hospital, came into my room. I knew who he was from being previously hospitalized there with rheumatic fever and later for a tonsillectomy. Dr. Callahan was a tall, thin man with a kindly face. When I had first seen him, his gray hair and full mustache made me think he must be somebody's grandfather. He always smiled as he passed people in the hall. I turned my head away.

"My nurses tell me that you're really a good kid and have been accepted to college after you graduate in a few weeks. I'm afraid if we can't find a way to get you out of here, that won't happen. I'm not going to ask you why you're so hopeless or you want to die, you probably wouldn't tell me.

After a lot of thought I've come up with an idea that just might get you out of this jam you're in."

Instead of threatening me in any way, he was offering me sanctuary. In return, he asked me to promise not to run away or attempt to hurt myself. I took a while to consider his offer. He waited patiently. When I seemed to agree, he took off the restraints. "I'm really sorry we had to put these on you to keep you safe," he said as he removed the leather cuffs from my chapped and reddened wrists. "Are they sore?"

I looked down, shrugging my shoulders.

"I'd like to help you sit up," he said.

Instinctively, I cringed.

"I promise you, the last thing I want to do is scare you. I have a feeling that trust doesn't come easy at this point."

After helping me to a standing position, Dr. Callahan suggested that we walk down to the end of the hall so he could point out a small cottage in the back of the hospital. Dr. Callahan explained that it would be mine for the summer if I kept my promise to stay safe and to return with my diploma when I graduated. I could not only live there for summer rent-free, but I would be hired as a nursing assistant and his nurses would train me.

That small cottage was the most beautiful building I had ever laid eyes on. It was brick with white shutters at each window, red flower boxes, and a red front door. Part of the arrangement was I had to promise to call Connie each week and give her a report on how I was progressing toward graduation. A few days later, Miss F silently drove me back to my mother's. "I better not see you again," was the only thing she said to me as she dropped me off in front of my mother's apartment building.

I walked up the stairs, listening for voices. My mother was passed out cold, couldn't be roused, it was 10:00 a.m. I grabbed what few clothes I had, stuffing them into several brown paper bags, took what money I found, and left. I used some of the money for a locker at the Chicago & North Western train station to store my things in, knowing that I could not survive or keep my promise if I stayed at my mother's. I was homeless for the next four weeks.

I had one of two friends who sometimes invited me for sleepovers. They had no idea I wasn't still in a foster home. Most of the time, I slept in unlocked parked cars, stairwells, the bushes under the front window of the Dominican Sisters house by Immaculate Conception Church. The best of nights were the ones warm enough that I could sleep at the

Me at my high school graduation

end of the lighthouse pier jutting out over Lake Michigan. It was a very long pier, and being a good swimmer, I reasoned that if anyone messed with me, I could just dive in the water and get away. I loved falling asleep watching the stars and waking to the long, drawn-out calls of the gulls that frequented the pier looking for fish. One morning I jumped awake to the sound of quiet conversation as two fishermen cast their line into the lake while the sun slowly grew, glowing over the lake. They looked at me with a smile and said to have a good day as I collected my things and left. I smiled back. "Hope you catch some good fish. You have a good day too," I responded. At that moment, I felt safer than any time in my life with my mother.

The Sunday of graduation dawned. I had no family in attendance or anyone there for me. I was numb to everything except my goal to receive the diploma. On Monday morning, the crowded cross-town bus took me to the hospital. I slowly walked down the hall. In the doorway to the main nurses' station, I gasped in surprise. The small area had been decorated with a bright banner that read in bold red letters: *Congratulations High School Graduate.* Crepe paper, colorful balloons, a large, decorated chocolate sheet cake with my name on it, and brightly wrapped presents greeted me. Dr. Callahan, wearing a warm smile, handed me a key.

"Welcome to your summer home and to your new job."

This was my first taste of real medicine.

***

I loved my work as a nurse's aide. The cottage became my first ever home, an oasis of sanctuary and quiet. The grounds soothed me. I came to know every tree and flower intimately. I bathed myself in all the senses and sounds that nature had to offer. Peace.

One of my assigned patients was a funny woman nearly ninety years old who had spent her life as an acrobat in the Ringling Brothers and Barnum Bailey Circus. She had snow-white hair that reached past her waist and was certain I was the only one who could braid it the way she liked. As I carefully braided the silver strands every morning, she told me stories of her life in the circus.

One morning, Connie was waiting for me when I arrived. She asked me to sit down because she had something difficult to tell me. "Marisa unexpectedly died during the night in her sleep, most likely from her heart failing. She wasn't in any pain. We waited to remove her body until your shift in case you would like to spend some time with her and say goodbye. I know you meant a great deal to each other."

Touched by this kindness, I was also saddened by the loss of someone I had come to deeply care about. I attended Marisa's memorial service with a small group of hospital employees a few days later.

The last day at the hospital came far too quickly, filling me with a mixture of excitement and trepidation. I had come to know Lake County Hospital as home and it was difficult to say goodbye. Dr. Callahan and Connie drove me to the train station. I was sent on my way to college with best wishes, hugs, and a new suitcase from Dr. Callahan and school supplies from Connie. A hodgepodge of feelings vied for attention, filling me with a mixture of excitement and trepidation, confidence and hope. If I had had even an inkling of the challenges that were to come, I might not have boarded the train that day.

Reflection

The Web of Life—Shirley and Carole

*To bring about change, you must not be afraid to take the first step.
We will fail when we fail to try.*

Rosa Parks

While writing about Shirley, I wondered if she might still be alive. I came across the following tribute written after her death in the *Waukegan Sun Times*.

> Project Headstart founder Shirley Tometz dies: WAUKEGAN, 2002—Shirley Tometz, a pioneer in the city's civil rights movement in the 1960s and founder of Project Headstart, died Monday at her home from cancer. She was 82. In 1964, Tometz, a founder of the Waukegan Area Conference on Religion and Race, was the spark behind Project Headstart, a pre-kindergarten school program for disadvantaged children. This program became the pilot for the national program of the same name that continues to this day. Tometz secured the location, got background on preschool programs, and recruited teenage counselors for the program which educators termed a success. In 1965, Tometz, along with several other parents, filed suit against the then-Waukegan Grade School District to end de facto segregation—caused by housing patterns—at Whittier School and extend integration to the city's entire grade school system.

As I read this tribute to Shirley, I felt waves of gratitude that she had chosen me as one of the counselors for the pilot program. It taught me lessons I'll never forget. I'm very grateful for her influence on my life and for being another one of my angels wearing skin and the face of compassion. It's only now that I fully appreciate what Shirley was doing to change the narrative on racism in the 1960s, and I feel honored to have known her and been part of a small brigade of high school students learning the value of making a difference.

As I wrote this, I felt saddened that I had lost touch with my good friend and teaching partner, Carole. I had tried unsuccessfully to find her a number of times over the years.

While I was editing these pages prior to publication, I had a bit of magic come that began with a dream.

I am in a room with Carole Robbins. I tell her how glad I am to see her and how much trouble I've had finding her and she replies, "I've always been right here for the past 30 years."

I ask her where right here is. Before she can answer, her father comes into the room and I turn to greet him. "Hello Mr. Robbins, it's so nice to see you after all of these years." He looks at me fondly. "Now that you're an adult, you can call me Glen," he responds. Mr. Robbins takes me aside and tells me he thinks now would be a good time to be in touch with Carole and she has been looking for me.

I woke from the dream and wondered if Glen could really be Carole's father's first name. I hadn't known his name as an adolescent—in the 1960s, adults were always called Mr. or Mrs. I wasn't certain if the name I remembered from the dream was true.

I went to my computer and entered the name Glen Robbins. I found myself staring at his obituary. He had died peacefully in 2012 at ninety-six years old. The obituary listed his next of kin, including his only child, Carole, and gave me her married name. I was quickly able to find her and by the end of that day we had our first of many conversations. Carole sent me pictures and a newspaper article with a picture of both of us with our little charges from the pilot Headstart program. I was surprised to see that I had been quoted from the application I had sent in to be part of the program as saying that I wanted "to give of myself to people less fortunate than me." When talking to Carole about this, I told her that it sounded so funny that I said that back then, as I didn't know of anyone any less fortunate than me. Carole agreed. "I'm not surprised because you never felt sorry for yourself. But you definitely had it worse than anyone I knew."

7.

The Sharp Edges of the World

The fairytale of happiness ever after cannot be taken seriously, it belongs to the never-land of childhood, which is protected from the realities that will become terribly known soon enough.

Joseph Campbell, *The Hero with a Thousand Faces*

When I turned eighteen, I believed my life would be my own. How wrong I was. Looking back, it's clear how unrealistic my thinking was. Or perhaps, even though I had no safety net or support, I was just hopeful, like most adolescents when finally set free to live on their own. My summer at Lake County Hospital had saved me and protected me. But in some unconscious ways, it also contributed to the fantasy I carried forward. I was supposed to be a grown-up, I told myself repeatedly as I stumbled over all the ways I didn't know how to be an adult, horrified and ashamed of my inadequacies. At eighteen, I was sure I was nothing but a big imposter, a fraud about to be found out. This assumption made me terrified to ask for help. It wasn't until much later in life that I began to see clearly what I was up against. It was then that I could look at everything that conspired against my success and begin to understand why I'd put so much pressure on myself, and why everything went so wrong.

When I read these statistics cited by the Children's Defense Fund in 2017, I grieved for the young woman I had once been:

More than 23,000 children will age out of the US foster care system every year. Upon reaching the age of 18, 20% of the children who are in foster care will become instantly homeless. Only 1 out of every 2 foster kids who age out of the system will have some form of gainful employment by the age of 24. There is less than a 3% chance for children who have aged out of foster care to earn a college degree at any point in their life. More than 70% of them have PTSD.[1]

The statistics outlined here by the Children's Defense Fund would have been far worse in the late 1950s and 1960s, given the lack of oversight. These statistics hint at the experience of millions of young people across the United States, even today, as they age out of the foster care system. Small programs of transition are cropping up for homeless young people and those raised in the system, but, when I was young, they did not exist.

The beginning of my new life started with disappointment and challenges. Other than a school outing in the eighth grade to a musical in downtown, I'd never spent any time in Chicago itself and the transportation system alone was overwhelming. The Chicago & North Western train had carried me south from Waukegan into the city, followed by two buses, an elevated train, and another bus, dropping me off several blocks from the school. Arriving with my suitcase at Northeastern Illinois University's freshman registration was daunting all by itself.

I was late and joined the long line waiting to register for classes. When it was my turn, I set down my two suitcases and shyly asked a woman at the table where my dorm was. The woman at registration was harried and I interpreted her brusque answer as anger or disgust as she asked if I ever read my mail and told me that I should have made arrangements months earlier. She had no options for me. Filled with shame, I was certain everyone was looking at me and could see how inept and stupid I was. "Sorry, I didn't know. I'll try to come back next year, I guess."

I moved aside, defeated and near tears, unsure what to do next. A woman stepped forward, introducing herself as the Dean of Women. "Come with me, we may be able to help you figure something out," she said.

As she walked me down long halls and up the stairs to another level, she asked me a number of questions, learning that I had a couple of scholarships and intended to find a part-time job as a nursing assistant at a nearby hospital. She introduced me to Miss Barbara, one of the school counselors. Miss Barbara said she thought she could help me and I wasn't as badly off as it might appear. To my great relief, within a few hours she found me a room to rent within walking distance of the school. She also helped me apply for student loans to supplement my scholarships, and to complete registration.

96

I rented a room in the home of a widow who had what seemed to be an endless list of rules. Her anxiety about renting her guest room for the first time to a local student matched my own discomfort. Grateful I had a place to stay, it nevertheless proved very difficult to make friends without the ready-made community a dormitory setting might have provided. There wasn't a lot of campus life to speak of, and being painfully self-conscious and shy made it extremely difficult for me to initiate conversations with other students. One of the many rules my landlady had was: absolutely no guests. I also had a strict curfew: 9:00 p.m. The few times I was invited to an evening event, it was impossible for me to say yes.

The summer I spent as a nursing assistant at Lake County Hospital paid off. I was able to quickly get a weekend job, despite not being able to work evenings or night shifts. In order to get to the hospital by the time my shift started, I had to leave the house by 5:00 a.m. every Saturday and Sunday. This displeased my landlady, who was a light sleeper and didn't want to wake up as I left the house. Before long, she asked me to find another place to live.

I found the next place advertised in the paper. A college student attending another university in the city was looking for a roommate to share expenses. The apartment was much further from my school, making commuting more difficult, and it turned out the roommate and I had nothing in common. She seemed to spend less time studying and more time giving parties filled with the smell of marijuana, alcohol, and a wide variety of recreational psychedelic drugs. She was highly critical of my boundaries and commitment to saying no to both the drinking and the drugs, introducing me to her friends as her "baby roommate." Despite the challenging living arrangements, I had begun to finally make a few friends at school and I found my classes interesting and enjoyable.

Just as I began to relax a little and believe things were better, an older, creepy male employee at the hospital started making sexual overtures toward me. Unwilling to accept my lack of interest in him, he began actively stalking me. It went on for months—he cornered me, followed me, and showed up in random places: the bus stop, the grocery store, outside one of my classrooms, in front of the apartment where I lived, although I hadn't given him my address.

Meanwhile, the school counselor, Miss Barbara, helped me to get put on a waiting list for one of the Parkway Eleanor Clubs that provided supervised, supportive, and safe dormitory living for single women going to local schools or working for the first time in the city.

To my great relief, a room opened up and I assumed the change in my commuting pattern and the move to a safer, supervised dorm would put an end to the man's persistence. The only downside was that my living situation came at a price of around $400 per month, including meals, which was still way over my already-strapped budget. To make ends meet, I increased my work as a nursing assistant to longer hours and more shifts. My living situation was the best it had been, with a roommate who was easy to be around, a lovely study area, a lounge, optional evening activities, and complimentary bikes. The dorm was much further from school, on the edge of what was then called Old Town, an interesting part of the city to live in but a long commute to and from school.

Within days of moving, I was walking home from the subway when a guy on a bike accidently bumped into me. He quickly apologized, introduced himself as Frank, and struck up a conversation. I learned that he was a senior at a nearby Catholic high school. I was charmed when I learned he still served as an altar boy several times a week, thinking this made him innocent in some way and safe, which he was. Frank would be graduating in June and had been accepted at the University of Illinois, Chicago campus, where he would start school in the fall.

We continued to talk as he walked me home. When we arrived at the dorm, we sat on a nearby bench, and before saying goodbye we made a date to see each other again. I was surprised at how attracted I was to his warm smile, his sparkling blue eyes, and dark Italian good looks. I felt at ease with Frank in a way that I had never felt with a male before. He lived in the neighborhood and we began to see each other in the late afternoons.

As the relationship grew and deepened, I found myself letting down my guard and for the first time in my life, I thought I was falling in love. We explored the neighborhood together, and enjoyed biking and walking along Lake Michigan's nearby beach. As the relationship began to bloom, I found myself enjoying Frank's easygoing flirtatiousness, affection, kisses, and warm intimacy, with all the thrills of experimenting with new boundaries of first love. We saw each other as often as we could squeeze it in.

I had let my guard down and relaxed my vigilance, and seemed to have successfully been able to avoid the guy from the hospital with my change of work patterns and move. Then one late, dark evening on my way home from an early evening shift at the hospital, the man appeared, waiting at the bottom of the steps of the elevated train. I had no idea how he had figured out my new route. He quickly grabbed me and tried to drag me into his car. A man descending the stairs startled him, yelling out, "Get the hell away from her! Let her go!"

He immediately let go and I ran the dozen blocks to the dorm. I became hyper-alert. Constantly on edge, terrified of what he might do if he found me alone again, I quit my job, skipped classes, and avoided going out for the next month. I had nightmares and flashbacks from childhood that overwhelmed me, leaving me gasping in desperation for relief. I spent time searching in the want ads and calling nearby hospitals seeking new employment. I became nearly obsessed with my fear of the guy who had been stalking me, always terrified he would find me again and the next time I might not be so lucky. I felt terrified and self-conscious and didn't talk to Frank, my roommate, or anyone else about what had happened. Anxiety began to slip into hopelessness.

An unconscious pattern I carried from my childhood was the belief that when life became completely overwhelming and emotionally unbearable, I would be better off dead and could escape by committing suicide. I had never fully closed off that option of escape, and now, overwhelmed with worry about finances, filled with terror of the man who had been following me, and unable to find a new job, I felt like a cornered and doomed animal and turned all my frustration and rage on myself. I impulsively swallowed a bottle of aspirin but immediately regretting it, I made myself throw up. Despite my fear, I told the dorm mother, who was understanding, and told me she had ideas for other jobs that we could talk about after I got checked out by a doctor at a local hospital. She called a taxi and sent me to a nearby emergency room, promising I could return to the dorm.

My vitals were normal and the blood tests came back clear. I was given a clean bill of health by the young ER doctor. A few minutes later he returned and explained they felt it best if I spent a few days in a nearby hospital and they arranged transportation to have me admitted "to a nice, modern, young adult psychiatric hospital for a few days of support." It wasn't presented as an option. I was transferred from the emergency room to Illinois State Psychiatric Institute, known as ISPI. Months later, I was still at ISPI, trapped within the psychiatric system and daily growing more frantic than the day before. The place seemed nice enough and the patients were indeed all young like myself. Initially, the staff seemed caring.

I knew I didn't need medication, but the assigned psychiatric resident grew angry and condescending when I questioned him. He was unbending, demanding that I take the daily prescribed pills. I was a model patient, except in my resistance to taking drugs. Three times a day I fought a battle of wills with the nurses when they dispensed medication to me in a small white "med cup" filled with pills. This eventually grew to two full cups of "antipsychotics." I was not psychotic, but the nurses insisted they were "just following orders." I thought of my mother's use of drugs and her barely functioning life. I would never be like her.

The first month or so, I did everything I could to avoid taking the pills. When refusal failed, I became sneaky, holding the pills in the side of my mouth until I was out of sight of the nurses and could spit them out. I was never sure how they figured it out. Eventually, they overcame me, giving me the drugs in liquid form and through injections. I ran away but was caught and brought back. Over time, the day nurses became clearly frustrated, intolerant, and demeaning.

Having not been ill when I was admitted, I deteriorated under these circumstances, both psychologically and physically. As the drugs began to work, for the first time I had episodes of dizziness. I became unbearably agitated, experienced heart palpitations, could not sit still or sleep, was increasingly exhausted—and always desperately thirsty. Overwhelmed with anxiety, I felt in mortal danger from the drugs.

I started to secretly cut my arms, my legs, my abdomen with anything that I could get my hands on. This offered a false sense of control. Enraged at my powerlessness and having no other language to communicate, the cutting temporarily released the pressure. It didn't resolve the feelings I neither understood nor could talk about. My very life felt threatened by even attempting to do so.

With decades of experience and insight, I know now that the cutting was also a way I could stake claim over my body. I felt objectified, unseen, and unheard by the psychiatrist and the staff. I didn't put it together at the time, but I'm sure the feelings of objectification that had lingered deep in my body and psyche from my years of abuse at the hands of Dr. L and the similarity of that feeling in ISPI are what led me to cut as a way of declaring "this body is mine."

I ran away again and was picked up by the police and returned to ISPI. Several days later, I was taken to court for a formal, involuntary commitment hearing. Sitting in the courtroom in a disconnected, distant daze, I listened as the medical resident lay out a list of reasons why he believed me to be incompetent. He claimed I was a danger to myself and others and he was petitioning the court for my commitment. The judge looked over the paperwork in front of him. Glancing up, he asked if I had anything to say.

For a moment, I hardly knew what courtroom I was in. As a child, every six months during the years I had been forced to see Dr. L, we had to reappear in court for an evaluation of how I was doing in "therapy." Dr. L taught me to lie to Judge Hulse. If I didn't, he threatened that he would kill my mother and me. He instructed me to say, "Your Honor, whatever you and Dr. L think is best." The Judge would turn to Dr. L: "Doctor, what is your professional opinion?" Dr. L would report that he thought we were "making progress." After that there would be a continuance of "care" for the next several months.

All of this flooded back as I sat in court again and my mind went blank. I simply could not respond while time slowed down and my life slipped away as the judge's voice rang out loud and clear. "By the Power of this Court and the State of Illinois, I hereby order the patient to be committed and removed to Elgin State Hospital." With the loud bam of the judge's gavel ringing over and over again in my ears, I knew my life was over.

A hospital security guard returned me to ISPI. I went straight to my room with the sound of the gavel and the words "state hospital" repeating in a continuous loop in my head. I was more alone than I had ever felt in my entire life. I sat unmoving through the late afternoon and into the evening. I looked away and ignored the dinner tray someone brought in. I could not eat and felt unable to even move. The evening nurse, Sydney, came in and out of my room until shortly before 11:00 p.m. she sat down. "My shift ends soon but I'm going to sit with you until you open up and talk to me. You won't survive where you're being sent unless you let yourself have some feelings. I'll stay all night if that's what it takes."

Sometime near dawn, the cemented dam of my feelings gave way in wracking sobs of despair, followed by pure terror about what was to come next in my life. Sydney told me she would do everything in her power to visit me, and to get me out. I wanted to believe her, but I didn't. I blamed myself and didn't believe I had the right to get help from anyone. It would be many decades before I learned the real reason that I was sent to ISPI and subsequently committed to Elgin State Hospital.

8.

Shattered

...Whom should I turn to,
if not the one whose darkness
is darker than night, the only one
who keeps vigil with no candle,
and is not afraid –
the deep one, whose being I trust,
for it breaks through the earth into the trees,
and rises,
when I bow my head,
faint as a fragrance
from the soil.

Rainer Maria Rilke, *The Blessing of Earth,*
The Book of Hours: Love Poems to God, 11,3

Six months later, my life in Elgin had become a long, drawn-out dying. The physical and sexual assaults continued, but, numbed by cocktails of drugs, I didn't care. One day, my brain vaguely registered a name being called on the speaker system. I didn't understand it as *my* name until I was jerked to a standing position by an attendant who said I had a visitor. He escorted me reluctantly out of the heavy, locked doors, down the hall, and into a small room. I experienced all of this as though within a world and self, bent inside-out and disjointed by all of the drugs they gave me each day.

As I shuffled down the hall I thought, *They must have made a mistake. There was no one who would visit me.* I froze in the doorway, shocked. It was Frank, sitting in the visitors' room. I was nudged from behind as the attendant directed me to sit down. Time seemed to bend as memory rushed through me like a tidal wave, knocking the breath out of me. Images rolled by like old movies stored in the basement of my brain: Frank and I walking along Lake Michigan, a first kiss, a bouquet of flowers, wandering through Lincoln Park Zoo, and the heady feeling of first love. My long months in Elgin had bombarded me with more than I could possibly handle, leaving me bloated with experiences I couldn't digest. I had sunk into the hopeless reality of my new life. Along with the combination of drugs and daily abuse, I had shut down completely. The deadness that grew in me daily made it impossible to feel anything other than complete terror of the resurrection of memories from the life I had once lived, outside the walls of Elgin. Without warning, Frank's presence had created a rupture in my defense system.

I thought I had left everything behind. Not only had I become dead to the past, I had assumed I was dead to anyone who had known me before. But there was this one person, Frank, who I had not dared to allow myself to think about. Now he was here. Through my detached, drugged haze, I observed the once-beloved face, sitting across from me, watching it move from shock, to horror, and then to pity.

Frank's voice seemed to come from a great distance, but I could see he looked concerned. He was explaining something about the long train ride and wanting to see me. My throat and chest constricted in agony and protest as my mind screamed, *go away*. Scalding tears raced down my face as I began to shake my head no, begging him to leave. "Please. Just leave. Just leave me."

Shame sucked me into a vortex—a deeper and darker place than I had already been. It was unbearable to see Frank. I had been stripped of everything and the girl he once knew was no longer here, replaced by a vacant, skeletal, hollowed-out, drugged woman with matted, lifeless hair and dressed in a state-issued, bleached-out dress. I couldn't listen to him as he tried to connect with me, tried to cheer me up with news from the outside. The shock of Frank bearing witness to Elgin, to who I had become while in the care of the state, was too much.

"No, no. Please, just leave." Those words were all I could manage to say as I shook my head, like some broken, mechanical thing, stuck on this one gesture. Hopelessness, regret, and loss ran like a river down my face as I tried to block out Frank's voice. Finally, he got up and, to my horror, reached for me, to hug or kiss. I stepped away, terrified of his touch, terrified that I couldn't bear it without breaking into millions of pieces. I don't think he realized there was no "me" to take in his loving gesture. He departed, leaving me gutted from the awakened memory of a young woman's first love.

I didn't know it then, but Frank and I would reconnect years later. One of the first things he asked me was if I had any idea how that visit had impacted him. He left the hospital hopeless and cried all the way on the train ride back to Chicago, certain I would die in Elgin and he would never see me again. He was unnerved by the building and the lack of care evident everywhere, as well as by how significantly I had changed. He had been studying psychology, but after his visit, after witnessing other patients shuffling up and down the long halls of the hellish, frightening building where we were housed, he began to reconsider his major.

Five months later, I was again called because of a visitor and found myself seated across from a woman who seemed vaguely familiar. It took a while to understand who she was or to comprehend what she was saying. It was Sydney, the nurse from ISPI, who had sat with me into the dawn on the night I had been committed, before I left ISPI for Elgin. She reminded me that she had promised to come and see me, and apologized that it had taken her so long to get there. As she talked, I struggled to understand her. Her words didn't register or have any bearing on my current condition. I

Sydney Krampitz, the nurse who risked so much to save me from the system

105

had difficulty not falling asleep, and desperately wished she'd leave. I was confused and wondered what it was she wanted from me.

It wasn't until we reconnected forty-five years later that Sydney told me she had been so appalled at my debilitated, drugged state that following her first visit, she went to the Elgin administration and threatened to reveal that I had been illegally committed. She told them she would bring a lawyer if she didn't see changes in me and a plan for discharge.

After several more visits had passed, and after seeing no changes in me, or in the hospital's response, she insisted that the administration allow her to take me home for the weekend, albeit with all the medication they required me to take. She told the administration that she feared for my safety. "If I don't get her out of here and find a way to give her some hope, we're going to lose her."

The drive to her suburban home was long and surreal. All of my senses were assaulted, overwhelmed by how vast everything seemed. Moving between sleep and terror, I remember little from the weekend. Sydney's husband and three daughters were caring and pleasant and tried to engage me, but the drugs overwhelmed my ability to stay awake or to track conversations. Anxious and so, so tired, I could barely stand the stimulation of this new environment. In retrospect, I recognize the risks Sydney took on my behalf by challenging a powerful and dangerous authority. At the time, however, I had little capacity for insight.

What stands out in my memory on the drive to her home is stopping at a beautiful setting with a lake, flowers, and a large weeping willow tree. Sydney and I sat under the tree near the water's edge and I had a few moments of peace while she talked about hope and patience. The words felt alien, like concepts from another planet—I had no way of understanding. Why did she bother? The psychiatrist said I was committed for life. In my mind, I was way beyond the possibility of "release."

Miserable and unable to function because of the drugs, I had doubts about my ability to survive outside the walls of the hospital. It was impossible for me to believe that she, or anyone, could possibly do anything. But, it seemed, Sydney was determined to free me. One visit moved into another, and many obstacles arose because of Sydney's unrelenting persistence. She was told I would have to return to court for a sanity hearing, but first would need to pass a battery of IQ and psychological tests.

I failed.

Dr. Radeloff, the psychologist who conducted the testing, informed

Sydney and I that she believed I had failed because of the amount of medication I was being given. They had skewed the results. "The IQ portion of the test was so low that if it had been accurate, you would have been in a sheltered workshop rather than college before coming to Elgin. You wouldn't have even been able to complete school with scores like this."

Again, Sydney visited the administration and requested that they find a way to reduce the medication. They said it was impossible. "It won't be when I bring my lawyer with a court order," she threatened.

It took time to wean me down from the high dosage of drugs they had me on, although I remained heavily medicated. During that time, Dr. Radeloff met with me weekly and petitioned my high school and college for grades and statements from those who had known my ability to function, as proof of my mental capacities in case it was needed. Later, I learned from her that by meeting with me and working with Sydney to get me released, she had nearly lost her job. She felt it was worth the risk; she agreed with Sydney's belief that I should never have been committed in the first place and didn't belong in Elgin.

Eventually, Dr. Radeloff re-tested me and I did better and passed. Sydney visited administration, again requesting a court date be arranged. She was told it was unnecessary after all. But now, a new hurdle was thrown up—I could only be discharged to a legal relative.

After considerable thought and encouragement by my two champions and several phone calls, my Aunt Myrtle's middle daughter, Sharon, agreed to take me for a short time, until I could return to school. Sharon was seven years older and newly married with a baby. I hated to impose on her. It seemed impossible to me that I could ever again live outside an institution or return to college. Although I lacked any confidence in this plan, I agreed to stay with Sharon if it meant getting out of Elgin.

Sydney and Dr. Radeloff felt hopeful for me. Terrified and unsure of myself and wary of everything and everyone, I shook inside with doubts. Dr. Radeloff and I met with a representative from the state Division of Vocational Rehabilitation whom she had contacted. They agreed to pay for my tuition and books, and give me a small stipend when I returned to school.

As a very young child, I was subjected to watching my Uncle Clinton eviscerate a deer. As he removed the heart, lungs, stomach, and intestines, he threatened to do the same to me if I dared to look away. He scraped the insides clean, down to nothing, as he made me watch, sobbing in horror. Elgin scraped me down to muscle and bone, leaving me eviscerated, empty. But there were no tears to shed on my own behalf. A derailed, destroyed nervous system jumped at the smallest things and left me feeling handicapped, disoriented.

Although I had experienced horrendous trauma as a young person, I had somehow stayed connected to a spiritual center of gravity. At Elgin, that center was taken from me. The extreme trauma of Elgin transformed me into a person who was numb and disconnected from myself and from others. There had been an amputation, if not of a limb then of light and soul. A lifetime of traumatic memories lay stored in my body and nervous system, impacting my life in subtle and not-so-subtle ways for years into the future. And yet, somewhere in the deepest and darkest center of that time was the memory of trees.

Emerging from the Abyss

There is a pain-so-utter-It swallows substance up-
Then covers the Abyss with Trance-
So Memory can step
Around-across-upon it-
As One within a Swoon-
Goes safely-where an open eye-
Would drop him-Bone-by-Bone.

Emily Dickinson, Thomas H. Johnson, 1955 edition of
The Poems of Emily Dickinson

A few weeks turned into a month as I stayed with Sharon, her husband, and brand-new baby. Exhausted, I mostly slept—whenever I could get away with it. I was sick much of the time with flu-like symptoms, nausea, vomiting, dizziness, muscle spasms, and tremors in my hands, keeping me immobile for days on end. At times, my entire body shook violently. Anxiety was my constant companion, with my mood swinging from flat apathy to ramped-up irritation. Or I'd be overtaken with deep, racking sobs for seemingly no reason. My body felt heavy, out of balance, and clumsy: I fell several times and bumped into things on a daily basis. I only learned fifty years later that these were the effects of abruptly discontinuing the medications I had been overprescribed and discharged with, tucked into a small, brown envelope. The doctor I'd seen for five minutes on admission and only again at discharge had given the pills to me without instructions, besides to take them and go to a community mental health center to get more. I immediately threw them away.

A pervasive feeling of alienation and loss filled me. I felt alienated from myself, the life I had once known, and the "normal" world. I was filled with toxic, crippling shame. Nothing felt "normal." Sharon did everything she could to encourage me to get active or connect with old friends, but I felt incapable of anything she suggested. Back in the hospital, cocooned in a drugged fog, people's voices had felt distant and filtered; now I was hypersensitive to any sound, light, or touch—raw nerve endings exposed. I was handicapped by physical discomfort, nightmares, and mood swings, and felt unable to complete even the smallest tasks. Incapacitated by shame and self-doubt made returning to school seem impossible. Prior to Elgin, I was determined to get an education; it now seemed insurmountable and unrealistic. I had difficulty imagining any kind of future.

One day, I begged Sharon to drive me back to Elgin. I'd been terrified of the hospital—but I was now even more terrified of the outside world. I simply had no idea of how to function. She refused and told me to "snap out of it." Several days later, near hysterical, I begged her again to take me to Elgin. Though she acquiesced, fortunately, I never got any further than admissions. They had called Dr. Radeloff, the psychologist who had worked so diligently with Sydney to get me discharged. She talked to me for a couple of hours and then strongly encouraged me to return to Sharon's and take one day at a time. She also suggested that we meet by phone during this time of transition.

Slowly, the symptoms began to disappear, and one morning, Sharon sat me down. "It's time for you to pull yourself together and get back to your old life." What life? I thought. "I'll plan on leaving in the next couple of weeks," I told her.

It was time to leave Sharon's. I couldn't imagine returning to school, but I had nowhere else to go. Whatever had motivated me to attend college before was now missing—I was hollowed out, lacking in the goals I had previously held dear, and some dynamic aliveness in myself was absent. I had few thoughts and no language to describe the feeling. *Vacant* is the word that seemed the closest to it. The me who had once lived in the body that now robotically navigated each day had disappeared.

When I returned to school, I temporarily moved into the YWCA since there weren't any available dorms. I walked through the lobby one day and ran into Melinda, the girl who had been prostituting herself while in Elgin. We began to hang out, sometimes eating meals together. She tried to set me up with a "date," but I had no interest. Just a few weeks after running into her as I left the YWCA, a man who had been sitting in a nearby parked car approached me.

"Excuse me, Miss, I need to talk to you a moment." He showed me a badge and told me he was a detective. He asked me what I knew about Melinda's boyfriend and her other male friends. I didn't know a thing. He told me that she had gotten herself involved in a "white slavery ring." I had no idea what he was talking about, so he went on to explain. "It's not just a date they're looking for," he said. "White slavery is about forced prostitution. You look like a good kid; you should stay as far away from her and her friends as you can. We're just waiting for the right moment to arrest them. Please don't tell her we've had this talk."

I tried to talk to Melinda about my concerns, without telling her about the detective, but she was as stubborn and determined about this as she had been about my discomfort and concerns for her welfare while in Elgin. I then resorted to avoiding her—I had enough problems of my own, trying to cope with each day.

A room in an off-campus girls' dorm opened and eventually I made a couple of good friends at school, especially Karen. She was supportive and needed support herself. Her mother had been committed to a state hospital since Karen was in grade school. She had been raised by her aunt, with whom she had little to no contact. Like me, she often felt out of place and self-conscious about her life and seldom talked about it. Karen asked me if I'd like to be her roommate, as she had just moved out of the dorm and into an apartment. She was a psychology major and wanted to teach high school. I was an education major but still uncertain of teaching or what I wanted to do. I had little confidence in myself and wasn't even sure I could complete school. Karen saw me differently than I saw myself.

I was in therapy at this time, which was always treacherous territory for me, given my history. I simply could not look at the past—my time in Elgin or my childhood—without suffering debilitating physical and emotional symptoms. Nancy, the therapist, was kind and supportive but simply didn't have the tools to help me fully recover. However, seeing her was a requirement of the Division of Vocational Rehabilitation grant I received. In the meantime, I was slowly building more ego-strength.

Several months after I moved in with Karen, she came home excited about job possibilities at Chicago State Hospital. It was a short bus ride from our college. They were seeking psychiatric aides, no experience necessary. I was unsure, but Karen talked me into applying. I grew more confident as I remembered my experiences in the high school summer program working with preschool children, and to my amazement, I was offered a part-time position on a children's unit, while Karen was placed on a ward for adult women.

I immediately loved the work. Although the physical facilities at Chicago State were awful—nearly as bad as Elgin—the staff, unlike the staff at Elgin, was kind and loving to the children and supportive of each other. I began to grow and thrive in my work. The children brought out my creativity and the need to nurture and care for someone else. I also used the many invaluable skills from the summer program with inner-city preschoolers.

At Chicago State Hospital, the children's resilience and openness inspired me. My creativity flourished, and hope and meaning slowly began to re-emerge and reshape themselves. I learned that kindness, love, a hug, or a soft lap did wonders from an older aide named Miss Foster who had worked at the hospital for nearly thirty years after moving to Chicago from the deep south. She was a no-nonsense sort of woman and held nothing back in her love of the children. I seldom saw her without a child on her lap. She'd croon and sing, referring to them—and to me—as "baby."

A little boy named Arthur drooled continuously from the medicine he was on. He was a lap sitter. One day, he climbed on my lap and of course drool began to cover the front of me. I squirmed, uncomfortably trying to distance myself from Arthur's wet mouth, and proceeded to try to get him off of my lap. Miss Foster noticed and came over. "Now baby girl, you just be still and hold that little guy in your lap. He's missing a whole lot of loving, and I know you can put up with a little bit of wet drooling. What's worse, you being wet or him being a lonely, achy little boy just looking for someone to sit by?"

I nodded in agreement, remembering the fleeting moments of care that had sustained me as a child. I've never forgotten her words.

I arrived one weekend when we were short-staffed, with Miss Foster and I the only ones working, to find that our oldest—a nearly fifteen-year-old boy named Henry—was in the seclusion room waiting to be transferred to a ward for adolescents. We hated keeping Henry in seclusion, but we were concerned for the much younger, vulnerable children on the unit. That week Henry had lost his temper and picked up one of the youngest children and hurled him against the wall, breaking his arm.

Sometime mid-morning, we noticed smoke pouring out of the

seclusion room. Miss Foster quickly filled a bucket of water, instructed me to call the on-site fire department and then bring another bucket of water. Henry had somehow gotten a hold of matches and lit the mattress on fire. The fire was quickly doused to a lingering, smoking mess. In amazement, I watched as Miss Foster held Henry by his arm and talked to him kindly but firmly. "Henry, you my baby, surely you are. You won't disappoint me again, I'm sure of it."

She firmly sat him down, instructing him to put his hands on the arms of the chair and not let go. She then lowered her voice to a near whisper and crooned to him. "If you do, Henry, you will see the angry side of your Miss Foster and will be very sorry, do you understand me?"

"I'm sorry Miss Foster, I won't move a muscle here, I promise," Henry stammered. Large tears began to run down his cheeks.

"There, there Henry, I know you're sorry and going to be a good boy now."

Miss Foster taught me the power of love in action. That love made an amazing difference to the children who lived in an environment of cracked walls, inadequate heating, poor lighting, and not a toy to be found. At the same time, I was learning in my Human Growth and Development class that play is the language of childhood. As I saw the real-life applications, my coursework gained more meaning. Whereas before I was a silent observer at school, I became involved, asking the professor questions and applying what I learned at work. I found myself, like Miss Foster, bringing games and toys for the kids, or inventing them when none was available. I was inspired by Miss Foster's love and generosity to the children and to other staff. This stood in harsh contrast to my experiences of cruelty at the hands of 'caregivers' in Elgin. Perhaps if Miss Foster had been there, I wouldn't have suffered as much.

Every shift, my first task after morning report was to get the littlest boys' teeth brushed. One morning, I went into the day room expecting to round them up, but the room was empty. I went from one dormitory to another, growing concerned, until I came to the last one and noticed that the beds were all pushed against the wall, whispering coming from underneath.

I got down on my hands and knees. "Hey you guys, what are you doing under there?" I said.

"Digging out," eight-year-old Vincent triumphantly answered. He scooted out from under the bed, majestically waving a spoon. Somehow,

Vincent, considered one of the most ill children on the unit, had been able to lead every little boy out of the dining room with a spoon. He then instructed them to crawl into their under-the-bed cave to "dig out." And the amazing thing is—they did.

At that moment, I had a flash of insight about this little boy. I knew his actions were important—they were speaking volumes in a way that he couldn't yet give voice to. He was not only creative; he was a strong little leader and most likely not as "sick" as his diagnosis might suggest. And for a moment, I had a glimmer of compassion for myself. I too was "digging out." For me, a process of excavation of what I had lost in Elgin had truly begun. And perhaps, like Vincent, I wasn't as "sick" as I had been led to believe.

10.

Fool's Folly or Angels in Disguise?

Before the inexplicable mystery of the universe, we are all the village fools. But in our choice to reveal our hearts to ourselves and to each other, we can all be masters and healers.

Agapi Stassinopoulos, *Unbinding the Heart*, Hay House.

The withdrawal symptoms I had experienced from the psychiatric drugs the first few months after my discharge from Elgin by now were more manageable, though not entirely gone. Days of contentment alternated with mood swings, anxiety and doubt, tremors, and stomach pains. I had no idea how to pull myself together and get on with life, but it seemed to be happening slowly, one day and one decision at a time. Some days, I made progress, and then the next it felt as if I'd gone two steps backward again, particularly on the days when some smell, sound, or circumstance would trigger me back to the past.

At the time, I had no idea I had post-traumatic stress disorder; I encountered and learned about that term and its protective function only years later. There was little understanding of the impact of trauma in the 1960s and 1970s. It was natural for me to compartmentalize life since I'd grown up needing to do so. This ability served me well during those years, when there was still no real safety in my life, nor a skillful therapist or community who could support my healing, as there would be many years later.

The medical community's ignorance of the nervous system and trauma made things much more difficult and longer lasting than they might have been just a few decades later. Flashbacks, triggers, and immediate ramping-up of the nervous system were all things I experienced on a regular basis. Without understanding these experiences, I held myself accountable for them in harsh ways that further crushed my fragile, growing self-esteem. It would take many years to develop ego-strength and skills for living in the everyday world, as well as for deep and full healing to come.

A few days before the winter holidays, the Dean's office summoned me for an emergency phone call. On the other end of the line, a nurse identified herself and told me my Aunt Myrtle had given her my contact information. She was calling about my mother. Startled, I listened to her in disbelief. "I'm calling because your aunt listed you as next of kin."

My thoughts ran in circles, clashing with long-suppressed emotions. I didn't want to be known as "kin" to Edna, let alone "next of." Reeling from the words, unable to digest them, my mind searched for something to say.

"Are you the biological daughter of Edna Dean?"

"I suppose so," I answered, hesitantly.

"That makes you her next of kin, so I'm calling to tell you that your mother was in a fire and is in critical condition. She suffered significant smoke inhalation and some second- and third-degree burns. She is lucky to be alive."

"My aunt should have told you, I lived in foster care and I haven't had a relationship with my mother in years."

The nurse acknowledged that my aunt said that we weren't in regular contact or on friendly terms. The word "friendly" was a heavy boulder rolling around and around in my brain. My mother and I had never even been close to being "friendly." For a moment, I wanted to scream at her all that had been so wrong between us, all that was other than "friendly." But I bit my tongue hard, shoving away the unbearable weight of the word "friendly," a word that encapsulated the unbearable fault line of sorrow that lay between my mother and me.

The nurse told me Edna had been living in a second-floor apartment over a grocery store and just after closing there was an explosion from inside. The fire had spread immediately to the apartment directly above, blowing a hole in the floor and trapping Edna.

I was surprised to hear myself ask if she could have visitors. "Not yet, we're concerned about possible infection, she's in isolation in the burn unit." They would phone me if there were any changes.

Disoriented, I watched as I hung up the phone—at the same time as I began to smell smoke, hear sirens, and loud noises. Looking at my hands in confusion, I was surprised not to see blistered burns. One of the women who worked in the office was talking, but her voice was garbled as I slipped further away, reliving the fire I had been in as a small child. Someone brought me a glass of water and carried me back to myself. The school counselor appeared. She asked if I could tell her what the caller said to me and I somehow managed to repeat parts of it—and found some relief.

I pulled myself together enough to attend my last class for the day and got home around 4:00 p.m., emotionally spent. I could barely remember the trip home, my mind filled with memories of the fire I had been in and the last time I saw my mother—the night I had fled in terror of killing her and the man to whom she had just sold me. I was disappointed that Karen was at work, so I nibbled on a little bit of food, then turned on the radio. It provided background noise, until Judy Collins began singing her newly released song, "Both Sides Now."[1] The words caught my attention. I stood listening, the words about love and its illusions permeating me. The song finished and I turned the radio off, craving stillness.

An inner voice reminded me that I once knew *love*—a clear image of the upstairs neighbor, Dale, came to mind. She had been the first and only adult to tell me she loved me. A luminous presence and vitality filled the room, and my heart swelled in epiphany. A realization flowered in the middle of my chest—the recognition that I loved my mother. I savored the memory of the child-me who had loved her mother. I pondered the words of the song and asked myself if I could tell my mother that I loved her.

I whispered a prayer for her survival. The realization that I had always loved her, even when it seemed I had not, moved through me. I had completely distanced myself from her because I was unable to bear the way she treated me, her pain, or mine. Waves of love and grief for us both filled me, a fire connecting me to my mother and to something more significant than I had experienced since Dale moved away. Held in grace, I realized loving my mother didn't mean I had to sacrifice myself to save her. I could simply love her—a liberating revelation. Old bitterness, outrage, and hurt fell away. In that moment of epiphany, something essential to my own being returned and filled me to overflowing—my soul gathered close.

Feeling the need to listen to the song again, I set out to buy the album in Chicago's Old Town district—a twenty-minute trip by the elevated train. Everything seemed magical and colored through the lens of the new feelings of love and life that were flooding through me. I bought the record and found holiday presents for my mother and Karen.

As I hurried back to the elevated train, my attention was caught by a woman on the other side of the street. The sight of her stopped me in my tracks. She was near the corner of Wells Street and North Avenue, selling art in the lightly-falling snow, dressed in bright fabrics, wearing a white winter hat and furry coat. She stood surrounded by a golden orb of light from the nearby street lamp. I was captivated, watching her animated face as she greeted people passing. Many seemed to know her and stopped to look at the paintings she was selling. I waited until the crowd moved away and then crossed the street to admire her art. "How much are they?"

She didn't respond. I studied several and asked if she had more. "It depends—I have a lot more, but first you have to tell me about yourself."

Her name was Lee. "Call me Goldie, if you like the sound of it better," she said as she dramatically flipped her golden-blonde hair. Her warm, throaty laugh was like a waterfall. She was mesmerizing and her voice reminded me of music. I slowly began to do as she requested. Eventually, I was telling her things I had never said to anyone before—about Dale, foster care, Elgin, and school. I told her about my hatred and fear of my mother, the fire she had been in, and, most importantly, the epiphany and discovery that I loved her. Although it was snowing, the night was mild as we stood together, and I was warmed by her presence and wisdom.

"About your mother, it's essential that you let yourself know that you love her," she said. Her pensive look was penetrating. "Sometimes, mothers just can't be good at it—can't tell their child they love them, they can't even see them, or be around them either—but that doesn't mean love isn't so. Their personhood can't love, but their soul loves the child—always the soul," she mused, turning slightly away as she paused, deep in thought. "It's an intense soul thing that sometimes a person just isn't able to bring up to the light of day. But you, keep being a good girl and love her no matter what she does—remember what I just said, now."

I nodded, holding back tears as I looked into her kind, wise eyes.

Although I didn't have the maturity or wisdom to understand everything Lee said, I hung on her every word, knowing they were important. We spent most of the night on that quiet corner. Snowflakes fell in silent benediction to what transpired between us. Their crystalized, snowy flakes kissed our cheeks and adorned our shoulders with prayer mantles as Lee shared a tiny portion of her light and her wisdom.

Occasionally, Lee would gesture to me and we would step into the entryway of the nearby brownstone to warm up before returning to the beauty of the outdoors.

Then, Lee told me about her art. She leaned close and lowered her voice like she was about to share a great secret. "My art, it's like that love energy that moved into you. It moves through me when I'm painting." She elongated the word "through", emphasizing it. "My calling as an artist is to show the real mysteries of life. We're a very complicated species."

There was something about her, some greatness and mystery she carried and inhabited, that moved me deeply. "Some days, I'm just the handmaiden of the gods," she laughed with her honeyed, waterfall voice.

We said our goodbyes as the sun was coming up. She thanked me for my company, and I promised to see her again. She gave me a small watercolor picture of flowers as a gift. "How will I find you? Where do you live?" I wondered aloud.

"I live everywhere and nowhere—here and there. Mostly I live here," Lee winked as she pointed to her heart. "You'll find me when the stars are lined up. Just pay attention and keep your heart as well as your eyes open."

As I walked away, I smiled, sure I had met someone who knew the secrets of the universe. She made me think of Sister Sebastian with her calm presence and wisdom. I couldn't wait to get home and tell Karen about Lee.

When I arrived home, Karen was still asleep. I quickly took a shower and set off for a therapy session. The therapist I saw on a regular basis was on maternity leave, but I was eager to tell the substitute therapist I had seen a few times before about the fire, the epiphany, about my mother, and about meeting Lee. The therapist's response to my experience, however, was to minimize. "This notion of suddenly feeling like you love your mother now after having described hating her previously makes no sense. It's magical thinking. You don't just go 'poof' and that hatred vanishes."

I was taken aback by her words. I knew with every fiber of my being that my life depended on not losing my new awareness. "It wasn't just a notion. I had a life-changing experience," I insisted.

"A person doesn't just snap their fingers and go from hating a mother like yours to love—without doing anger work in between," she countered. "And, I think you were very foolish to stand on a street corner all night talking to an old bag woman you didn't know. Anything could have happened."

She wasn't willing to believe I had been perfectly safe. I grew more and more discouraged in my attempt to communicate to her how monumental these events had been. I took a deep breath and I tried again. "I lost so much of myself in Elgin. But my center of gravity, my inner compass, has come back. I'm back."

She looked at me skeptically, her eyebrows raised and her arms crossed.

"I'm much more myself than I have been in years—maybe ever. I feel connected to God and Love again—I'm fully back."

A sound of utter disbelief, near ridicule, came from deep in the back of her throat. "Did you have these kinds of delusions before being sent to Elgin?"

Uncomfortable with where this was going, I knew it was useless to respond or keep explaining. She suggested that I go home and get some sleep. She wanted me to promise to see her the next day. "I'm concerned that you may be getting delusional and need medication, or need to be hospitalized for a short time."

Beginning to feel panicky, I knew I had to leave. Although she seemed to mean well, she could only see me through the lens of a psychiatric diagnosis, and as an ex-state hospital patient. Her certainty of being right deafened her to her ability to really hear me. Attempting to communicate any further would be a waste of her time, and mine. I took a deep breath and stood up calmly—I was leaving. "I'm really okay, better than okay," I emphasized.

She looked incredulous. Feeling generous toward her, I had the thought that she was probably doing the best she knew how within her field of work and narrow perception. She again requested that I make a promise to see her the next day.

"It's clear to me that neither you nor anyone else in your profession can help me at this point," I said. "The kind of help I've received is from a higher source. I'm going to depend on that for now. Thanks for your concern."

I left her office and quietly shut the door as I went out.

Needing some time to sit and think before walking to the subway, I went into a beautiful large church across the street from the mental health center. Memories of sitting in churches as a child flooded me with inspiration as words seemed to lift from the prayer book I sat reading, speaking to me and opening my heart further. Gratitude and genuine peace enveloped me as I started for home, knowing I had made the right decision.

On the elevated train, a very distraught man was talking aloud to himself. "I'm just invisible to all you people. You can't even look at me," he said. He rambled on about the war in Vietnam: he had just come back. He talked at length about all he had done for this country and no one cared. The person in the seat next to him got up and moved to the back of the car. The other passengers looked away. "Why don't you go ahead and spit on me like you want to. I may as well fucking kill myself. No one has ever loved me, or ever will, even less now that I came back from fighting your war. I should get off at the next stop and throw myself in front of the train."

Without hesitation, I got up and went and sat by him. I held his hand and told him I cared, I wanted to get him some help—if he would let me. He nodded, tears pouring down his face.

As he and I walked to my apartment from the subway, I made a plan to call the Salvation Army as soon as we got there. I wanted to help, to be a bridge for him, but I knew he couldn't stay with Karen and me. Looking back on it now, I can see why it made sense to me to bring this man home with me, but I also know it might not have been a wise choice, and why it was not seen as rational.

My shocked roommate was frightened and angry. When the man asked to use the restroom, Karen told me the therapist had called earlier and said she was concerned about me because I had left her office not making any sense. "Now you show up with a strange man from the subway. You say you want to help him. You can't even help yourself right now."

Karen called the police. They said they were taking the man to a shelter. They took me to the old Dunning State Hospital, now called Chicago State. I begged them not to. "I work in the children's unit. I don't want to lose my job."

"It's a big place. I doubt the folks you work for will know you're there. Sorry, it's the law you get checked out since a professional was concerned about you," he shrugged as if to say, "don't blame me."

It took several hours to complete my admission to Chicago State. The admissions worker was waiting for a call back from the therapist I had walked out on, and Chicago State's weekend psychiatrist, before sending me upstairs to the women's unit. When I noticed it was almost 7:00 p.m., I explained to the admissions counselor that I was an employee and worked on the children's unit next door. "While you wait for the calls, can I go over to the little boys' unit where I work and help put kids to bed? I know they are short-staffed on the evening shift. I'd like to help out, not just sit here. And I want to find a supervisor and let them know that something came up and I won't be able to work my shift tomorrow."

"Sure, go ahead, just promise you'll come back in a half hour or so." He chuckled. "Between you and me, I don't even think you need to be here, but it's not my call."

The little guys were excited as I read them a couple of stories and tucked each of them into bed. The staff was pleased that I dropped by to help, even after I told the manager I wouldn't be able to work that weekend.

When I returned to admissions, the paperwork was in order and they took me upstairs. The admissions worker apologized and said again that he saw no reason for me to be there, but when a therapist was concerned, they felt a professional obligation to check it out. He told me I would most likely get discharged early the next day.

Being admitted to another chaotic, crumbling state hospital and not becoming upset or triggered with memories of Elgin seemed incredible to me. As I drifted off to sleep, I marveled at how peaceful I felt, considering the circumstances of finding myself in another cramped room of wall-to-wall beds in a state hospital.

The morning passed as I continued to feel calm but eager to be discharged and get home and work on a paper that was due on Monday. Shortly before noon, I sought out the nurse and asked her if she knew when the doctor would be in since I was hopeful of being discharged. "The doctor doesn't come in until Monday or Tuesday. He just called and ordered some meds for you."

A lightning rod of tension immediately snaked its way through my body—fear. "I'm not taking them. I don't need any medication," I replied.

"You can do it the easy way by cooperating, or the hard way. I just have to say the word for a couple of the attendants to hold you down. Then I'll give you an injection." She seemed to study me for a moment. "The food cart just came up, and you have until after lunch to decide how it's going to be. Easy? Or hard?"

I kept eyeing the door, determined to find any means of escape as we formed two lines on either side of the large metal cart of food. My anxiety mounted and just when I thought I would lose complete control, a woman across from me reached over the cart and squeezed my hand and began talking in a honeyed, waterfall voice. The voice was unmistakable. Looking up, I was shocked to see that it matched my memory of the person it went with—the artist, Lee, from the night before.

"Calm down. It is a time for just a little affliction for your soul," she squeezed my hand. "Don't let them get the satisfaction of confirming you're crazy—you certainly are not. It will be over before you know it."

Surrounded by a glow of serenity, her presence soothed my panic. She turned to me and winked as she walked away with her lunch tray. I was reassured by her presence. She'd softened my experience of confinement, again being forced to take unnecessary drugs.

The nurse gave me a couple of pills after lunch. Fighting seemed like a lost cause. By the middle of the afternoon, I could hardly stand up straight or see. I accidentally lurched into another patient, who started screaming that I had attacked her, and was told to sit in a chair and not get up. I was too drugged to move and hadn't tried to get up, but they ended up securing my arms in loose restraints to the chair for the next two days. Lee occasionally walked over to me and with a glance or subtle touch calmed me.

The weekend passed and Monday morning brought a doctor. Lee was seen as one of the first patients. Before she left, she sauntered over to me, taking ownership of the room like she had the street corner the night we met. She sat down, her gaze intense, penetrating, as she slowly shook her head back and forth and released a long sigh. "You're too skinny, girl. Your soul is emaciated, full of holes from being in places it has no business being—like this," she gestured around the dayroom.

I knew what she was saying was important. Then she continued, seemingly on a tangent, and I could barely follow her words, let alone their meaning.

"Mary," she began, as she looked closely at me.

"My name isn't Mary," I corrected.

"Mary," she continued. "You're going to have to take the baby Jesus and get as far away from Herod as you can. Take a donkey, a bus, a train or walk, but just get yourself out beyond the walls of the city. It's not safe for you or the baby."

I wondered if she was psychotic, or if they had given her drugs. She continued. "The baby is too vulnerable and skinny—about whittled down to near nothing. Take yourselves to someplace peacefully small and away from the city. I have to get out of here myself. Now, take care and do what I said."

A few minutes later, I was called to the small office to see the doctor. After asking me a number of questions, I was relieved to hear him say he would take me off of the meds and I would be discharged the next morning. I was determined to make the time pass as productively as I could, and I was able to get some paper and a pen. I had been keeping a journal since adolescence and I spent much of the next several hours writing down the events of the past week. I was discharged uneventfully early the next morning.

Lee deeply touched my life that night in Old Town, planting seeds I would later harvest. She validated my experience of love and encouraged it to flourish, even—and especially—for my mother. She pointed me inward. Steering me a new direction through her symbolic language opened me to something mysterious and inexplicable.

Over the years, I would find myself thinking of her and the significance of our encounter. While telling the story of our meeting to a good friend or mentor, I always found myself hesitating and qualifying my retelling of the moment I saw her at Chicago State Hospital with the caveat that it seemed just too incredible and unbelievable that she was at the hospital. I sometimes wondered if I might have hallucinated her or experienced some kind of vision in those moments of extreme stress.

Reflection

The Web of Life—Lee Godie

Be not forgetful to entertain strangers, for thereby some have entertained angels unawares.

Hebrews 13:2 KJV

While writing this, I paused and on impulse began a Google search. I typed "homeless woman artist in Chicago sold art in Old Town in 1969–1970s." To my surprise, the screen opened to a *People Magazine* article titled "Baglady artist, Lee Godie is a wacky success—her paintings are off the wall and in demand."[1] From there, I found many other articles and recognized pictures of Lee immediately.

I learned that Lee Godie's work has been shown at the Smithsonian American Art Museum, galleries around the United States, and in the London Hayward Gallery. She became beloved on the streets of Chicago and is viewed as one of Chicago's most famous, self-taught, "outsider artists." She was active, selling her art on the streets of Chicago for almost thirty years, from 1968 through the early 1990s.

Lee was described as a clever businesswoman who saved her money, often having several thousand dollars tucked away with people she trusted. She chose to make her home outdoors, sleeping on benches or in transient hotels if the weather was too cold. Lee felt people had to be deserving to own her art, and frequently asked them to tell her about themselves before she was willing to sell.

Not much is known about Lee's private life, but I learned she had a daughter she had not seen since she was an infant. In Lee's later years, the daughter found her mother after reading an article about her in *The Wall Street Journal* in 1988. Lee eventually went to live with her daughter and died in her care on March 2, 1994.

My heart quickened as I continued reading how Lee had been picked up one weekend and was taken to a mental hospital. "Ken Walker, director of the influential Betsy Rosenfield Gallery, has dedicated an entire wall of his folk-art-filled loft to Godie. On interview Walker stated, 'I think a lot of people would describe Lee as mentally ill… But I think Lee is quite functional, and I think she is very happy in the life she is living."

I continued to dig, looking for the answer to the burning question I had carried for fifty years. Was Lee really at Chicago State with me?

I came across a trailer for a documentary of Lee's life. From there, I went to the website www.leegodiemovie.com and read, "Lee Godie, Chicago's French Impressionist—a movie by Tom Palazzolo and Kapra Fleming."[1] There was a telephone number listed. Without hesitation, I dialed the number. Kapra Fleming answered. By the end of our conversation, I had learned a good deal more about Lee—and had the answer to my most important question. Lee was frequently picked up by the police for "vagrancy," particularly in the harshest winter months, and taken to the hospital. Holding my breath, I asked Kapra the burning question.

"Kapra, do you happen to know what hospitals Lee was usually taken to?"

"It was always Chicago State—because downtown was one of its catchment areas."

Toward the end of the call, Kapra asked me if I would be willing to be interviewed for the documentary. She felt my story was important and would add another dimension to viewers' understanding of Lee. I returned to Chicago during the 2018 holiday season. I met with Kapra and was interviewed on camera—nearly fifty years to the month after meeting Lee.

I was really astonished to realize Lee was not only a real person who embodied some magical qualities, she was a nonconformist, living on her own terms. She chose to make her home outdoors and lived outside of the normal constructs and rules.

Lee used metaphor and symbolism when she addressed me as Mary, protector of the divine child, knowing full well that Mary was not my name. Jesus was the metaphor for my soul—as my divine child—as what was vulnerable and emaciated in me. Lee used the name Mary to encourage me to get as far from Herod (Chicago) as possible. Leaving the city became essential to my survival and ultimate healing.

In retrospect, I think of Lee as the archetypal Fool in the Tarot, a figure who has shown up throughout time, in nearly every culture and religion. Historically, "holy fools" lived in voluntary poverty because acquiring wealth is thought to build up the self and thereby block the "path to unity." The fool often rejects the norms of the culture, which makes them appear foolish to others. Though fools separate themselves from society and are often subjected to contemptuous treatment, they may also be regarded with respect and admiration—as was Lee by many people.

My encounter with Lee came at a critical time when I needed validation and support, a time that would then signal the need for a dramatic change. The archetypal Fool in the Tarot deck shows up at the beginning of a journey, pointing the way forward, asking us to leave everything we know behind and move into the unknown. This was a journey that Lee herself knew well. A journey on which I would soon embark.

11.

Enough

The moment one definitely commits oneself, then Providence moves too. All sorts of things occur to help one that would never have occurred otherwise.

W.H. Murray, *The Evidence of Things Not Seen*

In April of 1968, riots broke out in Chicago and across the United States, following the assassination of Martin Luther King Jr. Chicago was a tinderbox waiting to catch fire when the Democratic Convention took place two months later. This brought thousands to the city in protest against the war in Vietnam. Demonstrations and violence occurred throughout cities and on college campuses for the next several years, including at Northeastern State University, where I was a student.

Violence had broken loose daily at Elgin between attendants and patients when I was there. As much as I might want to join friends at the protests, I was too frightened, reeling from the experience. Forced off campus one day by tear gas released into the ventilation system, I witnessed the escalating hostility firsthand. What I had experienced in my life was being echoed throughout the country: people had grown tired of suffering at the hands of authority.

Antiwar and civil rights movements were motivated by the refusal of many to support an abhorrent political culture, outright racism, and inequity. Activism of the 1960s and 1970s took place within the broader context of social upheaval and unrest. I understood students' need to protest, although I wasn't yet able to articulate it. I often couldn't distinguish between the tensions of the city and my own, and began having nightmares and flashbacks.

I had a number of dreams where I became caught in the middle of violence, unable to escape. Sometimes the landscape of the dream was Elgin; others, it was the streets of Chicago. My nervous system was always on heightened alert. During the day I experienced overwhelming anxiety—my ability to concentrate or study suffered—and my nights were filled with terrors.

One dream was different from all the rest. It became a guiding light.

I am climbing the steps to board a train, unsure where I was going. As I sat in a seat waiting for the conductor to take my ticket, I was delighted to see that the conductor was Lee Godie, herself. She smiled and told me I had made the right decision, before patting me on the shoulder and moving on.

Upon waking, I remembered the words Lee whispered to me at Chicago State Hospital: "Take a donkey, train, or walk and get out of the walled city." Despite some questions about my decision, I knew it was time for me to leave Chicago, and school. While making preparations to leave the city I became more focused and energized with the rightness of my decision.

Still, I had many moments of doubt, I felt vulnerable. Small, underground fault lines shifted deep in my psyche. I had recurring nightmares of my time in Elgin and flashbacks from my childhood. I'd awaken drenched in sweat, assaulted by shards of images, sensations, and smells of men violently pressing my body into a hard floor as I stared at an ornate ceiling of sculpted rosettes. Sounds and the smell of urine and the urge to gag and vomit came in and out of focus. Specific smells ignited memory: cigarette smoke, liquor, and rotting garbage were the most difficult to endure

Just as they came, these memories receded to the underworld, followed by disorientation and a vague fogginess. At other times, I was filled with hope as my departure from the city grew closer. I never considered returning to therapy during this time, despite the frequency and tormenting quality of the nightmares and disquieting memories. I had agreed to see a therapist after I left Elgin and it had proven supportive, but of minimal help. The experience I had with the therapist after my epiphany and meeting Lee Godie had proven those systems of care to be rigid and undermining. The person I received the most effective help from was Lee, a woman living on the margins of society and judged by many as mentally unstable.

It would be years before anyone in mental health had the experience and training required to offer me a safe and effective form of treatment, powerful enough to support me in facing the complex trauma embedded in my psyche and nervous system. There was little to no understanding of trauma's impact in the 1960s: the words *trauma* or *post-traumatic stress* were not even a part of the normal psychiatric lexicon. I trusted my instincts that this wasn't the right time to face what had been done to me, but in the meantime I needed to move forward to create a stable, meaningful life.

The dream of Lee stayed with me and I half-way expected to see her when I boarded the Chicago & North Western train, headed northbound and carrying the same suitcases I had arrived with at college. I had less than one hundred dollars. With no specific plan for where I was going, I relied on the inner compass of my heart for what came next. That compass directed me to my mother. She had recovered from the fire, been discharged from the hospital, and was living with my Aunt Eunice until another place could be arranged. She had lost everything. The complex history between us was an open wound, now cushioned for me by the soft contours of the love for her I'd acknowledged to myself.

The closer the train got to Waukegan, the more anxious I grew. Distracted by racing memories of the last time I saw my mother, I almost missed my stop. Walking, hoping to empty my mind of images and the memory of anger, I took a shortcut through a park and sat, my body heavy, not ready to move forward as memories screamed and shuddered through me. The song of a bright red cardinal in a nearby tree caught my attention, shifting me from the past back into the present. I smiled, thanking the bird, left the park bench, and began the remaining walk.

The smell of stale cigarettes and beer overpowered me as I stepped into my aunt's kitchen. My mother sat immobile at the table with a beer in front of her. Taking one look at her, I was flooded with a kaleidoscope of feelings. Her broken, inert stillness shattered me—my legs almost gave way. She looked pale, disoriented, and so weak. My body started to shake and my throat constricted, making it difficult to speak. As a child, I witnessed my mom abused in many ways, but I had never seen her broken. She had worn anger and resentment wrapped around her like an old sweater.

I looked at the woman sitting at the table. Raw, undefended emptiness had replaced the mother I had spent my childhood studying. She didn't look up or respond to my voice. My life with her had depended on understanding her every mood, but this pale woman didn't look like the mother I remembered. My mother had been animated and energized by bitterness, insane passions, and addictions. But not one thing appeared to enliven the empty husk of the woman in front of me. Anxious, I dived into explaining why I had come.

"I wanted to see you and tell you I'm sorry you were in the fire. I'm relieved that you're okay," I stuttered, not sure if she really was okay—whatever that meant. "I love you, I've always loved you. Our life was just too painful. I'm sorry I said hateful things to you when I saw you last."

She stared off into space as though she had not heard me, or cared. My entire body wanted to curl itself around her, hold her together, and howl in pain from the inner emptiness I saw reflected in her face. As I looked at her, a mother-hole bigger than the universe opened in me. It threatened to suck me under—a giant sinkhole filled with longing and loss.

"Will you get me another beer?" she asked, turning toward Eunice.

At least this was something familiar. As I left, filled with inconsolable sorrow, I fully realized that this woman who had given birth to me was incapable of mothering me. She wasn't even capable of functioning as a normal person. In retrospect, I realized that my mother was not withholding anything. She had nothing to give, emptied as I had been at Elgin. I hadn't really expected anything from her, but I was undone.

With no idea of where to go or what to do next, I stopped in a nearby drugstore, ready to engage in the old default pattern of escape by buying pills. Instead, I turned away, deciding not to dull the pain as I had before—or even allow myself suicidal thoughts. Determined to handle my pain differently, I put ten cents in the payphone and made a call seeking support from a trusted adult I had known throughout junior high and the beginning of high school in after-school religious education classes. I had always known I could count on Mrs. Meier's calm centeredness during the rare times I allowed myself to ask for help. She picked up on the third ring and I explained to her I really needed help and someone to talk to. "I'll be there in a half hour," she replied without hesitation.

As we sat in the nearby restaurant, I learned she had just become a volunteer for a newly opened program for young women in trouble to learn and grow. She had been there once and described to me a large house on a lake in nearby Wisconsin. It sounded peaceful and a perfect place to go for a while. I trusted her. They agreed to accept me despite my problems not being related to drug addiction, as was the case for most of the girls they accepted. The following day Mrs. Meier drove me to Silver Lake Home.

Peace enveloped me as I was greeted by a large, inviting house surrounded on one side by trees and the first signs of spring growth, and on the other a shimmering lake. Mrs. Meier had found me a temporary respite. I was to be their fourth admission. For the first month I thrived in the slow routine: morning chapel, bible study, gardening, chores, afternoon prayer group, free time, and regular meals.

Still reeling from the visit with my mother, grief often overtook me. They instructed me to pray and put my faith in God. I was, however, forbidden to talk about my mother, and this increased my anxiety and isolation. We were continuously cautioned to not dwell on the past or even bring it up in any way.

In one of the group sessions, the assignment was to write specific experiences related to God in our lives. Then each of us read what we had written aloud. My list included each of my childhood experiences of faith, my meeting with Lee Godie on that snowy evening in Old Town, and my experience of love from Dale as a child. My writing also included my epiphany of knowing I loved my mother and having the courage to tell her.

I wasn't the only one who was punished that day. After reading what I wrote, they pushed me down to my knees, instructing me to pray— demanding Satan leave me. They believed I had to "relinquish and strip away" everything I claimed to have experienced as sacred. They pronounced me guilty of worshiping the false idols of psychology and education. They told me my experiences around belief and faith hadn't been genuine salvation. They prayed for me to "accept Christ as my Lord and Savior and instructed me daily to renounce the devil and all his legion."

"Get thee behind me Satan," the staff shouted as they laid hands on my head to exorcise the devil. "You are in spiritual warfare and being led astray by Satan. You must hand over your will to God and to us."

They took away my outdoor free time for the next week. My next punishment was to memorize twenty-five scripture verses and recite them to the group before I could again spend free time outdoors. I soon learned that the only way to survive and not lose free time in nature was to express no feelings, nor ask any questions.

Another time, I was ordered to honestly tell the group the list of drugs I was on at Elgin in order for them to determine if I was an addict. I replied that I didn't know the name of the drugs. They asked why I had been sent to Elgin. I answered as honestly as I could, given the missing information and my limited understanding of my court commitment. They argued that I was lying and refused to believe I was not withholding information from them.

The punishment this time was to run up and down the basement stairs fifty times, then spend the hours before dinner scrubbing the stairs with a bucket of water and a toothbrush. I would have liked nothing better than to scrub my mind free of any feelings related to the abuse and torture I had suffered. This was what they were asking me to do. I was so confused. Anyone who talked about feelings was publicly shamed and prayed over for not taking responsibility for what had happened to them. Trying to better understand your life and circumstances fell under the label of psychology, evil, and a trick of the devil.

This was not the Christianity I'd been taught to believe in. They acted and spoke in a manner that contradicted the doctrines they themselves claimed to follow. I would often find myself thinking about Sister Sebastian. My experience and understanding were that the core of the program consisted of an extremely rigid, fundamentalist belief system It was controlling, authoritarian, intended to indoctrinate. It demanded complete, unquestioning obedience from everyone, creating fear and self-alienation—not healing and love. It was frightening how much they considered to be "of the devil."

Yet I was grateful for the time and space they offered me. What sustained me, when I had access to it, was waking to the variety of bird song, the changes of light and shadows over the lake, the mirror images of passing clouds, and the reflections of the trees on the lake with the setting sun. I took long, meandering walks through the countryside during free time, savoring the smells of the earth.

One day, I watched from the side of the road as a black-and-white cow gave birth to a tiny calf and proceeded to lick the baby free from the fetal membrane. As I moved closer to the fence, she lifted her head and gave a small shake and drawn-out, low bellow. From out in the field, a nearby herd came and surrounded her and the calf. Each one faced outward, large, warm brown eyes focused on me as they bellowed in unison, reminding me of Latin chants, bidding me to stay away.

As they cared for mother and calf, they reflected how a caring community gathers when one member is in need. More often than not, this does not happen in the human family. Awed, I realized the sentient nature of animals for the first time. This small act of grace filled me with wonder and curiosity to learn and experience more of the natural world. I had yet to discover the many various realms in which spirit can appear. These insights were not welcomed in the environment in which I lived, but I knew by then to keep quiet.

I graduated from the program deemed "rehabilitated." I wondered what I was rehabilitated from. They had come nowhere close to providing a safe haven; the safety and healing I had hoped for came through nature.

After leaving the program, I reconnected with Sister Sebastian, who helped me get a job as a phlebotomist at St. Therese Hospital in Waukegan, Illinois. Sister Mary Margaret patiently taught me to draw blood in the lab and other random duties, and said I had "just the right touch." I loved being at St. Therese. I became good at this work, learning patience, and it helped me to focus my anxious and unruly mind as I learned how a kind word or warm touch can change someone's day, or the comfort of their blood draw. Living near my mother was challenging. One part of me always felt pulled, as though it were still my job to take care of her. I struggled when I was flooded with traumatic memories.

Within the year I moved to Madison, Wisconsin to stay with friends while I waited to return to college in a nearby small town that upcoming fall. My friends suggested that I volunteer at a local group home for boys. They were happy to set up an appointment and introduce me to Dave, an Episcopal priest, founder, and director of one of Wisconsin's first residential treatment/group homes. Dave was tall, with dark brown, almost black hair and deep blue eyes. I was immediately attracted to him as a person. There was an instant chemistry between us, but I quickly pushed the thought away.

Dave was trained in the Episcopal Church, an ordained priest and a biblical scholar who studied religions from around the world. He said he was open-minded and an ongoing seeker, believing there was much to learn from each religious tradition. In my initial interview, Dave asked pointed questions about my work history and also my family background. I answered honestly and spoke in a factual, straightforward manner about having been hospitalized. Dave saw it as an asset rather than a liability and only asked that I would meet with their local consultant, Dr. Mary Berg, every month, in addition to the consultation group the entire staff attended. This would give me a way to receive support in case my own issues might come to the surface and impact my work.

By the time our meeting concluded, Dave offered me a paid position in the residential treatment facility, suggesting that I could attend school in Madison, have a reliable source of income, and work around my class schedule. There was one stipulation for my role: I needed to learn to drive. I said yes. Little did I know, the day I accepted the job, I had just met the man who would one day become my husband.

Dave, the priest who would become my husband

12.

Beginning When the Past is Present

Believe in a love that is being stored up for you like an inheritance, and have faith that in this love there is a strength and a blessing so large that you can travel as far as you wish without having to step outside it.

Rainer Maria Rilke, *Letters to a Young Poet*

My life in Madison fell into an easy rhythm of work I loved, classes, and growing friendships. Over the course of months, I began to relax. The past began to seem like a distant memory as I was welcomed and integrated into the team at Christ the King Home. Several evenings a week we took the kids on outings to the park, swimming, roller skating, bowling, or on nature walks. We played flashlight tag, capture the flag, freeze tag, and other popular neighborhood games. Each of us had a strong relationship with the kids and helped each other out without complaint.

In our own ways, each of us looked up to Dave, who was not only an excellent administrator but also involved in the day-to-day care of the boys. I grew to like and respect him, and everyone I worked with as well.

Although difficult for me to admit at the time, I had a crush on Dave. We fell into an easy camaraderie. In the evenings I would join in the story hour he led. Enchanted by his melodious voice as he introduced us to the stories of C.S. Lewis, George MacDonald, and others, I was held captive with the kids. Dave's great impersonations and deep, resonant voice brought each story alive. Through my training and experience in mental health, I continue to be impressed at what an ideal program he had created, one that could have gone on to become an innovative and transformative model and standard of care.

Slowly, over time, Dave and I enjoyed each other's company as he drove me home when our shift ended at 11:00 p.m. He began to invite me to concerts and introduced me to classical music, symphonies, and jazz, as well as great choir music. We attended *The Music Man*, *Fiddler on the Roof*, and *My Fair Lady*. After seeing *My Fair Lady*, he teasingly complemented me and said I reminded him of Eliza Doolittle.

We took long drives and tried out new restaurants. For the first time in my life, I began to get an inkling of what normal people must feel like. With the wisdom of time, I wonder if our fates were indelibly cast in those moments, although, at the time, a part of me expected that once Dave fully knew me, he wouldn't like me anymore, or he'd turn out to be an exploitive jerk like nearly every other male I'd known. But instead, as the days, months, and a year grew into a life, mutual trust and affection grew between us. Occasionally, as gentle as a butterfly, he would kiss me on the lips.

A few months later, at the end of a Saturday afternoon drive and lunch, he slowly pulled the car over, turned, and looked at me. "My God has told me I'm going to marry you, but I have absolutely no intention of doing so," he said as he started to laugh.

I responded in kind, laughing with him. "I have no intention of marrying you, either," I teased back. But I honestly felt a tad disappointed.

Summer came, and everyone grew excited about a camping trip to the Black Hills. I had never been camping, or anywhere close to a wilderness area, and was both nervous and excited. To this day, the Black Hills are one of my favorite places—a small mountain range covered in pines rising from the plains as a glorious vision when you drive toward it from the east. Woven throughout are majestic views, ghost towns, caves, streams, and rivers. It was inspiring to watch the kids come alive outdoors. Something new came alive in me as well.

The next summer, returning from a vacation, I walked up to my front door and saw a note. It was from Dave, requesting that I call him right away. I was immediately concerned that something had happened to one of the kids. Dave picked up the phone on the second ring and asked if he could pick me up in an hour. "I have something really important to talk to you about and would rather not wait. It doesn't have to be a late night."

"Is something wrong? Is everyone ok?"

"This is really important and I'm not going to be able to relax about it until I see you."

I knew that he had been considering returning to graduate school to complete his doctorate in theology and thought he might want to talk about that, so I was surprised when he pulled up in front of one of the nicest restaurants in town. He studied me over the menu. We talked a little about my vacation. He filled me in on work and the kids, saying everyone had missed me. I was left wondering what was going on.

"So, what did you want to talk to me about?"

He reached across the table and took my hand. "All in good time," he said. "Let's enjoy the food, first."

He seemed a bit nervous, pensive, and unsure of himself. Finally, he took a deep breath and looked directly at me. "I've been accepted to Oxford in England and the University of Notre Dame in Indiana and have to get back to the one that's right with my acceptance."

"Congratulations, that's great," I stammered. "How are you going to choose?"

"I needed to wait for you to come back before I gave an answer to either one of them." He cleared his throat. "I wanted your opinion and thought you should be part of the decision."

I couldn't believe that my opinion would matter, let alone that he had waited to see me before making his decision. He reached for my hand and held it firmly before continuing. "I've come to realize that you're the love of my life. I can't imagine making a decision like that without you. I want you to be my wife. You'll make me the happiest man alive if you say yes."

He pulled a simple, elegant engagement ring out of its box and held it, waiting for my answer. He was sweet, flustered, and clearly vulnerable in a way I had never seen.

"Why would you want to marry me?" I asked, incredulous.

Frozen like a deer in the headlights under the gaze of his earnest, deep, sky-blue eyes, I can't remember his answer. I hadn't seen an engagement coming and couldn't respond.

I was thrown into inner chaos at his proposal. He couldn't help but notice my uncertainty and confusion. Reading my face, Dave asked if I needed a few days to think about it. He nervously acknowledged that he had spent plenty of time thinking about it. He was a little anxious because he hadn't dated much or ever had the kinds of feelings for anyone that he had for me.

I was touched by his vulnerability, as well as the sunbeam of love and hope in his searching eyes and the depth of character they reflected as he confessed that he was a virgin and had not found the right someone to share that intimacy with. I was pulled into a gravitational force field—I couldn't refuse. I said yes.

I thought I knew what Dave would bring into a marriage. The challenge was: I didn't believe that I had anything to offer in return. My unhealed childhood issues lay curled in my stomach. I was certain he would find me unlovable and lacking. On several occasions, when other clergy came by to see him, I overheard them debating philosophical or theological concepts. At times, I felt just plain intimidated by his intelligence, the breadth and depth of his knowledge, and his use of words I didn't understand.

I look back and feel compassion for that young woman—so unsure of herself. Although I had told Dave the facts around my commitment to Elgin, foster care, and some of my life with my mother, I wasn't capable of talking about many details. I believed I had to act as though I was more together than I ever felt. This reinforced the belief that if Dave, or anyone, ever saw how inadequate I felt, they wouldn't like me, let alone love me. It was impossible for me to see my strengths or what Dave was attracted to in me. He loved my creativity and connection with children, as well as my reverence for nature, music, poetry, and literature. These qualities were so embedded in me that I couldn't see at the time they were something that set me apart.

The months went by in a rush as I moved through the bliss and magic of our engagement, marred by only one thing: my mother and Bud. Over the years since the fire in her apartment, I'd written to her and visited. Bud was back and she seemed to have settled down, both of them in the late stages of alcoholism. I had reconnected with the last foster parents I had lived with before being homeless and graduation. They unexpectedly threw me a surprise bridal shower on a visit to Waukegan. When I asked the foster dad if he would walk me down the aisle, he said he thought it should be Bud, whom I hadn't planned on inviting. He looked at me sternly and told me to just get over myself and do it.

Intimidated, I agreed. Dave was supportive and left the decision up to me. My mother and Bud had no money for the wedding, so I bought them both something suitable to wear. I arranged for my aunt and uncle to drive them to Madison. They found a hotel on the edge of town with no liquor stores, to keep them from drinking. I wouldn't see them until the ceremony.

The morning of our wedding arrived. My maid of honor, Karen, helped me into the ivory, floor-length dress with royal-blue, deep-green, and gold flower accents around the collar and sleeves. She stepped back in appreciation after placing the crown wreath on my head—vibrant golden-orange roses, surrounded by a mix of small blooms and greenery. I looked in the mirror, barely recognizing myself.

I felt beautiful for the first time in my life.

My mind was racing minutes before I was to walk down the aisle when the priest who was conducting the wedding pulled me aside. "I'm sorry to have to tell you, but Bud is going through DTs. He's come to me twice begging for communion wine, I think I should give it to him or he won't make it down the aisle." I nodded my head in agreement.

As I waited for the processional music to begin, I saw Dave, standing at the end of that long aisle. He was strikingly handsome in a royal-blue velvet jacket that accented his eyes and his black clerical shirt and white collar. I gripped my flowers tightly, as though I was gripping a lifeline, my face fixed in a mask, strained and tentative. Glancing sideways at Bud, I noticed he looked solemn and awkward in his suit, just as terrified as me. He would wear that suit next when he was buried, a few months later.

The music began. I moved robotically down the aisle, hardly aware of Dave's smiling face, or the guests looking at me expectantly, except for my mother, who looked terrified too. Although my life was now anchored in the religious community of the Episcopal Church, that day I felt none of it. The scent of incense and the somber chords of the music faded into the

The day of my marriage to Dave

141

background as my panic escalated and I left my body. I didn't understand it then, but my unhealed past was as present with me at the wedding as the future I would be stepping into.

The wedding was small and the ceremony intimate, followed by a late-afternoon lunch buffet in the church basement. During the reception, Sister Sebastian pulled me to the side. Tears sprang to my eyes as she asked if I'd made a mistake, and if I loved Dave. I had no doubts about loving him, and was confused about the panic I had felt in the church. I didn't have the insight to understand how, in an instant, I had been triggered by my past trauma cascading into the present because of the close proximity to my mother and Bud and the attention focused on me that day, so reminding me of the parties with Dr. L. Sister Sebastian assumed it was fear of our marriage night. She told me to relax and remind myself that sex was a holy act, a receiving of the beloved. She reminded me that Dave was different from any man I had ever known and to keep my mind out of the past. This was easier said than done.

The first morning of our honeymoon in Naples, Florida we went to the local market for food to cook for dinner. It was in the shower together that my world tilted, wobbling out of control as a memory of terror in a shower with Dr. L emerged, followed by flashes of the Elgin shower. Past and present merged into that enclosed space and I became confused and terrified of Dave. I began to hyperventilate, and Dave reached out toward me. I hit his hands away and screamed in panic. "Get away. Stop looking at me."

Because Dave had no specific details about my past, he had no way of understanding what might be happening to me. I hadn't consciously withheld information from him. In my mind, I minimized and compartmentalized most events of my past as a coping mechanism. He couldn't possibly know the extent of the abuse I had suffered through my childhood and youth.

"What's wrong with you? You're afraid of your own husband? What on earth have I ever done to you so that you think I am someone to be afraid of?"

My tears and the water of the shower flowed together down the drain. I crouched in the corner, shaking. Dave grabbed a towel and left as I continued to heave up feelings and memories of the past. I was so out of touch with my body that I couldn't explain to myself, let alone to Dave, what had come over me.

As I write this now, after healing and integrating the past, and from the vantage point of professional training and experience with trauma survivors, I know I was experiencing a flashback to past trauma. I was triggered by the vulnerability of being naked in the enclosed space of the shower. My traumatic memories were laid down and encoded within my nervous system as sensate memories, rather than as a narrative. It was not until my sensate memories were recalled and healed that the full story could be constructed.

Flashbacks would come suddenly, replays of sensory memories too horrifying to integrate. It was as though a rubber band had pulled my past and present together and memories stored in my muscles, skin, and optic cortex created a perfect storm of accelerated heart rate, panic, and confusion. In those moments in the shower, I felt threatened and terrified—as though Dr. L, the male attendants gawking at me in Elgin's shower, and those who had raped me in the garage had all crowded into the small, confined space with me. Ripples from the underground of my past surfaced, leaving me gasping for breath.

The nervous, guarded, and distant young woman who emerged from the shower was a ghost of the woman who was married a couple of days before. Now, through the lens of healing and understanding, I can see and hear Dave's confusion. Nightmares, flashbacks, jumpiness, and anxiety increased, but neither Dave nor I had the tools to deal with them. There may have seemed to be brief moments of intimacy, but if he guessed that I wasn't really embodied or fully present during those times, he never let on.

A week after we returned from our honeymoon, I was cutting vegetables for a salad as Dave made dinner and I accidently made a cut into my finger so deep that it would require stitches. I didn't feel a thing. Staring as though at a distant scene of someone else, I observed the blood flowing out of my finger, across the cutting board, and down the side of the counter. Dave took the knife out of my hand, wrapped my finger, and drove us to the emergency room. Disconnected physically, emotionally numb, and exhausted, I watched this scene unfold as though seeing a movie.

Years later I came to understand that what I'd experienced was depersonalization, the felt experience of the mind being out of the body, the "freeze response." This response is one of immobility as the body undergoes huge biochemical extremes. A flood of endogenous opioids, the natural heroin-like substance of the brain, is released, killing pain, producing calm and psychological distance from what is occurring—dissociation. Post-traumatic stress disorder results from the undischarged chemicals and energy of hyper-activation in the amygdala and under-activation in parts of the prefrontal cortex, responsible for higher reasoning and problem-solving. This results in increased hypersensitivity to additional trauma because the system is always on high alert, with a decreased ability to think rationally or to stay grounded.

The first several months of our marriage were challenging. Times of connection and stability could, without notice, be disrupted and replaced by flashbacks hurtling me into the past and flooding me with anxiety, fear, and mistrust of Dave.

We moved to Indiana the following summer so Dave could finish his doctorate in Theology at the University of Notre Dame. After researching conditions of child welfare services, we found that Indiana was even more behind the times than Wisconsin had been regarding children's services. Following a home study, we were licensed as foster parents able to provide a home for three children who had been living in appalling conditions at the State Hospital.

A small, four-bedroom bungalow with a large family room and nice-sized backyard in a neighborhood of families, not far from the campus, would become our home. Family life, taking care of the kids, and running a home grounded me, whenever the storms of the past hit. We continued the story-hour tradition with our new little family in Indiana, as we had done in Madison, and quickly moved into a rhythm with the children who came to live with us. As the children grew and thrived in our first home, our marriage deepened and blossomed.

13.

The Majesty of the Great Plains

The first peace, which is the most important, is that which comes within the souls of people when they realize their relationship, their oneness with the universe and all its powers,

and when they realize that at the center of the universe dwells the Great Spirit, and that this center is really everywhere, it is within each of us.

Black Elk, Oglala Lakota Holy Man, *The Sacred Pipe*

During Dave's last semester at Notre Dame, he was recruited by the Episcopal Bishop of South Dakota to direct a failing educational institution for Native American youth on the Rosebud Reservation. We accepted the opportunity, a choice that would change our lives. We prepared by learning what we could of the history and beliefs of the Lakota people. We arrived at our new home mid-afternoon to a dry, flat landscape of sunbaked earth. The temperature was a punishing 112 degrees. The desolate, alien land felt hostile and threatening with its high season of rattlesnakes and unfamiliar terrain. Within a short time, we were both dripping with sweat, dehydrated, and temporarily daunted by the tasks ahead of us. We woke the next morning with dry, cracked lips, exhausted from sleeping on the floor in sleeping bags, covered with red welts from the biting of black flies from the nearby barn.

Our house was located on the property of Bishop Hare Home, which first opened its doors in 1927 as a mission project of the Episcopal Church and served as an alternative to government boarding schools. It sat on a small campus outside the town of Mission. The property consisted of dorms, an industrial-sized kitchen and dining room, a study area and community room, a chapel, staff housing, a barn, three horses, a herd of cows, chickens, and acres of vast prairie.

We moved into the director's house, as it was known: an old and poorly maintained two-story house. It was large, with three bedrooms and lovely woodwork and hardwood floors that, with work, would eventually shine. For the next several weeks, we immersed ourselves in the adventure of making our house livable. The closest town with access to decent shopping, lumber yards, and hardware stores was ninety-nine miles away. Still, we were able to fairly quickly transform what had seemed like a daunting task into a warm and serene home. We were conscious that those around us had so much less: there was visible, heartbreaking poverty on the Rosebud and neighboring Pine Ridge reservations, with the lowest per-capita income in the nation and an eighty to ninety percent unemployment rate as well as inadequate housing and resources—few even had heat or electricity.

I quickly fell in love with the moods and seasons of the sky. Clouds spun like cotton candy of filtered light could be replaced with rolling, dark cauldrons of energy, thunder, and lightning, filling the sky from hundreds of miles away. The magnificent, changing colors—golds, indigo, pink, deep reds, blues, and greens—made me long to paint. The kaleidoscope of constellations and the moon provided a shimmering, soundless brilliance that I often fell into. Floating out of time and the pull of the earth's gravitational force, I was anchored by brilliant pinpricks of light and the luminescent moon that provided a deep source of spiritual nourishment, wonder, and revelation.

We settled into our new home and Dave fell into his own routine when the staff and boys returned in the fall. With little to do while Dave was working, I found our new life challenging in ways I hadn't expected and eventually accepted a job as a teacher in the local preschool program. It was here I was immersed in the daily realities of the poverty those throughout the reservation faced. The winters were brutal, with snowstorms that a person could quickly become lost in dictating life through the winter months. But still, in the winter months, there were three- and four-year-old children with no coats or shoes, scantily dressed. Children who needed to be sponged down and given a change of clothing every morning before beginning classes because they were nearly flammable from kerosene on their clothing from the heaters in their overcrowded living situations.

As I grew to know individuals in the Lakota community, my admiration, inspiration, and awe of their deep sense of community and relationship to the land grew. I felt honored by the stories that were shared by the elders I came to know. Through them I learned the power of storytelling. Their quiet respect and connection to all beings never ceased to move me. The common greeting or farewell—*Mitakuye Oyasin*, All My Relations—reflects their belief in the interconnectedness of everything. The ceremonies, music, and dance called me into a deep place within myself. Their history of suffering and survival—against unspeakable odds—touched a deep and resonating chord.

In time, I fell into my own rhythm of relationship to the earth and sky and found it deeply rooted and grounded me as I drove across the prairie. Listening to a tape of choir music reminded me of the music of my childhood; tears of gratitude and connection would fall for this living cathedral I had come to call home.

In December we were overjoyed to learn I was pregnant and the baby was due at the end of August. Pregnancy filled me with both anticipation and fear. I had previously experienced a miscarriage, and with my sexual abuse history, the physicality was daunting. Before becoming pregnant, I barely noticed my body, but now I was aware of every twitch. During the last trimester, triggers from the past began to emerge, destabilizing me. I was excited about having a baby—it was the act of giving birth that I feared.

I explored these fears with my family physician, Dr. Spears, and told her about the episodes of depersonalization and dissociation I'd experienced shortly after being married. It was happening again and I was afraid I wouldn't even feel myself going into labor. She instructed me in exercises to create more body awareness in order to alleviate the split between my body, mind, and emotions—giving me a small sense of control.

At the end of August, I gave birth to a healthy baby boy. Dave and I were both ecstatic and named him after a long succession of Davids. The following morning, as I sat holding our new baby, Dave walked in. He leaned over, kissed me, then gently placed a small, wrapped present on top of the blanket that held our sleeping son. He whispered to our newborn that it was a gift for his brave mommy. The box contained a beautiful ring to mark the occasion of his birth. Dave returned home early the next morning.

Later that afternoon, Dr. Spears, dressed in jeans and tennis shoes, her arms filled with fresh-cut pink peonies, walked into my room and said she was visiting since I lived so far out of town and Dave had returned to the reservation. She pulled up a chair, took off her shoes, put her feet up on the side of my bed, and started to talk gardening, about her own son, and my new one. I was deeply touched. Dave returned a couple of days later to pick up baby David and me.

I spent those first nights at home watching the rhythm of my baby son's breath—fearful it might stop. The baby seemed so tiny and vulnerable in the cradle at my side. My chest felt near to exploding with love. Each day I floated through the house in a state of wonder, nearly weak in the knees with a feeling of spiritual connection.

The Bishop baptized David when he was a couple of months old in the small Bishop Hare Home chapel. I truly felt like a proud mother surrounded by a caring community. In a photo taken that day, baby David is held by the Bishop in a traditional star quilt made by his Lakota godmother, Mrs. Iron Cloud, who called him her *Takója*, which means grandson. We are surrounded by friends, the boys from the dorm, and other staff from Bishop Hare Home. It's difficult for me to look at this picture now. It's the only one I have from David's baptism, but it fills me with grief. I didn't know then that before long my life would begin to unravel in the most devastating ways.

14.

Earthquake

The world is indeed full of peril, and in it there are many dark places; but still there is much that is fair, and though in all lands, love is now mingled with grief, it grows perhaps the greater.

J.R.R. Tolkien, *The Fellowship of the Ring*

That July, the Bishop stayed with us for two days for a board meeting where it was decided to close Bishop Hare Home the following summer. Since more schools had been built throughout the Rosebud and Pine Ridge reservations, the board no longer saw the 100-year-old facility as necessary to reservation life.

It was late October. Dave was leaving for a conference the following day. He planned to network and inquire about possible job opportunities to teach at a divinity school or university. The Bishop was arriving the next day for meetings throughout the reservation and would be a guest in our home. I found myself smiling as the music continued to flow through the house as I cleaned, making it ready for his visit. I wondered if the upstairs guest room would be warm enough. The house was cool that afternoon. The radiators were slow to warm during the changing of seasons. I didn't know that a deep and lasting chill was about to creep into my life and marriage, like the prairie winds, ushering in the harshness of a winter nearly too much to bear.

Dave left for the conference that morning, kissed me goodbye, and said he was going to miss us. After putting David to bed, I watched the sunset—a canvas of various shades of red and blue—from the living room window, and saw the Bishop arrive. He put his things upstairs, then joined me in the living room. I was grateful for the counseling sessions with him and earlier in the day reflected on my growing trust—I still didn't easily trust men other than Dave. The Bishop had slowly gained my trust and I had grown to see him as the father figure I never had. We sat in the living room talking for a couple of hours about my feelings regarding the upcoming closing of Bishop Hare Home. The room had warmed throughout the day and was cozy as we discussed small challenges in my life, the business of Dave's schedule, and how little time we had together.

The Bishop said a prayer, bringing our counseling session to an end. He stood as though to go upstairs to bed and turned to give me his customary hug at the end of counseling sessions. Suddenly, without warning, what had always been a fatherly hug unexpectedly changed. Everything about him changed: his muscled arms, his hands and mouth. His entire body moved too quickly as he groped at my breasts. My mind raced out of control and then slowed down to minuscule heartbeats of horror, encapsulated in my heavy, frozen, and terror-filled body and brain. He pushed me hard against the hallway wall, hands all over me, roughly trying to remove my blouse. He shoved me down the hallway backwards. My scream of "No" rose up and was quickly silenced by his hard, insistent mouth, his heavy breathing. I tried to push him away. My heartbeat raced out of control and blood pounded in my ears.

He pushed me into the bedroom my husband and I shared. It was incomprehensible. I was unable to think—to make sense of this nightmare. I begged him to stop. I pleaded. He threw me onto the bed, knelt above me, holding me down with his leg and hand as he tore off my clothes and quickly removed his own. My mind and body shuddered, locking up tight to flee from the horror. I have no memory of him entering me. He grew distant in my mind, the ticking heartbeat and mechanical gears of the grandfather clock in the living room grew louder—the chimes rang a quarter to the hour. I floated outside of myself, too terrified to take in what was happening on the bed. But I do perfectly remember when he rolled off of me. The beautiful clock's Westminster chimes struck, followed by the heavier gong announcing eleven o'clock. It had only taken him fifteen minutes to tear my psyche and marriage apart.

The clock was the first thing Dave and I purchased after our marriage. We looked long and hard for just the right one and both agreed we loved the sound of the Westminster chimes. That clock had been a source of wonder and was a soothing companion through the days and nights. It was the heartbeat of our home. Where before this night I had loved its melody, now I would dread the sound of it. For my remaining time in its presence, I would frequently startle, my heartbeat racing and my mind growing numb whenever I heard it.

The Bishop laid on the side of the bed—where Dave normally slept next to me. He came up on his elbow and stared at me, his movement and look jarring. "How do you feel having just committed adultery with your Bishop?" he asked.

His words hung in the air like a knife, severing my heart, leaving me numb and stone cold. My body shook violently and my teeth chattered, blocking out any other words he might have said. Curling away from him into a small, still ball, everything went quiet. Very slowly I began to fully comprehend what had just happened as my body and brain caught up with each other, jarred by his voice and the question. "Well? How do you feel having just committed adultery with your Bishop?" he asked again.

"I just committed incest. You were a father to me," I answered, still numb and reeling from his question.

In my heart I knew I would no longer see him as a bishop. I can't recall his exact words, but he insisted that he hadn't even hurt me, that I was overreacting. He chuckled. At that moment, I felt as though God was laughing at me with him to further humiliate me. Something in me withered and died as he got up, dressed, and went upstairs.

My heart raced like a horse out of control. I got up and woodenly went to the front door and quietly opened it, hoping to find peace in the vast outdoors. I fantasized fleeing and realized there was nowhere to go and I didn't have a car. It was a clear night. I lifted my face to the inky-black sky, dotted with stars, hoping they'd anchor and ground me as they always had. But I couldn't find the wonder that had always greeted me; instead, I felt crushed and smothered by the sky I had so loved.

Dark, condemning shame flooded me, then my entire body emptied of all sensations. Throughout that night I was tortured by flashbacks of men my mother had given me to, the face and hands of Dr. L, followed by the rape in the garage at Elgin. My baby's cry in the morning was what saved my sanity and brought me back to myself.

The Bishop was there for another night—my memory of that is scattered and diffused. Wrapped in a shroud of shame, deadened to myself and anything other than the basic needs of my son, I longed to physically die. I could not live with the deception the Bishop insisted on. If I told Dave, he promised he would deny it and Dave would be convinced I was losing my mind. "Who do you think Dave is going to believe?" he said.

"Of course, it will be his Bishop."

I didn't realize it then, but he was manipulating me in some of the same ways Dr. L had. In insisting I not tell Dave or anyone else, he claimed I would not only be protecting him from scandal, I would be saving Dave, and the Bishop's own wife, Kay, and the people of the Episcopal Church of South Dakota, from deep pain and suffering. He told me that I had seduced him. The Bishop left, but the seeds of self-doubt he had planted began to eat everything in my path like the weeds in a garden gone bad, choking off anything living.

Exhausted and near mute with terror, I waited in dread for Dave's return from out of town. My mind moved between a whiteout condition of emptiness to wandering lost in a maze of static, confusion, and self-condemnation. *Why didn't I see this coming? Why was I so stupid to trust him? Why didn't I fight harder? What was wrong with me that these things kept happening? Why did men think they could do this to me?* I could not understand how the Bishop believed I seduced him. I could not imagine how I could possibly tell Dave, nor how I could not tell him—and live with myself.

I was caught in a double bind—I had no way to live with what had happened. The Bishop's warnings spun in my head like cotton candy, muffling my ability to think rationally. If I didn't tell Dave, I risked hurting him deeply, but at the time I had no language to describe what had happened with the Bishop. I didn't realize consciously how he had muddled my mind and activated the earlier programming Dr. L had inflicted on me. If I did tell Dave, I'd devastate him. The painful fault line that ran between us in the shower on our honeymoon was now a full-scale earthquake. I saw nowhere to seek safety or solid ground.

I had no idea at the time of how my early childhood abuse impacted my now-heightened nervous system. Dr. L and the Bishop had both implanted lies and self-doubt in my vulnerable psyche. They festered, bubbling to the surface and tainting my perceptions with faulty beliefs. Despite my horrendous experiences of sexual abuse, I believed that the sexual union of two people was holy: a sacrament of flesh and spirit coming together. With Dave, I experienced sexual union as deeply healing. The rape created in my mind and heart a severing from the deepest aspects of myself and from the God I thought was one of love. I couldn't separate what the Bishop had done and not involve the God I had been taught to believe in. These distortions created a spiritual crisis that would take years to heal.

Now, as I look back with a better understanding of the dynamics of sexual exploitation and rape, I understand that most women who are raped scrutinize themselves as I did, in order to circumvent the devastating feelings of powerlessness. I tore myself apart, examining every past interaction, behavior, and nuance that could have possibly led the Bishop to believe I would welcome his advances. I couldn't find one thing other than my respect for him and appreciation of the counseling sessions we had. But still, doubts haunted me.

As I attempted to cope, I told myself nothing in my outer life was different, but inside me everything had changed. As I rocked my baby boy, a lullaby turned into a song of supplication—a prayer. It was the last time I prayed for a long time. As I sang over and over, my grief and anger rained down on baby David's soft face, hounding heaven and a God I no longer believed in. Shaking his small head, back and forth, my son reached his chubby toddler fingers up to my lips. "No more sing," he pleaded.

I stopped singing. How could I have been so blind and so trusting? But my mind continued like a rat in a maze looking for a way out, a way to view it, a way to bear it. But I knew that without a doubt that in one act my marriage vows had been ripped apart. My trust was brutally violated by the Bishop and by the God I had believed in.

Dave returned. I felt caught between wanting to scream out what had happened and terror of losing him. I was so riddled with anxiety, I was certain he would see I wasn't myself. I convinced myself he and David would be better off without me. With no road forward and no way to undo what had happened, nearly incoherent with shock and grief, I reverted to my very old way of escape and attempted to kill myself. I took nearly every pill in the house and drank cleaning fluid. My thoughts were muddled with the words that *I was unworthy to raise a beautiful child and be married to such a good man.* I have no memory of being driven the one hundred miles to the same hospital where I had delivered David.

Awakening in a body I loathed to inhabit again, I found the room spinning for hours. Everything hurt. I didn't know being brought back from death could hurt so much. I was angry, disappointed, and ashamed I was alive. Thinking about my son caused a well of grief to rise within me. I couldn't believe he wouldn't be better off without me. I vomited off and on for hours as my shroud of shame wrapped itself tighter. I had failed at the simple act of ending my life and had only made things much worse.

Dave called and begged me to tell him why I had done such a thing. I said nothing. I could hear him crying. He was confused, worried, and angry. He had no way of understanding. He had said goodbye to a content and happy wife with a beautiful baby and a loving husband and returned a week later to a withdrawn wife he loved who'd just tried to kill herself. I tried to reassure him that he hadn't done anything wrong. I was deeply sorry and didn't know what had come over me. He said he had difficulty believing I loved him in the face of what I had done and quietly hung up the phone. Numb with the reality of the gulf between us, my anxiety ratcheted up to an unbearable level.

Dr. Spears walked in a short while later, her face solemn. Like a crazed animal caught in a trap, I was frantic. My attempt to escape from my own pain and disgust had not only failed miserably, leaving me with an ulcerated stomach, it had created suffering for those I professed to love and wanted to protect. I could see that in my desperation to relieve my own pain and run from the nightmare of the reality of what had happened to me, I had been utterly selfish. This thought filled me with unbearable self-loathing.

"You must've been in a hell of a lot of pain to try to kill yourself in the way you did," she said. "Well, I've got all the time in the world to listen. And you're not getting out of here until you talk."

My confusion and shame came tumbling out as I initially talked around what had happened and avoided naming the Bishop. Dr. Spears reached for my hand and asked me to tell her who hurt me. Flashes of the Bishop's tall, thin physique, white hair, and long, angular, unremarkable face flashed in front of me. I had always read kindness there. Now, his image conjured a dangerous, cunning man with little regard for me, my husband, or my child.

She held my hand firmly as she encouraged me to talk about how I knew this person. I explained that over our time in the Dakotas I met with him as a confessor and counselor. Unsolicited by me, he had made time in his busy schedule to meet with me. "Did this man force himself on you?" Dr. Spears asked.

Without warning, I froze in the light of her compassionate presence and heard the loud ticking of the grandfather clock and chime on the hour as I had heard it that night. My body began to shake, as she waited, the firmness of her warm hand steadying me while I hung over the cliff of memory and despair. The question the Bishop had posed right after he

154

raped me was seared into my brain: his words a branding iron of white, hot pain. I now spoke the words, hesitantly, to Dr. Spears.

"Afterwards, he asked me, 'How do you feel having just committed adultery with your Bishop?'"

"The bastard exploited you, seduced you into trusting him, and then raped you! Some Bishop he is, all right."

When I protested that I hadn't fought hard enough, she reassured me that it wasn't my fault and it wouldn't have mattered. She encouraged me to tell Dave and reiterated that she couldn't tell him, but hoped I would. She was adamant that she wasn't going to let me leave the hospital unless I agreed to see someone for counseling and Dave agreed as well.

Early the morning of my scheduled discharge, Dave called to tell me that he wouldn't be picking me up—the Bishop would. Aghast, I begged him to come himself. He explained that the Bishop was already in Pierre for meetings and he would drive me to Sioux Falls, where I would spend the night at the Bishop's house. Dave would pick me up the next morning and take me to my appointment with the psychiatrist Dr. Spears insisted I see. After the appointment, we would drive together to the small town of Aberdeen where the Bishop had set up an interview for Dave as a parish priest. How could I possibly endure a three-hour ride with the Bishop, trapped in the close quarters of a car? Memory of that horrendous night came rushing back, like a slow motion, badly made, fragmented black-and-white movie. I wrestled with myself, looking for a way to make sense out of what was incomprehensible.

When Dr. Spears arrived late in the morning, she asked me what time Dave was picking me up. When I told her the Bishop, not Dave, would be picking me up, she was furious. After making me promise her that I wouldn't hurt myself again, she wrote her home phone number on a piece of paper, insisting I had to call her if I became too overwhelmed, suicidal, or the Bishop did anything inappropriate. I nodded.

The Bishop arrived later in the afternoon, just as Dr. Spears walked in to give me the discharge papers. He turned to her in greeting and asked her if I had told her that he thought he had found a parish for us. I'll never forget her biting reply, dripping in sarcasm. "Great idea, get them off the rez—and into a fishbowl. That's just what they need."

The Bishop seethed all the way to the car, a thunderstorm ready to break. I felt terrified as he ordered me to get in the car and immediately began to bombard me with questions. He assumed that I had told Dr.

Spears what he had done and I didn't deny his accusation. He proceeded to lecture me throughout the three-hour drive about why I couldn't tell Dave or anyone else about our "little affair." I was nearly lost in a whiteout, foggy feeling of deep, dark, crippling fatigue—of hopelessness and nausea. I begged him to stop the car when he took my hand and placed it on his leg. After vomiting, I climbed back into the car and leaned my head against the cool window, eyes closed. His voice droned on and on, reminding me of his threats and my supposed responsibility not to tell.

These swirling thoughts evaporated like the mist as we pulled up to the front of the Bishop's house. His wife Kay quickly came out to welcome me and help me inside. Beyond exhausted, I stumbled and she clucked like a mother hen, wondering if the hospital had discharged me too soon. She quickly tucked me under a warm blanket in front of the living room fire and brought me a cup of tea. I couldn't drink it. The Bishop said that I had a weak stomach from what I'd done to myself. Kay sat on the floor beside me, stroking my head. "I've been beside myself worrying about you," she said.

Her tenderness undid me. My mind leapt to the deception I was living. I knew she would hate me if she knew the truth. I longed for a woman's comfort, but couldn't allow myself to receive it. Consumed by guilt and trying to shake off this cozy family scene, I struggled to a sitting position and took a sip of tea. Immediately, I knew this was a mistake and ran to the bathroom where I heaved my disgrace into the toilet. It felt as though my stomach and intestines were being devoured by both pain and the secret I believed would never allow me to deserve love again. Muttering an apology for not being able to talk, I made my way to the guest room.

Dave arrived around ten the next morning to take me to the appointment with the psychiatrist. Conversation between us was strained, his face tight; the secret hung as a heavy cloud between us. Dr. Gehlhoff seemed caring as he greeted us in the waiting room. I was wary and cautious before; now that I saw the psychiatrist was male, I was near panic. With every step I took toward his office, my body became heavier and robotic and my rib cage tightened in fear. By the time he had closed the door after Dave left the room, I'd been replaced by some windup mechanical thing. My mind scurried around the room like a mouse being stalked by a cat. It was nearly impossible to see him other than through my recently resurrected memories of Dr. L and the Bishop.

I told him that my life depended on not trusting him. He replied that my trust must have had a hell of a violation and been trampled on for me to reach that conclusion. When he asked what had precipitated my suicide attempt, I somehow kept my promise to Dr. Spears and told him the truth. He advised me against telling Dave; he cautioned me that it would be the end of my marriage. Dave's ego structure would never be able to bear it if I told him. I agreed to accept his counsel. My body began to shake in terror when Dr. Gehlhoff described what the Bishop had done to me as rape. Much to my relief, over the course of the next year and a half, Dr. Gehlhoff would continue to be supportive and helpful. He was always professional and didn't push me, respecting my boundaries.

When we left Dr. Gehlhoff's office that day, the highway stretched, endless. We spoke little. Dave's eyes were fixed on the road, but he seemed more relaxed—until he asked me a question.

"I'm only going to ask this once. Why did you do such a damn thing? Haven't I been a good husband to you? Don't we have a beautiful child, supportive friends? A rich life of faith? What more could you want?"

"No, nothing. You're a wonderful husband," I stammered.

He reached over and held my hand and said he was sorry for pushing me. Somehow, we got through the next several days. Dave was offered a position as rector and was given some time to decide.

Months passed, moving through our final winter and into our last spring living and working on the Rosebud. Spring gave way to the oppressive heat and dryness of summer. My inner season was dry and oppressive as well; I had lost what grounded me and provided meaning— my faith. Most days, I felt as though I was in a spiritual wasteland. Going to mass was excruciating and I could barely hide it from Dave.

One day, several months later, Dave suggested that when the Bishop arrived later that day, it would be appropriate for me to ask him to hear my confession. His voice was filled with kindness as he explained he had observed my discomfort in church and believed I was still suffering since my suicide attempt. He thought I'd feel better if the Bishop heard my confession. He went on to point out that the attempt to end my life had been an occasion of sin. I remember nodding non-committally, sickened inside by the thought of even being in the same room with him.

As soon as the Bishop walked in, Dave told him that he thought it would be a good idea for him to hear my confession. The Bishop agreed. The short, silent walk from our house to the chapel felt miles long as I imagined how a prisoner might feel walking to his execution. As soon as we entered the chapel, the Bishop turned to study me in the light streaming through the windows. My heart raced and I felt like jumping out of my skin, or through one of those windows. He sat down heavily in one of the ancient pews and said he probably shouldn't hear my confession; that we should just stay in the chapel and sit for a few minutes and then go back to the house and Dave would think it was done. We sat in silence in different pews, not speaking. For me, in those unbearable moments, another lie had been committed. The secrecy and deception deepened, the fissure between Dave and myself widened further.

15.

The Scarlet Letter

*She had wandered without rule or guidance, into a moral wilderness
… The scarlet letter was her passport into regions where other
women dared not tread. Shame Despair. Solitude. These had been
her teachers—stern and wild ones—and they had made her strong,
but taught her much amiss … She could no longer borrow from the
future to ease her present grief.*

Nathaniel Hawthorne, *The Scarlet Letter*

We moved from Rosebud to Aberdeen, South Dakota late that summer. I missed the Lakota people and the wide, open prairies. Over time, my son and the prairie skies had become my only source of comfort, so I grieved deeply, missing the vast skies of the reservation: the small rolling hills and flat land where earth and sky meet each other in the early mornings and in evening benediction. Some days my longing was palpable as I felt hemmed in by buildings, trees, and people. Dave became rector of the Episcopal church and life seemingly achieved a new normal. On the outside I functioned—I acted. Inside, I was empty, struggling to find meaning as I navigated a spiritual wasteland, always worried that I might be found out. Dr. Spears was right, our life no longer seemed completely our own as we lived in a fishbowl of others' projections and expectations. Dave seemed no more suited for it than I was. The land and town seemed stifling, locking us in—a reflection of my inner state.

Self-mutilation can be done in a number of ways. I hadn't cut myself since being a patient in Illinois State Psychiatric Institute, but I mutilated myself daily. Not with sharp objects, but with recrimination. Self-criticism became a sharp razor blade of thoughts: *If anyone knew who I really was, they would hate me.* Having to live in a way so alienated from myself and any inner source of spiritual nourishment was slowly killing me. I felt distant from most others, and from myself.

My marriage was falling apart in small, subtle ways: we seldom argued, but the connection, the passion, any form of emotional intimacy, were increasingly infrequent. If I did allow myself to appreciate or experience moments of closeness, or even the hint of intimacy with Dave, I battered myself with self-abuse and a litany: *If Dave really knew ... I don't deserve a good man like him ... No matter what, my marriage vows are still broken ... Dr. Gehlhoff warned me—it would be the end of my marriage and too much for Dave to bear.*

My bright-eyed, creative little boy kept me alive, just by virtue of his sweet spirit. I had grown to believe what Dr. Gehlhoff taught me about my son's need for me and was determined to be the best mother I could. I took a parenting class and a self-defense class for women, hoping it would help me feel more empowered. I vowed to never, ever again let anyone hurt me.

Over time, I was absorbed into parish life, teaching Sunday school and singing in the choir. Both were expected by the women's vestry as a responsibility of their pastor's wife. In time, I got a job teaching deaf–blind children part time. This too fed me in small ways, reawakening my creativity. Our second November in Aberdeen came and with it our seventh wedding anniversary, as well as the clergy convention in Sioux Falls. Increasing anxiety about seeing the Bishop mounted as the week approached.

Convention week was filled with workshops and luncheons for clergy and spouses and ended with a formal dinner and dance. That evening I wore a lavender, long-sleeved ballgown with a fitted bodice, a full skirt, and a modest but flattering neckline. Dave wore the same deep-blue, velvet jacket he'd worn at our wedding. As we dressed, Dave looked at me warmly and said I looked beautiful and that he was proud I was his wife. I was more touched than I could say by his sentiment.

Dave was charming at dinner, drawing me out as he had when we first met. It felt like the pain of the past had finally begun to resolve. I started to embrace the moment and enjoyed a conversation with the warm and interesting wife of another priest. The tables were cleared and a band started. I danced with Dave through several songs when he was tapped on the shoulder by the Bishop who asked if he could dance with me. Dave stepped aside as I tried to mask my panic.

The lights went down as a slow dance came on and the room filled with a white, slow-moving strobe light bringing magic and romance. Desperately, I wished to be back in Dave's arms. I excused myself and tried to pull away as the Bishop backed me into a cloakroom and tried to kiss my neck and put his hand down the front of my dress. For a moment I froze, then quickly my body remembered a move from the self-defense class and I managed to step on the Bishop's foot and at the same time slip out from under his arms.

I ran to the women's restroom to try to collect myself, and then sought frantically for Dave, about to tell him what the Bishop had done. Instead, I found myself telling him I didn't feel well and was going to go upstairs to bed. He kissed me on the cheek and said he'd be up shortly.

A week later, I had lunch with a friend I'd met at church. She was someone I had grown to like—she was close to my age and we shared a lot of interests: music, motherhood, and good books. Midway through lunch she asked me about the clergy conference and if I'd seen the Bishop. I nodded.

"I bet you're excited that he's coming in a couple weeks for the ceremony and blessing of the new church," she continued. "Father Dave told us at a meeting that the Bishop is going to stay with you while he's in town."

I froze mid-motion while taking a bite of my sandwich. Caught off guard, my face must have revealed something and she demanded to know what was wrong. I insisted that I couldn't talk about it and tried to change the subject. She protested that she had thought we were friends and felt insulted that I couldn't trust her after she had talked to me about many of her own problems. My fear and the story of what the Bishop did came tumbling out. She was horrified. "It must have cost you a lot," she said. "To keep a secret like that."

Two days later, I received a phone call at work. It was the Bishop. He was furious. He told me that thanks to my blabbing about what he called "our business," a group had formed at the church to examine the issue. He ordered me to meet him at the small airport on the edge of town at 4:00 p.m. He told me if I didn't show up, I'd live to regret it.

Looking back on it now, I'm astounded that I could so easily be persuaded to meet with him. And yet, I see the culmination of all the earlier ages of myself and the horrific events that came together, influencing that terrified young woman. I had been trained to give in to the demands of powerful men, so I met him—how could I not?

I was barely able to hear him, although he was shouting. He said that he had told the callers that I lied and had made up the story for attention. The words "lied" and "made it up for attention" reverberated off the walls of my brain. As a child, I hadn't lied about Dr. L, I'd told the truth, but still had not been believed. Now, as a grown woman, I knew: I could not give into his demands and lie for him. He continued ranting, threatening me that I'd better tell them that I had lied or it would be the end of me. He grabbed my arm and twisted hard. His face distorted with rage as he ordered me, as the Bishop, to end the mess I had created with my big mouth. He then turned and walked back toward the small private plane waiting nearby.

Saturday morning came. I received a call telling me that the committee planned a meeting, to "finally, and once and for all, get to the bottom of this." They wished to meet with the Bishop and myself, at a parishioner's home. Seated in the living room, surrounded by judges and jurors, I was interrogated. The Bishop eventually broke down, admitting that he'd had an infatuation with me and we'd had a brief "affair."

"It wasn't an affair," I said. "The Bishop forced himself on me."

No one said a thing. The Bishop immediately started talking. "Forgive me my sin of indiscretion," he begged. "Please don't let my confession leave this room. My only wish is to protect the diocese, to protect the good people of South Dakota."

But the Bishop had not only failed in his relationship and responsibility to me, my husband, and child, he had failed the people of South Dakota. At the time, I also believed I had failed them. But to my horror, I saw each member of the committee nod to him in agreement. They were complicit, unable to see the full scale of what he had done. Before I turned to go, disheartened and on edge, they left me with one final warning: don't tell anyone.

The next day was Sunday. I arrived to teach Sunday school and was told someone else had taken over the class for me: I wasn't needed. Upstairs, the choir director told me not to put on a robe for choir: the group had decided it would be too difficult for a number of congregants to see me at the front of the church. An invisible scarlet letter "A" had been stitched onto my chest, and even more painfully, seared into my heart. Like Hawthorne's Hester Prynne I had been labeled a whore by the church community.[1]

The underground tremors set in motion a year and a half earlier grew into a full-scale earthquake as my life fell apart. The next day I told Dave the entire story. He broke down, first sobbing and then becoming enraged that others knew before him and demanded that I leave the house. I begged to bring David with me but he refused. We argued, but in the end, I felt so awful—responsible for his devastated response—that I left alone and drove my car around until dawn. I didn't have enough money in my purse to stay at a hotel. The next morning, I quickly discovered that Dave had shut down my access to our joint checking and savings accounts. I tried to sleep in my car for two nights but riddled with remorse for not telling him immediately after the rape, I slept little.

After a second sleepless night, a sign in front of a building I drove by in the morning drew me in like a lighthouse beacon. It read "Resource Center for Women—Walk-in Counseling." I received the support I needed and the space to brainstorm options. Later, with the help of the counselor sitting nearby, I called Dave. He was gruff and distant but by the end of the conversation he agreed to leave an envelope with some money for me at a place I can no longer remember. He agreed I could call every evening and talk with David before bedtime. He told me he'd set up an appointment two weeks later in Sioux Falls with Dr. Gehlhoff. He would meet me there.

That evening I called at the agreed-upon time to say goodnight to David and was shocked when the Bishop's wife answered the phone. She didn't think I should be talking to him. She told me Dave was close to a nervous breakdown because of me. She accused me of being manipulative, a liar, and that I'd seduced her husband. I was undone by her attack. I replied that she could think what she wanted, but to please put my son on the phone. Every evening for the next two weeks I called and had my heart broken as little David begged me to come home.

The days crawled by until the upcoming appointment. Two days before, I drove to Sioux Falls to meet with Dr. Gehlhoff by myself. After sincerely asking me how I was holding up, he warned me that Dave would be arriving the next day with divorce papers. I hardly knew what to say—I had hoped the meeting the next day was about finding a way for the two of us to get through this nightmare together. I hadn't anticipated an immediate divorce. Dr. Gehlhoff told me he didn't want me to get railroaded by the Bishop's narrative and Dave's knee-jerk, hurt reaction. He said I needed a good lawyer since Dave, to my horror, was claiming

I was mentally ill and filing for full custody of David. Dr. Gehlhoff had contacted a good friend who was an attorney and knew mental health well. She'd agreed to see me that afternoon.

By the next day's meeting I was as prepared as I could be. Nervously perched on a chair in the waiting room with my heart beating against my rib cage, I gasped when Dave entered the room, still enraged, and handed me an envelope. He demanded that I sign. I refused to sign anything until my attorney had seen it. "You're not smart enough to have gotten yourself an attorney," he said.

I understood that in his hurt and desperation he needed to retaliate and diminish me. By the time Dr. Gehlhoff told him that he wouldn't support his petition for full custody of David, or the premise that I was mentally ill, he looked so much like a deflated balloon that I felt bad for him. But I was also relieved. Dr. Gehlhoff cited research that revealed that young children in a divorce did better by remaining in the custody of the mother, if at all possible. Boys did well by considering changing that arrangement around puberty.

By the end of the meeting, Dave had resentfully agreed to the recommendations Dr. Gehlhoff laid out. I would have custody of David throughout the school year; he would go to his father for holidays and summers. This arrangement would change when David moved toward puberty. Dave told us he would be moving out of state at the end of the following week. He agreed to let me pick up David on Tuesday.

In 1978, as unexpectedly as Dave and I had gotten married, shortly before David's third birthday our divorce became final. My biggest regret was not telling Dave that the Bishop had raped me immediately after it happened. I can see now why I didn't. The Bishop was a charismatic priest who had, slowly and skillfully, won my trust much as Dr. L had done. He made me feel important to him and worth spending time with, playing on the needs he had discovered. The Bishop, like every other perpetrator I have worked with or heard described by victims, escaped accountability for his actions by first manipulating my desire to not be the cause of hurt to Dave or others and then by demanding my silence and secrecy. When his actions had been made public, he attacked my credibility and tried to make sure no one would listen to me by using what I'd shared with him as a trusted Bishop against me.

Perpetrators like the Bishop always attempt to make sure, by whatever means it takes, that no one listens to the victim. The Bishop blatantly and artfully constructed rationalizations, telling others that I had lied and made up a story, and then that I had exaggerated and actually seduced *him*. "It wasn't that bad. We had a brief affair. If only you had screamed and fought harder, then I would have known to stop." He then threatened me in subtle and not-so-subtle ways, as often happens to victims of domestic violence and rape.

The divorce broke open old fault lines of betrayal, loss, and abandonment. The Bishop had taken everything from me, including my belief in a just and loving God. Coupled with the institutional abuse I had suffered at ISPI and Elgin, and the Bishop's rape, I found a strength and determination to heal at every level, whatever the cost.

Around this time, I had an important dream.

I'm walking in circles in a house that has been decimated by a tornado. I'm searching for something, but I'm not sure what it is. I walk into the bedroom Dave and I shared in Rosebud: there are large holes in the wall, everything is broken apart. A sound draws my attention to a corner of the room. A large tree has fallen through the wall and my son, curled in its arms, seems to be peacefully waking from a nap. He smiles at me as he stretches, cat-like. I am flooded with love for this little being—a result of the union of love his father and I shared. I scoop him into my arms, this little boy who looks so much like his Daddy. I notice small blossoms on the few remaining limbs of the tree.

I woke from the dream and lay still, savoring the peace that had stolen over me in my sleep. In an instant, I knew I hadn't lost everything after all. Not only did I continue to have the capacity to love, but the grip of the strangulating secret that had eaten me from the inside out for so long had loosened its hold and I was fully determined to recover from it all.

Reflection

The Web of Life—Does Anybody Hear Her?

Synchronicity is the coming together of inner and outer events in a way that cannot be explained by cause and effect and that is meaningful to the observer.

C.G. Jung, Synchronicity: An Acausal Connecting Principle (from Vol. 8 of *The Collected Works of C.G. Jung*

In the morning after working on this chapter titled, "The Scarlet Letter,"[1] I stopped at my favorite drive-through coffee shop. As I went to hand money to the server, he smiled and said, "The people in front of you already paid for you."

"This has happened to me before, but I'm always surprised," I answered.

"I bet you haven't had this happen before," he replied, handing me a folded piece of paper. "They asked me to give this note to you."

I glanced up, looking closely at the car as it pulled away, but I didn't recognize the vehicle or the two people in it. I pulled forward and off to the side in the parking lot and opened the note. It read, "Tune into radio station 98.5. Have a good day. God bless." Intrigued, I searched for the radio station I'd never heard of and began to drive. I nearly ran off the road as I listened to lyrics describing judgmental people from organized religions who damn women with a scarlet letter by the way they dress or their assumed sexual promiscuity.

The song could have been written about me during those long-ago years when I had felt branded with a scarlet letter by those in the parish. They seemed unable to lay blame at the Bishop's feet, finding it easier to blame me. Just the day before I hesitated in writing and labeling the chapter "The Scarlet Letter." I was moved by the way forces beyond me had again intervened as if confirming that I was on the right track.

16.

Beginnings—Excavating the Past

And the day came when the risk to remain tight in a bud was more painful
than the risk it took to bloom.

Anais Nin, Risk

Despite my grief, life marched forward into the 1980s with rewarding work with deaf–blind children and I returned to school, graduating at the top of my class with straight As and a master's degree in Clinical Psychology and Counseling in Education. To my surprise, I received the highest award, "Outstanding Counseling Student," for that year's graduating class. I went on to work as a therapist at a mental health clinic, followed by rewarding work as the first crisis counselor in Aberdeen's Central High School.

My mother was first diagnosed with cancer when David was three months old. I had flown through a snowstorm to see her one last time after being told she had suffered two cardiac arrests in surgery, another in intensive care, and would likely not recover. They allowed me five minutes in the intensive care unit, as her life dangled by a slender thread. I put my newborn into her arms and the lump in my throat grew nearly unbearable, until I took a deep breath. Somehow, she survived for nearly four years more—until cancer showed up in her throat.

Those years flew by, and I occasionally visited her. Two things stand out from this time: she loved my son in a way she had never been able to love me, and she stopped drinking any alcohol or using drugs after those near-death experiences around her first surgery. However, she had brain damage from the years of alcohol and drug use, making her seem very old for her years. On a visit three-year-old David and I made shortly before she died, I watched in pleasure as he played with small cars on her bed. As the afternoon passed, David grew sleepy, curled up close to his grandma, and fell asleep. My mother seemed content and appeared to have fallen asleep right along with him. Without thinking about it, I took off my shoes, crawled up on the other side of the bed, and lay down next to her nearly emaciated body. Wrapping my arms around her and my small son, something in me settled.

"I love you, Mom," I whispered, hoping to not wake either of them.

"I love you, too," her breathy, pain-filled voice replied. I marveled at the beauty of those words. I had longed to hear them from her since I had first heard them and experienced their meaning through the neighbor, Dale.

Several weeks later, my Aunt Myrtle called me one night saying my mother was actively dying. I drove through the night, arriving early the next morning, but too late. My mother had died and was buried two days later. After the memorial service, I went to her small, low-income apartment and saw how very little she had—hers was a small life.

My mother lost her life early to a war that was never really hers to fight, but one she was compulsively engaged in from age three. I've stopped that war in my generation. My grief was not in the losing of her—I'd never really had her since she'd been incapable of being my mother. My grief was in the fact that this was a woman who had never lived a fulfilling life. She had lived her life with an insatiable appetite born out of extreme poverty, abuse, and desperation. She had never healed. She devoured men, alcohol, drugs, and felt a ravenous need to fill a bottomless pit.

My mother attempted to colonize me with an identity of victimhood simultaneously with the belief that all men are no good and only out for sex and exploitation. She tried to instill in me the idea that outsiders of any sort are never to be trusted. She mistrusted education and ridiculed me for pursuing it, certain that I would think too much of myself and believe I was better than her and her relatives. I grieved for this woman who had never really lived.

My relationship with David's dad remained challenging as Dave continued to be distant and angry that I had the bulk of the custody of "his son." My heart broke every holiday and summer when I put young David on a plane to his father's, who by then had moved several times and lived in Ohio.

For some time, I experienced a nagging whisper from the underworld of my psyche through dreams, things I read in graduate school, and a deep yearning to fully heal from the past. Finding a therapist in the small town in which I lived was impossible. I realized there wasn't one person who didn't know me as a fellow student from graduate school, or from my internship placements.

The summer of 1983, David turned eight. While he was in Ohio visiting his Dad, I flew to Minnesota to take a two-week professional course in adolescent chemical dependency. I had been seeing an overwhelming number of students at Central High School challenged by drug and alcohol abuse. Given the scope of the problem emerging across the country, the course was intensive. The mornings were filled with lectures, and the afternoons we each attended a small group facilitated by a local therapist. At one point, we were each asked to "dive deep" and look at how chemical dependency or drug addiction had touched our lives. One day, my small group facilitator Judy told me she observed that when I talked about my history with my mother's chemical abuse, it sounded like I was talking about a distant cousin I'd never met. She invited me to see if I could get in touch with the feelings related to this.

Judy was a few years older than me, warm and caring, and clearly a feminist in her interpersonal, therapeutic approach. She practiced depth psychology and emphasized dreams, encouraging me to explore my own. Her observations and invitations to expand my self-reflections were timely and welcome. During the remainder of my time at the training, I did some deep inner work and decided I needed to get into therapy and face my past. By this time, I longed to do so, and I had the inner strength and determination.

The way forward revealed itself when Judy agreed to be my therapist and work with me once a month if I could arrange to see her in Minneapolis. The long five-and-a-half-hour drive each way for therapy sessions didn't deter me. Intuitively, I knew that it was time to heal the past. I made a vow to myself: I was unwilling to live with a leftover mental health history or diagnosis. I would commit myself fully—no matter the cost—to a healthy and whole life.

Although committed, I was naive about what it would really take. I trusted Judy as much as I trusted anyone. It soon became apparent that with my complicated history, therapy often felt like stepping into a war zone. An inner world of devastation slowly began to reveal itself. This was a place where I never knew if I would accidentally step on a landmine, resulting in flashbacks, nightmares, and increased anxiety. My life had been stable for a number of years as I reinvented myself after my divorce, but suddenly I was regularly catapulted into a past that had been partitioned off in my psyche—and for good reason.

At times, it was nearly impossible to recalibrate and ground myself following a session. As deeper defenses gave way, I became increasingly bonded with Judy and, every time I left a session, I was wracked with sobs of grief and the tearing open of the historic "mother hole" I had carried deep in my core. The flashbacks and body memories became difficult to contain. I desperately struggled to stay in the present and fully functional with the tsunami of feelings and memories that could overtake me without notice. I had been seeing Judy for over a year when summer came. David was with his father for the holidays, so I was able to do a series of more intensive therapy sessions. This seemed to help for a while and I again felt more stable.

Fall came, and with it more flashbacks. I felt physically ill much of the time, and I again was hospitalized with physical issues as I slowly recovered from another surgery. Judy was adamant that I meet with a chaplain while I was still in the hospital. She felt I needed help in healing the rift in my spiritual life. The hospital only had male chaplains and she had anticipated that this would be a problem for me, so came prepared with a list of female chaplains that she'd gotten from the Council of Churches.

The next day a woman named the Reverend Margo Maris visited me. Had I known ahead of time she was an Episcopal priest, I wouldn't have agreed to see her. Judy hadn't realized that either: she'd called the local Council of Churches looking for any female minister who could visit me in the hospital. By the end of Margo's visit, something deep within me, related to the Bishop's rape, began to ease. Margo proposed setting up a meeting with the Bishop of Minnesota, believing that this would help me move further in my healing. I was hesitant but said I'd think about it. We agreed to meet again in a few months.

Judy met with me in the hospital a few days before my discharge. She told me that she could no longer work with me long distance. I needed more support and to see her more often than one time per month. She'd be happy to see me for therapy if I ever decided to move to Minneapolis. I understood that it wouldn't have been ethical for her to continue under those infrequent circumstances. That night, my mind ran around in circles. My intuition told me that discontinuing therapy was not a viable option, logic told me it was insane to move my young son and leave a community where I had a good job and close friendships. A few weeks previously I had received an award from the board of education for an innovative multi-school program I created. Moving made absolutely no common sense and, yet, my mind continued to swirl in a cauldron of confusion. That night I had the following dream.

I'm in the house I live in and look out the window and see that a tornado is coming at the same time the sirens go off. I grab David, confused as I wonder if we will be safer in the house or in a small trailer, standing off in a distant field. We run back and forth as the tornado gathers speed and draws closer. Eventually, we hide under a small table in the trailer after I've decided somehow this is the safest thing to do. The tornado passes. We go outside and see that the house has been totally destroyed—flattened. We were safer in the structure that at first appearances seemed less secure than the solidness of the house. The trailer is mobile and doesn't appear to have a solid foundation like the house, but was clearly the place of greater safety.

I woke with the clarity that I needed to resign from my job and move. That morning my internist, Dr. Eckerly, told me that she was glad that I had made the decision; I needed some specialized medical treatment. If I didn't move, she believed I would die prematurely.

Everything seemed uncertain as I handed in my resignation letter and then prepared to move to an unknown city where I had no job and knew no one except the professionals who had cared for me. The only thing certain was that I believed with every fiber of my being that my life depended on this move. From the moment I made the commitment to uproot my life in South Dakota and fully embark on healing, Spirit was with me, throughout the intensive years, sometimes in subtle ways and other times in more overt ones.

Dave had left the Episcopal Church and was ordained in the Catholic Church within a few years of our divorce. He spent several years living in Kentucky at the Abbey of Gethsemani, until David's custody was changed. During those early years, young David enjoyed many summers and Christmas holidays at the abbey. Although Dave and I talked on the phone about our son, he remained aloof and guarded.

Although our custody agreement stated that it wouldn't be until David hit puberty that our arrangement would change, it seemed that the time had come early. I moved to Minneapolis and put David on a plane at the end of December to join his dad in Ohio. I knew the decision to have him live with his dad during the school year, and to visit me during holidays and in the summer, was now in his best interest, but it was the hardest decision I had ever made. My grief made it nearly impossible for me to leave the airport. Fortunately, I had an appointment with Margo that afternoon.

By the time I arrived for the meeting with Margo, the immediacy of the grief I felt after sending David to his dad's, coupled with the old unresolved feelings about the loss of my marriage, was overwhelming. In that moment, the full realization of just what the Bishop's rape and lies had cost me flooded me.

17.

The Interior World of Healing Trauma

The bodies of traumatized people portray "snapshots" of their unsuccessful attempts to defend themselves in the face of threat and injury. Trauma is a highly activated incomplete biological response to threat, frozen in time.

Peter Levine, *Interoception, Contemplative Practice, and Health,*
in Frontiers in Psychology

Throughout this book, you've read a cohesive narrative. However, it took years of deep, intensive, difficult therapeutic work to lead me to the integration of my past. As I reflect on my years of therapy, I am reminded of being nine and pushing through the upper glass of the window trying to get into the apartment we lived in. At the emergency room, shards of broken glass were carefully picked out of my arms and hands before the many cuts were sutured together.

Good therapy, which I finally had, is much like this. Initially, memory comes in fragments, images, sensations, isolated events, which can hurt and injure in return like shards of splintered glass—some very small and others large. Then, very slowly and not without pain, the context and broken images began to converge into a coherent narrative—torn psyche and memory stitched together. Over a matter of years, I completed my work with Judy and began work with Charlotte, another therapist who had more expertise with complex trauma and dissociation.

After years of being forced into therapeutic situations that were often themselves abusive, I was fortunate to work with therapists who were masters at working with emerging memories that had been splintered off. Good therapy requires great skill and willingness to care about the patient's needs. The therapists I worked with consciously created sacred space that could contain the terrifying images slowly seeping up from the underworld of my psyche. They came out through my body and my senses: the smell of cigarettes, liquor, sweat, vomit, or spoiled food. The sound of fire engines, angry voices, and certain kinds of music were all triggers. The ticking of clocks could immobilize me. These long-held back images and memories flooded me, creating agitation and panic and the immediate thought that I had to run and get away: "I've got to get out of here."

In the 1980s the profession of psychology knew little of the current emerging science of how trauma is imprinted into the body itself: into tissue memory, into the neurobiological systems, and into the senses where beliefs and life patterns are formed. But my therapists' compassion, commitment, and skill paid off, even though the understanding of trauma was more limited than it is today. The field has developed light years ahead of where it was when I was undergoing intense therapy and continues to rapidly develop today.

Patterns of rigidity and constriction formed early in my life. In order to avoid feeling overwhelmed by sights and sounds of abrasive stimuli, I learned to shut down. From age three, I had developed a propensity, when faced with unbearable physical or psychological pain, to leave my body. It was automatic. I felt as though my very life depended on getting away and out of my physicality. A constellation of reflexive survival beliefs and patterns had developed that had initially been protective. As an adult they created greater vulnerability and ongoing stress to my dysregulated nervous system. This is true of most victims of childhood trauma and must be fully understood in order to work with them toward resolution.

There were times I felt like a living zombie, observing myself from far away, dislocated from the physical body I had come to hate. Needless to say, such patterns are not helpful in adult life. It wasn't until much later that I began to understand that my symptoms were the language of my banished and suffering soul.

Dissociation is like escaping out the back door of the psyche in order to leave the threatened and painful body behind. The freezing response is a biologically driven reaction of freezing in the face of threat or unspeakable terror. This immobility is an unconscious reflex built into humans and animals that can't escape by fighting or fleeing. A flood of endogenous opioids is released by the brain. This natural, heroin-like substance kills pain and produces calm and a sense of psychological distance from what is happening.

In the short term, this is an amazingly effective system. However, when there isn't quick resolution, these systems become overactive and sensitized to many emotional, behavioral, and cognitive problems long after the event or events are over. A traumatized brain can swing from symptoms of hyperarousal with anxiety, panic, emotional flooding, digestive problems, chronic pain, sleeplessness, and ongoing hypervigilance. During this period of hyperarousal, the brain can feel amped up, like the dial is stuck on fast.

Once the adrenal glands have run out of cortisol, the system moves to a state of hypo (under) arousal, with symptoms like lethargy, inability to feel emotions, disconnection, low blood pressure, exhaustion, disorientation, depression, and dissociation. It's here that the system dials down, stuck on the off button. If there is a perception of danger, the thinking part of the brain shuts down and allows the doing part of the brain to take over. The ability of the brain to shift naturally to a calm state becomes impaired over time. Relaxation skills and meditation would later become essential for resetting my lifetime of living with a traumatized brain.

During the years of therapy, my life depended on learning to stay put and become increasingly self-aware. This was challenging because this tendency was part of my protective system, wired in at an early age and then reinforced repeatedly out of necessity. During flashbacks, time seemed to fold in on itself, creating confusion between past and present. Until I learned to distinguish the past from the present and recognize symptoms of hyperarousal and emerging memories. These times were terrifying and often debilitating for hours or days after a challenging therapy session.

Charlotte's dedication and creativity helped me to stay the course and invited me to cultivate the courage to listen to the unspeakable terror that I had experienced throughout my life. At times, the refuge of therapy quickly transformed itself into a chamber of torture, particularly as I relived specific events related to Dr. L and Elgin State Hospital. Many give up on therapy at this point when their therapists don't have the skills or commitment to stay the course. It's hard work. There were times in which I felt like I was drowning in a tsunami of painful flashes of memory.

There were times when my inner pendulum swung in the opposite direction, away from hyperarousal because of adrenal fatigue, leaving me more disconnected and withdrawn, avoiding others, and tempted to avoid therapy itself. During these times, I struggled with grief and depression and had little energy, making the navigation of daily and professional life challenging.

In addition to healing my nervous system, my thinking was full of faulty logic created at the time of extreme physical pain, terror, and anguish. These beliefs became the conclusions I had reached as a child and young adult, in order to try to even begin to understand and make any sense of what was incomprehensible. These misbeliefs were all disempowering. The brilliance of a dissociated system is that a part of you at times can act normally, but the inner conversation and flawed logic were breeding grounds for self-contempt and further fed my system with ongoing stress, creating a vicious, recurring, and exhausting cycle.

For years, I secretly believed I was defective in every way. In my mind, the proof was in all of the ways I had failed: my mother's inability to love me; telling Dr. L the truth about our life, which led to his exploitation; failed foster placements; ending up in Illinois State Psychiatric Institute; my commitment to Elgin; the Bishop's rape; Dave divorcing me; on and on the litany ran. Unconsciously, I had organized my life and myself in ways that dampened down and minimized the impact of what had shattered me. In response to the unbearable events in my life, memories and aspects of me had frozen in time, withdrawing consciousness itself from the unspeakable reality that was too overwhelming to face.

This is the challenge of anyone recovering from childhood trauma and, in many cases, of traumatized adults as well. I've worked with children, war veterans, first responders, adults with trauma histories, and rape victims. We humans cannot bear feeling powerless. Trauma is completely disempowering, so we struggle, making up stories related to how or what we could have done differently so that traumatizing events would never have happened in the first place.

Changing this destructive inner narrative is essential to developing self-love and compassion, but it is no easy task. I had been the victim of a series of failures of the courts, violations by others, and institutional abuse throughout my life. Not understanding this, I saw these things through the lens of a child's powerlessness and as my own failure. As a professional with thirty years of experience, I've learned the brilliance of the fight, flight, and freeze pattern built into all beings.

It takes tremendous courage, commitment, and grit to heal from the kind of familial, systemic, and institutional abuse and neglect I suffered.

So, of course, when as a young child I couldn't fight or flee, I froze. In the shower on my honeymoon, in the midst of a flashback triggered by nudity, I froze. There is no way the freeze response wouldn't have activated after living through the systemic institutional abuse of Elgin, where of course under that dehumanizing tyranny and powerlessness, I froze. Of course, when the Bishop raped me, I froze.

This immobility, a deer in the headlights response, is a part of every human's biological inheritance. In my case, it was immediate and woven into every part of me. For years, I avoided conflict in whatever way I could. I knew the freeze response incapacitated me emotionally as my mind went blank and I had difficulty finding words. It was so helpful to learn about this automatic protective function of the survival brain.

As I've worked with traumatized individuals and groups, when they learn this about themselves, the relief in the room is palpable. This is not only true with the adults I've worked with but also with traumatized adolescents. Looking back, I can see how my body became the storehouse of every form of violence it had suffered, holding memories as well as unfelt, unprocessed emotional pain. It also held the undischarged residual energy and chemistry within my nervous system. Whenever my nervous system fired up, I became aware of little else but my galloping heartbeat and terror of annihilation.

But the other thing I can now see is that the grave failures everywhere were not of my making: the court order to see Dr. L; the larger institution for which he was employed and the military base that provided prostitution, both on and off base; the foster care system; the juvenile system with those like Miss F who seemed to resent, rather than care for, those in their case load; the psychiatric system and institutions they served; the church, the Bishop, and Dave and the congregation who turned their backs. The grave failures of individuals and institutions I'd been taught to trust were everywhere. How could I have endured any better than I did, and most importantly, how was it that I not only survived but would fully heal?

With time, I came to see symptoms as red flags, bringing messages from the underworld, letting me know it was time to look at a particular emerging memory. Again and again a healing force within me pushed memories to the surface in order to give voice to, and metabolize, the previously blocked energy, in the service of healing. As the symptoms began, my initial response was to contract against them in protest. But as I gained experience and confidence, I was able to relax into them and expand my awareness in order to heal my lifetime pattern of pushing away pain. After moving through each traumatic event and consolidating the memory, I had more energy and felt lighter, as though knots were being unwound, leaving me with a feeling of more freedom and openness until the next time. This gave me confidence and more determination to finish the work.

Because of the gift of neuroplasticity, which makes the brain capable of healing and change, I learned to breathe through the panic and calm my thoughts, feel into my body rather than attempt to flee it, and ground into present-day awareness. Also, by learning to give voice to the senses, smells, images, and thoughts, I emerged more quickly out of the frozen terror or desire to flee. At times, I used healing imagery to coexist with, and eventually replace, some of the traumatic images.

Trauma creates fragmentation. It had restrained and restricted my wholeness. As for anyone who has suffered extreme trauma, it dislocates you from your body and disrupts continuity of connection with physicality, mind, and soul. It creates a vacuum of inner space and distance between yourself and others. As I became more embodied, my thoughts, feelings, and sensations became unified, and I felt a growing continuity and depth in relationships.

All of this is referred to in one way or another in the last chapter so I'm deleting it here. Therapy, body work, and eventually spiritual practice each helped me reconcile with my body as I began to see it as a sacred temple, the temporary custodian of my spirit and soul. I had always believed that the loss of my soul was one of the results of the trauma I experienced. Intuitively, I knew with my whole being that I would never completely heal unless I focused on this loss of soul and its recovery.

Studying different spiritual traditions and developing a spiritual practice would eventually become central to my healing. But before that could take place, I needed to begin to recover from the desertification that had occurred at the hands of an ordained Episcopal priest, a bishop in that tradition.

While continuing to see Judy in therapy, I met with Margo, and fairly soon after joined her in meeting with the Bishop of Minnesota. Bishop Robert Anderson wept in that first meeting and apologized to me for all I had been through. I was cautious as well as hopeful about his sincerity. My trust had been brutally violated but I still believed in the fundamental goodness of people. Before we concluded the meeting, he told me that if

I would find it helpful to have a confrontation, he would attempt to make that happen. This began an intense process of growth and preparation for a meeting that would change each of our lives.

Initially, the Bishop declined coming when invited by letter and a follow-up phone call by Bishop Anderson. He said that I was "manipulative and unstable and not to be believed." He also said that "he had tried to help in my healing before."

About a year after the first meeting with Bishop Anderson, my work and preparation culminated in a session with my rapist on July 26, 1985. Present with me were Bishop Anderson, Margo, Judy, Barbara, and a rape advocate. I was well prepared and reassured that each person in the room was there to support me. At that time in the history of the church, or in any state, there were no laws that had been set up to deal with exploitation or abuse within a church setting or abuse that had occurred years earlier. I had no idea that day that something larger than any of us was being set in motion.

It had been eight years since the Bishop had raped me. On his arrival, if he was nervous he didn't show it—he appeared cooperative and friendly to everyone gathered. I watched him as he appeared to take over the room, immediately beginning to talk, unsolicited by anyone. He stated vehemently that at the time of the event on the reservation he had made a mistake. He claimed that he genuinely cared for me. He said that in his mind, he had engaged in sex with me out of love: to help me because of my poor self-esteem and loneliness because of Dave's absence due to his working responsibilities. It took everything in me to not interrupt him. He continued and said he was willing to apologize to me again. Where before I couldn't see or hear his manipulations, now I could. He was either an incredible actor, or he truly believed what he had done to me was motivated out of "love."

I realized at that moment how difficult it is to heal when love, exploitation, and abuse are wrapped up together in the same package. His self-delusion was no different than that of incestuous fathers who often convince themselves of the same thing. My relationship with him was made up of looking to him not only as a father figure but as God's representative.

The Bishop appeared to listen as I confronted him about his exploitation and rape, his lies and the short-term and long-term consequences to me, Dave, my son, and the people in the church community. After I finished,

Bishop Anderson asked my abuser if there was anything he would like to say. The room was quiet as he looked around. Then came a defining moment for me and everyone present.

"When she stopped screaming and fighting, I took it as consent," the Bishop replied, looking at Bishop Anderson as though for support.

I swallowed as the bitter taste of bile rose to my throat and for just a moment, a flash of memory intruded, sharp and clear, as though he had just said the words. "So, how do you feel having just committed adultery with your Bishop?" In my memory, the clock with the Westminster chimes struck deafeningly. For a moment those chimes seemed so real that I looked around for the clock itself. The look on Bishop Anderson's face brought me fully back into the room. Then I watched as Bishop Anderson sat forward in his chair, his face incredulous, his words like a bell, so crystal clear that they would forever take up residence alongside the Westminster chimes in my psyche. Bishop Anderson pointed his finger at my rapist and responded with words I have never forgotten.

"I don't care if she sat on your lap naked, you were her bishop, confessor, and a father figure to her. It was up to you to set appropriate boundaries. What you've subjected her to is abhorrent and inexcusable. It was sexual exploitation, rape, and abuse, nothing less."

Before the meeting closed, I asked the Bishop for two things. I requested that he write a letter to Dave taking full responsibility for everything he had done. I also asked that he pay for the therapy sessions that had been dedicated to healing from the rape. He did neither of them. Did I feel he heard me that day? Not at all. But I left the meeting satisfied that I'd had the courage and ability to say what I needed to.

I had many feelings over the next several weeks: anger, grief, completion, and pity for this man, a wolf in sheep's clothing who clearly appeared to be unaffected, attached to his delusions, and only sorry that he had been caught. I wondered what he was looking for, what answer he hoped to hear that night right after he raped me. His voice was upbeat, with an arrogant edge, as he spoke. His face wore a smirk of self-satisfaction. "So, how does it feel having just committed adultery with your Bishop?" He asked not once but twice. I wonder what answers he had gotten before from the other women he had violated. This was a man used to getting his way, being fawned over. Was he hoping for gratitude from me? Was he shocked by my reply? An answer he hadn't seen coming. What kind of man would ask that question immediately after he had raped someone?

Was I supposed to feel honored by his attentions and lust? I felt humiliated, disgusted, and betrayed and he didn't even have the sensitivity to notice.

By this time, I had started to see Charlotte for therapy. Within the next several years Bishop Anderson and Margo began to lead an annual conference for bishops, who attended from around the United States, on sexual exploitation within the church. I was a speaker for four years. During that time, I never used the Bishop's or Dave's names, nor was I specific about where we lived when the rape had occurred. I thought at the time I was protecting Dave's privacy; he had not been willing to talk about the circumstances of our divorce at that point.

Charlotte and I talked a good deal in therapy about this ongoing protection of Dave. It was the fourth year I had been a speaker when I received a call from Bishop Anderson, the day after I had spoken, asking me if I would be willing to come back and meet with all of the attending bishops. They were very distressed that the Bishop who had caused such harm had never been held accountable by the church. They wanted to talk with me further, to see if I would consider giving them the Bishop's name.

I did meet with them and came, finally, to deep resolution of the ordeal. That meeting also led to awareness and accountability within the Episcopal Church, which paralleled similar inquiries in many religious institutions, including the ongoing investigations of global wrongdoing in the Catholic Church.

Not long after, I was eating lunch with a colleague and friend, Lyndall, and I told her about the rape, my relief following the confrontation, and then the recent meeting with the attending bishops. Lyndall gasped and told me her story.

During a time of depression and vulnerability following the birth of her first child, she formed a close counseling relationship with the parish priest at an Anglican-Episcopal church, an experience very similar to my own. Not long after, Margo Maris and Bishop Anderson were able to organize a meeting with her offender. Unfortunately, her meeting didn't go nearly as well as mine and it broke open long-buried wounds and feelings of betrayal by the church.

It was helpful to know this had happened to someone else whom I knew personally. Over time, I learned that we weren't the only ones. At that time both Margo and Bishop Anderson were doing whatever they could to change the tide and influence church law, which continues to be a struggle. After working in that unbending patriarchal system, a field of institutional exploitation, Margo left the church.

In 2018, an article by Melodie Woerman appeared in the *Episcopal News Service* titled "Bishops lament and confess the church's role in sexual harassment, exploitation and abuse." At a church convention in Austin, Texas on the afternoon of July 4th:

> Bishops of the Episcopal Church stood and collectively offered laments and confession for the church's role in sexual harassment, exploitation and abuse in a service called a "Liturgy of Listening." The service featured 12 stories – six from women and six from men – from victims of sexual misconduct perpetrated by someone in the church. These were among 40 stories… from those hurt by the church.[1]

Although this might be a step in the right direction, it has gone on for far too many years after the foundation work that was laid by Margo and Bishop Anderson in the 1980s. It's clear that the problem continues to exist to this day. Victims of clergy abuse continue to suffer, as I did, alone. The problem does not just exist in the Episcopal Church or the Catholic Church—it is rampant among Evangelical Christians as well. Bureaucracy and institutional enablement allow these patterns of institutionalized sexual exploitation and abuse to continue to this day.

Reflection

Confronting Clergy Abuse—Margo Maris

O ver the years, Margo and I have stayed in touch. Meeting me became the catalyst that changed the course of her ministry, as well as that of Bishop Anderson. They both became strong advocates for change within the Episcopal Church and for the way in which victims of sexual exploitation are treated.

I came across a book titled *The Episcopal Church of South Dakota* by Robert Prichard.[1] Here is a brief excerpt about the movement that Margo, with Bishop Anderson's support, began to lead after that first, fateful meeting in that hospital room.

> In October 1984 a priest from the Diocese of Minnesota paid a hospital call on a troubled woman. In the course of the visit, the woman revealed to the priest that she had been the victim of sexual misconduct by an Episcopal bishop. The priest, Margo Maris, began to search for ways in which to respond pastorally to the woman. In previous generations, those who had been sexually abused by the clergy kept silent out of a sense of shame; those in authority had often sought to shield the church from embarrassment, allowing offenders to resign quietly or to move to other areas. Margo Maris ... worked with the Minnesota Council of Churches and with an ecumenical team of attorneys to develop models for dealing with such situations.

That "troubled woman" was me.

But Margo's activism on behalf of victims of exploitation in the Episcopal Church didn't stop there. In the 1980s committees that Margo sat on were influential in the adoption of new laws that made clergy abuse a felony. In the mid-1990s, she played a key role as the co-chair of the General Convention's Sexual Exploitation Committee in advancing changes in church procedures responding to clergy sexual misconduct. Chicago diocese communication officer David Skidmore's 1996 article, "Sweeping revisions in clergy discipline canons prompt mixed reactions,"[2] details the changes, as well as Margo's passionate involvement. "The Rev. Margo Maris, co-chair of the General Convention's Sexual Exploitation Committee (SEC) ... has been reciting that message to bishops, chancellors, diocesan standing committees, and just about anyone else touched by the issue of clergy misconduct since 1988 when she worked with the Office of Pastoral Development in drafting the first comprehensive response strategy to sexual misconduct."

Margo's nuanced attention to the particular challenges and obstacles women like myself face are clear in Skidmore's article. He writes: "Maris sees false accusations as the rare exception, noting that barely one percent of charges are proven false. 'The highest percentage I've had is two percent,' she said ... For a woman or man to go public with charges against their pastor 'takes tremendous courage,' she said."

When clergy disciplinary canons were finally changed, Margo saw it as the reward of her hard work. And gave credit to "the compelling accounts by victims of their struggles to be heard and see justice served."

18

Harvesting the Gifts of Unknowing

There is an emotional current that carries us along through life creating an impetus to seek more, to dive deeper and live on more than the surface of our lives. This under-song creates a holy longing.

Ralph Waldo Emmerson, *The Portable Emmerson*,
edited by Jeffery S. Cramer

A pattern, an undersong of mystery's signature, has woven its way through my life like an underground river, influencing its landscape and geography. Although trauma had initiated a healing journey, death would come to mentor me through the evolution of my spirit.

By this time, I had turned away from formal religion where belief is concretized into a theory, a prescribed notion of God. This was not just because of the rape and what followed within the church community, but because of something intangible, a deep, instinctual soul-knowing beyond the teachings of most structured religious traditions that reached for me. The journey I was about to embark upon not only would take me into the ocean of my longing and the realm of spirit, but would threaten some of the beliefs around which I'd built a life.

Everyone's personal journey is unique as a thumbprint. In these pages, I share with you my own. Many of us have experiences of the sacred: something real but indescribable, something that transcends the ordinary. Such experiences do not depend on doctrine or dogma. As a direct experience, the numinous can feel electric, charged with life. I share my encounters with life's mysteries because it was an essential part of my healing that is far too often overlooked or misunderstood in mainstream psychiatry and psychology. The story would be incomplete if I neglected to tell this portion of the narrative and left you with the false impression that it was therapy alone that helped me become the confident and effective professional I am today.

Some may rush to find a new diagnosis for me as they engage with the next portion of this narrative. Instead, I ask that you open your minds and hearts to possibility. Psychiatric and psychological services routinely eliminate discussions of spirit. Traditional practitioners subtly define the parameters of what can be talked about and what can be paid attention to. The cultures of psychiatry and psychology are such that emotional distress and problematic behaviors are customarily seen as a disorder. My own experiences and those of clients I have worked with have taught me that this is a huge mistake. If we ignore talking about people's deepest nature, we do them a disservice and collude with an unexamined professional system that is concretized and formulated in much the same way traditional religions have evolved over the decades.

An oath is taken to do no harm, but, by silencing a person who has a need to speak of spiritual experiences, harm is done. If a person has had a transcendent dream or a moment of unexpected synchronicity, it's important to understand how that affects them, not to turn away and add it to the long list of symptoms labeled as pathological. Symptoms of the suffering of the soul are expressions of an authentic voice needing to be heard. But these symptoms are too often silenced and medicated in our current psychological system, one that often only looks for and sees pathology. There is a precedent set far back in history to attend to this aspect of an individual. After all, the word "psychology" once meant "study of the soul." The term comes from the ancient Greek word "psyche," meaning the mind, soul, or spirit, and "logos," denoting study.

If you are a mental health professional reading this, I invite you to entertain the possibility that we are all spiritual beings. An individual's spiritual reality cannot be organized or classified. This can create a dilemma for psychotherapeutic theories and practitioners. Psychotherapy based on a theory becomes an ideology, which creates a narrow orientation and preconceived notions of an individual's experiences and capacities. Religion is how we choose to practice and grow in community, but it does not always open an individual to their spiritual essence or soul, which is related to the deepest aspects of being a human being.

Traumatized patients are not suffering from a brain disorder. Instead, they are suffering from trauma's unique existential crisis, one that is both psychological and spiritual. Fortunately, I felt safe enough in therapy to talk about many of the spiritual experiences that you will read about in the next chapters. But it wasn't in therapy that I could even begin to understand, integrate, or develop a language with which to fully describe these experiences or their deepest impact and gradual and sustained transformation. I had to go outside of therapy for that. It would have been ideal had I not, because in doing so I often felt torn between two disciplines, two ways of seeing the events that began to occur.

The period of my life I describe in the following pages can best be understood as a time in which a divine form of alchemy was at work, transforming the darkness of my earlier life. It was a time when the energy that connects all living things reached out to me, so that I could learn to turn inward, recover, connect to my soul, and discover the fullness of my being.

In the early 1980s I was fully immersed in life in Minnesota. My professional work was deeply rewarding. Seemingly out of nowhere, I was recruited for a new job working with children who were medically fragile or dying. Accepting the offer appeared to make no rational sense. But, despite the voice of reason, I found myself leaving a thriving psychotherapy practice. At the time, I had no conscious understanding of why I let go of work that was both flexible and I enjoyed for a new role of providing both hospital and in-home family therapy at a children's hospital with a fairly rigid schedule. Meaningful work had always been a higher priority to me than salary, but I would be earning more than fifty percent less. Still, the compulsion to take the job trumped rationality. So once again, without understanding why or for what purpose, I left something with a solid foundation for something completely unknown that called to me. I entered what became a critical time of growth and learning, a cauldron of transformation as I sat next to death day after day.

As I recall this time of working intensely with the dying, I see how death had courted me my whole life from the time I was very little. Premature and fragile in my first moments of life, I'd encountered death as I came into this world, violently convulsing. Death stayed near me for those first weeks of life while I was maintained in an incubator and kept alive by machines. My uncle's suicide brought me close to death again, as did the days that followed, when I hovered near death until I was finally, miraculously, found by my aunt.

The pattern continued in elementary school, throughout the period when I snuck into churches to see funerals and eventually into a funeral home with the intent of seeing a dead person for myself. Death continued to court me through my first suicide attempt and afterwards, as I longed to die as Dr. L took me to that edge of life and dangled me over the abyss. I lived my childhood, adolescence, and young adulthood believing death was merely a back door I could use to exit the house of my body at any time, through either suicide or dissociation. Certainly, there had to be something *more* elsewhere—my suicide attempts were as much a longing for that something else as they were an effort to escape. Now I can look back with the wisdom of time and see that a wiser aspect of myself, unknown to me at the time, had needed this change—of intensely working within the crucible of dying.

As a child, I had spent hours and days on end in the wide-open spaces of my imagination where I lived a parallel life. The churches of my childhood created sanctuary, opening me to liminality as I sat reverently, certain God was raining down on me through the choir music sung from the loft above. These early experiences were foundational.

In accepting this job of in-home family therapist with medically fragile and dying children, I was called for the sake of others as well as myself in response to a sacred mandate. By working with others as they struggled at the threshold of life and death, I more fully began to understand myself. Witnessing life in the balance became a daily reminder of the precarious, unpredictable, messy randomness of being alive. It was a teacher, propelling me into a deeply spiritual life, a calling that became as formative as the horrors of my earlier life.

Over many years, my teachers were infants born so prematurely it was hard to believe there was enough-ness to their small, underdeveloped bodies, brains, and lungs to hold them together. Often there wasn't. Nonetheless, lives were changed, simply by being in the presence of their pure essence, in the brief time they stayed on Earth. Children and teens of all ages were challenged by cancer at various stages of the disease and struggled with the emotional and spiritual stages of dealing with it. Eventually, my work expanded to adults with life-threatening illness, all of it a daily reminder that we really aren't in charge, and that life is precarious and uncertain. Death itself became my teacher. First, it broke my heart wide open and then set it free, taking me directly into the cauldron of the great, unknowable darkness of transformation.

During this time, I had the honor of meeting many children, families, and individuals caught in their own terror and fear of the unknown—a foreshortened future. Some of those who crossed my path embraced each moment they had left, eventually transforming into light. Others came filled with anger and regret, teaching me that nothing in my professional training had prepared me for how to meet them. Others came impoverished spiritually or socio-economically, teaching me humility by their gratitude for the simplest of kindness. Some came from wealth and privilege and had the means to buy any kind of healthcare, but in the end there was no amount they could pay to buy more of the life they felt they'd squandered.

Only weeks into the new job, I was sitting with a young mother. Her nine-month-old infant, Meghan, lay in the hospital crib. The mother sat facing me and I was facing her. She told me the baby was stable and only in the hospital so she and her husband could have a respite weekend—this was not out of the ordinary for the families on my caseload to use the hospital on occasion for desperately needed respite from the full-time job of caring for a medically fragile child. Baby Meghan was sound asleep.

As the mother talked, I watched, mesmerized by a light gray energy moving out of the top of Meghan's head and hovering above her. At the same time, I heard an inner voice instruct me to talk about the possibility of Meghan's death, so her mom would be better prepared. I almost invited the mother to turn and look at what I was seeing, but hesitated in self-consciousness. I said nothing. As I left our meeting, I wished Meghan's mom a restful and nourishing weekend.

A little while later I saw the doctor talking to the charge nurse and said I wanted to check in on Meghan's status as I was leaving the following day for a week's vacation. They both told me Meghan had been admitted for her parents' sake, to give them a break. They assured me that she had a little cold, but nothing serious. Leaving the hospital, I let go of my concerns, doubting what I had seen and heard, and told no one, but throughout the vacation, my thoughts would return to that moment in her room. I came back from vacation a week later and was told by the person who filled in for me that Meghan had unexpectedly died while I was gone. It was troubling to realize that had I risked saying something to her mother, perhaps the death would have been eased in some way. Vowing to myself to work more conscientiously on my self-doubt, my work continued.

A week or so later, I was doing rounds on the newborn intensive care unit and a nurse informed me that one of my assigned babies, Trevor, was dying. His parents lived in western Wisconsin and had been called, but the nurse said that there was no way they would get there in time. I thanked her and continued on. Nearly to the door, I was stopped in my tracks with an inner sense that I couldn't shake. This time, I listened. I went back to the nurse and asked if someone could hold baby Trevor. She replied that they were short-staffed and just couldn't spare the time. I timidly asked if I could hold him. She seemed surprised and said yes, if I didn't have anything I had to do.

She pulled up a rocking chair and placed tiny, two-pound baby Trevor in my arms. His skin was a dusky gray, cool to the touch, and his flesh was mottled. She explained that this meant he was very close to death. She said his systolic blood pressure was very low and she hadn't been able to get a temp on him as his body was so quickly cooling down. It would take his parents at least an hour and a half before they would arrive.

As I sat rocking him, I closed my eyes and found myself sending out waves of compassion to his parents and waves of love to Trevor. Shortly after, I began to notice that I felt very hot—unbearably hot. The nurse touched my arm and asked if I was ok because my face was so flushed. I opened my eyes and looked down at the same time as the nurse—baby Trevor's eyes were open and his skin was a warm pink.

She asked, "What were you doing?" Not sure what to say and slightly embarrassed, I stammered, "Nothing." She smiled and said, "Well, whatever it was, keep it up." So, Trevor and I hung out in that chair—his skin stayed a rosy pink as sweat continued to pour down my forehead and out of every pore of my body. His parents rushed into the unit forty-five minutes later and I handed Trevor to his grateful mother. He died five minutes later in her loving arms. The parents had closure and were able to be with him when he took his last breath. This was the beginning of learning to deeply listen to my intuition and instincts, and to trust them.

✳✳✳

Missy, a seventeen year old dying of bone cancer, sat day after day in her darkened bedroom refusing to talk to anyone. Her oncologist had visited, her favorite nurse, her best friend, and others, but she refused to talk to them and often refused to even allow them into the room. One day her mother begged her to tell her if there was anyone she might be willing to talk to. She named me.

Nothing prepared me for what it was like to step foot into that room of dark despair. After a few minutes I hesitantly tried to start a conversation and asked her how she was feeling. But instead of answering, she shrieked at me. "Why does everyone feel like they have to make me talk and get me to feel differently than I do? Can't someone just sit and be with me?"

I spent the next hour with her in silence, conflicted and agonizing over how I could be helpful. When I awkwardly got up to go, Missy stopped me. "When are you coming back?"

I continued to visit Missy week after week, sitting silently in the dark with her. I was humiliated by my discomfort with silence, by my impotence in not being able to be helpful, to ease her pain, or to satisfy her parents' expectations and the referring oncologist. In time, as I began to let my needs go, I came to see the experience as humbling. As my initial agenda and expectations dropped away, I was filled with the realization that although she wasn't talking to me, my sitting seemed to matter because each time I prepared to leave, Missy asked me when I could return. So, I sat—with my discomfort, with her unspeakable suffering and anger. Occasionally, she would reach across the gulf of her grief for my hand. When I misunderstood it as an invitation to talk and asked her a question, she reacted like a frightened deer caught in the headlights of my expectation. Over time, although I wouldn't have known to name it as such, my time with her became meditative.

Initially, my own agenda, my anxiety-filled, overly busy mind that so easily jumped ahead with solutions, my ego-driven need to "solve the problem" or get the credit for fixing her, were obstacles. By learning to let Missy lead, and by getting out of the way, surrendering to the truth that there really wasn't anything that I could do to fix this, I learned to surrender to the present moment.

There was a mysterious something that began to open in me, in Missy, and around and through us. I experienced this mystery as a palpable form of Presence. It eventually opened up as a field of conscious awareness that infused light through and within the darkness itself and supported and enveloped the two of us—a space pregnant with possibility. One day Missy told me that she needed to tell me something, warning me that I better not say one thing back to her. "Something mysterious and magical is happening here. I feel lighter and hopeful."

Over time, as we continued to meet, Missy asked questions and began to speak about everything important to her. Although painful for her, a week before the night Missy made her transition, she asked her parents to take her shopping.

Missy had the space prepared as she wanted it and orchestrated each step of her death: who she wanted present, what music would be played, the flowers and essential oils that would scent the room, the scattering of candlelight, and the hundreds of butterfly mobiles and stickers surrounding her as she died. She gave instructions for how she wanted her body—that body she had hated but now felt grateful for—prepared and dressed in her prom dress before being taken to the mortuary. In her own sweet time, she had grown from being a tightly wrapped cocoon, slowly opening from darkness and uncertainty, until she finally grew her own wings and soared into light. After months of sitting in the dark with Missy and studying the nature of darkness, I felt more alive than I ever had. Witnessing Missy take her last breath was like watching a birth. When Missy died, her loving, radiant face lit up the room, transforming each of us present in its glow.

Like the caterpillar that instinctively begins to weave itself a cocoon yet has no conscious awareness of why, or to what purpose, Missy too had followed her instincts and done the very same thing, weaving herself into a cocoon of silence. At first, she might not have even been aware of why she had drawn this space around her or why it was important. But in doing so, she had created the perfect space for her transformation from one state of being to another, and then she marked this inner change with the ritual of decorating her room with the perfect symbol of transformation: butterflies.

I received a phone call early the following morning from her father. "I wish you were here to see what I see. It's a miracle. The evergreen bushes outside Missy's room are filled with butterflies. I don't know why, it's never happened before," he whispered, his voice choked with awe.

✶✶✶

When Cori, a tiny premature newborn who had spent months hanging on by a slender thread, slowly grew and was moved from the hospital's NICU to the transitional care unit, the staff and her family celebrated. When she was at last discharged for home, albeit still considered fragile, she was accompanied by only a ventilator and part-time nursing. Her lungs and immature organs were slowly growing and everyone was optimistic; the ICU staff even had a discharge party. Cori's mother was supported with weekly home visits from me.

Many months later, Cori had not only survived an uncertain beginning but was a thriving fifteen month old, on the cusp of slowly being weaned from the necessity of the ventilator. She was a happy and content baby. Although you couldn't hear her laughter in an audible way because of her tracheostomy, her dimpled, round face lit up the room and our hearts. Her mother and I talked about her developing personality, her laughter, her always-smiling face, and agreed that she looked like a buddha-baby radiating contentment and joy.

Early one Friday morning, Cori was unexpectedly admitted through the ER to the pediatric intensive care unit. She had suffered extreme oxygen deprivation during the night due to an error that a new night nurse had made related to the ventilation apparatus. Although doubtful, the neurologist took a wait-and-see attitude for the next several days about the possibility of Cori's recovery, hoping that perhaps the brain swelling would go down. The weekend was heavy with grief. Cori's family and many of the staff, including me, found ourselves holding our breath as time slowed down to an unbearable and unchanging landscape of dread and uncertainty. Hours and minutes seemed stagnant that weekend as nothing changed, and it became increasingly unlikely that anything would.

Dread hung like a gray cloud over the intensive care unit on Monday morning as we waited for the team of specialists to arrive. A somber group of us gathered in the conference room for the results of her most recent brain scans. Cori's family was told by the team of specialists that she had lost so much oxygen that her brain had suffered irreparable brain damage and would never recover, leaving her essentially "brain dead." They went on to explain that although her small heart was beating and lungs working because of the ventilator, she would permanently remain in a vegetative state because too much brain tissue had died due to oxygen deprivation. They recommended that she be removed from the vent and allowed to die.

Sorrow filled the room and Cori's mother protested. "This vent saved her life for all these months. I came to love it as a part of Cori. Now you want me to just unplug it? I just can't do that. I'd feel like I was agreeing to amputate one of her limbs."

The neurologist reassured her that it was her decision; he was only sharing the irrefutable facts, his recommendations, and her choices.

I left the hospital exhausted, sad, and disheartened. After parking in the underground garage, I went up to my apartment and threw myself across the bed. I don't think I fell asleep, but in a state between sleep and exhausted awareness, I was lucid dreaming.

I am back at the hospital and standing in the doorway of baby Cori's room. She is lying in the crib, pale, inanimate, the ventilator the only sound and movement in the room. No one else is present. I leave my body at the threshold. My spirit slides easily into her body. My consciousness joins hers. I experience dual awareness, both aware of each sensation and perception that she experiences—and simultaneously never losing a sense of myself. Within her body, I am aware of the rhythmic whooshing, tapping sounds of the ventilator, the feel of its expansion and contraction. I hear other sounds from within the room, a beeping, voices in the outer area, a distant phone ringing. I sense random individuals as shadows walking by the room.

And then, a pulsing and radiant light pouring through many various geometric shapes grows in front of us, dominating and pushing away everything else. This magnetic and compelling light pouring through each shape is reaching out for the little spirit—whose body I am temporarily cohabitating. Awareness of everything except them falls away for a few seconds as the light and energy envelop us in peace.

The peace and light are interrupted by a jarring physical motion as we are picked up, the tubing that was lying across the inanimate body is adjusted. We are handed into waiting, warm arms, swaddled and held close to loving familiarity. The shapes of light have moved to the farthest corner of the room. There's confusion, between longing for the emanating light pouring from the shapes and longing for the familiar comfort of the body holding us as tears fall from above. The arms holding us tighten, a murmuring voice of rhythm and sounds.

Slowly something changes as the softly spoken words are replaced by a distinct loosening of energy and emotion, a letting go filled with loving release and permission. In the same moment, the light becomes nearly blinding as the geometric shapes again draw closer, dominating the small room until only they exist. The diamond shape draws closest and clearer than any of the others, lit from within and radiating outwardly, calling and compelling me toward it. As baby Cori moves toward this light and crosses through the diamond threshold moving out of the hospital room, I begin to separate from her spirit. My last view of her is with hundreds of bluebirds in flight. I am crying as I sit up saying "fly baby bird, fly."

Slightly disoriented I looked at the nearby clock. I was so tired—the difficult weekend work had caught up with me, it was only 6:40 p.m. I looked for my hospital pager to place it by my bed in case I was paged during the night and realized that I had mistakenly left it in the car. I found the pager and saw that the hospital had already tried to reach me several times. When I called the unit, I was told baby Cori had just died. I drove back across town, numb with fatigue, not thinking of anything except getting to the family in a timely and safe manner.

I found Cori's family tearfully gathered in the visitors' lounge. Cori's mother asked me if I would go outside with her for a few moments while she got some fresh air and had a smoke. Her family waited upstairs in the lounge.

Cori's mother told me that she had sent her family for dinner, needing time to be by herself. She then asked the nurses if she could hold Cori. She described to me that as she sat weeping, her tears fell on Cori's baby face.

"I didn't exactly pray, it was more thinking and talking to her, but it was a prayer of sorts. I told her that I just couldn't take her off the vent, it was such a part of her and had kept her with me. I told her I loved her and, if it was time for her to go, it was okay and she could leave me. I said I would never forget her and had learned so much from her. 'You can let go and just leave,' I told her. 'I want you to be free, so it's okay to let go if you need to go now.' That's exactly what happened. I finished my little prayer, and Cori let go."

As she finished her story of the last moments of Cori's life, there, in a small tree, its branches covered in snow, sat a bluebird singing its heart out to the February cold and frosty early evening sky. I recalled my dream but didn't share it, not yet. I could not bring myself to speak it aloud, although for a moment I felt there might be a connection.

Cori's grandparents hosted a brunch following the memorial service a few days later. We were just finishing up when Cori's grandmother walked to the kitchen sink to rinse some dishes. She suddenly gestured urgently to us, pointing at the windowsill. "Come slowly," she cautioned. "Look, there's a bluebird sitting on my windowsill. It's February and so cold outside. There's not another bird around. I've never seen a bird like that in this part of the country. I think it must be a sign from Cori."

We gathered at the sink, arms spontaneously linking as we silently gazed in awe at the vivid, deep-blue bird on the snow-covered window ledge, each of us dazzled at the mystery as the bird opened its beak and we heard its faint song through the closed window. It was then that I found the courage to share my experience of the night that Cori lay dying in her mother's arms, drawn toward the diamond light and the promise of bluebirds.

"In the moment when the Cherubim lift up their wings from Below to Above (the sacred symbols by which the universe was created) Fly from above and below, and they meet each other in flight. They then merge together and kiss one another with the kiss of Love until all the universes become one and the Sacred Wellspring becomes one-unified in a total union that is without any separateness whatsoever."

I received a Christmas card from Cori's mother the following December of the painting "Night and Her Train of Stars." The picture is stunning. An angel is covered in blue feathers and is carrying a baby swaddled in a blanket of blue feathers. I was curious and searched, eventually learning that the painting was based on the poem by William Ernest Henley, "Margaritae Sorori."[1]

A late lark twitters from the quiet skies:
And from the west
Where the sun, his day's work ended,
Lingers as in content,
There falls on the old, grey city
An influence luminous and serene,
A shining peace.
The smoke ascends
In a rosy-and-golden haze. The spires
Shine, and are changed. In the valley
Shadows rise, The lark sings on. The sun
Closing his benediction,
Sinks, and the darkening air
Thrills with a sense of the triumphing night—So be my passing!
My task accomplished and the long day done,
My wages taken, and in my heart
Some late lark singing,
Let me be gathered to the quiet west,
The sundown splendid and serene, Death.

19.

Purification—The Inner Fire

*We only live, only suspire, consumed by either fire or fire ... And all
shall be well and
All manner of thing shall be well
When the tongues of flame are in-folded
Into the crowned knot of fire
And the fire and the rose are one.*

T.S. Eliot, *Four Quartets*, "Little Gidding"

Throughout this time, I began to experience subtle and then not-so-subtle energetic shifts in myself. At times the energy was like a slowly meandering river until I'd hit an eddy where the water slowed and dammed up around an obstruction before eventually opening again, pushing me into challenging rapids. Frequently, the feeling of obstructed energy took a parallel course of feeling blocked in my therapeutic work, followed by making huge gains in insight and resolution of long-held-back trauma.

The energy became accessible to me—visually and physically—with each death slowly breaking me open to see everything, including myself, in new ways. Over time, these experiences extended to every part of my life. A tsunami of energy overwhelmed me, with heart palpitations, pressure in my chest or head. Extreme fluctuations of energy—or depletion of it—colored my days. Light bulbs blew out when I walked into rooms as well as other odd phenomena. Naive and having no way to understand or even articulate what was occurring, I felt helpless and overwhelmed. I found myself worrying that the erratic, unpredictable fluctuations of energy might mean I had some grave illness.

I didn't see the connection between these gifts emerging from my work and the unbearable intensity and discomfort of my nights. My therapist had no idea what was happening. When I reported my concerns to my primary care doctor, he was initially concerned, and so began a series of evaluations. A brain tumor, endocrine disorder, menopausal symptoms, cardiac issues, and more were all ruled out. I was told there simply was nothing wrong with me, these symptoms did not seem related to any known physical or mental illness. I was both relieved and discouraged, still having no idea what was happening.

One night, I woke for the third time around two in the morning, drenched in sweat. Anxiety flooded me as I experienced music and light radiating throughout my bedroom from no physical source. After once again changing my nightwear, I paced. Finally, in desperation, I prayed like I had so often throughout my childhood. I begged for a guardian angel's protection. For a moment I grew still, exhausted from the effort. Then I heard a distinct, inner voice directing me to go to the closet where I stored old tapes and to get one. I pulled out an unopened tape, still wrapped in its original plastic—songs and lullabies for children, something I had bought when working with very young children years before in private practice. I began to put it back on the shelf and the inner voice unmistakably said: "This one."

Suddenly alert, I sat up straight and listened intently as the music began to play a simple lullaby about angels surrounding me. I played that song more than a dozen times that night. The lyrics soothed me, swaddling me in a deep peace I hadn't felt since falling in love with earth and sky in South Dakota and listening to the choir rehearsals I sought through elementary school. I turned off the tape player and sat, savoring the quiet. It was then that the inner voice directed me back to the storage closet.

For over a year, I had randomly experienced books lighting up in bookstores. The other books would seem dark and the text unreadable next to whatever book seemed to be calling my attention. When I had time to open the particular book, I found it held no interest for me. Slowly, over many months, books stacked up on the storage shelf in the closet. This night, I was directed to one of them. As I pulled it off the shelf, I remembered the day I'd bought it. My friend Lyndall and I had eaten lunch and then stopped at a nearby bookstore. As we walked out of the store, Lyndall asked me what I had purchased. I had stammered that I didn't know, it just kind of lit up. Curious herself, she suggested we take a look. "*Opening to Inner Light: The Transformation of Human Nature and Consciousness* by Ralph Metzner, Ph.D.," Lyndall read.[1]

I had no idea why I would buy something like that and asked Lyndall if she wanted it. She told me that she thought I should keep it and that there must be some reason it had lit up.

Sitting in the rocking chair, I opened the book to a random chapter and my eyes fell on the title, "Kundalini and the Yoga of Fire." I read: "When Kundalini is awakened, through conscious yogic practice, the fiery energy passes up though the body's energy centers, energizing them and burning off the 'coverings' that block or dwarf their expression, finally to unite with the spiritual consciousness in the 'crown chakra' at the top of the head."

I found myself entering a foreign territory where I couldn't understand the language, except the little I had begun to hear at work about energy in the form of Healing Touch classes that some of the nurses were taking. One day I was in a room with a young Hmong child with leukemia when some of the grandmothers from the Hmong community arrived with large baskets filled with warm, hard-boiled eggs. They took the eggs, peeled them, and placed them on the child's body, rolling them around until they turned black. They would then throw the egg away and begin with another. The child's mother explained that they were using the energy of the eggs like a poultice to remove blockages and heat from her boy's energy body. A few days later a shaman from Peru was using smooth rocks to pull out blockages from his nephew for the same purpose. It didn't matter if the practitioner used their hands, as was the case with nurses learning Reiki or Healing Touch, or eggs or stones. Each healer was working directly with energy, although using a different cultural lens and practice.

In Eastern traditions an understanding of the energy body is taught and worked with through ancient teachings and techniques. All spiritual traditions speak of a "fire" or "baptism by fire" that purifies and burns out impurities. In Buddhism, as well as in the practice of yoga and other forms of meditation, the body and psyche are purified and prepared over a long period of time by the purposeful activation of a reservoir of energy that lies dormant in the spine of every human.

This force of heat and fire is seen by many spiritual traditions and in the growing work of spiritual intelligences, mysterious and intelligent, transformative, evolutionary forces that purify, on a cellular level, everything that is no longer needed for each individual's transformation, and ultimately the evolution of the planet. In its journey upward through each of the chakras or gateways, the rising energy burns away blockages within that part of the individual.

Kundalini can be triggered by many things. In addition to devotion, longing, and the commitment that often accompany an ongoing spiritual practice, it can begin spontaneously during trauma, childbirth, and other experiences. For individuals who have no preparation or experience, the dramatic extremes and the puzzling symptoms create disruption and discomfort. Many of the symptoms are masked as physical problems, which increases confusion for an individual and for medical and mental health providers.

Throughout the next several weeks I learned more about this transformational energetic process known as "kundalini awakening," or in my case "kundalini crisis." There were others who had experienced a kundalini crisis with heightened perceptions, visions, inner pressure in the head, electrical charges, uncontrolled muscle spasms, pressure in the chest around the heart, sensations of burning, or intense heat concentrated on particular organs and areas of the body. I didn't have one symptom that had not been studied as a part of the experiences of those experiencing "kundalini crisis."

What was occurring as a normal, transformational process was actually accelerating my therapy and ultimate integration. It was now clear why I had recorded months of dreams about fires in my journal. At the time, I could see them only as related to the fire of my childhood, and then to the fire my mother was in. I began to sense that the pattern of buying books beyond my volitional thinking brain's decision to do so was being activated by an "evolutionary impulse," a term I had read in the chapter I had blindly opened to.

In the kundalini literature, St. John of the Cross and St. Catherine, who were both considered Christian mystics, wrote profusely about their experiences using words like "purifying fires of love," "the divine furnace," and "the soul's innermost fiery probe." The topic of unexpected kundalini awakening was researched in the 1970s by Dr. Lee Sannella, a reputable San Francisco-based psychiatrist who wrote *The Kundalini Experience: Psychosis or Transcendence* after seeing many cases of what he called "kundalini syndrome."[2] He worked on developing diagnostic criteria for distinguishing the difference between what he had come to see as a healthy transformational process when handled well with support and a true psychotic breakdown. It's unfortunate that so few psychiatrists know anything about this body of work and can see certain behaviors and human experiences only through the view of psychiatric diagnosis.

The next morning, I called my friend, Alla Renée Bozarth, in Oregon. In addition to being known as one of the first eleven women ordained within the Episcopal Church, she was a prolific writer and viewed by many as a mystic. I was hopeful that she might be able to provide me with some guidance.

Alla immediately said that she was happy I had called because she had woken in the middle of the night and been directed to pray that I would meet my angels. I described the sequence of events from the night before and asked her if she thought I might be experiencing kundalini. "Yes, and you need to get yourself to a good body worker who knows how to help you work with this. Don't go to someone inexperienced or it could make it much worse."

She told me about the Spiritual Emergence Network, an organization that started in California to support individuals experiencing psycho-spiritual difficulties, including kundalini crisis. They had no answers for me, but they advised me that it could be helpful to begin a meditation practice.

As the kundalini continued, it was essential to develop a spiritual practice as a form of reorientation. Within the next month, what I needed fell into place through another series of synchronistic experiences. I was led to a meditation teacher and then to Lois, a gifted body worker. In time, I took yoga classes and tai chi.

The ebbs and flows of the kundalini continued, but for the most part they were smoother, and less confusing and jarring. I grew adept at directing the energy. As I trusted this process, I saw the symptoms as the wisdom of my body, providing me with a source of information and shining a light on where I needed healing.

About a year had passed since I had first come to an understanding of the kundalini process. During this time, I experienced three distinct types of awareness: cognitive, intuitive, and transcendent. It was helpful for me to have a language to describe the different ways awareness came to me, particularly transcendent awareness. This type of awareness was described as an awareness unbounded by time and matter; a way of knowing that represents an exchange of energy occurring without rational thought and an awareness of expanded consciousness itself, or entering into the quantum field.

Later, I came across an insightful excerpt from *Holistic Nursing: A Handbook for Practice*, written by Barbara Dossey and Lynn Keegan.

> Transcendent awareness is that of spiritual awareness. Transcendent is not bound by time or matter. It is a way of knowing that represents an exchange of energy occurring without rational thought … knowledge that flows directly from one's soul or spirit. Within a person, each of these three types of awareness is synthesized into a resource of inner wisdom that may be tapped through self-reflection activities … Transcendent awareness or spiritual, transcendence, is the knowledge that one has a spiritual connection to something greater than the self—a fundamental unity with nature.

Reading this was validating and gave me the language to better describe my experiences. One afternoon, I was at work, sitting at my desk thumbing through a booklet that highlighted primary-care physicians in the new network our employee insurance provider was changing to the following month. I needed to find a doctor who could help me distinguish between kundalini and medical symptoms. I laughed out loud at how ridiculous that seemed, but read on and came to a page with a picture of a female family physician that grabbed my attention. There was something about her face that drew me in. I read through her brief bio, which ended by saying that Dr. Jan Adams frequently recommended yoga and meditation to her patients. This, in and of itself, was rare at the time. I got excited and noticed an increase in heat slowly moving up my spine. Perhaps I had found a doctor who might at least try to understand my experiences with kundalini. But her medical clinic was over an hour south of the Minneapolis, St. Paul metro area. My rational brain protested that this was too far to drive to see a doctor.

I struck a bargain with myself, between intuition and rationality. If she could offer me what I needed, I'd be willing to drive that far and, if not, I would find someone closer to home. The doubting part of me was skeptical about finding a physician who understood kundalini. A few weeks later found me waiting a little nervously in an examining room of the pleasant, small-town clinic for my new patient visit. Dr. Jan came into the room and sat down. She appeared to emanate an aura of light, an undeniable presence of compassion. She asked me to tell her about myself. I took a deep breath and dove right in.

"I know this might be hard to understand, or not in your scope of practice, but I'm looking for a doctor who can help me as I navigate through ongoing kundalini arousal states."

"Yes, please continue," she encouraged.

"I need a doctor who can help me distinguish the difference between kundalini symptoms versus symptoms that require a medical approach," I continued in a rush as I felt my energy quickening.

"Well, it looks like you've come to the right place. I've had my own kundalini awakening and believe I have a lot of experience and knowledge to help you."

That first visit continued for the next hour, during which I had the most thorough and complete interview and physical exam of my life. Dr. Jan talked to me about nutrition, synchronicities, and ongoing symptoms and progress with the kundalini, for which she had very specific and helpful suggestions. About six months after I began seeing her, I had a dream in which we were both at a conference. The next day at my appointment, the first question she asked me was about my dream life.

"Funny you should ask," I answered. "I had a dream about you last night."

"Tell me," Dr. Jan encouraged.

"We were at a conference of some sort together; I think it had to do with spirituality. I turned to you and asked you if you would be my mentor."

I suddenly felt very self-conscious as she patiently waited. I stalled, worrying that she might think that by even telling her about the dream would seem like I had an expectation. She finally broke the silence and looked at me. "You'll have to ask," she said.

My face turned red with embarrassment. "Will you?" I stammered.

"Of course. I said yes in the dream, didn't I, it's already been prearranged."

20.

The Cat from Hell, 1995

The dream is the small hidden door in the deepest and most intimate sanctum of the soul, which opens to that primeval cosmic night that was soul long before there was conscious ego and will be soul far beyond what a conscious ego could ever reach.

Carl Jung, *The Meaning of Psychology for Modern Man* (1934)

I grew in exponential leaps, both psychologically and spiritually, throughout the mid-1990s. Most important, this was a time when my rejection of all things spiritual fell away. I saw that my resistance had been embedded in the belief that spirituality was directly tied to religion. Unbraiding these two concepts was liberating and freed me up to devote myself to healing on every level.

The year 1995 was especially transformative as I experienced many out-of-the-ordinary, synchronistic, and ongoing experiences with kundalini. My nights were filled with vivid dreams, frequently waking me up in heightened states of consciousness. It pushed and prodded me toward continued healing. It opened the doorway to my body and its deepest physical, mental, and energetic blockages. For the first time in my life, I felt grounded and at home in my body.

Throughout this time, I had one tornado dream after another where I barely escaped their threat. In one, I hid under tables in a public place. In another, I was outside and just managed to find safety. At the time, I had a sense that the dreams were preparing me for another major life change, just as the tornado dream had initiated my move to Minnesota in 1984. Over the years, I came to trust that tornado dreams came to me when I was about to go through some kind of powerful turning point.

One night, I had a dream that initially left me both confused and intrigued.

I'm dreaming that Dave arrives in a white pickup truck; in the back is a gift for me. The parking lot is crowded with cars so he parks quite a distance from the entrance where I'm standing. Dave opens the tailgate and a white baby elephant jumps down and runs toward me, making a trumpeting sound of greeting. I gasp in dismay as it nearly gets hit by a car. This baby elephant seems to know me and comes straight to me and lifts its trunk and strokes my cheek while gazing deeply into my eyes. My heart opens. Dave stands slightly to the back of him and asks what I think of the present. I am overwhelmed with gratitude and uncertain what I'll do with it.

I tell Dave that I feel torn because I love his present but can't have animals in the apartment building where I live. He suggests some friends who live in the country and reloads the baby elephant back onto the truck. I drive to the country a few days later and the elephant is in a distant field. As soon as it sees me, it again runs toward me and gets tangled up in barbed wire. I hold my breath, concerned for this little one's safety, but it manages to untangle itself and come to the fence line where I'm standing. Its little white head again lifts its trunk and begins to stroke my cheek while gazing deeply into my eyes.

At the time, I saw the dream as a message that the loving gift of the innocent baby elephant was having difficulty getting to me: there were obstacles in the way. I had no understanding at the time of the meaning of the white elephant itself, or what obstacles I might be about to face, but the images and feelings of the dream continued to linger. The elephant would play a significant role in events as they played out several months later.

In June of 1995, Dr. Jan encouraged me to attend a retreat on "The Divine Feminine" in Baton Rouge, led by a friend of hers, Gloria Karpinski. Several years before, I had read Gloria's book, *Where Two Worlds Touch: Spiritual Rites of Passage,* deepening my understanding of spirituality as a birthright.[1] I now see clearly that what had happened to me within the Episcopal Church had been deeply traumatic and impacted my connection to religion, but the same connection with spirit that nourished me throughout my life was still very much vibrant and alive, even during the years of my anguish and despair. When I first read Gloria's book, I'd found myself drawn to her. One night, I'd even impulsively called her, but when she picked up, I immediately hung up in self-doubt.

On the first day we were each asked to tell a story about ourselves as a child in front of the entire group. I related the story of Dale and Diane. I felt cautiously empowered to speak for the first time of my mother's life of prostitution. This experience helped me begin to break down the walls between the life I'd lived with my mother and the life I now lived as a therapist and a spiritual seeker.

The last day of the retreat, I was sent on a wild goose chase, only to return to the large gathering room and discover it had been prepared for a coronation. I was deeply moved as it became clear that the room had been prepared for me and that Gloria and the group were about to crown me "Queen for a Day." Late-afternoon sun streamed through the windows as music played—the exact music my childhood friend Barbara and I had hummed as we crowned Diane queen all those years before. I returned home from the retreat filled with connection to community support, validation, and new friendships. I made internal shifts that I barely had the language for, but I knew something was changing inside me.

Before leaving for Baton Rouge, I had undergone a series of scans and tests for problems with my large bowel. After returning home from the retreat, I was seen by the colon surgeon who went over all of the test results and scheduled exploratory surgery a couple of weeks later, to rule out "likely colon cancer." Two days later, I was in a car accident that left me with a closed head injury and a year of rehab at the local brain injury program. Colon surgery was delayed until August when I would be stabilized enough to undergo anesthesia. Throughout the slow recovery

Dr. Jan Adams, left, with Gloria, both influential characters in my life, and me with Gloria

I experienced challenges with word retrieval and difficulty organizing anything sequentially. The kundalini energy seemed to accelerate and intensify during this period, as did my dream life. I had another tornado dream, significant in its differences from any of the others and which reminded me of a very similar dream I had as a child.

A tornado comes and lifts me into its very center where it is calm. There is a very old woman with a sunbaked, wrinkled face and a little girl, around six or seven, who looks much like myself at that age. I am in awe that it is so calm in the center of this giant beast of a storm. I watch as my furniture, my mother, and others are tossed around on the outside of the rotating column of energy. Initially, I'm enthralled by the awareness that it is calm in the center. Then I begin to worry that although calm now, I might get hurt or lost when the tornado drops me. As soon as those thoughts occur, I am swept to the outer edges of the tornado and am nearly hit in the head by the furniture flying around me. I try to remember the Twenty-Third Psalm, "The Lord is my shepherd …," but falter until the child reaches for my hand and recites the words for me until I can join in. We are then set down gently in a beautiful field of wildflowers. I awaken laughing aloud with the realization that I've just discovered that it is calm in the center when I turn my focus away from fear.

The week of surgery both took forever in coming and at the same time seemed to arrive too quickly. I did everything I could to get ready for it. I had a gathering of friends and hosted a meditation circle. The day before the surgery I noticed a male cardinal sitting on the tree outside the front door. I remember being told by my first spiritual teacher, an Elder in the Cherokee tradition, that cardinals often appear as spiritual messengers. As I left my appointment for energy work with Lois, another male cardinal was sitting in a branch hanging directly over my car.

My next stop was to meet with Jan. She explained to me that the surgery was going to be difficult, but if I could see it as a form of "spiritual initiation," and hold that concept central throughout whatever might happen, I would be alright and later find that I had moved to a new place on my spiritual path.

A male and female cardinal appeared on the railing of her deck when Jan stepped out of the room. I sat thinking about her words as the cardinals began to sing in unison. Jan returned with a cup of broth and a bowl of warm water filled with floating rose petals, and proceeded to conduct a ritual of anointing me with essential oil and then washing my feet in the rose water. The cardinals stayed watchful throughout the ritual. I later read the following quote from Dr. Jean Shinoda Bolen's book, *Close to the Bone*.

> Sometimes I wonder if a life-threatening illness or condition is a last-ditch opportunity to pay attention to soul needs for authentic expression, for creativity, for intimacy, for solitude, for retreat inward, for something significant to happen. Perhaps when all else has failed to call attention to pain at the soul level, disease not only may result but may become the means through which we go inward to find buried feelings and cut-off or dismembered aspects of ourselves.[2]

The next day, the surgeon told me that the good news was that he had found no evidence of cancer. The bad news, he had found yards of necrotic/dead colon. He explained that my entire colon was dead and he had no idea why. "It's as though you've already had radiation treatment," he explained.

He had removed all but a few inches of my large bowel and left a very small portion so that I wouldn't have to have a colostomy at that time. Although that portion was also dead tissue, he thought I would have gravity on my side to keep my food moving.

I was discharged several days later. I asked the doctor what kind of diet I should be on and he said that I could eat whatever I wanted, there were no restrictions, but he would have the dietician come up and talk to me before I left. The dietician reiterated what the doctor had told me and said there were no special orders for me, so I could eat whatever I wanted and to just pay attention to what I was hungry for.

I took the dietician and physician at their word and asked the friend who picked me up from the hospital to stop at a nearby store and pick up fresh-squeezed orange juice and a few other things. The first thing I did when I got home was pour myself a glass of orange juice. Within several minutes I was vomiting blood—a lot of blood—bleeding that wouldn't stop. I was rushed back to the hospital and back into surgery to close the ulceration at the surgical site caused by the acidity of the orange juice.

I remember very little of this time in intensive care, except one thing remains inspiring to this day. Over the next several days, both in and out of consciousness, awake or asleep, I dreamed.

I was in the presence of the now fully grown white elephant from my earlier dream. Also, a very old weathered-looking indigenous woman and little girl were there. A gold box descended through a stream of light while we were sitting on the elephant's back. It was filled with jewels, ribbons, and paints of rich colors of gold and silver, and other decorative objects to be used to adorn the elephant. I felt pure joy and laughed out loud as the older woman, child, and I embellished the elephant in jewels, soon to remove them and begin again, and again. The elephant and these activities of sacred ritual seemed to act as a symbol between the divine realm and my hospital bed.

The second time I was discharged, I asked the doctor if I should go home since I was running a temperature. He told me not to worry about it, that wasn't uncommon. I kept rapidly losing weight, had little tolerance for food and difficulty keeping it down. A couple of days later, weak and light-headed, I was running a high fever. My friend Barb insisted I call Jan, who admitted me to the hospital in Shakopee. My lab tests revealed a urinary tract infection and "medically induced malnutrition." Despite having a colon surgeon and upper GI specialist, records revealed that neither one of them had ordered total parenteral nutrition (TPN), usually given through an IV when a patient is recovering from surgery and can't ingest enough nutrients by mouth for a significant period of time.

Discharged several days later and free of infection following IV antibiotics, and happy to be home, I was nauseated much of the time, making it difficult to eat. My energy started to ramp up to a level I hadn't experienced before. A week passed with no relief and I intended to phone Jan, but she was out of town.

Light bulbs burned out every time I entered a room. I saw energy around the plants in my apartment and circling the trees and flowers out the window. One long, sleepless night, I filled a journal with inspiration I heard through the song of a grasshopper on my balcony, teaching me things I hadn't previously known about, like how geometric shapes are the matrix of everything. In my journal I recorded things I saw happening in the future: a time we would have a need to remember passwords for everything, the manufacturing of cell phones, two controversial wars the United States would enter into, food that would be genetically modified that wouldn't be healthy to eat, and even how my small, inexpensive countertop microwave was leaking radiation. I managed to carry it to the basement dumpster myself that night.

Barb stopped to check on me the next day. I told her about the grasshopper and how I wrote through the night. She noticed my missing microwave and told me I was manic and should go to the hospital. However, another friend arrived who understood energy and thought she could help me get stabilized from the kundalini crisis I was in. I agreed with her and saw no reason to go to be medically assessed, but Barb disagreed and called 911.

The police arrived with paramedics and strongly suggested, since Barb clearly believed I was in trouble, it wouldn't hurt to get checked out. Although upset about this, I agreed to go. On the way to the emergency room, I was concerned when I noticed the direction they were driving. "What hospital are you taking me to?" I inquired.

"Southdale."

"It's not in my insurance network, please don't take me there," I replied, concerned about out-of-pocket expenses.

On arrival at Southdale, the ambulance driver was told they couldn't see me because I was not in their network. We were redirected to my in-network hospital. A physician met with me in the ER. After a series of questions, he told me I was suffering from "a post-surgical reaction to extreme weight loss and inability to sleep." He recommended that I stay in the hospital for a night or two so they could check my labs and get me stabilized. It was my choice. I agreed and was admitted to the psychiatric unit. They gave me a sedative and I slept deeply. By the next day my thinking had slowed down to normal.

Jan came to see me later in the day. She brought me her two-hundred-years-old Tibetan prayer beads that had been in the monastery with His Holiness the Dalai Lama before he fled Tibet. She said that I could use them for as long as I needed to keep my energy grounded. She also suggested that if I laid them on my abdomen when I was in pain, they would help. The beads acted like a poultice, becoming warm and pulling out abdominal discomfort. I went home the following day.

I continued to recover over the next number of months. At Jan's recommendation, I started to attend weekend retreats several times a year with a spiritual teacher named Barbara, a friend of hers who would be starting to work with a new, select group of students in Minnesota. Barbara was gifted at bringing together the mystical teachings from many diverse spiritual traditions. In her view, the years of psychological and spiritual exploration of my interior landscape had provided the preparation for the time of spiritual acceleration I was experiencing.

In ancient mystical traditions, death and rebirth, either symbolic or literal, were signs of initiation. In any true initiation there is a place of transition. What I had experienced was just such an initiation. Jan in her wisdom was able to discern this possibility in creating the ritual of blessing and washing my feet in rose water as she prepared me for surgery. She had set the stage for the ultimate positive outcome and a way to make meaning of the challenges throughout the experience. The cardinals appearing that day were messengers that bore witness as they sat watching on her deck. The dreams had also helped prepare me for surgery and its subsequent obstacles to healing. This period of time anchored me and deepened my spiritual life as well as giving me an ongoing spiritual community along with the meditation groups that Jan led.

During an individual session at a retreat with Barbara, I was surprised when she singled me out and instructed me to get a kitten. Although hesitant, I trusted Barbara. So, I looked in the local paper and found someone looking for homes for kittens and that day brought home an adorable, striped-orange tabby with golden eyes. I named him Honey.

Within days I was frantic. Honey wasn't as sweet as the name might convey. He repeatedly pounced on me in the middle of the night. I tried to lock him out of the bedroom, but he scratched on the door, crying so loudly I was certain the neighbors would complain. One night I was jarred awake when he landed on my chest and sunk those sharp kitty claws into me. Half asleep, I angrily pulled him off my chest, drawing blood, and hurled him off the bed. Furious, I'd thrown him a little too hard and he hit the wall and wailed as though he were injured. I felt terrible and decided that I had to get rid of him the next day because he was bringing up a level of anger I had never experienced before. I might really hurt him the next time. I took a picture of him, put it on the bulletin board at the hospital, and delivered him to his new home late that afternoon, relieved that I was done with him.

Barbara called shortly after I returned home—minus one annoying cat. "How's things going with the new kitten?"

"I just gave him away. I couldn't keep him," I confessed.

"Well, you'll just have to get him back," she scolded.

"But why? I'm afraid that I'll hurt him or even kill him. He wakes me in the middle of the night and I get so furious when he wakes me out of a dead sleep," I confessed.

Barbara was quiet for several minutes. "You need to call the woman you gave him to and explain you made a mistake and would like to pick him up."

"But why?" I protested.

"He's exactly what I had hoped for, he's perfect for you at this time in your life. He's helping you get in touch with your injured instincts and your anger," Barbara said.

Reluctantly, I agreed and hung up the phone. He was back with me late the next afternoon. It was amazing how something so little and so darn cute could activate such unbridled rage in me. He became known to friends as "the cat from hell" or "the little shit." He woke me at night by jumping up with his paws and turned on the overhead light, jarring me awake, my entire body shaking. While taking a shower in the morning, he jumped up and turned the lights off with his paws.

I hadn't seen Lois for bodywork in a while and I resumed seeing her as well as working with my anger in therapy. Within a short time, I had several realizations. The most important one was a promise I had made to myself as a child: that I would never be like my mother, never be rageful like she was or many of the men that came into our lives. I had repressed my anger and Barbara had intuited my need to come to terms with it. Honey became the catalyst for all of my repressed and uncomfortable feelings of anger to emerge. As a child, I'd so often been violently awakened from deep sleep, my normal instincts to protest in anger or cry out had been frozen and stored deeply in my nervous system. Being suddenly jarred awake in the middle of the night by Honey activated all the years of pent-up, frozen anger that I seldom expressed as a child. I realized that Honey indeed was my teacher and was allowing me to access "state-dependent memories" that could be reached only when I was in a similar state—vulnerable and unexpectedly awakened from a deep sleep.

In an intense bodywork session with Lois, I finally *truly* moved through all the rage. It was that day that Honey calmed down and the "crazy cat" behavior ended. I then nicknamed him "Velcro" because he became such a loving boy, always sticking close by in the same room, sitting on my lap or cuddled up next to me. I didn't know that in splitting off my anger and numbing myself to it, I cut out other aspects of my fullness. I began to notice subtle changes in myself. I felt bolder about stating my opinion or preferences. I also felt more joy and spontaneity.

At Jan's encouragement, I wrote a short story entitled "Queen for a Day," which was published in the literary journal *Scrivener's Rampant*.[3] After writing about Dale and Diane, I found myself thinking about them and set out in search of each of them. In the early summer of 1986, I found Diane, the woman I had crowned Queen for a Day in the Osco drugstore. We enjoyed a wonderful afternoon together. She not only clearly remembered me but told me how much I had helped her. She had never been very good in school and hadn't gone on to college because she didn't think she was smart enough. She told me that she felt inspired by my trust in her. After seeing me all these years later, she told me she would never again underestimate how you can impact another person's life by small acts of caring.

After reconnecting with Diane, I became even more determined to find Dale, longing to thank the woman who had made such a difference in my life. After months of searching, I remembered she had said she and Dick were moving to Blue Island, Illinois, a small, blue-collar town south of Chicago, so that her husband could become a policeman. I called the local police department and was told that Dale and Dick had divorced but that Dale still lived in town. I dialed the number they gave me, trembling with excitement and also with worry that she might have forgotten me. She picked up on the first ring. I recognized her voice immediately and told her who I was. She didn't seem surprised. She said that I had always been her "heart child" and of course she had never forgotten me and had hoped that I would get in touch with her one day.

Two weeks later, I flew to see her. I had carried her image, voice, words, and touch for thirty-eight years. Her striking, simple beauty and presence again moved me. It was as though all those years of longing and separation fell away. I was no longer a child wearing a face immobilized by fear, but she recognized me. And I remembered and re-experienced the directness of her gaze, and the love that poured forth from her. Once again, her presence enveloped me.

For years following Dale's move, I had imagined her living in a big house, surrounded by loving children of her own. But Dale had suffered through domestic violence of her own and eventually a divorce. She had given birth to one child, a troubled alcoholic son. She told me she had barely graduated from elementary school; she had always had difficulty learning and had been labeled as borderline retarded. She was very poor; she lived in an economically depressed neighborhood, hardly making ends meet on a maid's salary. In spite of all this, she had a deep serenity about her. Our first visit led to another and another, along with weekly phone calls. It became increasingly clear that Dale needed me in her life as much as I had once needed her.

Five months after our first visit, it became apparent that Dale was very sick. She had a wracking cough for several months that didn't stop. Soon after, she was diagnosed with advanced lung cancer. One day, Dale sat across from me, pale and barely eating. I began to cry and reached across the table to her, gently taking her hand. I told her how badly I felt that I hadn't found her years before. She answered me by saying that it was ok because I had found her and, now, she wasn't afraid to die because she had one good thing in her life. Dale smiled proudly and told me that her one act of kindness was like a ripple that went out in my life to touch others, so she felt ready to die knowing that. Over the next several months, I visited her as often as I could. On one of the last of those trips she was in the hospital. She asked me if she needed me, would I come, and I reassured her that of course I would.

One night, weeks later, I had a dream. *Dale was calling for me over and over again.* I woke around 5:00 a.m. remembering her words: "If I really needed you, would you come?" I reached for the phone and dialed the hospital where she had been undergoing palliative radiation treatment. The nurse informed me that Dale was actively dying and wasn't likely to make it through the day. A flight and several hours later, I walked into Dale's hospital room and told her I had heard her calling and had come. She nodded and weakly squeezed my hand.

As midday moved to afternoon, I sat next to Dale's bedside in vigil. At times the past and present merged as I contemplated the loss of her yet again. After being given something for pain, Dale slept deeply for a short while. There had been so much I'd wanted to give her, share with her, so much time we had missed together. And I thought of all the times I'd longed for her loving presence throughout my growing-up years.

Afternoon passed into evening as I watched the magnificent changing colors and patterns of the sky outside Dale's window. Time became measured by each of Dale's inhalations and exhalations, her life reduced to minutes, seconds, and heartbeats. As her breathing became increasingly labored, for a few moments my chest felt so full and tight that I could hardly breathe myself. I moved between grief and gratitude until they commingled and became one emotion. My heart and breath began to fall into rhythm with Dale's. I began to savor the intimacy and fullness of each moment: every inhalation, every exhalation. The air and energy between us became palpable, energized by a loving connection much greater than the two of us.

I felt Dale's body slowly shutting down, moving from the base of her spine upwards, beginning to pull away from the solid comfort of her physical form. I put on some music, hoping to help carry her to the edge; it seemed to calm her body's struggle. It calmed me. As Dale explored the outer limits of her consciousness, I too made a little more progress in my spiritual awakening, becoming a little less afraid and more awed by the territory expanding in front of me.

Dale grew bright red with heat and I began to notice a pattern. She seemed to be burning off around each chakra or energy center. I had seen this before with patients in my work, but was never able to be present for long enough to fully track it. The heat of this transformational fire slowly moved upwards in a distinct pattern, like a forest fire snaking up to the top of tall pine trees. It began first in her legs and then her torso. Eventually, the heat focused only in her face and the top of her head; her limbs had grown cold, still, and empty of any sign of life force.

Each breath became shallower and farther apart from the last. I prayed aloud the twenty-third psalm, the Tibetan prayer for the dying, anything and everything to stay focused and keep this bridge between us alive and intact. As I breathed with her, I felt more solid and anchored in the poignancy of every moment, awed at the territory of loving consciousness expanding in front of her and between us as she continued to slowly shed the skin of her body.

At 4:00 a.m., Dale took her last breath and left her body through the top of her head with a sigh and a small, peaceful smile. I had been with her for about sixteen hours. I witnessed the opening of her crown center at the top of her head and the birth of her spirit as she burned herself clear, her face radiant. As her body broke open, I was sprinkled with a little bit of that light.

Moving calmly and deliberately, I pushed the call button for the nurse. She came in briefly and said that I could stay as long as I wanted. I called Dale's son, focusing on compassion rather than anger at his inability or unwillingness to be present. I slowly and lovingly bathed Dale's body, put lotion on her hands and feet, honoring her life and our brief time together. I kissed her cheek one last time and left the body of the woman who had saved my life and opened me to love. I had carried her in my heart for nearly forty years and would continue to carry her the remainder of my days and beyond.

Outside, I was greeted by the sound of birds, singing to the golds and reds of a rising morning sun, as a full moon descended against a backdrop of fall-colored trees. As a child, I had learned in a deep sensate way that love is as essential to my life as oxygen, food, and water. On this glorious October morning, I was enveloped again in love's presence, connected to the essence of life and all things holy.

Dream Portal

If a man could pass through Paradise in a dream
and have a flower presented as a pledge
that his soul had really been there.
If he found that flower in his hand when he awoke;
Aye, and what then?

Samuel Taylor Coleridge, from the Unpublished Notebooks (1772–1834)

I returned to work two days after Dale's death in the autumn of 1997, the first of far too many deaths to keep count of over the course of the next few months. For a number of years I had been diligently working to integrate kundalini's ongoing presence in my life through meditation, acupuncture, psychotherapy, and energy work. Rather than getting stressed when I had trouble sleeping, I found it far more helpful to get up and use the creative energy that kundalini brought. Whenever the energy became heightened, or new "symptoms" occurred, it meant that another major clearing and integration of my psyche, spirit, and energy body was taking place. By now, I had experienced many spiritual teachings and had a better understanding of what was occurring in my life: an integrative transformation.

I had just emerged from the challenging memories of Thanksgiving. On top of my intense work schedule, I was spending the rest of the season alone as David was traveling with his father that year. Feeling disillusioned with the materialism and Hallmark attitude around the holidays, I yearned to make peace with it, to break free of all the associations and memories Christmas also held for me. I was frustrated with myself that after years of therapy, meditation, and serious spiritual practice I still couldn't overcome the associations with the ghosts of Christmas past.

Finally, as bedtime approached after a long and lonely Christmas Day, I was beginning to breathe a sigh of relief for having gotten through the day when the phone rang. "Lora, this is Dee, the charge nurse in the intensive care unit. Baby Anna unexpectedly died. Her family is beside themselves and really needs you. Can you come in?"

I groaned in response. "Oh no, those poor parents!"

I felt the devastation of Susan and Jack who had lost baby Anna's twin, Ashley, several months earlier. Since the birth of their premature, disabled twin girls over a year ago, I had come to know them intimately and we met regularly. At first, they were overwhelmed, but over time they had made peace with the reality that this unplanned pregnancy had resulted in the birth of extremely medically fragile babies who would always need extensive medical care. Just when they had finally moved to a place of acceptance, the first twin, Ashley, had died. The intervening months had been filled with grief. I had just met with them the week before Christmas and knew they had been looking forward to it, having found ways to honor Ashley's death and celebrate Anna's life. Now this! "All right, I'll be right there."

Hanging up the phone I was filled with panic. This would be the thirteenth death within a very short six weeks and I wondered if I was beginning to feel the effects of burnout. I felt overwhelmed and awash with fatigue and helplessness.

Going into work after what had already seemed like a long Christmas Day was the last thing that I wanted to do. On the drive to the hospital, I alternated between despair, confusion, and simmering anger. Something began to give way inside of me and I found myself screaming within the confines of the car to the cold night air. *Why on Christmas Day for God's sake? Why two babies in one year? How much can anyone be expected to bear?*

I shrieked my despair and confusion through the cold night at a God or higher power in which I had just rebuilt my faith. I suddenly no longer knew if I believed in anything. Surprised by the force of my feelings, I also felt resentful at being called out of my own apathy and darkness to attend to someone else's needs. I felt guilty at having such selfish feelings. It suddenly occurred to me that the scaffolding supporting the wall of beliefs I had been constructing all my life had started to fully give way. The professional beliefs with which I was able to make sense of trauma and crisis in other people's lives began to disintegrate in front of me. Any faith or belief in a spiritual source had evaporated.

By the time I reached the hospital, I had a sense of being surrounded by ruin. As I met with the family, I was near speechless with the certainty that I had nothing to offer. It was all I could do to move through the routine tasks my role demanded. These impotent feelings persisted throughout the rest of the evening after leaving the hospital and continued into the following days. The very foundation of how I had begun to perceive my world continued to implode throughout the week. I couldn't bring myself to go to work. Both physically and emotionally ill, I called in sick.

I lay in bed staring at the ceiling for hours, drowning in a dense inner darkness. I surfaced six days later, feeling as though I should get myself to work at least once that week, after all it was January 31st. I convinced myself that I could tolerate that one day. Witnessing so much death was undoing me. I had loved my job, felt valued and fulfilled. At the same time, I realized that a large part of my ego was invested in my professional role. An identity crisis was under way. Who was I anymore? Nothing came to me, other than overwhelming hollowness, lethargy, and doubt as I hoped that nothing significant would be required of me, since I had nothing left to give.

When I arrived, I couldn't bear to see my colleagues, so I used dreaded, overdue paperwork as an excuse to hide in my office. There had been several messages left over the past week by baby Anna's mother, Susan, but I held off returning her calls. Instead, I started to write a letter of resignation.

Towards the end of the afternoon, the phone rang. I picked it up without thinking and instantly wished that I hadn't when I heard Susan's voice on the other end of the line. "Lora, I'm so glad you're back at work. I've tried to reach you all week. Tomorrow is Anna's memorial service and we want you to be the main speaker."

Her words triggered absolute panic. "I can't! I absolutely can't," I stammered.

"But it's really important to us, you've been with us from the beginning. You can't just abandon us now."

"I'm sorry," I said. "I had nothing to offer you on Christmas Day at the hospital and have nothing now."

"You were there. That's what we needed, your presence and your tears."

"But I'm empty. I'm going through a spiritual crisis."

"Well, have it on your own time," she said, about to cry. "Please, please don't say no, we really need you to do this. It is so important to us. I'm begging."

Somewhere inside my darkness, a spark of compassion flickered. Hesitating, I sighed and agreed to come up with something. As I hung up the phone, I cursed myself for giving in.

That evening, I paced like a trapped animal. I couldn't come up with even one meaningful thing I could say the next day. Perhaps, I conceded, it is because there is absolutely no meaning to be found in any of it. My world had become devoid of mystery, meaning, and hope. By midnight, I was exhausted from the hours spent in unproductive effort. As I lay in bed, restless and filled with anxiety without any resolution in sight, I began to let go of my lack of understanding, my frustration, and my need to feel competent. At the bottom of this dark night, I surrendered. In desperation, I pleaded, *please, if there is anything real out there, help me, not for my sake, help me for theirs.* I prayed for the grace to know what to say on behalf of Anna's family and then I completely let go. Exhausted, I fell into a deep sleep.

The dream began with a voice:

"Meditate on This, Meditate on Me, Meditate on This, Meditate on Me." The voice chants into the darkness. I somehow understand that I am in sacred space and fall to my knees. A near blinding Light slowly emerges in front of me, until my inner and outer eyes adjust to it. I become aware of vibrant, slowly moving energy—I am standing before a room, alive and glowing, a holy place, a living, vibrant rose of pure light, the size and energy of an ancient, sacred temple. The rose is vibrating and pulsating. As though breathing in rhythm with the voice of the chant, it is both of form and formless, "Meditate on Me. Meditate on This." The voice continues to softly chant throughout the dream. The space in which I kneel is filled with the scent of rose gardens. This energy holds a distinct presence.

The rose calls to me, surrounds me, and penetrates me. Consciousness opens to me as the rose's petals slowly open, blossoming in ever-expanding concentric ripples of widening energy and luminescent light. I sigh in deep surrender and am pulled inward toward the center of the rose—the heart of pure love. A sound with an unearthly, ethereal quality fills the air and moves through me, emptying me of all but Itself. The life force—love—the essential nature of life itself, calls me and penetrates my every thought—every atom and cell of my being. I am caressed, held and carried on a current as one by one, each petal continues to open, drawing me more deeply into the heart of the rose.

Finding myself in a brilliant sea of light and moving with the dancing energy, my life as I have known it passes quickly before me. Reviewed in the light of this moment, I understand the entire record of my life in a new light: each death broke me down and open, available for THIS. In a heartbeat, I am filled with understanding. Just as quickly as understanding has filled me, I am emptied. Emptied of all thought and knowledge, I rest in the wisdom of the unknowing. Nothing else matters. Left only with the presence of this moment, I have a sense that I am being rearranged. My thoughts, perceptions, feelings, and the very cells in my body begin to dance in a new way. I am held in the heart of eternity. It is enough.

I am gradually moved from the center of the rose to outer space as the rose slowly begins to close. The voice encircles me, weaving through me, continuing to chant "Meditate on this. Meditate on me" as I fall effortlessly out the other side of the rose into velvet darkness.

I woke sometime later, the air infused with the scent of roses, the memory of lingering words and sounds I will carry within me for the rest of my life. The image of translucent rose petals opening and deep, spacious peace had replaced the fear of the night before. The agony and sorrow of the past lay knotted in the dampened sheets. My thoughts flickered, glowed, and caught fire as I became more alert. I could feel my body vibrating, pulsating slowly, and then quickening, sleep no longer possible. The clock read 3:10 a.m. as I recorded the dream in my journal, then randomly picked up a book from the stack on my bedside table. It had been a gift from a friend and I hadn't yet looked at it. I opened a page to a poem titled "The Visit and the Gift" written by a 13th-century Sufi poet, Mahmud Shabistari:

At dawn, the moon, like a creature of fantasy stole into my room
and woke me from some lazy and unproductive sleep.
Her face quickly illuminated the underside of my soul and my
own being stood revealed in the naked light ...
Sighing in wonder, I faced my Self, which said:
Your life so far has chased the illusion of control. You will not
meet me on that path ...
Sometimes, from sheer habit, I'm back on the compost heap.
And sometimes, when that glance finds me again, I am back in
the Rose Garden.[1]

I read the poem several times. It seemed to have been written for this moment. I meditated on it. Picking up my journal and pen, I wrote until dawn when my writing hand began to cramp. I opened another book at random and the words written in Wendell Berry's poem "To Know the Dark" began to speak to me. "To go into the dark with a light is to know light. To know the dark, go dark. Go without sight, and find that the dark, too, blooms and sings, and is traveled by dark feet and dark wings."[2] Setting the book aside, I found myself going back over the dream. The energy of the chanting voice and rose seemed to linger. I reflected that indeed I had gone "into the dark" and the dark had bloomed and sung to me, forever changing me. My heartfelt prayer asking for help had been answered in a most unexpected way.

I now felt full, enlivened, and deeply at peace. Preparing myself for the funeral became a sacred ritual—a holy event. I moved slowly, meditatively, as I showered and began to approach the day with deliberation, intention, pregnant with the holy. The anxiety of the evening before seemed like a distant dream, replaced by a state of deep calm. My fear of speaking at the funeral had become an inconsequential memory. I still had no idea of what I would say, but I intuitively trusted that the right words would come when it was time. I didn't need to plan ahead.

As I left the house for the funeral, I heard the dreamscape voice instructing me to stop at the florist. *"Buy two white roses and one red rose."*

In the flower shop, some breathtaking baby-pink roses caught my attention. I reached for them. The inner voice spoke again. Firmly. Insistently. *"I said the red and the white."* I dropped the pink roses like a hot potato and picked up two white roses and one red. Back in the car, I turned on the radio and Bette Midler sang "The Rose" as I continued my drive to the Catholic church where the funeral was to be held.[3] The words moved me, as they reflected the journey of the past week, as well as the subsequent transformation of winter into the blossoming of the rose within me. I arrived at the church and greeted the bereaved parents, Susan and Jack. They expressed their relief and gratitude that I had come. There was a small table in front of the podium, empty but for a picture of Anna and Ashley. I asked if I could place the vase of the red and white roses next to it.

The memorial service began. When the time came for me to speak, I did so with complete faith that I would know what to say. I had been opened by an unknowable mystery. Words came as a gift. I don't recall precisely what was said; the words scarcely seemed my own, they effortlessly flowed through me.

Following the service one person after another came up to tell me what my talk had meant to them. The priest said that he was moved beyond words and had experienced a true epiphany in his own time of wavering faith. He was touched by my use of the symbolism of the red and white roses. I was vaguely aware that I had talked about the white innocence of the small, closed buds—of the twins' brief lives—and the red passion with which their parents had come to love them as the red rose, fully open. I recounted Jack's words from Ashley's death earlier that year. "We have learned to bear what most people could never imagine and have learned to love it."

Because they had learned to cherish each precious moment, they accepted what their hearts knew, that their baby girls were here on borrowed time. The girls had been used in the way of a Bodhisattva, the anointed one, "The Christ," to wake each of them from the hypnotic slumber of winter and to teach us all about what is most important—the way of love. In this season known as a holy time by all spiritual traditions, a time associated with birth, death had come. In both birth and death, love breaks open, an exploding star scattering light everywhere.

In time I came to understand that beginning with the week of Christmas, I had come to a place where I found myself stripped of all of my resources, hopes, and expectations. The place of ego—my conscious understanding of myself—from which I had been living my life had come to a precipice. There lay a gap before me that no amount of plotting, bargaining, or thinking could help me cross. It was only in the discovery and declaration of this utter state of inner poverty that something else began to open and the way became clear.

A shift in my identity had taken place, an awakening that transcended explanation. I, too, had been broken open and touched by love. Sorrow had completely emptied me and left me in a barren place of psychological inner darkness. In the act of letting go and falling completely into the darkness, surrendering to the unknown, to what I couldn't comprehend with my small mind, I was caught by grace and shown the way. A slow blossoming of my inner and outer life had begun. Waking from my dreamtime "visitation," I was pregnant with new life.

Jan called the following day wondering why she hadn't heard from me over the holidays, concerned when I hadn't come to the meditation group. I found that it was now easy to tell her about the challenging time I had over the holidays. She assured me that a spiritual path is not straightforward and people often experience ups and down and move through times of darkness. She explained that this is a normal part of spiritual development and that I was entirely too hard on myself.

As I began to tell Jan about the rose dream, I became porous and permeated by something so inexplicable that I couldn't do it justice by trying to describe it as I again felt enveloped in that same energy from the dream. It was difficult to explain how dramatically my perception had changed, but she seemed to immediately understand what I was trying to convey and quite clearly knew more than I did about it. She asked me if I had any idea what the dream signified. Other than being completely changed by it, I confessed that I didn't have a clue. She instructed me to get a symbol dictionary and look up rose as well as other symbols that spoke to me and said she'd be in touch soon.

22.

Hidden Treasure

And all shall be well and
All manner of thing shall be well
When the tongues of flame are in-folded
Into the crowned knot of fire
And the fire and the rose are one.

T.S. Eliot, *Four Quartets*

*D*ear *Lora, I have been instructed to tell you more about the initiation you are currently embarked upon. Your experience with the rose is the first part of a twelve-part initiation called "The Great Initiation." It might be viewed as the progressive opening of a twelve-petaled flower—that great flower contained within us all, that is for the most part still closed in the majority of the species. The complete opening of this flower can be compared to "the lifting of the veil," so that once completed, one's consciousness is in "full flower"* …

Jan introduced me to the concept of initiation in August of 1995, the day before my colon surgery, in the ritual she had conducted. Her letter was validating and also issued an invitation to stay open, continue to learn, grow, and be present throughout subsequent smaller "initiations." She ended the two-page letter with, *I ask you always to remember the infinite ways in which you are supported by the universe in this endeavor. I wish you Godspeed. With love, Jan.*

A weekend soon after this moving dream of a rose, my friend Sandra invited me to drive with her to a small town about an hour east of the Twin Cities to help her look for an antique table for her bedroom. As we walked into the antique shop, I felt a compelling tug of energy pulling me toward the back corner of the store. Not wanting to be rude, I asked

Sandra if she was ok if I caught up with her in a little while.

Like an animal tracking a scent, I couldn't keep myself from following the unmistakable pull of energy that called to me. I quickly found myself in the doorway of a small corner room filled with dusty old books. As I stepped into the room, I was overwhelmed with the sensation of intense heat from within, noticing as I moved to different spots in the room that the heat either intensified or subsided. Experimenting, I closed my eyes, surrendering to an inner compass that moved me randomly around the room, my body a Geiger counter. I took a deep breath and settled into stillness, instinctively following the heat.

Time ceased to exist as I slowly moved toward the bookshelves, surrendering to the palpable energy growing increasingly warmer the closer I got to the books. As I moved back toward the center of the room, my body grew cold. I repeated the experiment several times until the energy was so compelling, it seemed I had no choice but to keep tracking the growing warmth and insistent pull of something that wanted to be found. I closed my eyes, focusing on the increasing heat as I slowly moved along the wall of books to my left, my body growing cooler with each step. I took a deep breath, eyes still closed, and moved to the right; the energy and heat increased, dramatically.

The smell of musty books and dust momentarily broke my concentration when I sneezed. Re-centering myself, I again followed the heat, moving to the right. The heat became even more compelling—enclosed me—fenced me in. Blindly, I continued slowly, cautiously, to the right; the energy and heat grew increasingly more intense: hot, hotter! I grew sweaty, burning up with an inner fire as my body began to shake and the top of my head pounded, pulsating with heat—volcanic energy seeking an outlet. Scarcely able to breathe and light-headed, I leaned forward, resting my head on the books while reaching out to steady my hands on the bookshelf immediately in front of me. My fingertips burned as though I'd touched a hot stove.

My eyes flew open. My fingertips were red hot. Right in front of me, my fingers had touched the bindings of two books, *The Rose-Garden Game* by Eithne Wilken and *The Symbolic Rose* by Barbara Seward, and there in front of me were three shelves of books.[1,2] I realized these were no ordinary books on roses, they were books on the mystical history and meaning of the rose, ranging from works on the rose in literature, in fairy tales, and across religious traditions. I gasped in wonder at the immensity of the treasure trove in front of me. I took *The Rose-Garden Game* off the shelf, opened it, and my eyes fell on the following words:

> Whatever form it takes and wherever it appears, the rose has extraordinary symbolic potency. It is the flower older than the human race ... It is in the twelfth century that the rose-garden becomes the standard image of Paradise.

I sat on the floor facing the shelves filled with books on roses. Time slowed and stopped as I began to page through one book after another, words and phrases catching me in a net of wonder. I opened *The Symbolic Rose* and read:

> In Carl Jung's view it is both the rose's circular shape (suggesting the sun, wholeness, and perfection) and its relation to fertility (birth or rebirth in beauty) that accounts for its repeated preeminence. For the rose is a part of what Jung calls the mandala, a symbolic design recurrent in myths and dreams ... Since the mandala is to Carl Jung the principal symbol of completion or end of the integrative process, the rose in his theory symbolizes rebirth, psychic harmony, and the fulfillment of man's being.

Carl Jung's emphasis on archetypes and symbols that appear in cultures around the world is especially relevant when it comes to the rose, associated with every spiritual tradition from ancient Egypt, Islam, Sufi mysticism, Native American culture, East Indian and Ayurvedic medicine, through early Christianity and the mystics. The rose has been called the Lotus of the West. It was associated with the ancient Greek Goddess, Aphrodite. The rose was a symbol in Roman, pagan rituals, where it was known as the flower of Venus, the goddess of fields and gardens, and revered as the goddess of love, beauty, and wisdom. The Virgin Mary was associated with plants and flowers by the early church fathers. The Catholic practice of praying the rosary and reciting 50 Hail Marys was known as a rosarium, the Latin term for rose garden, believed to be a meditation designed to take one into "the garden enclosed," an interior space of open receptivity.

A bit overwhelmed with the range of material on the floor in front of me, I suddenly remembered that I'd promised to catch up with Sandra and I didn't have a clue how much time had passed. I quickly gathered four or five books in my arms, trying to mentally calculate the price. The haunting words from my dream returned: *"Meditate on this. Meditate on me."* I became aware that the books I'd been led to were priceless. In that meditative moment I was consumed by awe. I looked around in disbelief at the books and the room now returned to normal. The pressure in my head, and the heat, had completely subsided, but my entire being was filled with reverence, embraced by spiritual mystery. Whoever would believe that spending time in a dusty corner of old books would be stepping onto holy ground? I gathered the books in my arms and went looking for Sandra.

The rose dream had shifted the way I worked and lived in the world. From that time forward, it also began a time of the study of symbols, myth, and archetypes in my life. I continued to bask in long periods of peace and appreciation for my life. My work changed and became effortless. Metaphorically, life as I had known it had been dismantled, then reconstituted into something new. In the dismantling, it seemed as though what I had lost was my perfectionism, self-consciousness, shame, and inability to love myself, as well as some of the ways I continued to protect myself. I had been riddled with self-judgment for so long it seemed like a normal part of me. What replaced these aspects of myself in the reconstitution was a deep serenity, trust, and a kind of acceptance that I never knew was possible.

There was a consistent feeling of being pushed and pulled along on a path by what I came to call *mystery* or *spirit* as this presence continued to speak to me through my dreams, intuition, and synchronicity, the sacred moving through me, and moving me forward day by day.

That theme of movement showed up in a dream soon after.

I'm walking on a winding circular path laid in stone; the direction keeps changing as the path spirals back and forth. I notice one, two, three ... inner locks being opened up at the center of my body, energetic waves spiraling upwards, creating a fire from inside my core. Each time the direction of the path changes, my body goes through a distinct physiological change. Four, five, six; another turn, the energy growing stronger. Another turn, the seventh ... the top of my head fully ignites, becomes the flame. The heat and heightened awareness nearly overwhelm me, as I find myself at the end of the path and step into the center of a rosette laid out in stone and flooded with the scent of roses. I drop to my knees.

When I woke at dawn, my nightgown was soaking wet. I was filled with the memory of walking round and round until I reached a sacred center, fully opened and aglow. As I moved toward the shower, I felt like a seven-story, walking lighthouse. A warm shower cooled me down, the number seven reverberating in my head like the beat of a drum. The seven energy centers in my body known as chakras had fully opened in the dream. Seven days of the week, seven sacraments, the seven dwarfs, seven notes to the musical scale, seven stations of the cross, seven colors of the rainbow, seven alchemical stages of transformation, seven sorrows of the Virgin Mary, seven ancient initiation sites of pilgrimage scattered throughout Europe—on and on the drumbeat continued.

Although I had never walked a labyrinth and knew nothing about them, my body now seemed to know it intimately. The realization that I had just been walking one in my dream created an intense desire to know more about this ancient meditative path. Labyrinths have served as a place of ritual, a form of pilgrimage, and a portal to the sacred unknown from ancient times. There have been many designs of labyrinths stretching back thousands of years. The simplest and oldest classical designs are believed to date back to somewhere around 2500 BC and have seven circuits. The classical labyrinth design is found throughout the world, inscribed on rock, laid out on the ground in stone, etched or painted onto ancient artifacts. In the center of many of the classical designs there is a depiction of Theseus and the Minotaur and an open space. Simple, classical labyrinths have also been found carved into rock on the Hopi reservations in Arizona.[3]

At least five labyrinths from the early Iron Age (750–500 BC) have also been found carved into rock in northern Italy, possibly connecting it to the Mother Goddess of fertility, new life, and compassion. The myth of Theseus, Adriadne, and the Minotaur is considered to be the central story associated with labyrinth in Europe. Labyrinth designs have been found on Cretan coins and pottery. They have been found made of mounded earth in fields in England, Ireland, and Scandinavia. Some labyrinths are round, some square, some octagonal, and the patterns vary. The paths in some church labyrinths form a cross. Labyrinths were walked by pilgrims in medieval times in churches throughout Europe.[4]

The modern labyrinth movement in the United States was begun by the Reverend Lauren Artress after she encountered labyrinths in France while at a seminar with the writer Jean Houston in 1991. She eventually brought the dimensions and patterns back to the United States where an indoor and outdoor labyrinth was built at Grace Cathedral in San Francisco. Since then, labyrinths have proliferated throughout the US, spreading to churches, healthcare facilities, places of work, gardens, and playgrounds. It is believed that walking a labyrinth balances both sides of the brain, lowers blood pressure, opens individuals to insight, and expands consciousness. The labyrinths installed at Grace Cathedral are designed from the pattern of the most beloved and sought-out labyrinth in the world, in the Cathedral Notre-Dame de Chartres, in France.[5]

Chartres Cathedral is the home of an eleven-circuit labyrinth laid in stone dating back to the thirteenth century. As you approach the center, embedded in stone is a "rosette" made of six flower petals radiating outward from an inner center. The labyrinth lies directly below a majestic rose window, a mandala of sunlight streaming through the deep blue and red glass, depicting the mysteries of the mother of Christ. She sits like a throne, holding her son; on one side of her is the moon, on the other is the sun. It is made to the exact same dimensions of the labyrinth. The rose window signifies the divine feminine as represented by Mary, known as the Mystical Rose.

The energy and influence of the rose continued to show up in my life almost daily in one way or another over the next several weeks, in odd and unexpected ways, like the day Lyndall brought me home following cataract surgery. I had fallen asleep on the couch when I woke with a start from a dream, reminded where I was by seeing Lyndall sitting quietly nearby in the rocker reading. Lyndall told me I'd been talking in my sleep.

"What does hopscotch mean?" I asked her.

"It's a child's game. You remember, you hopped in squares made in chalk on the sidewalk," she answered.

"I know that, but it must mean something. It was amazing. I was doing it in a large cathedral. What does it mean?"

Always the skeptic, she gave me a look. "It means the drugs from the surgery haven't worn off, go back to sleep!" she teased.

Two days later, I again had the same dream of hopscotch in an ancient cathedral.

I am playing hopscotch in a huge cathedral. I am hopping on one foot, one, two, three, then two feet, and so on straight to the top of the pattern— the destination I recognize from childhood—named Heaven.

Captivated by the image of hopscotch laid out in a cathedral, I pulled out several of the books I had found in the antique store. As I began to browse through *The Rose-Garden Game*, I came across a discussion on the importance of contemplation and turning inward:

> To contemplate, then, is to mark out a space, a circle, and fix one's attention on what is within it, uniting oneself as far as possible with the numinous forces thus concentrated … Is this what the children are doing, bobbing round in their ring-a-ring-of-roses, or chalking out on the pavement, for hopscotch in the spring, what is called a "temple" (in Germany the game is called Temple-Hopping, *Tempelhüpfen*, or Heaven-Hopping, *Himmelhüpfen*, and in Austria the "temple" is called "Paradise." Are they magically constructing a correspondence to the wonders of outer space and the intricacies of the psyche? Children are natural contemplatives.

But it wouldn't be until several years later, in 2001, when living in Washington, DC, I met Dr. Irene Gad, a distinguished Jungian analyst and writer, and was brought back to the dream of hopscotch in the cathedral. As we talked over tea, I began by asking her if she could tell me more about symbols and why they seemed to show up in the work of spiritual transformation. "They are the language of the Soul," she explained. "They convey not just an idea of the infinite, but can become a source of direct realization that makes manifest the radiance of the world. They serve as a bridge and are vehicles of light, of consciousness, itself."

She then asked me where such questions were coming from, and we talked about the rose dream and other experiences I'd had and still not fully understood. I found myself telling her about the hopscotch dream.

"Hopscotch was used in the Eleusinian Mystery Schools on a remote island in ancient Greece as a temple initiatory ritual of death and resurrection," she explained. "It also symbolized the overcoming of obstacles between earth and heaven. In German, it is called Temple-Hopping, *Tempelhüpfen*, or Hopping to Heaven," she explained. "By some they were considered a precursor or very early form of a labyrinth path because of the hopping forward and backward and so forth as you worked your way to a specific destination."

Toward the end of our afternoon together I had just gathered my notebook and was about to say goodbye, when I changed my mind and on impulse found that I had another question. "I'm wondering if you would be willing to see me for therapy?" I asked.

Dr. Gad smiled and looked at me thoughtfully. "In the Navajo tradition, a sand painting is created and used for ceremonial healing. It is a long and exacting process that is accompanied by a chanter who calls in the exact medicine and symbols for healing of the patient. This depicts the story of the illness and the healing symbols necessary for that specific individual to heal. The ceremony goes on over several days. In the Navajo language, a sand painting is said to depict the places where the gods come and go. The Navajo believe that a sand painting heals because the image attracts the Holy People and serves as a pathway for healing and identifies the patient with the Holy People that is depicted in the sand. The ritual is a dynamic, alive process that enables the patient to transform by focusing on the powerful symbols created in the ritual. There is one way to destroy this process. Do you know what that is?"

I shook my head.

"If someone, like myself, came along prematurely and took their hands and scattered the sand, like this." She took her hands and pantomimed the scattering of the sand. "My dear, you may come for tea and a visit any time, but if I were to accept you as a patient, I would be destroying the sand painting that is the dynamic and transformational process within you before it is complete. The gods come and go in you and have been very busy at work with you and will continue to be. I don't dare step into that process and scatter the sands of what the spirits have been up to. But please feel free to call and come for tea anytime."

I nodded my head and thanked her as I stood to leave, deeply touched by her words.

"You know, my dear, many don't realize a fraction of what you've experienced or are beginning to apprehend, even though you are still working it out to make sense. We're all longing to 'hop to Heaven' in one way or another. You are very fortunate to be learning and dreaming such deep mysteries. Be well and I look forward to seeing you again."

My dreams continued to be filled with symbolism. One dream stands out in particular.

I arrive at Jan's house for a board meeting and let her know that I have to leave for work at a particular time. There are guests sleeping throughout her house and Jan asks me to help wake them so we can get started—we are already late. I wake people up, but they are not in much of a hurry to begin. Jan suggests that I go into the room where we will be meeting and they'll soon follow and join us.

I step into the room and immediately notice that the floorboards have separated and I can see a body of water directly under us. Jan comes into the room and smiles. The walls expand and float away, shimmering into nothing, leaving the house open, and the floorboards float off, so that Jan and I are walking on top of the water—a rippling, clear, luminous lake. As we walk, we can see to the bottom of the lake and watch fish swimming directly under us in the brilliant blue water. It is exhilarating and beautiful. The sun is shining on the water and clouds float serenely above and are reflected in the water. We walk for quite a while until we arrive at a place where the water ends abruptly. In front of us is a mountain of sheer rock that appears to go straight up into the sky. Jan looks at me kindly.

"I have to leave you now," she says. "You must continue by yourself for a while now and just start climbing."

"I can't. I'm afraid of heights," I protest.

"Follow the exhilaration rather than the fear," she instructs me.

Jan suddenly vanishes and I am alone.

I look up and notice there are small ledges and what seem to be caverns or caves, and at the entrance of each of them is a door—there are hundreds of doors. They appear to go back through time and cultures, calling to mind ancient Egypt, Africa, China, Europe. Some of the doors are made of stunning wood and intricate door knockers. Others appear Gothic, embellished with a variety of elaborate scroll work. Some are made of bright metal, some of warm-grained woods, and others of deep earth tones and startling reds. There are doors that are round, some square or rounded at the top, others with sculpted, elaborate tops of great artistry, some covered in elaborate gold fixtures, others of vines.

As I begin to climb, I notice the beauty of each door and that some seem to indicate protection with statues of demons, angels, or other small heads carved into the rock itself. Although each one seems to call out to me, I know intuitively that although I'm tempted to stop and explore, none of them is my destination. As long as I keep climbing and look upward toward the very top, I am fine by following the exhilaration as Jan had instructed.

I finally arrive at the top and can go no further, I've reached my destination. In front of me is a structure carved into the rock, a head— much like the heads of the presidents of Mount Rushmore carved into the Black Hills of South Dakota. The head, however, is that of Jan's friend and my spiritual teacher, Barbara. Where the eyes would normally be, there are two ornate doors. I slowly approach, murmuring a prayer. I instinctively step through the one on my right and find myself in a sanctuary, filled with more doors—one after another—until I step through the last one. I become feather-light as I float in open space and bask in oneness.

Then, I'm back in the water, trying to swim to Jan's house. My arms ache and I am afraid that I will be unable to make it. I become so tired I begin to tell myself I can't do it anymore, when, from nowhere, emerge three women on each side of me. With the tips of their fingers barely touching me, I know I am being fully supported. I slowly feel a surge of energy from their support and know that I can make it, and begin to vigorously swim again, repeating the words "I can" over and over. As I complete this journey, I know that I have all the support that I need.

My inner compass pointed me in the direction of wholeness and of the divine presence that had been revealed to me through the Mystical Rose. It moved me deeply into the heart of symbolism, myth, archetype, and metaphor. It took me into the world of the divine feminine, sacred geometry, and teachings from antiquity and, always, an ongoing, inner voice and numinous presence. It required me to slow down and pay attention as I surrendered and opened both my mind and my heart to a realm of filtered light.

This journey required me to breathe deeply, meditate regularly, and surrender to an ancient, inner rhythm in order to make myself available to better understand my own longings and to experience in the deepest sense that we are all connected and all One. The living, energetic manifestation of the feminine face of God served as a vessel, a bridging function, that transported me to a life I could never have imagined. I began to realize that I had always been carried on the ocean of my longing, cradled in the arms of the Great Mother, even when I thought I was alone and abandoned on the sea of life.

23.

Exploring the Heart of the Mystical Rose

The rose must be revealed as a profoundly symbolic link to divine aspects of the universe, as a sort of quantum theology in a flower. A select few in every generation have understood the messages and have attempted to live and even teach to those who are ready to understand ... The red rose is an enduring, providential symbol that bespeaks the work that each aware individual can and must do to connect with Cosmic Consciousness ... symbolism is divine language, the keyholes to doors in the walls of space.

Frankie Hutton, *Rose Lore*

The next two decades continued to unfold as I worked with the energy and the archetype of the rose, while simultaneously my professional and personal lives expanded and grew in unexpected ways. I had written in a journal since junior high at least once a day, but now I found myself writing at least three to four times each day as one compelling experience and dream came after another.

My friend Lyndall, who had teased me about hopscotch, also had an unexpected spiritual experience—a vision—and, like me, she was exploring the archetype and symbolism of the rose. We were to learn that Chartres, France contained important mystical teachings we needed to discover. We hadn't sought resources to support our expanding interest; instead, resources sought us. Soon after, a woman at a local labyrinth-focused society learned what Lyndall and I were exploring and her family foundation offered us a grant to support our further exploration in France. On a spring day, we flew into Paris and from there boarded a train to Chartres to visit the Cathedral of Our Lady of Chartres. As we disembarked from the train, I noticed a young man on the platform who stood, sobbing. Somehow, he ended up in my arms and cried with his head on my shoulder. When I felt his energy grow still, I helped him to board the train.

"I think you've just helped a mentally ill man get on the train to god knows where," Lyndall teased.

I shrugged. I wasn't sure what had happened that he ended up in my arms. There were no words exchanged between us, but I somehow knew with certainty that comforting him had been the right thing to do.

During this first trip to France, we learned a great deal about the ancient science of sacred geometry and the mystical teachings that had been embedded within Chartres Cathedral, one of the oldest, most famous, and largest of the great cathedrals. Since the thirteenth century, individuals have made pilgrimages on their way to the Holy Land, stopping in Chartres to walk the ancient labyrinth embedded into the stone in the nave. One night we were given the opportunity to walk the labyrinth by candlelight. I experienced something so moving that by the end of the evening, as I approached the high altar, I felt compelled to prostrate myself fully in front of it and spiraled into an indescribable expanded state of consciousness. There were similarities that brought the rose dream to mind—but this was no dream.

A year later, I was back in France doing research and traveling with a friend from Paris. In a different cathedral in southern France, a young man briefly caught my attention as he knelt deep in prayer in one of the side chapels. For a moment, I wondered if it was the young man from the train platform the year before, but I quickly dismissed it as impossible. The mass ended and we stayed inside to take pictures of the stained-glass rose windows. As we left the church, the young man approached me.

"Excuse me mam, my name is Michael and my God has told me to tell you that you are in the wrong cathedral."

"But how do you know I am looking for any particular cathedral?" I countered.

He shrugged. "I was specifically instructed to tell you that you are in the wrong one."

I laughed and told him that I actually was looking for a specific cathedral and although this one had felt wrong to me, it was the only one in the guidebook for that small village. I explained that I was looking for a cathedral I had read about, built on top of an underground river and ancient druid site.

Michael and his female friend grew excited because they knew the church I was looking for. We followed them across town to a church so old it wasn't in any of the guidebooks. It had the very history I had been looking for and the most marvelous statue of the Black Madonna. Michael asked me if I would take a picture of him in front of the statue and send it to him as he didn't have a decent camera.

When I returned home, I told Lyndall about my trip and the encounter with Michael. She asked me if it was the young man who had been weeping when we stepped off the train in Chartres. I explained that I had no idea, it seemed unlikely, and I never really got a close look at him because he was crying on my shoulder so I never asked him. Lyndall yelled, "Are you kidding me?"

I remembered the picture and pulled it up on my computer. "Oh my gosh," Lyndall gasped, "it's the same guy. I'm positive!"

I emailed Michael later that day and asked if an unknown woman in the spring of the year before had helped him onto a departing train from Chartres. He replied several days later and said that it indeed was him. He'd thought I'd looked familiar but he hadn't gotten a very good look at the woman who had comforted him and helped him on the train. He wrote that he had just had a powerful mystical experience at Chartres and was sad that he had to leave and go back to school. I had served as a bridge and helped to ground him before he got on the train.

***

Although my work life and location changed, the theme related to the Mystical Rose continued to dominate my waking and sleeping life. February 2007 found me back in France with Lyndall, leading a pilgrimage of nearly thirty individuals to specific sacred sites. We began the trip in retreat, spending several days in a lovely countryside villa that had once been a school of culinary arts where my friend Jane had completed her cuisine education on a Julia Child scholarship. One of the nights we were there, I had a dream that I was actively in the process of dying. At the time I didn't think too much of it and saw this as a transformational dream.

From the villa, we went to the town of Chartres, arriving mid-afternoon. The Cathedral of Notre Dame de Chartres has been a place of pilgrimage since the Middle Ages. It is built on a hill overlooking the city on the left bank of the Eure River. We were able to stay in lodgings next to the cathedral where we also had a room reserved for teaching. That night I taught about the symbolism of the pregnant virgin and asked people to ponder what they were about to birth in their own lives. After the teachings, Lyndall and I decided to go for a walk, but the cobblestone roads were slick with rain and I slipped and fell, excruciating pain reverberating through my right arm and left hand, the left side of my face badly scratched and bruised. A couple came along and quickly drove us to the hospital. A homeless man was lying in front of the emergency room doors and sat up as we approached. "It's a nice evening for a visit to the emergency room," he paused, "as long as you don't take it too seriously."

Despite the pain, Lyndall and I laughed.

I had a compound fracture that required hospitalization and surgery that was scheduled for the next day. Because I'm allergic to all narcotics and no one in the ER could speak English, when they put the French physicians' *Desk Reference* in front of Lyndall, indicating that she should show them which drugs I could be given, Lyndall shook her head and declined any drugs for me. The doctor immobilized my arm and readied us to be transferred to a room in the maternity ward since there were no other beds. I had just lectured on the symbolism of the pregnant virgin. We didn't miss the irony of this.

Meditation became my medicine throughout that long night. Lyndall and I both came to the conclusion that perhaps my dream of dying had not been metaphorical and prepared as best we could for possible complications. I dictated a letter to my son and a list of people to be notified if I did not survive the surgery. There was no anxiety or urgency in me, just trust in what was unfolding and that I needed to have as much in place to lighten Lyndall's load if something did happen to me. Lyndall left me in the morning to tell the others where I was and to pick up the pieces of the pilgrimage. As she left, she promised to send another friend, Norma, to the hospital.

Although none of the nurses spoke English, I felt well taken care of. Later that morning the surgeon arrived and introduced himself. Fortunately, he spoke some English and explained the extent of my injuries, as well as what he would have to do in surgery, including inserting a metal plate and screws into my right arm and wrist.

Shortly after noon a man arrived with a cart to take me to surgery. After exiting the elevator, he parked the cart against a wall and proceeded to fold his hands in prayer, then bowed to me before kissing me on each cheek and indicating that he would pray for me. I had no idea if he did this with all patients or if something else was amiss.

A few minutes later, as the anesthesiologist asked me questions and explained the surgery further, I was flooded with an overwhelming feeling of compassion for him. "I want you to know that four days ago I had a dream I was dying," I told him. "I don't know if the dream was alerting me to something or merely symbolic."

I paused. "It's important that I tell you: if anything happens to me, it wasn't your fault."

This dear man thanked me and told me he believed in the importance of listening to our dreams, then folded his hands in prayer for several minutes. He left saying he wanted to speak to the surgeon and then he'd come back and talk with me further. He returned a little while later and told me that he and the surgeon had spoken and decided to do the surgery using a block—similar to an epidural during childbirth—and not traditional anesthesia. He confessed that although it was done in other hospitals, they had not taken this approach with a complex fracture surgery before.

The surgery went well. I was awake throughout and the surgeon informed me of every step of the process. While in the recovery room, I was very relaxed and semi-awake in a meditative way when two things caught my attention. To my left was a brilliant tunnel of light and to my right was the actual monitor. As I began to move toward the light, I noticed all my numbers on the monitor going down. When I moved away from the light, the numbers slowly came back up. I did this several times, until I stepped over the threshold of the compelling light and into the tunnel.

From a distance I heard alarms going off. I saw that the monitor numbers were all zero when suddenly someone was there, tearing my gown from my body and beginning to do chest compressions. I knew I could make a conscious decision to continue further into the tunnel or to return to my body. I was flooded with feelings for my son, for Lyndall and the others on the Pilgrimage, the surgeon and the anesthesiologist. I made the choice to stay alive and stepped back across the threshold, just as they had placed the defibrillators on my chest.

With my decision to return to my body, all of the numbers began to rapidly rise again. I heard the doctor's voice say in French—amazingly I could understand it—that they should hold off and see if I continued to stabilize since my numbers were rising. A nurse sat near my bed for the next several hours, monitoring me. They kept me in the hospital for three more days which were restful and without incident. The rest of the group moved on to Paris and from there would go to the French village of Amiens. Norma stayed back with a rental car and the day I was discharged, we drove to Amiens to rejoin the others. I was able to step back into a leading/teaching role and finished a meaningful and transformative trip for all.

I often found myself pondering the question about the energy and force that were guiding me as a flow that I found myself completely moved by. I was a seeker and at the same time I had the persistent feeling of being sought after myself as I followed a trail illuminated by an ancient mystery, scented with roses

✱✱✱

On a chilly day in March, a few weeks after returning from France, I received a call from David. "Mom, I'm at the hospital with my dad, he was just diagnosed with advanced pancreatic cancer. The doctors only give him a couple of weeks to live. He wants to go home to die, but they say hospice only does home visits. I feel bad because I don't know how to take care of him, so he'll have to go into a nursing home."

"David, tell your dad if he would like me to come to Cincinnati and help you take him home, we can take care of him together. I would be happy to do that," I said without hesitation.

It hadn't been until the summer following David's graduation from college a number of years before that Dave and I had finally been able to talk about the circumstances of our divorce. By then tremendous healing and closure had occurred between us. As I told Dave about my confrontation with the Bishop, and then being asked to speak at the annual conferences on sexual exploitation in the church and changes in church laws, he reached across the table between us for my hands. He apologized for being unwilling to talk about the circumstances of our divorce for so many years. He told me that his immediate reaction to hearing about the Bishop had brought him to his knees in grief, and then anger. Out of his pain, he'd felt it necessary to cut me out of his life entirely. He thought that amputation of our life together would make the pain easier to bear, but it hadn't. He'd spent years trying to cover his real feelings about losing me through distance, sarcasm, criticism, and anger.

He confessed that it was easier to choose to believe the Bishop's narrative, that I had been the instigator of events. By blaming me, in the immediate aftermath, his deep betrayal by the Bishop was temporarily softened. He confessed that the Bishop was not only his Bishop but also a father figure and mentor whom he had looked up to in a way he had never looked up to anyone before. He was deeply sorry and asked for my forgiveness. I told him I had forgiven him years before.

Arrangements were made and the next afternoon found me in Cincinnati helping David prepare the hospital bed that had been delivered. For the next week, we cared for Dave. Dave's sister and friends arrived, people I had not seen since before our divorce. David's partner, Amy, brought food, peace, and comfort.

One afternoon, Father Matthew Kelty was driven the more than two-hour drive from the Trappist Monastery of Gethsemani Abbey in Bardstown, Kentucky to Cincinnati to spend the afternoon with Dave. At ninety-one years old, Father Matthew Kelty had lived a long, full life of faith, including walking the 235-mile trip to Washington, DC to protest the Vietnam War in 1972. He was probably best known as the confessor of the Trappist monk, writer, activist, and Catholic theologian Thomas Merton. Father Kelty had also been Dave's mentor and confessor, both while Dave lived at Gethsemani and over the years when he returned on yearly retreats. Father Kelty was a poet and prolific writer and a revered spiritual master to many.

Father Kelty sat with Dave behind closed doors for much of the afternoon. As he was leaving, he approached me and said he would like to have a few words with me before they started the drive back to Kentucky, if I agreed. I assumed he wanted to tell me something about Dave's end-of-life care and was somewhat surprised when his serene, gentle, and humble eyes looked deeply into my own. "I want you to know I have prayed for you every single day since I first heard from Dave the circumstances of your divorce. Seeing you here with him is the answer to an old man's prayers. I hope by now you no longer blame yourself for the circumstances of your divorce."

He paused. "I believe you understand reconciliation in a very deep, personal way, in a way many others have difficulty comprehending. Dave is a truly fortunate man and is at peace now."

Dave passed away several days later with our son and me in the room. He and David had been listening to one of Dave's favorite albums by Johnny Cash that played as he took his final breath. As I listened to the words, I recognized the appropriateness and truth of them. Dave had indeed walked the line as he kept a close watch on his heart. And yet he had always felt love for me, and I for him, despite it all. And then with his last breath came the great silence and the chasm of what had been left unsaid between us. Moments later, like a great sigh, the chasm was filled with the only thing important—Love.

A couple of hours after Dave's body had been taken to the mortuary, Amy's five-year-old daughter, Morgan, solemnly approached me. In her hands she held an old cereal box covered with pictures she had drawn and cut-outs, of windows and a door. "I made a little spirit-house for Father Dave. Now that he doesn't have a body anymore, when he comes back to visit, his spirit will have a nice place to land."

24.

Consolidation of All Things Healing

I will set fire to the temple of your body
and make of its thorns a bower of roses.
Each humiliation, I bless, each loss, each agony.
Only death after death could have brought me
To this bare sun-dazzled desert where
You gush up in Everything.

Rumi, *The Way of Passion*, Andrew Harvey

The next several decades were marked by many inner and outer changes as the rose continued to hold its grip on my life in myriad ways. In early 1999, I accepted a job I had been recruited for by a woman I knew from Jan's meditation group. At that time, Abbott Northwestern Hospital was one of the first in the Twin Cities to get on board with the growing world of what was then known as complementary medicine, soon to become known as integrative medicine in academic centers and hospitals throughout the world. Although I was conflicted about leaving my work at the children's hospital and clinics, my curiosity and instinct to open myself to a new challenge paid off, so I said yes when they offered me the job.

In my new role, I worked with individuals, couples, and families. I facilitated small groups as well as developed programs at Abbott Northwestern in a new role as a healing coach with individuals with cancer. This was a role I was able to develop and fully define as I created a variety of supportive programs. The combination of creating a new program and being present with those making difficult choices soon became as rewarding as my work at the children's hospital had been.

Penny George, who had first envisioned my role and was part of the interviewing team, called me one day and asked if I had ever heard

245

of Dr. James Gordon, an author and leader in the growing world of complementary medicine. I hadn't. Penny said she had been telling Jim about the innovative and creative work I was doing, and that he was going to get in touch with me.

After we spoke, Jim decided that my work could indeed be the model for a national training program for cancer guides that he hoped to create. What had grabbed his attention were the innovative ways I worked with children and families with life-threatening illnesses through different stages of their journey, as well as transformative ways to work with those on the threshold of death. Patients benefited from understanding that cancer brings on an existential crisis, both psychological and spiritual in nature, creating the opportunity either to "just get through it" and return to your old life or to grow. Patients became open to working with both the psychological challenges they faced and the spiritual ones. Jim's hope was that I could help him train others to do the same.

While my work at Abbott Northwestern continued, I became part of a team of national experts in the field of cancer care to create Cancer Guides for the Center for Mind–Body Medicine (CMBM). Although housed in Washington, DC, CMBM conducted training throughout the United States and around the world. Jim invited me and Penny to attend that year's Professional Training in Mind–Body Medicine in order to experience that work and see if any of its elements should be integrated into the Cancer Guides program.

The training was rich with research on the neurobiology of stress, trauma, guided imagery, movement, spirituality, and various forms of meditation. In addition to the lectures and large group experiences, each day we participated in a small group experience. I was enjoying the program and learning a great deal until the day there was a lecture on genograms and learned we would each be constructing our own family genogram and sharing it in our small group. A wave of anxiety, followed by anger, moved through me. I recognized it as a defense because I had kept my life so compartmentalized. At times, I secretly felt like a fraud and wondered whether colleagues would respect me if they knew about the history of my family of origin. It was clearly time to test my assumption that if people knew my history, they wouldn't think well of me.

I thought about the recording I had made when I met with my Aunt Ethel as she told me about my family's history of war, death, poverty, and incest. In the small groups we were to look at our genograms as a unique portrait that could be explored to deepen our self-awareness, discover challenges and strengths in ourselves and in previous generations, explore and clarify family patterns, expand our perspective, see personal issues in a new way, and recognize past and current sources of support. We used various symbols for males and females and to indicate relationships, death, alcoholism, divorce, connection, or disconnection. Once I hesitantly sketched out the basic pattern and looked at my family picture in this way, I remembered that we were told we could add our own symbols. Here I added a symbol for church, my mothering tree, books, Dale, and many of those who impacted me in positive ways. I was beginning to see that again and again, it was love that outweighed the suffering.

I'd made a commitment to myself to practice honesty and self-awareness. However, I struggled with how much of my family history to share. I went to the group session aware of how reluctant I still was to talk about my family history, but I trusted that this was an opportunity for more growth.

Joel Evans was a wonderful physician whom I'd gotten to know a little as a part of the Cancer Guides initiative. As my group facilitator, Joel was knowledgeable, authentic, honest, funny, and gentle. We started with an opening meditation followed by check-in. Then Joel asked if anyone would be willing to volunteer to go first. When no one did, he turned to me. "Lora, would you be willing to share your genogram first?"

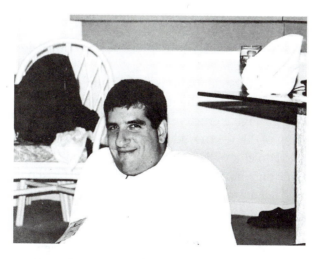

Dr. Joel Evans, part of the Cancer Guides initiative

Still working up the courage to share my genogram at all, I dove in. I began by admitting to the group that sharing my personal history in the group was challenging as there were some things that I had never talked about to anyone, other than in therapy. I took a deep breath and let go in a free fall of surrender to being in the moment and vowed to learn something from the process. In short order, I felt accepted and heard.

Several important realizations came to me as I talked about my family history. I unexpectedly was filled with admiration and pride for the ingenuity of the child I once was. I was able to appreciate my creativity in creating a parallel universe within the chaos of my life. While my mother was devouring beer, cigarettes, drugs, and men, I was fed on the books that filled me with the possibility of other ways to live. After reading a book, I'd retell it in my mind, then replay it in a make-believe universe that took me away from the daily fear. If I could easily create a new life in my imagination, I could find a way to do that in real life. As all this dawned on me, I looked around the room and felt gratitude for the group, as well as for myself. I had indeed created a new life and I saw it mirrored in the faces sitting in the circle with me.

As I pushed through my discomfort with sharing so much, I had an insight about my complicated relationship with money. I often felt guilty about being paid for anything enjoyable that I did. Of course, this was in large part because my mother bartered her body as well as mine for money, so, to me, money was dirty. I had never before connected my ongoing struggles with money to my history—it had been hidden in plain sight. I talked about Dale and how her presence awakened me to love for the first time, answering my continued childhood wish to understand why I was on this earth.

By the time all of the genograms were completed, I knew without a doubt that I really was not so different from others. Every person in that room had gone through a crucible and many had experienced trauma.

In the spring of 2001, I moved to Washington, D.C. to work full time as the Associate Director of the Center for Mind–Body Medicine. Nothing had prepared me for what it would be like to live in D.C. I'd only been there twice before and felt the intensity, but moving there rocked my world. Other than facilitating professional training programs, my work life required administration and organizational skills I lacked. I missed working directly with clients and children, and my learning curve was steep.

One night I had a bad belly ache. When the pain became unbearable, a housemate took me to a nearby emergency room where I learned that I had a full bowel obstruction. The attending physician wanted to rush me into surgery. I don't know what it was, but I had the sense that if I had surgery in that hospital, the outcome would not be good. The physician who saw me in the emergency room appeared too eager to get me into surgery. My colleague Amy was able to reach Jim Gordon, who promised to get in touch with a colon surgeon he knew for another opinion. The ER doctor insisted on keeping me in the emergency room, believing that no matter what I thought, I would be going to surgery that day.

I had Amy wheel me to the wall phone. I had missed a flight that morning and was supposed to be arriving in Minnesota for a retreat with Barbara that afternoon. When Barbara came to the phone, I explained what was going on.

"Lora, I want you to get very quiet inside, this will be over before you know it."

"But how can I do that when I'm in so much physical pain?" I protested.

"Didn't the doctor give you anything for the pain?" she asked.

"No, I won't take anything. I've had such bad allergic reactions to pain medications in the past."

"Let them give you something, it will be different this time."

I reluctantly agreed.

"If you can trust me, I can promise it will be different. Your job is to work on staying quietly centered and to pay attention. We'll be holding you in our hearts and working with you every day," Barbara promised.

When Amy wheeled me back to the area I had been in before, I explained to the ER doctor that a colon specialist would be coming later to give me a second opinion. The physician inserted a gastric tube in my nose to pump out some gastric juices from my very distended abdomen and started an IV in order to give me some pain relief.

As Amy sat in a nearby chair, I dozed on and off. As the pain subsided and the drugs took effect, I suddenly sat up. "I'm hallucinating now," I announced, laughing as I observed myself watching an unknown man's head bobbing around and looking at me from the top of the IV pole, then floating across the room.

Although I continued to have a few more visual hallucinations over the next several hours, I was able to remain unconcerned, thinking about various states of meditation I had experienced where I could simply watch, without judgment, what was rising and falling away, breath by breath, in each moment.

That afternoon, I was admitted to a room on the surgical floor and a colon surgeon Jim trusted came and looked over my labs and scans. He agreed to let me delay surgery for a day or two as long as my white blood cell count didn't go up. From the moment I had talked with Barbara, my ability to stay grounded and quiet internally continued. I became aware energetically of the exact moment each day when Barbara and those at the retreat center were prayerfully dedicating meditation on my behalf. First, there would be a quiet quickening of my energy and focus of attention, then an expanded awareness of the group that was beginning to gather on my behalf more than one thousand miles away. Despite uncomfortable tubes going in here and there, these times during the day I felt enlivened, more present at the retreat center with Barbara and the group than I felt in the hospital. I experienced the walls falling away. I was with the group in consciousness. It was as though I had changed the broadcasting channel and was transported to where the broadcast was emitting from.

A couple days later, the surgeon stopped by on his rounds and told me that he felt that since nothing had changed, he believed it was best for me to have surgery the next day. A few days earlier, I had been deeply concerned about surgery, both from my previous experiences of colon surgery and because, according to the ER doctor, it would require a colostomy and I couldn't quite bring myself to trust him or the hospital, which was dirty and extremely short-staffed. But by this time, I was in a space of such deep trust, I felt it didn't matter if I had surgery resulting in a colostomy, or even if I died. I completely trusted that only that which was for my highest good would come to pass. While the surgeon was talking, I felt that quickening I'd come to trust when meditation was about to start at the retreat. I was impatient for him to leave the room so I could begin to meditate with them.

The surgeon had no sooner left the room to write the order than I unexpectedly felt an overwhelming urge to go to the bathroom. Although conflicted by wanting to be in the meditation, I knew my body's need wouldn't be put off. I'd just made it to the bathroom when I had explosive diarrhea. I pulled the cord on the wall and told the nurse I wouldn't be needing surgery.

"I better hurry and catch the doctor, he was just writing the order," the nurse said.

"She couldn't have had spontaneous diarrhea, she had a full bowel obstruction. They don't just unblock on their own," the doctor said as he walked into the room with the nurse. "I don't believe this is possible. Do you mind if I just take a look?"

"Go ahead," I replied, a little embarrassed.

"I'll be damned, you've got some powerful prayer friends out there," he said. "I'm going to keep you in the hospital a few more days just to make sure you can handle food without another obstruction."

Jim Gordon visited the next day, bringing his encouragement, support, and acupuncture needles. I continued to tune into the retreat group meditations each day. I had no further problems and was eating solid food by the time I was released three days later. I called Barbara and the group to tell them my good news, but they already knew. They too had intuited my presence each day as they meditated on my behalf and as a group had felt the release of the obstruction. What I was doing on a physical level, they were doing emotionally and energetically within themselves and as a group.

On the morning of discharge, the doctor asked me if I had ever heard of Dr. Larry Dossey. I hadn't. He told me I might be interested in learning about Dossey's work as a cardiac surgeon and what he discovered about prayer, described in his book *Healing Words: The Power of Prayer and the Practice of Medicine*.[1] In the 1980s, Dr. Dossey discovered that patients being prayed for did much better than those who weren't. Dr. Dossey searched the research and analyzed over 100 scientifically well-designed experiments on the impact of prayer. He discovered that many of them showed that prayer affected everything from bringing down high blood pressure to healing wounds, the activity of leukemic white blood cells, and a positive impact on cancer cells and tumors. He asked himself, given the evidence, if he should begin to pray for his patients before surgery and whether it would be unethical if he did not. Each morning, he went to his office, earlier than usual, lit a candle, and while meditating prayed that his patients would achieve the best possible outcome.

Soon after, I read the following from Dr. Dossey's book, *Reinventing Medicine: Beyond Mind–Body to a New Era of Healing*:

I believe the vital ingredient is love—a state of caring and compassion that is so deep and genuine that the barriers we erect around the self are transcended ... When our focus is toward a principle of relatedness and oneness, and away from fragmentation and isolation, health ensues … Health and healing are about more than the eradication of disease. Health is related to wholeness and holy-knowing who we are and how we are connected with the world.[2]

I was discharged to home and packed that evening to leave for upstate New York, where the following day I was to do training with firefighters who had been at Ground Zero and their families. My colleague Debbie Kaplan and I were in charge of working with all the children. This was an exhausting training as well as satisfying and successful. The children's model that Debbie and I developed for the weekend was built on the CMBM model for adults, modified and expanded with skills tailor-made for children of all ages. Since then, it has been expanded and contributed to by other faculties. It continues to be used in the Advanced Professional Training Program in the United States and around the world. The manual that was eventually developed has now been translated into Hebrew, Arabic, and Spanish.

My work with CMBM continues to this day. Although I no longer live in D.C. or work full time, I continue to be a faculty member and this work has taken me around the world, to the Middle East, Haiti, and throughout the United States to work with traumatized communities.

Although I could fill a book with stories of the transformations I have witnessed and how the work continues to impact me, I share the following brief stories because of their relationship to my own ongoing healing, genograms, and the unexpected and spiritual aspects that can show up in this work.

Several days into a national training program, I was facilitating a small group that had begun to share their genograms as I had at my first training. That night I had the following dream.

I am in my hotel room, sleeping. I awaken in the dream, surrounded by my male ancestors; in a larger circle around them are the females. My Uncle Clinton, who caused me great trauma when he killed himself when I was three, steps forward and says, "Thank you for doing the work that you are doing. It's sacred work, that is not just beneficial for those who come after you but for those of us who have gone before you. I'm beginning to heal now. I'm sorry for what I did and am grateful to you and this work."

I realize that all of my male ancestors died before age forty. The room

*slowly begins to expand outward and appear as a series of holograms. I
see other hotel rooms and sleeping individuals. Surrounding them as they
sleep are their ancestors. Near them are the drawings of their genograms.
I recognize these sleeping people as members of the group that I facilitated
earlier that day. For some of them, they are mostly surrounded by male
ancestors, for others female, others a more mixed group. Those closest to their
sleeping body are the ancestors where there are blockages in the bloodline
caused by unhealed relationships. Holographically the scene widens into
rippling out into circles of ancestors. In a chorus they say, "Thank you, we
are beginning to heal now."*

We began the morning session with a breathing meditation and then
an opportunity for everyone to check in. Our talking object was a small
glass heart, reminding each person to speak and listen from their heart.
The first group member who wished to speak picked up the heart from
the table in the center of the circle and began. "Last night, I dreamed that
I was surrounded by some of my dead relatives. I felt they were there in
some sort of way blessing me. I feel lighter and freer than I ever have felt,
both because of the dream and because I shared my genogram yesterday.
My discomfort with my history feels more resolved."

We continued in clockwise fashion. One by one each member spoke
of what was most important. Seven out of the ten group members spoke
about dreaming that their deceased ancestors appeared. The heart came
to me. I knew we're in sacred time. I began to speak. "Last night I dreamed
that I was surrounded by my deceased male ancestors," I said. "My Uncle
Clinton who shot himself when I was three stepped forward in the dream.
He told me that this is sacred work and that he is beginning to heal now.
What we do, we do for those who come after us and it impacts those who
have gone before."

We sat in silence, the room filled with appreciation for the sanctity of
that moment.

A few months later, I was attending a training in San Diego. On the
last day, as the closing ritual was about to begin, a drunken, disheveled
young man reeking of alcohol wandered into the room and walked up
to the microphone. Jim graciously handed him the mic. The young man
began to cry and was nearly unintelligible as he thanked us for our work
with returning vets and those who work with them. He had recently
returned from Afghanistan.

As I was leaving the room for a faculty meeting and dinner a short while later, the young man came up to me and threw his arms around me, weeping. "I'm sorry, mama, I didn't want to kill anyone. Forgive me. I'm sorry, I'm sorry."

I murmured to him that it was okay. I pulled away so that I could look him in the eyes as my heart opened with compassion. "It's ok, you did what you needed to then. You're forgiven. It's okay now."

I had just fully forgiven my uncle Clinton through this man.

I learned a short while later that this vet had been living under the bridge behind the convention center; many of our training participants had been sharing their lunch with him throughout the week.

The CMBM model is a resiliency model that has brought my personal and professional lives together in an authentic and empowering way. For the past twenty-plus years, this work has been a gift that keeps on giving, no matter how many times I've led a group or been on the team and asked to do a lecture. At this time in history, we know that complete healing from trauma is possible. There has been a great deal of research written on what has been termed "post-traumatic growth." I'm fortunate to be among those this applies to. The gifts that have come from post-traumatic growth are not only increased resilience but others that continue to change my life. I have also witnessed how the CMBM model continues to change lives throughout the country in each training I've been privileged to be a part of.

***

I moved to Tucson, Arizona in 2003 after accepting a job as a Retreat Services Director for a new program. I would be creating and facilitating retreats for adults as well as children with cancer. I also designed programs for couples, family retreats, and specialized retreats for young adults with cancer, and helped facilitate equine retreats. I loved this job and found it to be creative and stretching me in more new ways of working with others.

In 2005, however, I knew it was time to return to Minnesota. I had grown both personally and professionally in more ways than I could ever have imagined. For the next several years, I was invited back to do trainings and facilitate retreats. Since returning to Minnesota, I have done a variety of things, including being part of a team that designed and taught the Health Coaching Program at the University of Minnesota

Center for Spirituality and Healing. In addition to serving as a consultant and educator and designing programs for a variety of organizations, I've conducted trainings and workshops throughout the state of Minnesota.

After working as the director of an Integrative Medicine Program which abruptly closed in 2009 because of the financial crisis, I accepted a role at PrairieCare, an innovative mental health organization dedicated to transforming psychiatric healthcare by providing every individual patient with the care they truly need. It was here that I met Dr. Stephen Setterberg, a psychiatrist who would come to have a significant impact on my life, one that continues to this day. Our first meeting took place through video conferencing. I was impressed by his insightfulness and presence. Toward the end of our meeting, he asked if I had any questions for him. I thought about it for a minute.

"What makes your heart sing?" I found myself asking.

"What an interesting question, no one's ever asked me that before."

For a moment, he grew quiet and appeared to be thinking. "But I can tell you exactly what it is. Sometimes, I'm sitting with a patient or family and this space opens between us. I don't have the language for it, but it's an alive, almost electric space of real possibility. This is sacred space. And that's real medicine."

25.

Weaving the World Together

The creative carries us. It takes us on the journey to wherever it is that we must go. Sometimes, the way is arduous, sometimes it is terrifying, sometimes too swift. But these conditions are compensated for by the beauty and meaning that also belong to this journey. It never occurred to me to reject the gift of the dark horse, no matter what loss I sustained to have it. Nor would I reject the presence of the wounded artist within myself, as the wound is one means by which we reach compassion.

Deena Metzger, *Writing for Your Life*

Listening wove my world together and became the gateway to all that matters. The essence of life continues to call to me in myriad ways. It called me through dreams, synchronistic experiences, through my longings, books, nature, and people. It was through deep listening that a book called to me from the crowded bookshelves of a local book shop. I first learned of Deena Metzger in 1992 through her book *Writing for Your Life: A Guide and Companion to the Inner Worlds*.[1] It was unlike anything I had read about the art and craft of writing. It spoke to my soul. I felt a gravitational pull toward her and knew that sometime, in the future, I would meet her.

One day in August of 2013, for no particular reason, Deena Metzger's name came to mind. When I had read her book twenty-one years previously, if she had a website back then, I hadn't found it. The day she came to mind, I discovered her website, where there were images of elephants everywhere—I'd been dreaming of elephants at the time. There were words like "healing stories" and "peace making" and I knew it was time to connect with her, so I arranged to attend a weekend retreat in

September that Deena would be facilitating, near Nashville, Tennessee. At the time, I didn't think I was drawn to the topic of the weekend, but I wanted to be in her presence to see if my instincts to connect with her were right. If so, I intended to ask her if she would work with me around my writing. I felt a charge of energy and excitement after signing up for the workshop and eagerly anticipated meeting Deena.

That evening, I was sitting in bed, when I noticed a large spider sitting on the top of the curtain rod. I have been squeamish about spiders all of my life. "What am I going to do with you? I don't have a clue how to get you down from there and I sure can't go to sleep with you in the room," I found myself saying aloud to the spider.

The spider obliged and moved halfway down the curtain. Now at eye level, she seemed to be looking right at me, as though communing with me and trying to tell me something. Unfortunately, my squeamishness around spiders got in the way of any message that I might otherwise have been able to receive. In the end, I confess, I called David to come over and remove her. I was relieved that he captured her between a piece of cardboard and a glass and carried her outside, releasing her back to nature. I don't normally talk to spiders and I hadn't seen one since a very large tarantula appeared on my windshield shortly before I left Tucson.

But that was just the beginning—over the next several weeks, dozens of spiders came into my life. One spider after another appeared in various sizes and varieties. They showed up in places where I couldn't ignore them: attached from the hand railing of the steps to the door handle of my car, one built a web right across the door into the house; another scurried around the bathtub as I ran water for a bath. I encountered them in many places, not just at home but on walks in the morning dew, their webs shimmering and calling out to me. As September grew close, my growing comfort and intrigue with spiders was amplified, right along with my excitement about finally getting to meet Deena Metzger.

As I checked into the retreat center outside of Nashville, I turned on the lights of my assigned room and the first thing that greeted me at perfect eye level was a large, black spider hanging from the top of the bedroom window by a single silken thread. I had no idea what to make of all of these sightings at the time, but it appeared as though something was amiss. I seldom saw spiders, so I found myself wondering why I was seeing so many of them at this time in my life.

The weekend was nothing like I had imagined—it was far better and

Deena Metzger, my writing mentor

a good lesson in not making assumptions. I felt perfectly at home and, as soon as I met Deena, I knew my instincts had been right. Before the weekend was over, she had agreed to work with me. The morning after the retreat, I woke to a stinging pinch and reddening bite. A spider sat in the center of my chest, right at heart level. Over the weekend, a participant, Danelia, was stung in the exact same place by a wasp while drying off after a shower. She wrapped herself in a towel and gently extracted the wasp from her chest and carried it outside, releasing it with a blessing and gratitude for the gift she'd received from it, although she didn't know what the gift was yet. She told us that wasps don't die following a bite like bees do, so she felt it was important to release it. I admired her presence of mind and ability to do that. A traditional Chinese medicine practitioner in the group told us that the acupuncture points that Danelia had been bitten on are called "the hall of spirits" and the "central altar."

In our first phone meeting after the retreat, Deena gave me an assignment to look back through all my journals and my memory and jot down significant experiences I had over the years with Spirit: through dreams, synchronistic events, people, and anything else that came to mind or grabbed my attention. Once that was done, we would begin to look for patterns and to see in what ways Spirit communicated with me and the ways I had been taken by Spirit. We also talked about my spider sightings before the weekend and the bite I received the morning after. As I began to write this book, I looked in my journal notes from that call and what immediately jumped off the page, grabbing my attention, were the words, *I was bitten by Spirit in spider form. I need to yield to carrying the spider's intelligence with heart … Her web is a home for the future. We weave webs and things that are not of us get stuck and are caught in our web and they feed us and are transformed into nourishment.*

In the February 5, 2020 edition of *New Scientist*, I read that spiders *possess an extraordinary kind of consciousness, including minds that extend beyond their bodies.* This consciousness extends throughout their entire web. It is humbling to witness mystery's divine signature in such a small and intelligent being. It serves as a reminder for me to continue to be open and learn from anything that I'm afraid of. I think about how writing this book has taken my full awareness and I've had to look at every single aspect of my life, leaving out nothing essential, continuing to open my consciousness. The fear, the good and the bad, light and dark, all caught in the web of my life, have needed to be fully digested in order to make sense of it and see it within a larger context. The web of my life was becoming the home to my future.

I met with Deena throughout 2013 and into 2014, revisiting significant experiences in my life, looking for themes and ways I might begin to write this book, and then we would discuss them. One theme was certain: repetition is one of the ways Spirit talks to me through strangers, dreams, and the great mystery of coincidences. It was important to appreciate the events that might seem like exotic moments, but I would need to appreciate them in a humble manner and in the right relationship. Deena also instructed me to pay attention to ways resistance would come up and to challenge myself to meet it. We were having our last phone consultation before Deena embarked on her summer sabbatical to devote herself to her own writing. The call was winding down when Deena asked what I was doing over the summer. I replied that I was thinking about a road trip; I had a lot of vacation time to use or I would lose it. Deena asked me what I thought about a road trip out to her place in southern California to drive with her to the Yakama reservation in Washington state to interview elders for the book she was working on. She also hoped we could get reservations to visit Hanford Nuclear Site, a uranium enrichment/plutonium manufacturing facility, built in 1943, near the town of Richland, in south-central Washington state. I immediately agreed. I went to bed early the night before departing for Deena's. The dream began.

I am at a party. Many people I know are milling around, intent on socializing. I become aware of a woman off to the side, standing in a far corner in tremendous pain. Others are avoiding her. No one is acknowledging her. I point her out to the hostess who tells me that she doesn't have time for that, she's busy throwing a party. I seek out another friend who I think might know the woman. She replies: "That's her problem, I'm here to have fun tonight." The last person I approach looks disgusted and tells me yes, she knows this person, but she's not taking care of her or anyone else tonight. She's there for a good time.

I decide to leave the party, but before going, I slowly approach the woman in pain. I gently touch her on the shoulder and gaze deeply into her eyes. She momentarily tears up and quietly replies. "Thank you, I'll be ok now that someone has seen me."

I leave the building and begin walking down the street, and look up noticing strange, very low, gray swirling clouds. It occurs to me that those aren't clouds, that's another level of consciousness. The clouds part, an opening appears, at first like the sun when the clouds part. From this other realm of consciousness, long-robed beings begin to move downward in two processional lines as though coming down a staircase of light. At the back, and in the center of the two processional lines, one being is carrying something in his arms; radiant light is pouring from whatever is being carried. My first thought is that he is carrying the ark of the covenant. Not certain what that means, I continue to watch as the procession grows closer, the one in the center moves forward through the line. I can now more clearly see what he is carrying. It looks like a very old (perhaps ancient) skeletal woman whose skin is very thin, like parchment paper—her life essence is pure luminous energy, radiating outward in all directions and enclosing her companions in radiating light.

The man carrying her moves gracefully toward me. He steps forward and indicates that I'm to take her. He places her in my arms and nods. She is lighter than a feather and lovingly gazes at me. The beings all disappear back the way they've come.

A limo pulls up and the door opens. I step into the back seat. I am still holding her—more energy than flesh—as she continues to look in and through me. In front of us is a small video monitor. It comes on. I watch as one holy person after another moves through it: Buddha, Christ, Gandhi, Black Elk, the Dalai Lama, Mother Teresa, Nelson Mandela, Desmond Tutu, and many more. The luminous skeleton serenely gazes at me.

As I began my drive across the country the next morning, I discovered I would never be able to look at clouds in the same way because of the dream. As I drove across South Dakota, I was reminded of falling in love with the wide, spacious vastness of the sky when I lived there while married to Dave. I found a track of Gregorian chants on my iPhone and began it in honor of Dave and our time together, and the honor of being with him as he died. Throughout my three-day drive, I had a strong sense the luminous skeletal woman from my dream was accompanying me.

A few months earlier, Deena and I were on our monthly call and the topic of my colon surgery came up. I told her the story and repeated what the surgeon had said about the good news of not finding cancer, just yards of dead, necrotic colon that looked like I'd already had radiation treatment. Deena stopped me, remembering that I had lived on the reservation in South Dakota while I was married; she wondered if perhaps I had lived close to where uranium mining had taken place. I checked into it and we lived too far away and it didn't seem likely that I could have had any exposure, but it got me thinking. I remembered that I heard from my cousin, Sharon, that she and her mother had also both had their colons removed. I wondered what we had in common. What came to me was that my aunt and cousin had lived for years very close to a major drug manufacturing plant. I lived near them for a year and remembered that in third grade, the teacher would hand out small squares of white fabric to cover our noses on the walk home from school on the days that black smoke and ashes would pour from the tall chimneys of the plant.

Deena suggested that I speak to a friend of hers, a scientist who spent a lot of years in the Chicago area on the board of a nuclear regulatory agency. The phone call took place as I sat in a rest stop halfway to Deena's. The scientist told me there was no way I could have lived that close to that particular drug manufacturing company on Lake Michigan and not been impacted. This company, which I'm choosing not to name, had received a number of violations regarding toxic waste, and there are many other superfund sites in that area being monitored by the Environmental Protection Agency. It seemed like a possibility that my aunt, cousin, and I had all lost our colons because of living in such close proximity to this place. Knowing that Deena and I were setting out for the Yakama reservation and Hanford, the scientist also suggested some research that we might want to look into.

I rested at Deena's and spent a day on the computer following up on the research her friend had suggested. I began by educating myself about Hanford as I had never heard of it. I learned that the Hanford nuclear facility sits on land that was once the hunting and fishing grounds for a number of Northwest tribes, including the Yakama Nation, Walla Walla, Cayuse, and Umatilla, since time long before the government took over the land to build Hanford. The waters of the Columbia running through Hanford are spawning grounds for chinook and, prior to Hanford, provided bountiful salmon that those nations harvested in abundance.

Although first settlers and now farmers occupy much of the land once home to many Northwest tribes, 1855 treaty rights guarantee American Indian people "usual and customary" access to much of the land and river that Hanford occupies. Hanford contains millions of gallons of toxic waste that has been leaked by wind, land, and air into the ecosystem for the past seventy years. For decades Hanford brought water from the Columbia River to cool its nuclear reactors, then without treatment funneled it back into the river, creating devastating effects to those living downwind and on the nearby Yakama reservation, directly affecting fish and wildlife, food and economic subsistence. The effect of Hanford on the Columbia's salmon population has disproportionately affected the health of American Indian people whose livelihoods and spiritual life are centered on the salmon.

I was sickened to read about radiation experiments conducted on human subjects without their knowledge or consent, summed up by this statement made in the US Government Report "American nuclear guinea pigs: Three decades of radiation experiments on U.S. citizens, Congressional Subcommittee on Energy Conservation and Power," published in November 1986:

> Although these experiments did provide information on the retention and absorption of radioactive material by the human body, the experiments are nonetheless repugnant because human subjects were essentially used as guinea pigs and calibration devices.[2]

This committee was chaired by Edward D. Markey of Massachusetts, who detailed tests conducted throughout the United States from the 1940s to the 1970s. "They involved injecting uranium and plutonium into human subjects. At times, experimenters fed subjects both real and simulated fallout from atom bomb tests, had them breathe radioactive air, and gave them radioactive fish."

As I continued to read, I stared at the computer in shock—the words "Elgin State Hospital" rose like a ghost in the middle of the screen in front of me:

ANL-1. Radium as an Experimental Therapy for Treating Mental Disorders at Elgin State Hospital in Elgin, Illinois —Patients in a state mental hospital were injected with radium as an experimental therapy for mental disorders. The experiment appears to have been conducted at the Elgin State Hospital, in Elgin, Illinois, between 1931 and 1933. Documents indicate that 70 to 450 micrograms of radium226 (Ra^{226}) were injected.[3]

Although I read that the research was conducted decades before I was in Elgin, it triggered the memory of having been drugged, both at ISPI and at Elgin. It caught my attention and wouldn't let go. For years, the sound of rattling keys, the smell of urine, food served cafeteria-style on battered plastic trays, drugs, the sight of dilapidated buildings from the late 1800s had occupied my dreams and hurled me into terror. Elgin State Hospital was now ancient history and a time I'd designated as insignificant. I had once dealt with it extensively in therapy and even returned to Elgin with my therapist at the time. Then why had I started to tremble and my body gone cold? I quickly moved on to the research for Deena, but somehow could not shake the feeling of being haunted and unnerved by what I'd seen.

"How's the research going?" Deena asked when I saw her a few hours later.

"It's ok," I replied.

I shrugged, trying to indicate, no big deal. Deena caught it though.

"What's going on?" she asked.

"I was just a little bit shaken to see something of my past in the research," I hesitantly explained.

"What part of your past?" she asked.

I found myself thinking that there was no place to hide. "I stumbled onto some research they were doing at a state hospital I was committed to while in college," I explained, trying to minimize this time in my life.

But Deena doesn't miss much. "And just why is it I've never heard you were in a state hospital?"

She asked so gently, it nearly split me open. But the secret I'd carried for decades curled itself into a tight ball in my belly. I realized I felt shameful about that period of my life. I'd convinced myself that my time in Elgin had nothing to do with my current life—there had been no reason for me to look back at this part of my history—but I know delusion to be sneaky. I carried the negative stigma deep inside me that I had been committed to a state hospital—thrown away by the state. I wanted to minimize its importance, bury this ghost, where it belonged and get back to the present. But when that ghost came back into my life like that, I found it impossible to rebury. And I would have missed out on so much that was important to who I have become and what I would learn from facing this part of my past. Had Spirit not made me consciously aware of its presence over the next several months, I don't know if I would have survived facing the full truth of my life as it presented itself to me.

A group of individuals who had been connected to Everyday Gandhis, founded and directed by Cynthia Travis, a non-profit, grassroots peace-building project that also works with former child soldiers in Liberia, came together at Deena's in a council to share their concerns and to listen deeply, including to recent pertinent dreams, in order to see how to respond with their colleagues in Liberia, given the growing Ebola crisis. Although I wasn't part of this group, I was invited to participate, but I was distracted thinking about what I had read earlier in the day. We would begin our trip the next day.

That night as I slept, I dreamed.

I am back in the council room where we'd gathered earlier. I look around for someone who seems to be missing, but I'm uncertain who it is. Then I see him standing in the doorway and recognize him as someone I had met at a conference years before, but I can't remember his name. We have a very deep spiritual conversation over lunch. He looks at me and says, "I'm Orland Bishop, please ask Deena to be in touch with me."

The next morning at breakfast, Deena asked me if I had any dreams. This was not out of the ordinary for her. I answered in the affirmative and asked her if she knew someone by that name. She told me yes and that she had hoped he'd attend the council the night before. I explained that I dreamed about him and told her the dream and his request that I ask her to get in touch with him. She didn't have a telephone number for him. I thought that was that, end of it, but on our drive Deena expressed concern about leaving town while there was so much worry about Ebola in Liberia.

That evening we stopped for the night at the house of a friend of Deena's outside of San Francisco. After introductions, Jaune invited us to sit on her lovely terrace together, unwinding with a glass of wine before dinner. She also knew Orland Bishop and the organization he had started, Shade Tree Multicultural Foundation. Deena asked me to share my dream.

"I have Orland's number right here in my phone, he seldom picks up, but let's call him," Jaune said as she reached for her phone. Orland was on speaker phone and we listened as he answered immediately. Deena explained that I had a dream that he had come to me the night before and she asked me to speak about it. I reminded him that we'd met a number of years before at a "Ways of Knowing" conference put on by the University of Minnesota Center for Spirituality and Healing, and then related the dream to him.

"Lora's got this just right," he said. "I really wanted to get there and couldn't get away from the city in time. I didn't have Deena's number and had reached out looking for a conduit and you were it, so I asked you to have Deena contact me."

I have no idea about the subsequent private conversation that Orland and Deena had after that, but I'm certain it was important and seemed to ease Deena's concerns about leaving her community for the trip. Spirit had used me right after I'd had the experience of the Pandora's box of Elgin opening; somehow the dream had soothed me with the realization that although there was still work to do around that period of my life, I had all the help I needed in Deena and in Spirit. My discomfort and unrest slowly unwound itself as Deena and I traveled together, talking about many things. I think of that trip now as time out of time, living in parallel realities as we talked about my time in Elgin, my shame and trauma. Deena would continually pull me back from remembering the past to remind me of all the ways Spirit had intervened in my life. And soon it became obvious that I had been sustained through every negative event through some spiritual intervention, often subtle, often without which I would not have survived. I had finally recognized Spirit in every step of my life and on this trip, in unbelievable ways. This also gave me the ability to re-enter my past and understand what the horror of it had really been, and to begin to see the bigger picture.

As we drove the back roads across Oregon and then Washington state, I found myself wondering whether there was anything else I hadn't shared with Deena. I realized I had never told her about my experiences following surgery so many years before. I began to tell her about the conversation I had with the grasshopper on my balcony. I told Deena how Cathy and I drove to Jan's and how as I told Cathy about my journal full of grasshopper messages, one had suddenly jumped on the windshield.

"At the time, I'd thought of it as just a random coincidence," I said to Deena.

"Stop the car! Look!

There was a large grasshopper sitting on my windshield, so close I gazed into his eyes.

"We have to make an offering." Deena reached for her tobacco pouch and opened her side of the car. After the offering was made, we sat together in quiet meditation, surrounded by the gentle song of grasshoppers encircling us.

That night, I dreamed. *An indigenous medicine man is circling me with a rattle. His headpiece looks like the head of a grasshopper and his rattle makes the rhythmic chirping sounds. He tells me that the sound is balancing and grounding for me and that I am to walk in beauty and balance.*

Hanford Nuclear Site allows only a small number of people to visit each year. Deena had placed us on a long waiting list; nonetheless, our names came up with two openings for a tour on the very days we would be available. We found ourselves in the most eerie, catastrophic, and polluted of places in America. One of the ten most toxic places on the planet. The land is nearly ghost white, the suffering of the earth palpable. As the tour bus drove through the property, a building stood off to the side marked with the same identification as the drug manufacturing plant I had lived close to in third grade.

Deena pointed out that I had arrived at her house on August 6th, the anniversary of the bombing of Hiroshima in 1945. We were in the redwood forest together on August 9th, the anniversary of the bombing of Nagasaki. The Hanford Nuclear Site mined and synthesized uranium into plutonium which went into the making of the atom bomb tested at the Trinity site and later dropped on Nagasaki. I carry that history in my body and lineage because of my Uncle Clinton's military service, bearing witness to his suicide, five years after the atom bombs were dropped, and the loss of my colon because of living in such proximity to the drug manufacturing plant.

We spent several days visiting with Yakama Elders, including Russell Jim. In 2017, he was awarded an honorary doctorate degree from Heritage University for his work on decades of monitoring Hanford regarding nuclear waste. John Basset, president of Heritage University in the state of Washington, spoke at the ceremony and honored Russell Jim's work by saying, "He speaks for an injured land that couldn't speak for itself."[4]

For nearly four decades Russell Jim was one of the sharpest critics of Hanford and at the same time made constructive progress in creating awareness and fought to clean up the aftereffects of Hanford. He fought so that no further harm could come to his people. He knew his science well and on behalf of the Yakama tribe he led the Environmental Restoration and Waste Management program to study the impact of radiation and nuclear waste. Over the years, he was able to rally the support of senators and congressmen alike, and was instrumental in giving tribes a voice at the congressional table.

Deena and I had the honor of spending several hours with Russell Jim. He was not only passionate about the environment, but also faithfully carried the traditions, culture, and language of his people to the next generation. Russell Jim told us a number of stories, but I'll share only two of the ones that impacted me. The first was about his uncle who was in prison for a petty crime and was lured into agreeing to a radiation experiment on his testicles in exchange for $25 cash and an early parole. He died within weeks of being released. These experiments went on in both Washington's and Oregon's prisons between 1963 and 1973. It was later learned that the University of Washington had been conducting the experiments on behalf of the government. When I heard about his uncle, I felt a mysterious pang. Russell Jim and I looked at each other with mutual understanding.

Russell Jim also told us about days of toxic plumes of radioactive material released over Yakama land. Days or weeks later large trucks arrived with X-ray machines and everyone would be herded into line to get X-rayed, most likely so that the government could learn where the toxicity had landed in their bodies. The incidence of cancer in both children and adults is high throughout Indian country and the problem is compounded by scarce medical services.

Russell Jim is quoted in a report to U.S. President George W. Bush, "Facing cancer in Indian country: The Yakama Nation and Pacific Northwest Tribes: President's Cancer Panel 2002 annual report." He stated: "[We] have in our front yard down here the oldest and largest nuclear facility that has … bombarded this area with radioisotopes for 60 years. And we do not know what has happened to the gene pool of the Yakama Nation."[5]

On our drive to and from these places, Deena and I talked a great deal about Elgin and my history. My mind went round in circles, making connections I couldn't put into words: the nuclear industry, pharmaceutical companies, electric companies, destruction of values, lethal substances, mind-altering substances, erasing of cultural values, banished whistleblowers, lack of principles, abuse of power, and rape of the land slowly wove their way through my psyche to the Second World War, Dr. L, military bases, prostitution, experimentation, ISPI, Elgin, and Hanford. They were all the same—examples of exploitation and corruption. It became clear that the book I was writing would be missing an essential piece if I left Elgin out. I was beginning to understand more deeply just how important this history is, not just to me but to the world.

On August 28, 2014, one week after leaving Deena's, I had a dream.

I am walking in a forest and I hear and see things I've never noticed before. The land is a living, breathing being. Everything is animated, the trees are interconnected and reach out to each other and to me. I see other connections and the circle of life everywhere. I look around and notice a large spider busily weaving a web. She pauses, then scurries down from the center of her home and hangs by a single thread, staring at me. I am given a mandate that I am to enter into the right relationship with all of life. We are to live together in respect and harmony if survival is to be possible. I'm to weave the threads of my life into a mantle of authority—a ritual robe while I become fully spirit-informed by the matter of my life, and become generative—light informing matter—the materialization of alchemized gold.

As I woke, I saw quickly, in a gestalt, how everything was changing: my relationship to myself, others, history, my body, experiences, my story, and the larger world. The realization hit me that I was one of many now carrying the soul of the world. In accepting the mandate of authority given to me in the dream, I knew that I must carry it into my writing, including the horrific circumstances of Elgin, with love and compassion for that young girl I once was, and with humility, integrity, and ongoing connection to Spirit. I knew that it would require everything of me and it would change everything. I vowed to begin by finding Sydney Krampitz, the nurse who had been able to obtain my release from Elgin.

26.

Return

I have walked through many lives,
some of them my own,
and I am not who I was,
though some principle of being
abides, from which I struggle not to stray.
Stanley Kunitz, The Layers, The Collected Poems

I'm alive today because of Sydney, who risked both her professional life and graduate school grant to advocate for me to be released from Elgin State Hospital. Following my release, Sydney and I had initially stayed connected—I frequently visited her and she flew to South Dakota to attend my graduation when I received my master's degree in 1983. I eventually lost track of her due to multiple moves on both our parts and I had started using a cell phone, unlisted in any directory. In 2016, after a week of searching, I located her daughter, Becky, and learned that Sydney was living in a small community south of Kansas City.

When I had met Sydney at ISPI nearly fifty years before, she was a psychiatric nurse who worked part-time evening shifts and was working on her master's degree. She went on to become Dr. Sydney Krampitz, Associate Dean of Nursing at the University of Kansas Medical Center and Director of Graduate Programs. She had then moved to Reno, Nevada, becoming Dean of the School of Nursing at University of Nevada. She eventually returned to Kansas. Sydney authored several books on psychiatric nursing and worked in a variety of leadership and clinical roles until her retirement. She was also a retired colonel of the US Air Force Reserves, and was appointed as the assistant to the USAF Surgeon General for Mental Health.

Sydney did not have email or a house phone, but Becky gave me her cell phone number. After connecting by phone, I drove for a long weekend to Kansas to visit her, eager to reconnect. During that first visit, we talked about the intervening years and the book I had started to write. During times we'd spent together in the past we talked little about Elgin. I kept the discussions pretty short and superficial, and Sydney never pushed, understanding I wasn't strong enough then to know the truth. I was now ready to really talk about Elgin and learn as much as I could from her. I sat in shock as I listened to her begin to fill me in on the critical gaps in my own story.

"Lora, what you need to understand is that ISPI was a research hospital. Local emergency rooms were sent flyers, recruiting appropriate research candidates to the many research projects they conducted through different universities in the Chicago area."

She stopped, letting that sink in before continuing. "The emergency room that you were sent to had to have known it was sending you to a research facility. Each floor was managed by a different university and each one was conducting a variety of different kinds of research projects. It was assumed that ISPI only kept its doors open through the support of research grants and provided their hospitalized patients as the research subjects. You were placed on a unit run by the University of Illinois designated specifically for young adults who had no family support—this meant you had no one to look out for you or to advocate on your behalf. It was a perfect setup for them to do whatever kind of research they wanted and have no one to answer to."

Sydney shook her head in disgust.

"They never told me. They never requested permission," I objected.

"I'm sorry to say that happened a lot back then and still goes on today in some places," Sydney told me.

"Even though I didn't know any of this, I knew my life was in danger," I said.

"They only allowed a select few nurses access to the patients' charts and I wasn't one of them, so it took me a while to figure out what was going on, but, over time, I grew concerned and frustrated at what others were saying about you in the nursing report. They were furious that you kept thwarting their attempts to make you take the medications," Sydney continued.

"But how did they know I wasn't taking them?"

"You may not remember this, but urinalysis and blood draws were done routinely several times a week. This was part of the research in order to track the absorption of the drugs that each individual was on. Through those tests, they repeatedly discovered when you hadn't been taking the prescribed pharmaceuticals they gave out each day."

"I remember those tests, but I never made the link between them and the medications. I had no idea that's how they found out I was spitting them out. I even tried to spit out the liquid Thorazine when they put me on that—what nasty-tasting stuff that was," I interjected.

"In report, they complained about you all of the time and I watched them grow increasingly bitter, more frustrated, and eventually outright angry at you. They took it as a personal affront to them that they couldn't make you take the drugs, and then on top of that, you had the audacity to run away. One day in report one of them actually said, 'How dare that brat.' I couldn't believe how unprofessional they were when they talked about you. I believe that you were committed to Elgin primarily as a punishment for that. Your non-compliance was screwing up their research," she said with disgust.

It wasn't long before Sydney resigned from ISPI. "That Thursday evening when I came to work and learned you'd been court committed and would be transferred the following morning, I was furious and very concerned. Everyone knew that Elgin had the worst history of any hospital in the state. It was a place where people who were given up on were dumped and seldom ever got out. I was outraged and committed myself to seeing to it that you were released. I'm just so sorry it took me so long. I was so busy with school and family that I just kept putting a visit off. I really thought they would see you were a bright college student and quickly discharge you.

"One Saturday morning, I woke up with you on my mind. I had this nagging need to confirm once and for all that you'd been discharged. I wanted desperately to believe that was true. I called and to my horror learned you were still a patient. I vowed that no matter what it cost me, I had a moral obligation to visit you as I'd promised and find a way for you to be released. So, I drove the two-and-a-half, maybe three hours with traffic to see you that afternoon. I can't even begin to tell you how shocked I was when I saw how drugged and minimally responsive you were. I don't think you recognized me at first."

"I'm just so grateful that you came and worked so hard for me to get me out."

"I am too—look at where life has taken you. I would have trouble living with myself had I not kept my commitment to you."

Sydney was in full support of my writing endeavors and wanted to make a contribution and be involved, using her background in research to help me. Together, we began to explore the history of research and experimentation at ISPI and Elgin. Eventually we broadened our efforts to include other state hospitals and medical centers around the country. ISPI was not only a research hospital, it received funds funneled through the University of Illinois from the CIA, beginning after the Second World War through the Cold War.

A book titled *An Illustrated History: Illinois Public Mental Health Services, 1847–2000* by Joseph J. Mehr, Ph.D. confirms what Sydney had said:

> The role of ISPI was to conduct research and provide training to the staff of the state hospitals ... Researchers at ISPI or its affiliated universities would make important contributions to knowledge about mental illness in the many areas of neuroanatomy, neuropathology, neurophysiology, neurochemistry, biophysics, psychophysiology, clinical studies and electroencephalography. The peer-reviewed papers from 1959 to the late 1990s are filled with the publications of ISPI staff .... the basic sciences were important, and biologically oriented research (particularly with new drugs) ruled supreme at ISPI.[1]

Although the ER doctor had said I was being sent to ISPI for rest, and to "get my feet under me," I had been nothing but an unwitting research subject.

By the following spring of 2017, Sydney and I had visited each other several times and had both compiled a great deal of information. When I told Sydney that I was planning a trip to return to Elgin, without hesitation she said that she wanted to accompany me. Not only were her support and company helpful, but her experience with research would prove invaluable.

After driving to Kansas to pick her up, our journey began with a visit to the Glore Psychiatric Museum in St. Joseph, Missouri. Sydney had often taken her psychiatric nursing students to the museum every year when she taught at UMKC School of Nursing. The museum chronicles the

145-year history of the state hospital, as well as centuries of mental health treatment devices going back to the sixteenth, seventeenth, and eighteenth centuries. One of the many devices we looked at was the "Lunatic Box," an erect coffin or clock case where in the eighteenth and nineteenth centuries patients were placed, standing, for long periods of time, often standing in their excrement, until their caregiver deemed them calm. There was also the "Tranquilizer Chair," complete with a built-in portable toilet, a hood that went over the head, and hand and feet restraints. The sign above it read that it had been created by Benjamin Rush, known as "The Father of American Psychiatry." Also on exhibit were various leather restraints and straitjackets, such as the ones I had been placed in while at Elgin. There were exhibits of lobotomy instruments, dental chairs, and instruments used for research from when it was believed that removing people's teeth could cure them of mental illness.

I found it hard to believe that people who supposedly cared for the vulnerable could possibly justify that these so-called treatments were humane and anything other than instruments of torture, no matter what era they had lived in. They must have viewed the patients as less than human, otherwise how could they rationalize causing such extreme suffering? The pain that had been inflicted on me in the name of "treatment" was a continuation of this same inhumane, sordid history embedded in the growth of psychiatric care.

From Missouri, we drove to Springfield, Illinois. We spent several days going through the files at the state library, where the librarian was extremely helpful, and then headed to the state archives, where we went through one box after another of archival materials. We found much more than I had anticipated. We discovered no lack of documentation of the poor conditions of Elgin State Hospital, as well as in other Illinois state facilities for both children and adults. In the evenings, we went back to our hotel and pored over the reports we had obtained.

"Patient deaths at Elgin State Hospital," a report by the Illinois Legislative Commission given to the Illinois General Assembly in 1974, was particularly relevant.[2] We learned that the commission had been formed to investigate untimely and unexpected deaths of patients after complaints were filed by family members. This report revealed an appalling history of Elgin. The wards were chronically understaffed: at times just one attendant for a ward of 50–150 patients. There was a shortage of physicians and nurses, frequently leaving one nurse or doctor per 300–500 patients. The doctors, with very few exceptions, had "limited licenses and experience." Most could only practice in a state hospital as a newcomer to the United States. Few, if any of them, had psychiatric training.

Minimally trained attendants routinely dispensed the medications because of the shortage of nurses. They had not received training regarding contraindications of medications. Patients were frequently overdosed. Charting was often missing and lacked significant details in all areas of patient care. Now, it made sense why I had only seen a doctor twice, for less than ten minutes: once upon admission and then at discharge. The nurse, Miss P., was seldom seen on the ward, usually early in the morning, and appeared to have little to do with patients, except on the day new admissions arrived.

Severe overcrowding was common, along with physical deterioration of buildings, poor staff morale, and outright abuse of patients. There was an overreliance on restraints and seclusion, and the overuse of drugs: particularly, chlorpromazine, marketed under the trade name Thorazine, an antipsychotic consistently used to control the overcrowded wards. Thorazine was seen as providing a similar effect to a frontal lobotomy, rendering patients immobile, lethargic, and emotionally disengaged.

The Legislative Commission report was comprehensive and included detailed patient autopsy results, leaving no room for the imagination. One "physician" was found guilty of involuntary manslaughter after three patients died because of his incompetence in the use of pharmaceuticals. It was discovered that he had no medical license: his diploma had been forged.

One investigation insisted upon by relatives of an unexpected death provided a detailed account of a healthy, developmentally disabled eighteen-year-old male who had died within thirty hours of admission, from neglect and over-medication of Thorazine. The supervising attendant had stated on admission that she did not want any "retards" on her unit. After playfully turning over several trash cans, the young man was immediately placed in restraints where he remained for no reason until his death. He had aspirated on his own blood after shredding his tongue from agitation while in restraints that shackled him to the bed. Testimony and the scant records revealed that he was not fed, offered water only once, and allowed once or twice to use the restroom. The on-call physician gave orders over the phone without examining the patient, even when it was reported that he was bleeding profusely and continuously biting his tongue. Although Sydney had the tolerance to relentlessly plow through the material, I had to take it much slower and read it over several weeks after returning from the trip. It was the most horrendous thing I had ever read.

I had visited Elgin State Hospital in 1992 with my therapist, Charlotte. At the time she believed that it was essential in order for me to move forward in my therapy and believed that I had suffered soul loss while there. Although Charlotte had made arrangements ahead of time for our therapeutic visit, we were required to stop at the administration building to pick up passes. The administrator had seemed encouraging and told me that she thought I'd find things much improved since I'd been a patient in the 1960s.

We were able to walk through some of the buildings, but not the actual Kirkbride building where I had lived—it was considered dangerous because of leaky pipes and falling plaster, and it was filled with asbestos. It was torn down a year later. On that earlier visit, I could hardly tolerate being on the property, but I was able to identify the building where I had been raped, with its ceiling of tin-tiled rosettes. It was exactly as I had remembered. I quickly became overwhelmed and fled outside, gasping for breath, as a flashback began of the events that had taken place in that garage.

Charlotte helped me to calm down. When I looked up, there standing in front of us were two large dumpsters. They were probably much like the one I had been thrown into on that dreadful night of my rape. Perhaps these stood on the very spot as the dumpster I'd been carried to and thrown into as easily as garbage. I stepped forward with Charlotte to look into a metal container that could have served as my coffin. Perhaps I shouldn't have been surprised, but the two dumpsters were filled with whiskey bottles and beer cans. My grief and fear were replaced with a quiet, burning flame of righteous indignation as I began to collect a bag of bottles and cans. When we returned the visitor passes, I took a bag of liquor bottles and another filled with beer cans and set them on the administrator's desk. "You told me things had changed since I was a patient, but not much change could have happened if I found this kind of shit in your dumpster. It would be inappropriate if patients on medication were drinking it and even worse for the staff on duty. We didn't have to look far to find this, it was in plain sight, and there's still a lot more in the dumpsters." I turned and walked out the door, believing that would be the last place on earth I would ever want to revisit.

Twenty-six years later Sydney and I concluded the research part of our trip and arrived in the town of Elgin midafternoon with heavy hearts, full of the images laid out in the reports we had read. The images that indicted Elgin's dysfunctions and shame stood in harsh contrast to the idyllic feeling of the town of Elgin, located along the Fox River. We drove out to the state hospital, located on the edge of town. I was filled with the memory of how traumatic it had been when I was there before, with Charlotte. The illusion of serenity that had once emanated from the park-like setting, with its manicured lawns, central fountain, and bright, beautiful flowerbeds, was gone. The remaining original buildings looked shadowed and heavy, like they could no longer bear the stories they had held inside for so long. Many were decrepit and abandoned, with broken glass and falling bricks. The grounds seemed stark, barren, and the few newer buildings looked cold and unwelcoming, and made no pretense to be otherwise.

We met with William Briska early the next morning. Bill is the president of the City of Elgin's Historical Society and he was an employee of the state hospital for twenty-seven years. He is also the author of a major historical book, *The History of Elgin Mental Health Center: Evolution of a State Hospital*, published in 1997.[3] I had talked to him on the phone a few weeks earlier after discovering his book. Bill was gracious with his time and information, taking us on a driving tour of the hospital grounds, pointing out where some of the old buildings that had been torn down once stood. He answered our questions and pointed out the newer, intimidating forensic buildings, now housing the "criminally insane." Bill explained the ways that Elgin had slowly changed over the years after a number of federal investigations, such as the one we had just read about in the state library. He told us he thought that newer mental health laws and guidelines were more clearly written and more strictly enforced than they had been when I was a patient.

I had arranged for Bill to take us to Elgin State Hospital's cemetery, explaining that I once knew a person named Mary Nolte who was buried there. As we drove to the cemetery, a sadness enveloped me as I thought about the last time that I had seen Mary.

Hillside Cemetery provided the Elgin state hospitals' unclaimed dead a final resting place through the 1980s, Bill explained. He had an uncanny

Mary Nolte's grave in the cemetery at Elgin State Hospital[3]

memory for dates and history. He told us a number of stories of people who are buried in the nearly one thousand graves, including a man named Robert Wilson, who was born in 1836 as a slave and died in Elgin in 1948 as the oldest patient at that time. Confederate records established his age as one hundred and twelve. He also pointed out graves of eight unnamed, newborn infants.

Bill had a registry for the cemetery and was easily able to find Mary's grave. A simple headstone, covered with bird waste, dead leaves, and weeds, marked the spot. Bill crouched down and began pulling weeds and clearing away the dead leaves. Sydney stood nearby in quiet support, her face a map of feelings, mirroring my own. My hand shook slightly as I laid white roses and a small, heart-shaped stone near Mary's faded name. Bill asked if he could take a picture and returned from getting his camera from the car with a water bottle and a rag. He knelt down, moved the roses and heart-stone aside, and slowly poured water on Mary's grave, cleaning off dirt and bird feces before replacing the roses and stone. I was deeply moved as Bill performed a simple act of human kindness. As he gently cleaned the gravestone, Bill asked me to speak about Mary. Reluctantly, I began.

"I became friends with Mary at ISPI. She had been diagnosed with untreatable grand-mal seizures that couldn't be controlled. She had been a concert pianist and suffered an embarrassing seizure on the stage, leading to a near-fatal suicide attempt and her admission to ISPI. Mary wasn't much of a talker. She'd always expressed herself through her music. Her only family were her music and fellow musicians. The doctor told her she would never be able to perform publicly again—her career and life were over. During our time in ISPI together, whenever I or anyone else became upset, she would sit down and begin to play the small upright piano that stood against the wall in the day room of the hospital. She also used the piano to express her feelings. Sometimes she played heavy somber music for hours until the staff made her quit."

Deep in thought, I paused, wondering if I should tell the whole story.

"I had been a patient at Elgin for some time when Mary arrived at the same unit, on a court commitment. A few days later, she had a severe seizure and was transferred to a medical ward. One day, another patient came up to me and handed me a grounds pass that she had been given by an attendant for whom she had provided sexual favors. She may have thought this would motivate me to provide sexual favors to them, considering she had been pestering me, telling me I'd have an easier time in Elgin and get passes and other favors if I did so. Although I didn't condone her behavior, I was grateful for the pass. I was allowed a half hour to see Mary. I found her on a very overcrowded ward contained in an adult-sized crib. Between the time it took to walk to her ward and back to mine, we only had about ten or fifteen minutes to visit."

Taking a deep breath, I looked at Bill and Sydney before continuing.

"As I was about to leave my visit with Mary, I told her I'd try to find a way to see her again. She told me to not bother. I asked her if she was getting discharged. She smiled the most radiant of smiles and slowly lifted the corner of her pillow and revealed a stash of pills. She placed her finger to her lips, whispering, 'Shh.' I received one more grounds pass a week later and went to see her—her bed was empty. The attendant told me she had committed suicide by taking an overdose of pills. Mary had shown me the pills that would end her life. I felt torn about not having reported her intentions."

"It was probably best you didn't report it," Bill said. "She wouldn't have wanted to live with a seizure disorder, in a place like Elgin, when there was no cure in sight."

Sydney agreed. I was grateful for their understanding and lack of judgment.

For Mary, a life without music was no life at all. The last time that I had seen her, her chronically sad and hopeless face had been replaced by one of peace. She wasn't asking to be rescued, she had cared enough to say goodbye.

At lunch, one of the questions Bill asked me was if I knew what medications I had been on and what my discharge had been like. "There was no plan for discharge as I recall, other than a five-minute meeting with the same psychiatrist I met briefly on admission. The female physician gave me a small packet of pills. She told me to take them and find a community mental health center to get more. The discharge report says I was on with Thorazine, Stelazine, Mellaril, Librium, and Dilantin."

"Did the doctor at least tell you what the withdrawal symptoms would be like if you didn't take them?" Bill asked but went on and answered his own question. "No, of course she didn't," he said, with an exasperated sigh. "It's amazing you survived the hospital in the first place and then I bet you went into classic withdrawal. I can't believe we're having this conversation, it's hard to understand how you ever got out. In those days, it was near impossible to get released. I'm surprised you aren't dead," Bill said. "How did you get out?"

Sydney jumped in and told Bill all she had done on my behalf.

Until Bill's question about my discharge, I hadn't ever thought about the possibility that the drugs I'd been on could cause withdrawal symptoms when I discontinued them as soon as I'd been released. That evening, a little research led me to the conclusion that it had been outright dangerous for me to stop taking the medications so abruptly. It was irresponsible for the physician not to have told me the ramifications of stopping the meds or at the least given me instructions on how to titrate them if I did choose to go off of them. She did neither one. Suddenly all the symptoms I'd experienced the first several months following my release made sense.

While Sydney was resting the next day, I drove back to the hospital on my own. I had a sense that something was missing—a longing I couldn't quite identify. I pulled the car up close to the foundation of the original building, where I had spent all of those horrible months. We'd learned from Bill that this front part of the property had been sold to the city of Elgin, so I wasn't concerned about security kicking me out. The grass was spring green. I sat touching the corner edge of the old foundation of the Kirkbride building I had lived in and let myself begin to search back in time. I thought about all that had occurred, everything I had suffered on that property. As I looked around, I saw that what I longed for was what was missing. The beautiful tree that had once stood outside the women's south ward was gone. The tree with the filtered light streaming through her branches that had called to me through the barred window so long ago, when I'd returned to the ward from dinner before any of the other women. I didn't know it clearly back then, but *that tree* had helped save me by reminding me of a world before and one outside the imprisoning walls of Elgin. I wanted to see her, thank her, bow down before her. She was gone.

Her presence had reminded me that there was more than the stagnant, slow, dying days I was surrounded by. Memories had rushed back: the smell of fresh-mowed grass, the colors of flowers bursting with life, the beauty and symmetry of the bark, green leaves, and the scampering life of insects and squirrels in the branching arms of a tree. She had reminded me that life moved on, through the seasons, and perhaps she had given me a small dose of hope. All these years later, most of the old trees have been cut down, the grounds are slowly dying, just like those of us trapped inside had been in a long-drawn-out daily dying, from neglect, toxic pharmaceuticals, individual and institutional abuse.

A fault line cracked open my long-held grief, opening me to waves of outrage and sadness. There was little beauty left to anchor my grief or the earth's sorrow in this place of nearly two hundred years of human misery. I lay full-bodied on the body of the earth, in need of solid ground. The earth's mourning reached up to join my own. Grief for the tree turned into grief for the girl I had once been and for all living beings who suffered on that property.

For the next hour, deep tidal waves moved through my heart, my muscles, my guts, and out through every pore and cell. Earthquake shudders passed through me as the horror and violence done to me, and to so many others, came to mind. A deep cleansing of my entire being was taking place. I was now strong enough, and had lived long enough, to be able to fully see what had happened to me for what it was, as I vomited it out in an animal, low keening wail that took my breath away.

The tears and deep wracking sobs continued to come throughout that day and into the following week at unexpected moments. I wept for all those buried in the cemetery and the babies buried with no names. I raged about the inadequate resources and everything that had kept the employees at Elgin from doing a decent and humane job. I thundered fury about ISPI which had at least seventy-five times more resources and staff because of its research dollars. I spit out fury about the staff at ISPI who sent me to Elgin to punish me for being a confused college student who refused to take unnecessary drugs. I cried in grief and anger at the pharmaceutical companies that exploit animals and humans in the name of science and for the ongoing ethical violations by medicine, corporations, politicians, and psychology. The memory of the tree outside the window at Elgin had been a catalyst for what had been building in me for days. I sobbed for that tree and for all of mother earth. When it seemed as though I had emptied myself and there were no tears left, what came next were sorrow and compassion for the employees of Elgin State Hospital. I cried for those who had lost themselves as they worked in such soul-numbing circumstances for an honest wage, in a system of cruelty, broken stories, broken promises, broken hearts and lives. I wondered just how much it must have cost them.

You can't go to a place like Elgin State Hospital and come out the same. At least, I couldn't. Not the first time as a patient, and not so many decades later as a visitor. The first time I left Elgin with a small, brown paper bag just big enough to hold a two-by-four-inch envelope with pills and my state-issued toothbrush, toothpaste, and comb. The bag was too small to hold much of anything, but it was too large to hold what little remained of the young woman who held the reverberations of a judge's gavel shuddering through the geography of her entire body. You can't go to a place like Elgin State Hospital and come out the same. I didn't the first time, I came out with a lot less of myself.

This time, I left with something much bigger than a small bag, bigger than a suitcase, bigger than Elgin State Hospital. I left with *outrage* and *compassion* wrapped together in a large prayer bundle for the world and for all those who have never had a voice.

27.

Presence

When fully present with another, you activate the potential of becoming a healing environment, by offering yourself as an environment in which the individual can dwell. The gift of presence takes place in this dwelling place and serves as "home." Your presence enables another's being to be unconcealed, your own being is more fully revealed.

Holistic Nursing: A Handbook for Practice,
Barbara Montgomery Dossey and Lynn Keegan

Early Summer 2017. A couple of days after returning from Elgin, I had a pre-scheduled meeting with Dr. Stephen Setterberg. From our first meeting, when he had thoughtfully answered my question about what made his heart sing, our relationship had deepened and grown over the years as we met many times as colleagues to discuss staff and patients in the PrairieCare psychiatric hospital and clinic system, leadership development, and other issues. Through the years, he was someone I had come to truly trust and admire.

On this day, I arrived on fire, with a heart and face filled with sorrow and other things that I hadn't yet fully given voice to. The meeting had initially been set up so that Stephen could meet Sydney and hear about our trip to Elgin. Unfortunately, Sydney was so undone by the large body of the investigative report we'd discovered at the state library and exhausted from the trip itself, she decided to return home right after leaving Illinois rather than come to Minnesota as originally planned. So, Stephen and I had the time and space to ourselves, seated comfortably in his light-filled office.

As I talked about my sorrow and outrage for the young woman I had once been, my grief felt alive and intense. Stephen leaned in and asked potent questions, genuinely interested in everything I had to say about the trip. As he listened to me, I knew all my feelings and revelations were welcome in this place of trust and safety.

My outrage and anguish grew as I described to Stephen what was revealed in the 1974 Illinois Legislative Investigative Commission Report on patient deaths at Elgin. I held nothing back as I talked about some of the most horrific findings revealed in the report, the incredible responsibility I felt to speak for others, like Mary who had died in Elgin. It had been made clear to me that I was one of the few who had made it out of such places during that era of Thorazine, and other pharmaceuticals, non-consensual research, abuse, and neglect.

There came a moment in which I looked up from my rant and noticed that Stephen was weeping along with me. He asked if I would pass him the Kleenex box which was closest to me. Time slowed down, urging me to savor this moment. Here I was speaking about the psychiatric abuse and the rampant cruelty in the psychiatric system and Stephen, a psychiatrist himself, was weeping. As I handed him the Kleenex, the irony of it swept over me. I started to laugh a bit and pointed out that I was giving *him* the Kleenex. He joined me, laughing too. I could almost feel the invisible wounds of betrayal and injury while in Elgin come together, like scar tissue healing. The space that Stephen had described as "real medicine" during our first meeting enveloped me that day when I needed deep listening and compassion, freshly returned from Elgin.

As I reflect on these moments, I know that this is indeed a portion of the "real medicine" that everyone longs for—a deep presence. I can see that I'd first experienced it with Dale as a child, and then with so many other human angels throughout my life. Stephen and the others couldn't do anything to fix me or take away my anguish or the challenges of my life, and they didn't even try. They were present and became *presence itself* in their deep listening and attention, so that for precious moments I felt held in the larger body of humanity, and no longer alone. It wasn't one encounter, or one person present in that way, but many individuals over the years who shared with me a treasure beyond price that can change the tapestry of a life as, over time, the golden threads of light and love outnumber and heal what has been broken.

Several years ago, the full realization of the potential impact of my story on others hit me in an unexpected way when my professional life took me to working with a small group of sixth- and seventh-grade girls. They sat around a table in a school library, near-mute with despair following the recent death of a friend to suicide and the burden of their own traumatic lives. I attempted to engage them in relaxation techniques and encouraged them to talk about their emotions. They had barricaded themselves against feelings, and appeared flat and depressed, but I could see they were nearly paralyzed in their grief and anxiety.

A girl sitting across from me, whom I'll call Stella, looked up, studying me, and threw out a challenge, punctuated with a sarcastic, biting cadence to her speech. "Why are you *really* here?" The "really" dripped with sarcasm.

Although introductions had been offered at the beginning of the group, intuitively, I knew it was something else she sought. "I've come with my heart open, in the hopes of bringing my ability to listen, and perhaps some helpful tools."

She shrugged indifferently. I repeated some of the themes that had emerged in the other groups of over two hundred young people I had worked with over the course of the week: hopelessness, anxiety, isolation, loss of meaning, bullying, abuse, family members who had fallen victim to drug and alcohol addiction, fear of loss of drinking water, extinction and climate change, and fear of the future.

Stella released a long, drawn-out sigh before looking away, seeming unmoved by my words. My heart and mind stuttered with the realization that it all sounded, well, pretty lame. An inner voice whispered that I had to go deeper and be more authentic with her. After several seconds I responded. "When I was your age, I lived in the kind of darkness and loss of hope that I see in your eyes. I tried suicide more than once. I remember what it was like to feel completely hopeless and unable to be with the pain that life threw at me. But there were people who came into my life and held hope for me until I could find it for myself. They held a candle in the light of my darkest despair. If they hadn't been there for me, I wouldn't be here today."

Stella shrugged and met my gaze with a forcefield of hopelessness. "I don't believe you. You look too happy. Too peaceful."

For a second, I wanted to defend myself from the intensity of her despair and disbelief. "I don't know if I could have believed what I just said to you back then either. It took me many years to feel the peace and happiness that you see, to escape from the darkness that held me hostage.

For a very long time, I never thought I would feel the way I do now or have the life I have."

She looked away.

It seemed time to move on and I handed out paper and markers and suggested it might help to draw or write about how they were feeling if it was too hard to talk about it. They slowly began to draw and then to talk about their concerns. Before concluding, I asked each girl to identify one person whom they felt they could talk to if they needed support. It became clear that most of them felt isolated, even from each other, though a couple had trusted adults they named.

Stella was last. She slowly rolled up her sleeves. With a mixture of fear and defiance, she held out her freshly cut arms. A roadmap of living, oozing flesh revealed her rage, self-hatred, and pain. Her mask fell away as she bit off words of challenge. "This is who I talk to. I talk to my flesh. I do this to let out the pain. This is why I'm still alive. I can at least talk to my flesh."

I could barely breathe as I looked into her pleading eyes. I inhaled deeply. Very slowly, I rolled up my sleeves and exposed my own scarred flesh. An offering of fifty-plus years of proof that I, too, had felt that alone and hopeless. "I talked to my flesh too, when there was no one else. I did this to release the pain and because I hated myself. This is why I am still alive. I could at least do that when no one else would listen to me."

Suddenly, in a flurry of movement, Stella got up, ran around the table, and threw herself into my arms, sobbing. In that moment, as I held this small bundle of heaving misery in my arms, I was grateful for my scars. After she calmed down, I admitted that I had felt very vulnerable showing her my arms. It was the first time I had ever done that—I had always kept them hidden.

"I believe you now," she said. And then she paused. "Before, I thought you were just another white bitch who didn't know anything," she said shyly.

She'd called me out, daring me to be more authentic, more aware, and to become a better healer. As I looked into Stella's nearly smiling face, it became clear to me that one of my greatest gifts for others is my history— including my scarred body. That day, in those moments, my history had been transformed into medicine.

Fishing for Fallen Light

If each day falls inside each night,
there exists a well
where clarity is imprisoned.
We need to sit on the rim of the well of darkness
And fish for fallen light
with patience.

Pablo Neruda, *The Sea and the Bells*

As I began writing this book, I was searching for clarity through the darkness of my childhood and eventual commitment to Elgin State Hospital. The journey has opened me to a depth of awareness about the circumstances in which cruelty breeds and grows, to disease proportions. It has opened in me a deeper state of compassion for those who work in exploitive systems without adequate training, burnout prevention, or fair wages. In my thirst for understanding my life, that of my ancestors, and those who have had no voice, I have sought answers to a number of questions. Did institutions like Elgin begin with good intentions and change over time? Is there a dark history of psychiatry and mental health that needs to come to light? What have been the dominant influences on mental health attitudes and treatment that would have led to my experience? Have there been treatment models other than those that have dominated psychiatry's troubled past that have been tried with success? And how can change occur so that we no longer build on the mistakes of the past?

At first, I conducted the research for my own understanding without any intention of presenting it here. However, as more and more accumulated, it began to reveal a pattern that I couldn't turn away from.

The same invisible, ineffable force you have met throughout the book, particularly when I discovered books that lit up revealing what I needed to learn about kundalini energy, archetype of the Mystical Rose, and all things related to the spiritual world, insistently guided me to the books and research you are about to read. All of this was bringing me to what I really needed to begin to understand. As I began to look at the years of research and books in order to decide if, why, and how to reveal what I had discovered, a strong sense of guidance seemed to hover nearby as the material began to easily fall into an order. A story emerged that insisted on being included.

My quest was to better understand, and to bear witness to, the darkness of our collective history, especially the ways that the most marginalized among us have been systematically abused. As my own story proves, it is only by excavating our concealed history—one scarred by suffering—that we can fully embrace the light that is possible in the present, and that awaits us into the future.

As Pablo Neruda's poem suggests, I've sat on the rim of the well of darkness, fishing for fallen light throughout both my personal and my professional lives, sifting through the deepest dark of history for answers. The history of the United States is not what appears in history books, and the complete history of psychiatry and psychology is usually not taught in academic centers. It is necessary to face their complex past if we have any hopes of surviving and transforming into a better future for all beings.

But before sitting on the edge of that darkness with me, we'll begin with a time when a small group of Quakers had the moral courage to deeply care and to act accordingly.

American journalist and author Robert Whitaker provides a well-written and thorough description of the complex history of psychiatry in his book *Mad in America*. In Chapter 2, he writes that following the French Revolution, the idea of moral treatment for mental illness was planted in 1793, when Phillipe Pinel was assigned by the French government to attend to the insane. Up to that point, lunatics were treated worse than animals, shackled to walls by chains, ridiculed, abused, neglected, and starved. Shortly before the time Pinel began his new role as lay superintendent, a man named Jean Baptiste Pussin had begun to treat the insane more humanely by increasing their allotment of food and reducing the use of restraints. Pussin quickly noticed that when the insane were not treated with cruelty and were given more adequate food each day, they began to act more rationally. He realized that many of the manifestations of their madness, such as ranting, tearing of their clothes, screaming, and smearing feces, were most often out of protest over the ways in which they were being treated.

Inspired by the early work of Pussin, Pinel thought deeply about the care of the insane, and he began to take careful and detailed histories. He believed that the treatments recommended at the time in medical books were seldom helpful and perhaps even made patients' conditions much worse. He decided rather than using the physical remedies of the day to instead focus on understanding and managing the mind. He talked and listened to his patients' concerns and noticed that patients behaved more appropriately when treated with kindness and care. At some level Pinel believed it was his moral duty to care for them in this way.

As Robert Whitaker details, in 1791, Hannah Mills, a Quaker woman, died through neglect in the York asylum. From then forward, the Quakers began to quietly open small homes to care for the mentally ill in retreat-like settings and were quite successful. One was established in Boston, opened by the members of the Congregational Church, which later became known as McLean Hospital, and continues to this day as a center of excellence. Another moral treatment asylum opened in New York City as well as one in Hartford, Connecticut. Each of these asylums was privately funded and primarily catered to the wealthy. Visitors to these institutions came away impressed, including the writer Charles Dickens. Moral treatment was known to create good results. The incidence of success and return to the community was high in each moral treatment center during this period. In Worcester State Lunatic's Asylum, within a year of admission, more than 80 percent of patients left the hospital, recovered.

Whitaker goes on to write about a time in which moral treatment appeared to rise and take precedence, representing more humane attitudes for the care of the suffering. As Erica Lilleleht, Psy.D. writes, drawing on the work of scholars of moral treatment such as Samuel Tuke and Benjamin Rush: "Moral treatment came to encompass an approach to madness that rejected the Renaissance notion that those who had lost their reason had lost it permanently, and thus partook of 'the nature of … animals'" (1997, page 175). However, Whitaker goes on to tell us about a counter movement that had begun to discredit moral treatment as a viable option.

The forces that would lead to the downfall of moral treatment began appearing into the 1840s and before the end of the century, moral treatment would be disparaged as a hopelessly naive notion. Yet it was during this period of downfall that moral treatment, in a new form, would remind the future of its potential to heal, and was best practiced. For more than forty years from 1841 to 1883, moral treatment held sway at the Pennsylvania Hospital for the Insane, during which time, the asylum was continually governed by a memorable Quaker physician, Thomas Kirkbride ... Kirkbride embraced all the usual methods of moral treatment, applying them with unflagging energy. (pages 31–32)

The more I learned about Thomas Kirkbride and other examples of moral treatment, the more I saw how humane and successful that model had originally been. It was a far cry from the lack of treatment and abuse I'd received at Elgin and the crumbling, drafty, asbestos-filled buildings, stinking of decades of human waste.

Whitaker and other historians of moral treatment, including Lilleleht and historian of psychiatry George Mora, describe Kirkbride's influence, his innovations, and systematic approach to the treatment of the mentally ill. Whitaker (2002) writes:

Thomas Kirkbride was a founding member of the Association of Medical Superintendents for the Insane, which was considered a forerunner of the American Psychiatric Association .... What most distinguished the care at the hospital was Kirkbride's skill as a healer. At this asylum, the doctor patient relationship was the critical element in the curative process. (page 32)

Unfortunately, this humane form of treatment as developed by the Quakers and deepened by Kirkbride was short-lived, signaling a missed opportunity for the profession of psychiatry.

What *could* have been an effective way to treat human suffering was snuffed out by excessive concern about finances, and because, simmering in the background, there was an ideological virus indoctrinating people to believe that the mentally ill were defective, undeserving, and not in need of humane treatment. No longer were devoted physicians hired; instead facilities were led by superintendents who could manage lean budgets, rather than hiring and training attendants in the moral treatment model with the capacity for compassion. As Whitaker writes: "Criminals and vagrants weren't likely to coddle the noxious patients … Attendants turned to maintaining order in the old way—with coercion, brute force, and liberal use of restraints … The care and optimism of the 1840s was replaced by pessimism in the 1870s and belief that moral treatment had failed" (page 35).

I found this decline described in detail through the eyes and ears of a patient in the 1860s in an official report archived in the Illinois state library, titled *The Prisoners' Hidden Life, or Insane Asylums Unveiled.* As described therein, on June 18, 1860, Mrs. Elizabeth Packard was committed without the benefit of a hearing to the Northern Illinois State Insane Asylum by her husband, a Calvinist minister, because she began to express liberal religious beliefs that differed from his own. Mrs. Packard spent three years in the asylum documenting "her imprisonment." After her release, she separated from her husband and began to campaign for the rights of women and the mentally ill. She founded the Anti-Insane Asylum Society, published numerous books, and was instrumental in the 1867 passage of an Illinois law, "Bill for the Protection of Personal Liberty," which guaranteed the right to a public hearing to anyone, including wives, who was accused of insanity. She testified to witnessing the daily abuse of patients by attendants who would beat patients around the head and face with keys, leaving them black and blue for weeks, pulling off hair, kicking, punching, and scratching patients. They were punished for the least thing and without provocation by having buckets of water poured down the front of their dresses and not allowed to change them for the remainder of the day. She testified that "this behavior and others even more cruel was the norm and the brutality toward patients occurred daily and created insanity where it had not previously existed" (Packard, 1868, page 52).

Eighty years later, Albert Deutsch, an American journalist and social historian, found similar abuse and deplorable conditions that he described in a groundbreaking exposé of state mental hospitals in the 1940s. In his book *The Shame of the States*, accompanied by horrific photographs of the neglectful, demoralizing conditions in state hospitals throughout the United States, Deutsch called for a public reform movement as the only way to enact significant changes in the state mental hospital system. He emphasized lack of funding as well as overcrowding as the causes of the problems he witnessed, and pointed toward a lack of public pressure on state representatives as the ultimate reason for the hospitals' limited budgets.

Deutsch writes about the Nuremberg trial of Dr. Karl Brandt, personal physician to Adolf Hitler, who calmly declared before the American military tribunal in Nuremberg on February 5, 1947: "The life of an insane person is not in keeping with human dignity." Dr. Brandt, on trial as a war criminal, was presenting the philosophy underlying the program that put to death 275,000 "lunatics and cripples" as "useless eaters." It was an act of mercy, he said, to shorten the lives of these miserable creatures. The cost of maintaining German "insane asylums," he explained, amounted to 350 million marks a year—"a great price for the state to pay." A battleship could be built for that sum, he added (1948, page 96).

Deutsch made a stark observation: "The spines of many American readers were chilled when the Nuremberg dispatches recounted the details of the Nazi euthanasia program, as narrated by witness Brandt. The thought flashed through many a mind: Thank Heaven, we are not like that. No, indeed, we are not like the Nazis. We do not kill off 'insane' people, coldly, as a matter of official state policy. We do not kill them deliberately. We do it by neglect" (1948, page 96). In my experience of Elgin State Hospital in the late 1960s, neglect was rampant: the lack of adequate heat in the winter months; closed, locked windows in the summer; dirt and filth everywhere, including dried feces; lack of privacy in the toilets; the lack of drinking water; and the overcrowding without sufficient chairs for all patients. Treatment of any sort was non-existent, and attendants ran the ward without supervision or adequate training.

As Whitaker (2002) writes, moral treatment:

> … was replaced by a belief—touted as grounded in science— that the severely mentally ill were carriers of defective "germ plasm," and as such posed a perilous threat to the future health of American society. In a stream of scientific articles, newspaper editorials, and popular books, the mentally ill were described as a degenerate strain of humanity, "social wastage" that bred at alarming rates and burdened normal Americans with the expense of paying for their upkeep. (pages 41–42)

Both Dr. Brandt's heartless comments in Nuremberg and Whitaker's well-researched description of the perceptions of the mentally ill are expressions of the movement now known as eugenics. Eugenics first became active in England and was named by Sir Francis Galton, a half-cousin to Darwin, in the late 1800s. Galton was an English intellectual whose work included statistics, psychology, meteorology, and genetics. In England and Canada, the eugenics movement promoted selective breeding of desirable traits. In contrast, once the eugenics movement moved to the United States in the 1900s, its focus was on eliminating negative traits, "degeneracy," and the continuing decline of the "human stock." Deutsch's first book, *The Mentally Ill in America*, written in 1937, critically assesses attitudes throughout history toward the mentally ill and mentally deficient. In it, Deutsch describes the way in which foundational beliefs regarding defectives influenced mental health in America and the growth and popularity of the eugenics movement. Through early times into the founding of colonial America, infants were frequently killed when born defective in any way. Deutsch chronicles the murderous opinions about the mentally ill and disabled children, describing how early Christianity—including Martin Luther—taught that children born defective were of the devil and should be drowned. Deutsch likens this recommendation to families to get rid of defective offspring to the early practice of negative eugenics.

When immigration to America increased in the middle of the nineteenth century, the ruling and predominant culture was that of white, Anglo-Saxon Protestants. The newcomers from Ireland, Italy, Germany, as well as Jewish people from around the world, were ideological fodder for the fire of eugenics as the ruling race and class increasingly felt threatened by the presence of those they deemed inferior—"others." All of this resulted in the white and well-to-do believing that they were bearing the burden of immigration, which they believed was the cause of increased social problems, that resulted in the need for systemic solutions, including orphanages, prisons, and especially insane asylums. Whitaker draws on one voice from the era, writing: "As early as 1891 ... Victoria Woodhull ... argued that the 'best minds' of the day agreed that: 'imbeciles, criminals, paupers and the otherwise unfit must not be bred'" (page 46). These kinds of sentiments have persisted, embedded deeply in the fabric of American society.

Reading Deutsch's work (1948), and learning more about the eugenics movement, I have a whole new understanding about why I was so often teased as being "white trash"—disposable, disgusting, something to be gotten rid of—as a child labeled by the parents of children I played with.

They disapproved of me, and at the time it made no sense; now I see how these kinds of passing comments were an expression of the same thinking as that which led to practices of discrimination throughout history and to eugenic thinking of a grouping of people as being superior versus inferior. Although we didn't live literally by railroad tracks, I frequently was dismissed as "living on the other side of the tracks," or "the wrong side of the tracks." A friend recently told me that she was adopted and would often overhear discussions by her new extended family inquiring about her adoptive parents: "what kind of stock does she come from?"

In *Against Their Will: The Secret History of Medical Experimentation on Children in Cold War America* Allen Hornblum, Judith Newman, and Gregory Dober document that many of the most highly-respected academic centers in the United States offered eugenic theory and curriculum classes emphasizing the importance of eugenic theory and practice.

By the start of the First World War, more than forty-four major universities were offering eugenics courses. This number would mushroom to hundreds, reaching 20,000 students annually. Eugenics became so commonplace in American institutions by the 1930s that Leon Whitney, secretary of the American Eugenics Society, proudly claimed, "Eugenics is being taught now in three-quarters of our five hundred colleges and universities, and in many high schools and preparatory schools" (Hornblum *et al.*, 2013). The upshot was that at least two generations of college students—the future lawmakers, teachers, doctors, and medical researchers of America who had sworn to do no harm—were being imbued with an air of superiority and a condescending disdain for the weak, the infirm, and the institutionalized of the nation (page 37).

Over time, eugenics would come to be seen as a way to protect society from anyone deemed inferior or defective, including the mentally ill, people of color, the disabled, and many others. They would be referred to as "social cancer" in the booklet *Tomorrow's Children* written by Ellsworth Huntington (1935, page 46). In sharing my history, my aim is, in large part, to speak for many of us who have suffered the violent consequences of the influence of eugenics on American life. Ambitious legislators, social reformers, physicians, and scientists pushed legislation to pass in thirty-three states making forced sterilization legal—64,000 Americans were unable to bear children and left dehumanized and devalued.

The eugenics movement appeared to have lost its influence and popularity following the horrors of Nazi Germany. The core belief and practice of "medicine" under Hitler was that "all people are not created equal, and some people are not considered humans at all, they were known as Untermenschen—subhuman" (Huntington, 1935, page 122). This designation referred to non-Aryan, inferior people, which included Jews, Gypsies, homosexuals, the handicapped, and the mentally ill. They were seen and treated as laboratory animals, whose bodies were only valuable for research—to advance the goals of the Third Reich: perhaps the purest expression of the eugenics ideology. This racial ideology was used to justify torturous experiments and genocide. The Nazis first sterilized and then euthanized its entire population of "mentally ill," including thousands of innocent children.

Unknown by most, however, eugenics didn't disappear; it merely went underground, with the attitudes and beliefs that made eugenics what it is—to continue out of sight. As I write this in the summer of 2020, we can see its dark shadow and perhaps unconscious influence in those who continue to oppose equality for all, while at the same time others are stepping forward and waking up and taking to the streets to protest and rally for an end to discrimination. However, as has become all too clear with the recent rise of the white supremacy movement and neo-Nazi ideology, many in the United States are being led back to the roots of eugenics, learning to support hatred and the same ideologies of superiority that fueled both Nazi doctrine and America's psychiatric past. It's a bitter pill to swallow, but, as the real expressions of this hidden interconnectivity of eugenics ideology bubble to the surface across continents, it becomes even more essential that we work to better understand how we got here in the first place.

In the book *Operation Paperclip: The Secret Intelligence Program that Brought Nazi Scientists to America*, Annie Jacobson tells us that beginning in 1945, over 1,600 of Hitler's top scientists and their families were secretly brought to the United States through a classified program called "Operation Paperclip and Project 63." These scientists—with expertise in rocket engineering, chemical and biological weapons, aviation, space medicine, psychological warfare, mind control, and weapons of mass destruction—were often the recipients of top scientific awards while serving the Third Reich. More than half of them were tried and convicted as war criminals. The United States government justified the decision to bring them to the U.S. as the lesser of two evils. The justification at the time was: if we did not recruit them, the Soviet Union would, meaning a potential "win" for state communism. These scientists left behind a long legacy of missiles, sarin gas, cluster bombs, weaponized bubonic plague, and secret mind-control programs hidden in the annals of the American military, and the fields of medicine and psychiatry.

This period, and the decades preceding it, dramatically influenced scientific research in America. It was a time in which fear and greed impacted our moral compass, which slid to a new low as the soul and conscience of this Euro-centric nation accelerated even further in a downward spiral as we conducted experiments on our own. Robert Whitaker and others look specifically at the influence of eugenics in the experimentation of techniques and pharmaceutics on the mentally ill. Whitaker (2002) asserts:

> Although eugenics had become a thoroughly shamed science by the 1950s ... the therapeutics it had spawned didn't suddenly disappear. Approximately, 10,000 mental patients in the United States were lobotomized in 1950 and 1951, alone. Electroshock remained a mainstay ... and was often used to deliberately reduce patients to confused states ... Dr. Ewen Cameron, who was named the president of the American Psychiatric Association in 1952, utilized electroshock in this way, shocking his patients up to twelve times daily, which, he wrote, produced disruption of memory "so massive and pervasive that it cannot be described." Approximately 4,000 mentally ill patients were sterilized in the 1950s, which was about the same number as in the 1920s, when eugenic attitudes toward the mentally ill were at a feverish pitch. This was the therapeutic milieu that was still in place—the value system, as it were—when chlorpromazine (Thorazine) made its debut in the state mental hospitals. (page 142)

Having been given high doses of Thorazine, I was interested—and horrified—to learn of its history as laid out by Whitaker. I had the opportunity to speak with him shortly before my visit to Elgin with Sydney. He told me that he had searched for a long time to interview individuals who had been subjected to Thorazine for his book and had few results. He told me that I was fortunate to be alive and healthy given that so many others died and never made it through that era of pharmaceutical research. Whitaker writes:

> Chlorpromazine ... belonged to a class of compounds known as phenothiazines that were developed in the 1800s for use as synthetic dyes. In the 1930s in the U.S. the Department of Agriculture employed phenothiazine compounds for use as an insecticide and to kill swine parasites .... In the 1940s, phenothiazines were found to sharply limit locomotor activity in mammals, but without putting them to sleep. Rats that had learned to climb ropes to avoid painful electric shocks could no longer perform this task when administered phenothiazines. (page 142)

In attempting to unearth anything I could find about the research that was conducted specifically during my time at Illinois State Psychiatric Institute, I looked in Whitaker's index and, to my surprise, found the following about another drug that was used on research subjects at ISPI:

> In 1991, doctors at Illinois State Psychiatric Institute injected methylphenidate into twenty patients who'd been in the hospital for two weeks (some of whom had become asymptomatic and were successfully off neuroleptics) and found that it caused "moderate or marked deterioration" in most of them. This proved, they concluded, that "methylphenidate" can activate otherwise dormant psychotic symptoms. (page 240)

I learned from a physician friend that methylphenidate is sold under many names, including Ritalin. It currently has an "ALERT: US" boxed warning that it should be strongly monitored for abuse and dependency. It comes with many warnings and contraindications, including possible hallucinations and psychosis, Tourette syndrome, or tics, heart arrhythmia, and heart attacks, as well as bowel dysfunction. It is currently overprescribed and misused in the quest for our control over children, throughout the U.S. Like eugenics, the roots and history of Ritalin are concealed, while many of the negative impacts remain, simply packaged and given inappropriately to millions of our children.

As I continued my research, an unmistakable pattern began to emerge regarding a history of the United States' willingness to experiment on, and even sacrifice, its own citizens in the name of science, political dominance, profit, and military might, especially when it came to the use of mind-altering substances. John Marks' book (1979) *The Search for the "Manchurian Candidate": The CIA and Mind Control, A Secret History of the Behavioral Sciences* is one such discovery of just how far our country went. As Marks writes: "The National Institutes of Mental Health had an interest in LSD's relationship to mental illness, and CIA officials wanted to know how the drug affected other populations as well and how it might be used on the enemy for interrogation and other measures. This research was done under the CIA code name MKULTRA and MKSEARCH, and other subprojects" (page 63). In order to keep secret its involvement, the CIA passed the money through "middle-men" and foundations. "There was a huge new market for grants in academia ... One of the early recipients of grant funding was released to Carl Pfeiffer at The University of Illinois Medical School for research regarding LSD. Pfeiffer was not alone" (page 63). There were far too many research projects and grant recipients to name in this document, but I mention those that I do specifically because of my experiences at Illinois State Psychiatric Institute and the University of Illinois, which was running the research on my floor as well as others when I was a patient at ISPI.

Although I didn't realize I was a research subject at the time, when we reconnected Dr. Sydney Krampitz revealed to me the true nature of my commitment and reason why the staff were angry at me: when I didn't take the drugs, I was "non-compliant" and was thwarting the research outcomes. Although I don't know which research programs I was unwittingly subjected to, the declassified records of the MKULTRA and MKSEARCH programs make clear the *type* of research that was happening through the University of Illinois—with Illinois State Psychiatric Institute as a research site.

My research revealed specific references to the University of Illinois and Illinois State Psychiatric Institute. Marks' work explained the reasons behind the vagueness of the studies. Marks remarked: "Most of the CIA's academic researchers published articles on their work in professional journals, but those long, scholarly reports often gave an incomplete picture of the research. In effect, the scientists would write openly about how LSD affects patient pulse rate, but they only told the CIA how the drug could be used to ruin that patient's marriage or memory.

Again, in *The Search for the "Manchurian Candidate"* I came across Pfeiffer's name: "$20,000 of CIA money was also channeled to Carl Pfeiffer when he was the head of the Pharmacology Department at the University of Illinois Medical School before he moved on to Emory University and tested LSD and other drugs on inmates in the Federal Penitentiary in Atlanta under MKSEARCH" (page 215).

There was a specific reference to Illinois State Psychiatric Institute in the book *Mass Murderers in White Coats: Psychiatric Genocide in Nazi Germany and the United States* by Lenny Lapon (1986), who writes that "John M. Davis of Illinois State Psychiatric Institute received $104,170 in 1970 by the government for a research project titled, 'Psychology Depression Program'" (page 102). He also reveals that "Robert L. Sprague of the University of Illinois was a recipient of $113,711 for a study on the Use of Psychotropic Drugs with the Retarded in 1980" (page 103).

In the Name of Science: A History of Secret Programs, Medical Research, and Human Experimentation (2003), Andrew Goliszek explores declassified information regarding both voluntary and involuntary experimentation on human subjects in the United States and throughout the world in the past five decades. Goliszek looks deeply into documents regarding chemical and biological weapons, and human radiation experiments, including the ones conducted at Elgin State Hospital. The book covers the efforts of unscrupulous researchers and physicians to test dangerous procedures and useless drugs on many human subjects, including our own military, unbeknownst to them. And it reveals the CIA's extensive programs in mind control and behavior modification while using universities and medical centers around the country to provide the human subjects.

> On April 13, 1953, MKULTRA was established for the express purpose of researching and developing chemical, biological, and radiological materials to be used in clandestine operations and capable of controlling or modifying human behavior. During its life, MKULTRA projects also included radiation, electroshock, harassment, substances, and paramilitary devices and materials. In a proposal describing MKULTRA, Director of the CIA, Richard Helms wrote, 'We intend to investigate the development of a chemical material which causes a reversible nontoxic aberrant mental state, the specific nature of which can be reasonably well predicted for each individual.'" (pages 155–156)

There were many prominent universities, in addition to the University of Illinois, conducting research and receiving funding through back channels of the CIA. In some cases, the grant recipients didn't know the true nature of where their money came from; many others colluded with the CIA directly, such as Dr. Carl Pfeiffer and Dr. Ewen Cameron, whom I wrote about earlier. Cameron took extreme risks, abused his patients, and created irreversible harm, in the name of treatment, in many of his human subjects at McGill, Allan Memorial Institute in Canada from 1957 to 1964. "The CIA had followed his widely published, questionable research practices for many years and eventually approached him with an offer he didn't hesitate in accepting. In 1988 the United States paid out thousands of dollars in out-of-court settlements to nine individuals experimented on by Cameron" (Goliszek, 2003, page 163).

Goliszek writes: "Dr. Cameron seemed the perfect candidate for recruitment to MKULTRA … Cameron used the CIA … as an excuse to expand his already inhumane research and some of the most hideous experiments since World War II" (page 164).

Although I am loath to form any conclusions without undeniable proof, I'm chilled by the similarities of research that Cameron and others were conducting with what I suffered at the hands of Dr. L and the pharmaceutical research that was being conducted on me at ISPI. Goliszek continues: "The CIA had known about Dr. E. Cameron's methods since 1956, the year he'd published in the *American Journal of Psychiatry* entitled 'Psychic Driving' … Operation Knockout had become a part of MKULTRA, subjecting unwitting mental patients to modern torture and stripping them of their memories and identities. The experiments ended abruptly in 1964 when Cameron unexpectedly left Canada and returned to the United States" (page 164).

At the time of his death, Cameron was widely esteemed and followed by other psychiatrists as he had published "140 papers. He served as President of the American Psychiatric Association (1952–1953), Canadian Psychiatric Association (1958–1959), American Psychopathological Association (1963), Society of Biological Psychiatry (1965), and The World Psychological Association (1961–1966)" (pages 164–165).

I could find nothing written that indicated Cameron was ever censured by the American Medical Association, American Psychiatric Association, or any other of the prestigious organizations of which he was president. *The CIA Doctors: Human Rights Violations by American Psychiatrists*

Dr. Colin A. Ross, M.D. (2006) provides over 15,000 pages of documents he obtained from the CIA through the Freedom of Information Act. This looks at the pervasive, systematic violations of human rights by American psychiatrists over the last sixty-five years. Dr. Ross describes the experiments conducted by psychiatrists to create amnesia, new identities, hypnotic access codes, and new memories in the minds of experimental subjects:

> These extensive violations of human rights by psychiatrists in North America throughout the second half of the twentieth century were perpetrated by leading psychiatrists, psychologists, pharmacologists, neurosurgeons and medical schools. Mind control contractors with TOP SECRET clearance include the American Psychological Association, Past Presidents of the American Psychiatric Association and the Society for Biological Psychiatry, and psychiatrists who have received awards from the American Psychological Association and the American Psychiatric Association. (page 11)

In Appendix C, Dr. Ross provides a comprehensive list of institutions and names of those receiving funding through the CIA. This includes the University of Illinois and the Office of Naval Research.

> The participation of psychiatrists and medical schools in mind control research was not a matter of a few scattered doctors pursuing questionable lines of investigation. Nor did the experiments occur in a previous era, governed by different ethical standards than those prevailing at the beginning of the twenty-first century. Rather, the mind control experimentation was systematic, organized, and involved many leading psychiatrists and medical schools ... These human guinea pigs were never told that they were research subjects in military and CIA mind control experiments, and they never gave informed consent. They received no systematic follow-up to document the harm done to them. The welfare of the "human subjects" was not a relevant variable in the academic equation. What counted for the psychiatrists, I think, was money, power, perks, academic advancement and the thrill of being a spy doctor. (page 122)

The variety of behavioural and pharmacological research conducted throughout this period is too vast to outline here, but it's important to know that it exists. What I found the most disturbing and reprehensible was the research conducted on vulnerable young children.

In *Against Their Will: The Secret History of Medical Experimentation on Children in Cold War America* (2013), authors Allen Hornblum, Judith Newman, and Gregory Dober write:

> Institutionalized children were used for experimental vaccines, research into radioactive isotopes, lobotomy and electroshock, untested pharmaceuticals such as curare and Thorazine .... Researchers—many motivated by the noblest of causes, others by the prospect of fame and fortune—gravitated to orphanages, hospitals, and institutions for the "feebleminded" when in need of test subjects to conduct a clinical trial. The ethical constraints for such dubious acts were sorely lacking—a direct result of an exploitive ethos that reeked of both eugenics and paternalism ... It should also remind us that a too ruthless search for knowledge is accompanied by significant human and societal costs, and that children—society's most vulnerable and defenseless group for purposes of research—were often sacrificed in that quest for advancement. (pages 163–165)

More difficult than living through my own abuse at Elgin was the horror and helplessness of watching others abused. As a child, I witnessed Bud and other men abuse my mother and would try to come between them or distract them in any way I could. In the beginning at Elgin, before the drugs took effect in me, I was frequently put in restraints for trying to intervene on behalf of other patients. Where did that instinct come from? Also, why were the staff at ISPI and at Elgin complicit? What was it that made Sydney Krampitz so different that she was willing to risk her career on my behalf?

As I read about the research on children, I wondered why other observers or caregivers appeared to have done nothing. Did they have no human feelings for the children in their care? Was fear of reprisal of losing their jobs a major factor that kept them from speaking out? I reflect on Miss Foster at Chicago State Hospital where I had worked with children. She led by example. I cannot imagine her keeping quiet and, of course, I'm sure she must have at times or she wouldn't have survived in that system for as long as she did.

Hornblum *et al.* (2013) address this question:

> Much is written about the "blue wall of silence" in the police departments and the inner city "street codes" that silence witnesses of violent crime, but an argument can be made that the moral amnesia and ethical paralysis of those in the medical and psychological research professions were equally formidable. As Dr. A. Bernard Ackerman often argued, "A conspiracy of silence emerged to protect the profession from the perversion of principles that had taken place in the medical community"... Why were there so few who had the moral capacity to discern a wrong being committed and the personal courage to speak up about it? Thousands have suffered as a consequence. (page 224)

It is essential that we learn from this history. That we each look at times and places when our silence becomes complicity, places where we feel the inclination to step forward in protest but pull back out of fear, lack of trust in ourselves, or any number of other reasons. The truth is, unethical experimentation on the vulnerable continues and is addressed by Hornblum and colleagues. This kind of unethical research continues, shifted from US soil to the most vulnerable communities in the most underdeveloped and undeveloped countries. It is our propensity to marginalize our least valued members, our cavalier attitude toward protecting those most in need, and our willingness to jettison inconvenient ethical constraints in order to follow the path offering the greatest rewards. That history, as uncomfortable as it may be, must be acknowledged and made available to forthcoming generations (page 227). To this day, Big Pharma conducts research in the Global South, such as impoverished countries in Africa.

Returning my focus to the most marginalized in the United States, I have become aware of the ongoing problem of the mentally ill in prisons, who are far too frequently without resources and suffer ongoing exploitation. Curious, I expanded my search to the mentally ill in prisons and Illinois. In "Report: Mental health care in crisis in Illinois" (2015), Phil Kadner writes that "between 2009 and 2012, Illinois cut $113.7 million in funding from mental health services ... Cook County Jail has become the largest mental health provider in Illinois. Of approximately 76,400 people who were admitted to Cook County Jail in 2012, 45,840 were people with mental illness." This is just a taste of the many articles written since then, and, so, the neglect and abuse of the mentally vulnerable continue in Illinois.

The problems and challenges continue to this day, as illustrated in a more recent article. In a January 2019 piece for Illinois Public Media called "Prisoners with mental illness still waiting for treatment," Christine Herman wrote about a mentally ill man who spent twenty-six years in prison, much of it in solitary confinement, where he had hallucinations, engaged in self-mutilation, and tried to kill himself.[1] In 2007 he and 12,000 other inmates sued the Illinois Department of Corrections for not treating them but using corporal punishment. Herman's article includes the following quote from a prominent psychiatrist, Stuart Grassian, M.D., who has spent nearly three decades at Harvard studying the harm solitary confinement causes for the mentally ill. "They're not the worst of the worst. They're the sickest of the sick, the wretched of the earth. Maybe they weren't even that bad before they got [into prison], and they just get worse and worse. It's a tragedy ... absolutely immoral to see that happen to people." There is inadequate treatment of the mentally ill in prisons throughout the United States, and according to a July 2014 report by the Pew Charitable Trust: "The problem is particularly bad in Illinois which has long ranked near last for health care spending on inmates."

Kenneth Wooden conducted a three-year investigation into the inner workings of the juvenile justice system and found the conditions were as bad with juveniles as with adult inmates. By now, I shouldn't have been surprised that Wooden spends a considerable amount of time focused on Illinois, and of course, Elgin State Hospital jumped out at me in his book, *Weeping in the Playtime of Others* (1976).

> In Cook County, Illinois, Pat Murphy, an Irish attorney with both intelligence and courage, clashed with the State Department of Corrections. Murphy litigated, resulting in the closing of Sheridan, an infamous youth penitentiary. But he soon discovered that the Illinois Department of Children and Family Services simply started using Elgin State Hospital and others ... At one hospital, Murphy found that at least 80% of the children needed no psychiatric care. In others, he found the figure about 65% .... As of August 1973, more

than two thirds of the patients at the Chicago Tinley Park Mental Center were unnecessarily hospitalized. Almost half of the children at the Chicago State-Reed, Elgin State Hospital and Madden State facilities should not have been incarcerated either. Yet because two thirds of all "direct-care staff" were nonprofessionals, and because their job was to control the behavior of the child, well over 70 percent of the inmates were on psychotropic or narcotic drugs by order of a staff physician. (page 52)

Gail Hornstein, a Professor of Psychology at Mount Holyoke College in Massachusetts, writes in both of her books about the importance of story. In *Agnes's Jacket: A Psychologist's Search for the Meanings of Madness* (2009), Dr. Hornstein begins with the story of a Victorian-era German asylum where Agnes Richter was a patient who painstakingly stitched a mysterious autobiographical text into every inch of the jacket she created from her institutional uniform. Despite every attempt to silence them, hundreds of other patients have managed to get their stories out, often in disguised form.

Hornstein should know—after all, she has spent her career teaching her students in psychology through the use of first-person narratives. Her bibliography of *First-Person Narratives of Madness in English* (now in its fifth edition) lists more than 1,000 books by people who have written about madness from their own experience. It is used by researchers, clinicians, educators, and peer groups around the world and is available on her Mount Holyoke College website at no cost.

A vast gulf exists between the way medicine explains psychiatric illness and the experiences of those who suffer. Hornstein's luminous work helps us bridge that gulf, guiding us through the inner lives of those diagnosed with a mental illness and revealing nothing less than a new model for understanding one another and ourselves. Two quotes from this book were meaningful to me. In the first one, she is speaking about two individuals who facilitate groups for the Hearing Voices Network in the UK. Hornstein spent a good deal of time in Europe attending these groups and talking to individuals like those named below, and brought the Hearing Voices Network idea back to the United States. She writes:

Patients see testimony as a crucial part of their effort to create an appropriate language to frame their experiences. As Jacqui Dillon and Rufus May wrote recently: "Clinical language has colonized experiences of distress and alienation." For survivors to make sense of what has happened to them, they must "decolonize" their experiences and create narratives framed outside the medical model of their doctors." (page 120)

The second book written by Gail Hornstein, entitled *To Redeem One Person Is to Redeem the World: The Life of Frieda Fromm-Reichmann* (2002), is also inspiring. In this book, Hornstein meticulously researched the life of Frieda Fromm-Reichmann, through her journey as a German-Jewish refugee child to becoming a brilliant analyst. Dr. Fromm-Reichmann treated patients with compassion, care, and dignity in ways that others thought were impossible when the resources of the times were medication, lobotomy, or shock treatments.

One of her patients was the bestselling author Joanne Greenberg, who wrote *I Never Promised You a Rose Garden*, released in 1964, after being discharged from four years of treatment at McLean where Dr. Fromm-Reichmann worked with her. She went on to complete college, get married, have children, and write the bestselling book about the years she experienced psychosis. As a patient, her real name was Hannah Green.

Hornstein talks about the kind of individual Frieda was and what drove her in her work with others, where she adopted an unusual approach, far different from that of her peers.

From earliest childhood, Frieda had been imbued with a deep sense of responsibility ... The worldview of her Orthodox upbringing was embodied in this story, told by the great sixteenth-century rabbi Isaac Luria. During the process of creation, God's divine emanations were gathered together and stored in sacred vessels. But the vessels, unable to contain the light pouring from them, shattered, fragmenting the divine sparks, which fell to earth. The world became chaotic: nothing was in its proper realm. The task of human history and the responsibility of everyone is to rescue the divine sparks and restore order to the world. This is the work of *tikkun olam*. When it is fully accomplished, redemption will come to everyone ... To redeem one person is to redeem the world. (Hornstein, 2002, page xxvii)

Although I doubt Sydney Krampitz saw her responsibility from this perspective, she did indeed help rescue the shattered sparks of the young woman I once was. I believe she was guided by the same kind of inner moral compass that motivated Dr. Fromm-Reichmann, whose work was clearly done in the best interests of each individual patient. Even with those who appeared the most ill, she saw their potential and worked in creative and new ways rather than allowing the challenge to eclipse her hope for them. I deeply resonate with Dr. Frieda's calling to do her part in restoring the divine sparks and to contribute in healing the world.

In 2018, I attended a conference hosted at The Retreat at Pacifica Graduate Institute, titled "Trauma and Transcendence: Depth Psychology, Spirituality and the Sacred." I was drawn to the conference by the unusual title pairing of the word's "trauma" and "transcendence" in the flyer and this accompanying quote: "Depth psychological pioneers from William James and Frederic Myers, to Sandor Ferenczi and C.G. Jung have described the intimate relationship among spiritual, paranormal, or otherwise revelatory encounters, and the psychological fragmentation caused by trauma and dissociation." I had a sense that two worlds intimately known to me but unexplainable from a psychological perspective might have an opportunity to come together intellectually if I attended the conference.

Over several days I listened to lectures by some of the most well-published, respected, and brightest minds in the world of Jungian analysis and took copious notes. Dr. Ann Belford Ulanov talked at length about the sense of annihilation that trauma can cause, and the frequently resulting *soul loss*. I had not read or heard any respected professional talk about how trauma can result in *soul loss*. Dr. Ulanov's lecture brought to mind how I had once witnessed a group of indigenous individuals I was working with in a group call another group member's soul back after she had spoken of recent devastating trauma. The difference in this woman was obvious—a striking contrast afterward to the woman who had sat in our group initially. We could each see how she was now embodied and enlivened in a way she hadn't been before.

One of the things Dr. Ulanov said was that in most cases trauma damages the ego but not the psyche—the Real (the Soul)—the essence of the child, the creative, relational, authentic spark of life at the very core of each individual frequently goes into hiding, deep in the unconscious, which through the gift of dissociation removes itself from everyday reality in order to save itself. Depth psychotherapy is about "sitting on a precipice of soul rediscovery."

On a break from the conference, I discovered a treasure trove of books in the bookstore, including one that seemed to be waiting for me. *The Dark Face of Heaven: True Stories of Transcendence Through Trauma* (2014) by Janet Elizabeth Colli, Ph.D. I opened it to Dr. Colli's words:

> Transpersonal psychologists such as myself have much to teach. Transpersonal states of consciousness are precisely where reality is constructed and deconstructed ... So the spirit world and the material world are both eminently real. But they are not equivalent. Not interchangeable. Their crossover should give us pause ... Their *meeting point* is where authentic miracles of healing happen ... transpersonal therapists help translate those states and realms into healing ... we bridge the gap between. (page 12)

Transpersonal development is the development of the self beyond the egoic or personal self which involve experiences of connectedness with phenomena considered outside the boundaries of the ego. Over time, these developmental stages can include increased intuition, states of transcendence, peak experiences, and the development of the whole person—the spiritual self. This theory is congruent with some of the newer work now being written about in the emerging field of spiritual intelligence.

Dr. Colli writes:

> Transpersonal psychology has been described as a discipline that bridges science and the spiritual traditions. Yet transpersonal findings remain largely un-integrated within psychology and psychiatry. (page 212)

I have a very strong conviction that my trauma could not fully heal without both psychological and spiritual work. It is also my experience in working with others that those who go on to experience post-traumatic growth and thriving have utilized and worked with the spiritual dimension.

Dr. Colli continues:

> It is through the mechanism of dissociation that consciousness unfolds, and through healing dissociation that consciousness expands. Ordinary people now perceive what used to be deemed *non*-ordinary, and regardless of the widespread cultural denial,

the extraordinary threatens to become the ordinary—with trauma as the initiatory event. The veil between realities—material and subtle—is thinning. Reassurance that these natural human domains is needed now more than ever. (page 214)

Spiritual awakening and psychic opening, out-of-body experiences and other altered states are often revealed during therapy. Transpersonal psychology is the psychology of the sacred. And trauma initiates the transpersonal. When the skin-encapsulated ego is "split open" through trauma our capacity to heal is unfettered and unbound. Trauma can initiate one into altered states and otherworldly realms that support healing. Yet this revolutionary finding is largely unappreciated within traditional psychology ... [page 16]. Simply put, the disorder itself carries the seed of its cure. (page 17)

Dr. Donald Kalsched, who wrote *Trauma and the Soul: A Psycho-Spiritual Approach to Human Development and Its Interruption* (2013), spoke about how it is through the soul that trauma and transcendence find a meaningful connection. Those who have experienced severe childhood trauma dissociate to the world of the transcendent, infinite, the sacred, beyond space and time. This other world is where the soul goes when it is no longer possible for an ensouled life in the material world, and it becomes a holding space for the soul. There is an intermediate space between the material world and that of the transcendent. When it is open, the flow of energy and affect are available. When memory and affect become unbearable, the system shuts down, the intermediate space is closed, the individual is cut off from their feelings, and access to the transcendent is occluded. Something in the unconscious oversees this dynamic, a self-care system that regulates how much experience, memory, and affect get through the stimulus barrier of the ego. Therapy is about going back and retrieving the soul that has been encapsulated by this spiritual defense system and emotionally and energetically detached from the outside, material world.

When an individual is met with skill, compassion, and safety, as I was with Charlotte, recovery increases in earnest. Kalsched explained that there is frequently an influx of increased and heightened spiritual energy in the form of dreams, synchronicity, supernatural powers, and transcendent experiences, which was also my experience. The individual must learn to live in both worlds. He writes in *Trauma and the Soul*:

> We need a psychology that does justice to the human soul, i.e., a *depth* psychology, and *ipso facto*, this involves the inner world. C.J. Jung reminds us that: "the aim of the great religions is expressed in the injunction "not of this world." ... symbolized as the "treasure," as in the parables of the "pearl of great price" and the "treasure in the field." (Jung, 1921: para. 423, p.250). This treasure in the field is the human soul—that evanescent reality that Christian Mystic Meister Eckhart claims bears the imprint of God. And this mysterious reality has always been located in man's inner life. (page 193)

I was heartened to learn of this work. It validated my own experiences and helped me to more deeply understand them, as well as giving me hope for the world of psychotherapy, currently dictated by insurance, pharmaceuticals, and universities that primarily teach brief therapy and cognitive–behavioral techniques, and seldom teach today's therapists about presence and exploration of the inner worlds or the life of dreams and spirit.

Kalsched relates the story of "The Woman Without Hands" from Grimm's fairytale as a metaphor for the inner work and experiences of a number of his patients. He unpacks and amplifies the story in relationship to extreme childhood trauma that leaves the individual psychologically dismembered—without wholeness, as was the Woman Without Hands.

> The girl is accompanied by an angel—a suggestion that her wounded innocence is the mark of her divinity and has attracted its representative from the "spirit world." Such wounding of innocence seems to draw angels down into time and space reality ... St. Augustine is reported to have said (see Romanyshyn, 2002:36) that to be an orphan is to be related to God. Or to put it in psychological language, when an essential God-given core of the self is split-off (orphaned) and banished to the unconscious as happens in trauma, it is "care-taken" there by archetypal powers angels ... that feed it on the "ambrosia" of the Gods until such time as it can come back into the world and start to eat real food. (page 301)

This brings to mind my memories of age three when I saw an etheric, other worldly presence—an angel—after I opened the door in a desperate attempt to escape the house filled with the horror of my uncle's suicide, after my mother fled the house, leaving me injured and alone. Opening the door and this visitation of an angelic presence have been the foundation of my life.

✳✳✳

It is my hope that increasingly ethical, innovative therapies and programs will emerge. I feel hopeful as I hear about mindfulness-based psychotherapy, as well as those techniques that incorporate spirituality and include a 'whole person' approach, such as transpersonal development. I understand the consequences of soul loss that can result from some forms of trauma. Edward Tick has developed an innovative program, which works with traumatized war veterans dealing with soul loss on their return from war. He is author of *War and the Soul* and *Warrior's Return: Restoring the Soul After Trauma*. There are some emerging innovative therapies that are skill based and developmentally appropriate for children and adolescents that deemphasize the use of pharmaceuticals, except when absolutely needed and well managed for short periods of time. But children like me need more than techniques— they need someone like a Dale in their life, or the quiet presence of a teacher or kind librarian. They need someone to tell them clearly, it's not their fault, that they belong and are loved.

Another innovative program is that of the Hearing Voices Network, popular throughout Europe, brought to the US by Gail Hornstein. It is gaining notoriety. In Minnesota, PrairieCare, an innovative mental health system, is working with patients in life-changing ways and working with the system itself in promising ways.

Also gaining attention are programs like Deena Metzger's "ReVisioning Medicine," one guided deeply by a spiritual approach, which includes dreams, visioning, and ceremony. Preceding the practice of Narrative Medicine, "ReVisioning Medicine" recognized from its inception that the complete story of an illness includes personal, familial, communal, social, political, and environmental histories. These must all be explored and understood in order for the healing path to be fully revealed.

It is my experience and professional belief that trauma creates an existential crisis, one that is both psychological and spiritual in nature. It cannot be addressed and resolved without attention to both areas of an individual's life. In some cases, trauma incurs a deep loss of soul that can only be restored and understood from a spiritual perspective. It's my hope that many more ethical, spiritual, and narrative-based programs will continue to emerge, programs that deeply listen to the story that holds both the suffering and the antidote. I pray that medicine as we know it—for those suffering from physical issues or mental health concerns—will begin to transform into that which is truly healing. In the meantime, we must also revisit the past in order to learn from it, and not continue to make the same mistakes as those who have come before us.

We cannot deny the history of our country. All of it, even the lesser-known parts, is woven into our country's DNA and nervous system, lingering in our poisoned lakes, rivers, and streams from the toxic waste dumped by pharmaceutical companies, and in our dying wildlife and changing weather patterns. People are taking to the streets in protest against racism throughout the world in greater numbers than they did during the protests of the 1960s. Kindness, solidarity, and increased awareness are rising along with the call that to do nothing is no longer acceptable. Ongoing news tells us of ethical violations by psychology, medicine, pharmaceutical companies, corporations, and politicians. At this time in history, everything hidden is rising to the surface to be looked at, on both the collective level and a personal one. Ultimately, this holds the potential seeds of transformation.

Over recent years, I've met individuals who have told me about a secret they've carried out of shame for their entire lives regarding a parent or grandparent who had been in a state hospital when they were children. This impacted each of them greatly. My story is a small reflection of a much larger story. It is crucial that we citizens of this great nation confront our past if we are to survive. History can reveal vital clues to understanding and increases the possibility of learning from the mistakes of the past. Change begins with this awareness.

Confession is good for the soul. Let me tell you, I have been the keeper of secrets, and come from a long line of secret keepers. Secrets ruled my life since I could talk. What I now know to be true is that secrets give way to a great silence, creating an enormous gulf between soul and body, and they give way to shame, which disables and disconnects us from ourselves and each other.

Starting this book, I felt called to hold nothing back. Yet I was hesitant as I touched on tender secrets still held in my body and soul. It can be grueling, painful work to excavate what's been buried and hidden. As I've released each secret to the pages that you hold in your hands, a great transmutation has taken place. The leaden weight of the dark secrets I carried as I began telling my story has been successfully, alchemically transformed into gold.

The underground currents of unconditional love planted within me by my neighbor Dale when I was a nine-year-old child in 1956 created a flame of longing that eventually became the fires of transformation.

Once we've been given a taste of that love unburdened by expectation and obligation, our experience of love changes. Its original nature of living energy can inhabit our soul and create the conditions to shift our relationship to ourselves and to the world and to assist in healing any kind of trauma. Love created a portal and way through which messages from spirit woke something in me, the conversation between the visible and the invisible. We have created lives in which we long for our essence and hunger for more soul-filled lives.

Throughout my life, I have been fortunate to recognize the glimpses of my soul's longing—this longing kept me alive. As we each faithfully mine and tend our inner worlds, we will be rewarded with glimpses beyond measure—of the shining filaments of light that connect us all.

Afterword

The Gifts of COVID-19

Work in the invisible world

at least as hard as you do in the visible.

Rumi, *The Soul of Rumi:*
A New Collection of Ecstatic Poems

April 1, 2021 was the day my life came to a complete stop. While receiving fluids in the emergency room for dehydration, my oxygen
dangerously plummeted. I was rushed by ambulance to the hospital with
COVID-19. I had been so careful that I had no idea where I could have
picked up the virus. I didn't know anyone who had it.

Many days are hazy from the month-long hospitalization that followed,
but a few stand out. Upon arriving at the hospital, I was immediately
moved into a high-pressure isolation room. The hospital staff came in
and out in their full protective gear like visitors from outer space. The
constant sounds of machines helping me breathe and filtering my air, the
eerie lights and sounds, were initially overwhelming, but slowly this lulled
my consciousness into a womb-like liminal space. My skin felt paper thin
and I was sensitive to everything, including the food. I had little appetite.
To make matters even more complicated, I am deathly allergic to MSG
and soy and it became clear that soy was in all the hospital food except for
cottage cheese and cream of wheat.

Hearing this, my dear friend Sandra began a "Feed Lora" campaign
and healthy, nutritious food was delivered to the security desk in the
lobby each day. A nurse or aide made smoothies for me each morning

with high-protein powder, a fruits-and-greens mix with a shaker that Sandra had dropped off. Not only was the circle of support of friends and acquaintances deeply moving, it helped my weight to stabilize after I dropped twenty pounds in a week.

Even with this nourishment, I continued to grow more ill with life-threatening COVID pneumonia. As days went by in this surreal and increasingly exhausting state, I realized that I had entered a realm of suspension between life and death. I found myself hanging by a thread of indecision about dying. I was no longer able to care about much of anything, including the completion and release of this book. Even on a high-pressure oxygen machine, my breathing was laborious and exhausting. Increasingly, I felt swaddled in a soothing state of darkening inner stillness. This was not at all frightening; on the contrary, it was soothing except when I was unexpectedly startled back into awareness of the room as the all-too-frequent alarms went off.

It's only in looking back that I realize that when I stepped into the borderland between living and dying, the force that created the Universe was at work with all of its primal powers and currents of energy. Although I didn't physically die, this period signaled the ending of one stage of my life and the beginning of another—a rite of passage. This opened a door; an unspoken invitation was issued. The illness of COVID and my extreme physical vulnerability created an opening to fully face myself within a community of support I had seldom known.

One night an unfamiliar physician woke me in the early hours and told me it was time to decide if I would allow the doctors to put me on a ventilator. If I did not want that or was unwilling to receive chest compressions, defibrillation, or advanced cardiovascular life support interventions, I needed to sign a document expressing my wishes.

It didn't take me long to decide to sign the "Do Not Resuscitate, Do Not Intubate" orders. I realized in those moments that I was not giving up, I was trusting the Universe with my destiny. The quality of my life is more important than the number of years. Having been present during my previous work for so many deaths, I was not afraid; I believe that death is a natural, sacred process. Many personal experiences and with others have taught me that I am more than my physical body. Death is not an end but a continuation, in a new form. For me, it would have been sacrilegious to have others attempt to save my life no matter the burden of cost or impact on my physical and spiritual being. It was important for me to trust that universal intelligence, God, the ground of my being—however I refer to it—had my best interests at heart, even if that meant I would die.

The following afternoon, I had a beautiful conversation with the female hospitalist who was caring for me. She sat down in the chair next to my bed and asked if I would be willing to tell her how I had made my decision the night before. She didn't want to second-guess me but to understand and learn from me. She explained that in medical school doctors are seldom taught how to be of assistance to others when navigating these kinds of difficult choices. They were usually given a checklist to go over in a rather cold, detached way. I was deeply touched by this interaction and in the end, she held my hand and we connected human to human, with tears running down our faces.

There was a turning point over the next several days as the ebb and flow of my life shifted. I intentionally emailed AlexSandra Leslie, a coach I had been working with since early January, and requested prayers and more energetic support for complete healing. As days passed, I began to feel held in an ocean of energy and loving prayers from her and the community she had rallied on my behalf as well as from the Center for Mind–Body Medicine community, ReVisioning Medicine, and others in my life. Later, I learned that many of my closest friends and colleagues had tapped into my energy so deeply that they could literally sense that I was in the borderland between life and death.

In order to be discharged to home, I needed to be weaned from the high oxygen level I was on. This took time and a dedicated nursing supervisor who wasn't afraid to push me a little and take some small risks, helping me turn the corner in the right direction. Then the other nurses followed. I was discharged to home with oxygen and other medical supplies at the end of that long month of April. Weak as a newborn, a criterion for discharge had been that I needed someone to be with me at all times those first months. I was profoundly moved by the volunteers who showed up to fill that role, some for a week, some for two, but always openhearted and wanting to be there for me. Initially, I also received intensive home-care services. I had a massive, very painful infection on my backside that needed to be taken care of daily.

On the days the nurse didn't come, it often fell to whichever friend was with me to change my dressings. This activated self-consciousness and age-old body shame. I learned many things in those early days. I learned that confronting body shame takes a radical act of courage. I learned that allowing others to care for me required being open to their attentions. It required a form of self-love and humility, which I committed myself to developing. Work on self-love and the embrace of others' love for me began dismantling old and entrenched, indoctrinated body shame.

The generosity of friends was an unexpected gift from COVID. I'd had no idea how many people would show up and create a community of such widespread support. They were generous with their time, energy, financial support, food, cleaning, companionship, and so much more. Thanks to them, in addition to the intensive home-care services, my care and recovery included weekly acupuncture and massage, functional medicine testing, and prescriptions of IV infusions and supplements my body needed to heal. It also included cranial sacral work from a dear physician friend and eventually pool rehab that is helping to strengthen my body and create more stamina.

Another unexpected turn was when I started to lose handfuls of hair. One day the aide who helped with my showers and cleaned up the piles of hair plugging up the drain said, "I can't stand watching this happen to you." I could barely stand it myself and decided to do what I had often coached cancer patients to do. Rather than grieving for each handful of lost hair and over the rapidly increasing number of bald spots, I decided to have my hair shaved off. A few days later, on a beautiful sunny day, five friends joined me in cutting some of their own hair, adding it to what I had brought of mine. Together we conducted a ritual of letting go.

Following my intuition, I looked in several symbol dictionaries and learned that historically hair was considered one of the first ways to register transformation and has long played a part in initiatory processes. Cutting off hair or shaving the head has often denoted a dedicated person renouncing an egoic way of life in favor of soulful living. The act represents higher powers, inspiration, and corresponds to sacrifice and surrender of the personality. Hair is often seen as a message to the gods and is linked to life force and the soul. The head itself is considered a vessel of transformation.[1] What began as a way of dealing with hair loss invited me to consciously acknowledge the transformational process. The loss of my hair became a visible representation of that journey.

In January, my publisher had asked me if I was ready for all of the unforeseen ways in which my life would change with the publication of this book. My tentative answer was, no. One day shortly after, an email popped up about a workshop opportunity that I intuited might support me through this. This was followed by a phone call from a dear friend who had no idea about the email but called to explain that she was sending me a gift and the only allowed answer to her was, yes, thank you. This friend's financial generosity, and the synchronicity of her call, inspired me to take a huge leap and I registered for the year-long program called "A Year of Miracles (YOM)" with Marci Shimoff, Dr. Sue Morter, and Lisa Garr.

I intuited that the YOM program was about personal transformation, setting goals, and so much more. From the initial session and my first coaching, I knew I had made an important choice. Although I now know that this program arriving in my life a few months before I contracted COVID was a way in which my intuition and spirit had prepared me and were giving me the tools and community to learn and embody COVID's lessons. I'd had no idea how much I needed the support and teaching of YOM, nor how essential the program and my assigned coach would become as I navigated the remainder of 2021. One of the Five Foundations of the program was to practice seeing and accepting divine perfection at work in every situation, and letting go of control and everything that keeps us from believing that we live in a benevolent universe and that we are always taken care of. This spoke to me in the early months of the program. It helped to center me while I was in the hospital and throughout my long journey of recovery.

COVID became the catalyst for deep inner work on every level. My physical vulnerability brought me to my knees, creating the openness to do the work, giving me the space and time to fully face myself. It brought up an extreme sense of vulnerability, both because I was physically fragile and because the underworld of past vulnerabilities reactivated old wounds. Once I was home, even with full oxygen I couldn't walk two steps before becoming extremely light-headed and gasping for breath as my oxygen levels plummeted. Because breath is essential for physical life and is related to Spirit, I not only felt at risk, but a bad fall a few days after I was home confirmed my fragility.

What was unforeseen was how much my physical vulnerability brought up again the vulnerabilities I'd experienced throughout my childhood. Although I'd done years of work on this, there always remains the possibility that radically new challenges reactivate old wounds.

On one of my coaching calls, AlexSandra used the analogy of holding a small butter ball, like those served in some restaurants. She explained that you can hold one between your fingers and flick it away and it is gone—like my trauma. I had been completely trauma free for many years. But there will still be some butterball grease residue on your fingertips, she explained. It was helpful to remember this was "residue" on the days when I was way too hard on myself.

There were many days in which tears began as soon as I woke and continued to pour out of me throughout the day. Sometimes, I had no idea of their origin; other times, I was able to get to the source and release the trapped emotions. I grieved for my mother, for the child in me that felt as though I had exposed her to the danger of Dr. L, abandoning her when I was taken away by the court. A litany of unconscious self-blame, feelings of inadequacy and abandonment came up. I realized by continuing to listen to this narrative, I abandoned myself. At times, a deep tsunami-like longing and grief for something unexplainable would take over. Slowly, I was able to treat this sorrow and longing with a deep sense of reverence and an invitation to move more deeply into my interiority.

Each time tenderness was spoken to me or came in an email, such as "dearest one," I'd end up in tears and feel as though my heart was shattering. The realization that an essential attribute of love is tenderness came to me. I'd had little to no tenderness growing up and had created an adult life and persona of complete independence. I told myself a number of things about this: I'm an introvert, I don't really need many others. I need to be strong, not weak. I seldom asked for help of any kind. As I began to take off the filters with which I had unconsciously created my reality and allowed my heart to break open, I realized this was the energetic component of Love that Dale had given to me as a nine year old. My calling from that point on had been to discover the waters and light of love and to embody and become Love itself.

I began to share these vulnerabilities with AlexSandra. She was consistently a gentle, calming presence and clear mirror for me. Over time, I was able to begin to see myself differently. I came to see the painful emotions that were emerging as a portal to unconscious material that finally needed to be felt and released. As I realized how the deepest aspects of me had been walled off and how I filtered emotions, thoughts, or perceptions I'd named as unacceptable, I began to share this with several friends. I was more open to taking in their care, compassion, and tenderness, and our conversations deepened.

COVID taught me I am part of a larger body and my life impacts others, and they, in turn, were gifted by my allowing them to give to me. It also taught me the lessons of ambiguity and stretched me to stay centered in the paradox of life.

Earlier in the book I wrote about how, in the 1990s, kundalini energy became an insistent messenger calling me inward. Like COVID, it had pushed and prodded me more fully into my body and opened a doorway to physical, mental, and energetic blockages. It was initially disruptive and disorienting, with my nervous system barely able to handle the amount of energy pouring through it. I became sensitive to everything. So, too, with the aftereffects of the virus. As I recovered, energy again became an insistent messenger, as did my emotions, some of which I had never allowed myself to experience before.

Breathing is something I took for granted, until I couldn't. It is connected to the autonomic nervous system and works automatically. It is also something that can be directed by the voluntary (conscious) nervous system. Breath is something I know how to work with and understand the mechanics of because I've taught breathing techniques to both adults and children.

One night while I was in the hospital, the machine I was on failed. An aide, trying to be helpful, had made a critical mistake. He was beside himself with anxiety and remorse. By the time the nurse came in, I was gasping for breath. My scrambled brain couldn't fully take in her words as she instructed me, to no avail, to breathe in through my nose and out through my mouth. Several minutes later, I remembered I could do this the way I'd often taught little kids. "Imagine your finger is a flower. Smell the flower and now it becomes a candle, blow out the candle." I slowly got back on track as the staff brought in a different high-pressure oxygen machine.

The intentional breathing shifted my consciousness inward and initiated an inner journey in which I traveled for what seemed like a very long time throughout the world, seeing, touching smelling, and feeling in a very somatic way—the quality of the air, the temperature of woodlands and meadows, the rain forest, oceans, desert life, and a forest of eucalyptus trees. Eventually, I encountered and somehow talked with COVID itself. This was a profoundly visual, sensory, and spiritual experience, connecting me on a micro and a macro level to the Oneness of all things. I could feel her desperation to survive and her connection to the earth. I felt myself enter into an alliance with her as I grasped that we desire the same communion and reciprocal relationship with

Mother Earth. This numinous, parapsychic journey left me committed to mindfully letting go into each and every breath, each day and moment, trusting that exactly what I needed for my highest good and ongoing growth would come to me. I would choose each day where to focus my attention, a concept and skill I'd learned from the YOM program. One of the vivid smells I brought back from that journey was from a forest of eucalyptus trees. Later, when I was home, a friend brought me eucalyptus essential oil, as it helps with breathing.

Again, trusting my intuition, after listening to one of the YOM workshops, I signed up for a parallel five-week course, "The Energy Codes, Level I," with Dr. Sue Morter, based on the work in her bestselling book by that title. The breathing and meditative practices I learned in these classes began to shift everything, bringing up more emotions and beliefs that needed to be transformed. I came to understand that the healing journey I was on was not just about a return to my previous condition but something beyond it. It was about life-changing transformative work that would open me to a much deeper understanding of spiritual principles I'd believed I understood but had barely scratched the surface of. It would also bring into awareness another aspect of myself. As I do the daily breathing exercises, I experience each inhalation as an invitation to unite the groundedness of the earth with energy from above and to activate an awareness that connects me to many levels of reality. This wasn't entirely new to me, but it activated an inner energetic component in which breathing in specific ways is becoming fundamental. My awareness of the reciprocity we have with the trees and plants as they recycle our carbon dioxide into food and oxygen brought me into a sense of deep connection with Mother Earth and the cosmos that I had experienced on my healing journey while in the hospital.

The work with the Energy Codes is both physically and energy based, as my work with kundalini had been. I saw that while kundalini had opened me, it was a beginning, not an end—now the work was continuing and deepening in a gentler way because of all the work I'd done in the intervening years. What I was learning in each of the groups fit together like a gigantic puzzle. I realized that I hadn't yet done the healing of the residue in my physical and energy body. I committed myself to do the deep work of surrender and accepting whatever came to the surface. I possess few words to even begin to describe the mystery and alchemy of how I am growing with the space and support to explore what needs awareness, light, and healing.

Over time, through this process, I've been removing energetic residue of old trauma and updating my energy system with a more open, expansive capacity. Throughout the Energy Codes classes, I've been able to come to deeper understandings and precise practices regarding my (everyone's) true nature. The language used is that of "the Soulful Self" and the teachings are that this aspect of each of us can come into full embodiment. This is not an entirely new concept. Based on the decades of previous spiritual work I've done, I've come to understand that many spiritual teachings talk about our True Nature, Higher Self, Eternal Self, Buddha Nature, the Divine Within, Christ Consciousness, the Tao, and many more. I realize that I understood them as concepts. I remembered that I had frequently been touched by experiences of this aspect of my Higher Self, but I'd had no real idea of how to attain embodiment. Embodiment was the missing word and missing piece for me. I knew that my body had been the holdout or last frontier of my work. Focus on my physicality took me right into the source of the greatest traumatic residue and violations. The Energy Codes work was exactly what was needed.

What is different from other teachings I'd received is the precision of the language, my readiness to take the teachings deeply in, and my commitment to doing the practices. I'm working on the belief that I, too, can achieve greater freedom and live as an embodied Soulful Self.

Instead of talking about ego-death as other teachers had, in this work the language is gentler and kinder, using terms such as "protective personality." This language invites me to be gentler with myself. In doing the ongoing work, awareness replaces habit and my consciousness has begun to awaken on a daily basis to a level that I'd previously known only briefly. I am able to live increasingly in the present moment, in flow for longer periods of time. Experiencing life by responding in the present without the planning and filters of the past is creating a greater sense of freedom, peace, and the ability to hear the voice of my Soulful Self.

My intuition tells me that something within me is both breaking down and breaking through. I don't believe that any of my previous teachers had ever explicitly told me not to allow emotions to come to the surface. But I realize that at some level, I had come to believe that I would be less spiritual or less likely to become enlightened if I acknowledged or felt them. I also had a history of shutting down my emotions as they had often been unwelcomed, ridiculed, or brought up what I had been incapable of dealing with as a child and young adult. This had become a habit I'd struggled with for many years. Unknowingly, I had fallen into the trap of creating a spiritual bypass. This is a common shortcoming in western spiritual practices that allows deep elements of trauma to remain unresolved by relying on a partial dissociation to generate a sphere of solace and peace—a bypass of the deepest work.

When these emotions emerged, I'd be flooded with shame and self-reproach, but the ongoing teachings from both programs and coaching helped me to practice being as gentle with myself as those I was working with were. Slowly, this pattern has started to shift.

One day, in a deep and expansive meditation, I had a profound experience of my consciousness *as* the consciousness of the world. As my indigenous teachers and friends have shared, we are all ONE. It's one thing to understand and even believe that as a concept and completely another to experience it.

According to the *Oxford English Dictionary*, "psychology" is defined as "the science of the nature, functions and phenomena of the human soul and mind." The word psychology comes from the Greek word "psyche," which originally meant breath and then included the soul or spirit and logos indicating the study of. When an individual experiences trauma, there is often a split off or dissociation. In my case I had done a lot of psychotherapy to heal my ravished nervous system and post-traumatic stress. What I hadn't understood was that although this had been timely and good work, I was ready for another level of deeper, transformative work to occur. Although the world of clinical psychology takes itself very seriously, it doesn't take its role and impact in the soul and spiritual life of others seriously enough. In current practice, the soul or spirit is not seen as important or talked about in the consulting room, with the exception of Jungian therapists and those who work with transpersonal development. It is not included within the biomedical psychological paradigm. It was not present or available in all of the previous healing work I had done—my spiritual work was sought outside of traditional mental health.

For decades, I've understood and believed in the power of dreams. This understanding deepened in my work with Deena Metzger. Some dreams can give us a glimpse into the path of the soul and open a window to our transcendent self. Some dreams are given for the benefit of the entire community. I've repeatedly experienced dreams that have been a bridge between the invisible and the visible, and have connected me to the world of soul.

Following on from the new level of deep trauma release and energy work that the months of recovering from COVID had brought me, I was about to come to an apprehension and understanding of the powerful significance of a repeating dream that I'd had over the past six years. AlexSandra had connected me with a woman named Dr. Lorri Beaver-Mandekic for some bioenergetic synchronization work to further support me. Dr. Lorri was extremely skilled and caring. The work was consistently both gentle and effective. The few times that more came up than I could process on my own, she was quickly available and effectively navigated me through the challenges I was experiencing. In one session she was doing some energetic clearing with me. In between each one of the areas she had worked on, she would instruct me to focus my attention on visualizing " a clear blue sky." Each time she did, images from a dream about the being I called the "luminous skeletal woman" came to me with the background from my dream, opening from a bank of clouds to "a clear blue sky."

In Chapter 25, "Weaving the World Together," I wrote about the dream I had the night before I was to begin the cross-country journey to accompany Deena to the Yakama reservation and to visit the Hanford Nuclear Site. In the dream, *I identify dark, low-hanging clouds as another level of consciousness. As soon as I have that thought, the scene opens to a beautiful, clear blue sky. There are two lines of white robed beings in a procession slowly coming toward me. In the center, another being is carrying something. As he draws closer, I gasp. He is carrying, in his outstretched arms, what looks like a skeletal woman with very thin parchment paper skin. She is surrounded in pure light, her life essence, pure luminous energy radiates outward in all directions, enclosing her companions and me. The man carries the luminous skeletal woman to me and indicates that I am to take her, placing her in my arms. She is light as a feather—more spirit than flesh.*

I didn't write earlier about the next dream in which she appeared, but will share it now.

I am running away, trying to escape, fleeing for my life, traveling from one state to another. I call ahead to friends and colleagues as I move across the country, trying to find refuge and unable to. I know "they" are after me. I believe they are connected to the government in some way. I say to myself that this isn't paranoia, this is REAL. A dark car with two men has appeared repeatedly.

I find myself in a small western town and duck into a movie theater, hoping to sit and rest for a bit. The theater is dark and there is a historical documentary playing. Ireland, the Potato Famine, then the First World War, other countries and cultures, South America, Africa. The scenes of each movie clip depict humanities at the crossroads and the choices that were made. The movie continues to unfold in the years of the depression and Dust Bowl years, the Second World War, and so on.

Poor choices are made, feeding fear, death, and destruction. A disembodied voice from the movie asks, "Will you do it differently with what is coming? What will you do this time?"

As I walk out of the theater feeling empowered, determined to stop running and hiding, I walk down the street and the black car pulls up. One of the two agents harshly orders me to get in, roughly pushing me into the back seat. I nearly gasp aloud as I see there is someone else sitting there. It is the luminous skeletal woman sitting beside me, quietly and peacefully radiating light and compassion. After taking a breath, I knock on the window between the front and back seats. I lean forward and gently place my hand on the man's shoulder. Warmth and light are emanating from my hand.

"You don't have to do things this way anymore. You can do it differently."

I then turn to his companion in the driver's seat. I tell him the same thing. Again, warmth flows from my heart and hands. The luminous skeletal woman radiates strength and pure love toward the three of us.

I had this dream shortly after returning to Minnesota following the trip with Deena. I was still getting used to the fact that it felt like a spiritual mandate that I write the truth of my life, things I'd had no intention of ever discussing, let alone writing about before that trip.

At the beginning of the YOM program, I had to come up with a personal theme for the year. What came to me in January was—Luminous Presence. I deeply desired to be a healing and luminous presence in the life of others. At that time, I did not connect the words to anything. But they came from deep within.

A huge revelation swept through me as the words from my dreams jumped off the page. *luminous … skeletal … more spirit than flesh … radiating light … another level of consciousness, dressed in light.* Some of the same words used to describe the "Soulful Self." As I gazed at a beautiful image that AlexSandra had frequently shown me, and Dr. Sue used in her teachings, I saw that the luminosity and background of clouds, the clear blue sky, overlaid by a figure dressed in a blanket of light descending from above, were similar to my dream, minus the skeletal figure. I realized that my Soulful Self had been communicating with me for a very long time and preparing me for the exact inner work I was doing. She had been hiding in plain sight all along. As awareness broke through my denial, every aspect of my being was filled with a vibrating radiant light. The luminous skeletal woman *is me—my Soulful Self.*

Curious about why she had appeared as a skeleton under her dress of light, I went to several symbol dictionaries and searched for bones and skeletons, and found the following. The Latin for "bones" refers not only to the substance of the skeleton but metaphorically to one's soul. Ezekiel's vision of the valley of dried bones that are restored to life seems to associate bones with the dew-like marrow of hope that can reanimate what seems defeated.[2] Bones represent what is indestructible, a medium that connects life and death, the conscious and unconscious. The skeleton symbolizes spirit that has separated from the body, enlightenment with intelligence, and has the durability to mediate between personal and transpersonal realms. In dreams, skeletons foreshadow an imminent event, which will transform the dreamer's life, by shattering a state to which the dreamer is accustomed without yet knowing what is to succeed it.[3]

Each of the descriptions added to my understanding of the dreams. But it was this last one that pulled the undeniable power and message together—it had provided the foreshadowing of what became an imminent event in my life. An event that shattered my previous state of denial and pointed toward an unknown future. The first dream occurred the night before I was to depart on the trip with Deena. That trip changed everything, including myself and what I was willing to face and write about in this book. It shattered my ability to undermine my own experiences and hide my true history, and gave way to an unimaginable writing and research journey.

Not long after that life-changing trip with Deena, while going through old journals in order to decide what I should tear up and recycle or keep, I came across some writing from a writers' retreat in May of 2016. Looking back again, now, I realize that part of me sensed all along that the luminous skeletal woman was me—my Soulful Self—and that she had always been with me.

At age three, the sound of gunshot moved me into a time of deep inner stillness. A solitude and disengagement from the world. For several years, I watched everything from the sidelines of my mute, seldom-animated three-year-old-form. This was my visible self.

There was another more ethereal me whom I observed as she filtered from the inside out, mesmerized in watching dust motes dance in filaments of light. Her skin was merely a thin covering for this radiant love of beauty and luminosity. This me continued to somehow thrive, internally fed by the memory of the silence of falling snow and the filtered, dancing light of the angel lady whispering to the toddler body to carefully go back up the stairs to warmth and safety.

She helped me to never forget.

That summer my mother continued to be absent from my life, but my skin grew honeyed from the stroke of sunlight that fell over me as my aunt set me in the sandbox most afternoons. I sat. But my ethereal self played in the shafts of sunlight streaming through the leaves of a nearby tree and was enthralled by anything in flight. As I grew in years, she came out as a free-spirited, make-believe ballerina, lover of spiderwebs, flowers, and the smell and colors of autumn leaves. She rode free on a neighbor's bike when riding downhill with the wind and sun streaming through her hair and her arms raised in salutation to the sky. She came in the freedom she found under water—the golden threads of silence and light opened her to awe. And she came in the silence of the stairwell as she listened, enraptured, to the God of Mystery raining down on her head from above as the choir rehearsed on Saturdays. It didn't matter that she couldn't understand the Latin words; she felt them throughout her entire body and knew that this holiness was real life and it held her in its embrace. She knew even in the darkest nights that darkness was a candle that held her in good stead, accompanied by angels to soothe her lonely heart as the stars and moon smiled from above.

Endnotes

Introduction

1. Heraclitus, On the Universe, Fragments 44. Heraclitus, born c. 535 BC

Chapter 2

2. A children's television program created and produced by R.E. Muir, NBC television (1947–1955).

Chapter 4

1. A game show created by J. Masterson, NBC television (1945–1964).
2. The show "Queen for a Day" had a host called Jack Bailey.

Chapter 5

1. *The Washington Post*, Dan Lamothe, October 31, 2014, "The U.S. military's long, uncomfortable history with prostitution gets new attention."
2. *New York Times*, Winston Williams, February 26, 1982, "Navy is cracking down at biggest training base."
3. *Chicago Tribune*, Jerry Thomas, September 30, 1962, "Prostitutes are blamed for N. Chicago's woes."

Chapter 7

1. "The State of America's Children," 2017 Report (Children's Defense Fund).

Chapter 10

1. Judy Collins sings "Both Sides Now," a track from the 1967 album *Wildflowers*. Arranged by Joshua Rifkin and produced by Mark Abramson, written by Joni Mitchell.

Chapter 15

1. Hester Prynne is a character mentioned in *The Scarlet Letter* by Nathaniel Hawthorne.

Chapter 16

1. Lee Godie, Chicago's French Impressionist—a movie by Tom Palazzolo and Kapra Fleming. www.leegodiemovie.com [Accessed on 18th November 2021].

Chapter 17

1. Melodie Woerman, "Bishops lament and confess the church's role in sexual harassment, exploitation and abuse." The Episcopal News Service, July 5, 2018. https://www.episcopalnewsservice.org/2018/07/05/bishops-lament-and-confess-the-churchs-role-in-sexual-harassment-exploitation-and-abuse/ [Accessed 18th November 2021].

Chapter 18

1. William Ernest Henley, 1849–1903, *Margaritae Sorori*, https://englishverse.com/poems/margaritae_sorori [Accessed 18th November 2021].

Chapter 19

1. Metzner, R. (1986). *Opening to Inner Light: The Transformation of Human Nature and Consciousness*. United States: J.P. Tarcher.
2. Sannella, L. (1987) *The Kundalini Experience: Psychosis or Transcendence?*. United States: Integral Publishing.

Chapter 20

1. Karpinski, G. (1990) *Where Two Worlds Touch: Spiritual Rites of Passage*. New York: Ballantine Books.
2. Bolen, J. S. (2007). *Close to the Bone: Life-Threatening Illness as a Soul Journey*. Ireland: Mango Media.
3. 'Scrivener's Rampant' (1995). Volume 2, Edition 2, pp. 37–43.
4. Jung, C. (1934). 'The Meaning of Psychology for Modern Man' is from a lecture given in Cologne in 1933.

Chapter 21

1. Shabistari, Mahmud (1288-1340). "The Visit and the Gift." Translated by Neil Douglas- Klotz (1995). *Desert Wisdom*, p. 237. San Francisco, CA: HarperSanFrancisco.
2. Berry, W. and Pohrt, T. (Illustrator) (2015) "To Know the Dark" in *Terrapin: Poems by Wendell Berry*. Berkeley, CA: Counterpoint Press.
3. Bette Midler, "The Rose." Written and performed by Amanda McBroom.

Chapter 22

1. Wilken, E. (1969) *The Rose-Garden Game. The Symbolic Background to the European Prayer-Beads*. London: Victor Gollancz Ltd.
2. Seward, B. (1960). The Symbolic Rose. United Kingdom: Columbia University Press.
3. "Labyrinths: Their Origins and Development," Loyola University of Chicago—Medieval Studies, www.luc.edu/medieval/labyrinths/index.shtml [Accessed 18th November 2021].
4. Sands, H. R. (2001) *The Healing Labyrinth: Finding your Path to Inner Peace*. Hauppauge, NY: B.E.S. Publishing.
5. Artress, L. (2006). *The Sacred Path Companion: A Guide to Walking the Labyrinth to Heal and Transform*. New York: Riverhead Books.

Chapter 24

6. Dossey, L. (2011). *Healing Words: The Power of Prayer and the Practice of Medicine*. United States: HarperOne.
7. Dossey, L. (2009). *Reinventing Medicine: Beyond Mind-Body to a New Era of Healing*. United States: HarperOne.

Chapter 25

1. Metzger, Deena, (1993) *Writing for Your Life: A Guide and Companion to the Inner Worlds*. San Francisco, CA: HarperOne.
2. Government report "American nuclear guinea pigs: Three decades of radiation experiments on U.S. citizens," Congressional Subcommittee on Energy Conservation and Power, published in November 1986.
3. "Human Radiation Experiments Associated with the U.S. Department of Energy and Its Predecessors: Oral History of Biophysicist Robed Edmund Rowland, Ph. D.", DOEEH-0491, July 1995. https://inis.iaea.org/collection/

NCLCollectionStore/_Public/27/062/27062022.pdf [Accessed 18th November 2021].

4.   Phil Ferolita, "Russell Jim of Yakama tribe spent decades monitoring Hanford." AP News, June 8, 2017. https://apnews.com/article/2bf0978712ce454e9d-c0d6e2bad2b2ed [Accessed 18th November 2021].

5.   "Facing cancer in Indian country: The Yakama Nation and Pacific Northwest Tribes President's Cancer Panel 2002 annual report." www.loc.gov/item/2005452631/ [Accessed 18th November 2021].

Chapter 26

1.   Mehr, J. J. (2003) *An Illustrated History: Illinois Public Mental Health Services, 1847–2000.* Bloomington, IN: Trafford Publishing.

2.   "Patient deaths at Elgin State Hospital," a report by the Illinois Legislative Commission given to the Illinois General Assembly in 1974. Chicago: The Commission.

3.   Mary Nolte's gravestone: died April 11th 1968.

4.   Briska, William, *The History of Elgin Mental Health Center: Evolution of a State Hospital*, published in 1997.

Chapter 28

1.   Christine Herman, "Prisoners With Mental Illness Still Waiting For Treatment." www.sideeffectspublicmedia.org/access-to-healthcare/2019-01-22/prisoners-with-mental-illness-still-waiting-for-treatment [Accessed 18th November 2021].

Afterword

1.   Ronnberg, A. and Martin, K. (editors) (2010). *The Book of Symbols: Reflections on Archetypal Images.* Cologne: Taschen.

2.   Gheerbrant, A. and Chevalier, J. (editors) (1996). *The Penguin Dictionary of Symbols.* London: Penguin.

References

Barks, C. (2010). *Rumi: The Big Red Book: The Great Masterpiece Celebrating Mystical Love and Friendship*. New York: HarperOne.

Barks, C. and Moyne, J (editors). Jalāl al-Dīn Rūmī (2001). *The Soul of Rumi: A New Collection of Ecstatic Poems*. New York: HarperCollins.

Brown, J. E. (1989). *The Sacred Pipe: Black Elk's Account of the Seven Rites of the Oglala Sioux* (Vol 36). (The Civilization of the American Indian Series). University of Oklahoma Press.

Campbell, J. (2012). *The Hero with a Thousand Faces* (The Collected Works of Joseph Campbell). 3rd edition. Novato, CA: New World Library.

Coleridge, S. T. (2019). *Anima Poetæ from the Unpublished Notebooks of Samuel Taylor Coleridge*. Sheridan, WY: Creative Media Partners.

Colli, J. E. (2014). *The Dark Face of Heaven: True Stories of Transcendence Through Trauma*. [Self-published]: CreateSpace.

Dickinson, E. (1960). *The Complete Poems of Emily Dickinson*, edited by Thomas H. Johnson. 8th Edition. New York: Little, Brown & Company Limited.

Deutsch, A. (1937). *The Mentally Ill in America: A History of Their Care and Treatment from Colonial Times*. New York: Doubleday.

Deutsch, A. (1948). *The Shame of the States*. New York: Harcourt, Brace and Company.

Dossey, B. and Keegan L. (2015) *Holistic Nursing: A Handbook for Practice*. Burlington, MA: Jones & Bartlett Learning.

Eliot, T.S. (1942) *Four Quartets*. New York and London: Faber & Faber.

Emmerson, R. W. (2014). *The Portable Emmerson*, edited by Jeffery S. Cramer. London: Penguin.

Goliszek, A. (2003). *In the Name of Science: A History of Secret Programs, Medical Research, and Human Experimentation*. New York: St. Martin's Press.

Greenberg, J. (1964). *I Never Promised You a Rose Garden*. New York: St. Martin's Press.

Hawthorne, N. (1850). *The Scarlet Letter*. Boston, MA: Ticknor, Reed and Fields.

Harvey, A. (2013). *The Way of Passion: A Celebration of Rumi*. Berkeley, CA: North Atlantic Books.

Herman, C. (2019). "Prisoners with mental illness still waiting for treatment."

Illinois Public Media, 23 January. Available at: will.illinois.edu/news/story/prisoners-with-mental-illness-still-waiting-for-treatment [Accessed on 9th November 2021].

Hornblum, A. M., Newman, J. L., and Dober, G. J. (2013). *Against Their Will: The Secret History of Medical Experimentation on Children in Cold War America*. London: Palgrave Macmillan.

Hornstein, G. A. (2002). *To Redeem One Person Is to Redeem the World: The Life of Frieda Fromm-Reichmann*. New York: Free Press.

Hornstein, G. A. (2009). *Agnes's Jacket: A Psychologist's Search for the Meanings of Madness*. Emmaus, PA: Rodale.

Hornstein, G. A. (2015) *Bibliography of First-Person Narratives of Madness in English*.

Huntington, E. (1935). *Tomorrow's Children: The Goal of Eugenics*. New York: John Wiley & Sons, Inc.

Hutton, F. (editor) (2012). *Rose Lore: Essays in Cultural History and Semiotics*. Germany: Uncut/Voices Press.

Jacobson, A. (2014). *Operation Paperclip: The Secret Intelligence Program that Brought Nazi Scientists to America*. Boston, MA: Little, Brown & Company.

Jung, C.G., *Synchronicity: An Acausal Connecting Principle*. Vol. 8. *The Collected Works of C.G. Jung*. London: Taylor & Francis.

Kadner, P. (2015). "Report: mental health care in crisis in Illinois." *Chicago Tribune*, 28 May. Available at: www.chicagotribune.com/suburbs/daily-southtown/opinion/ct-sta-kadner-mental-st-0529-20150528-story.html [last accessed on 9th November 2021].

Kalsched, D. (2013). *Trauma and the Soul: A Psycho-Spiritual Approach to Human Development and Its Interruption*. New York: Routledge.

Kunitz, S. W. (2000) *The Collected Poems*. New York: W. W. Norton & Company.

Lapon, L. (1986). *Mass Murderers in White Coats: Psychiatric Genocide in Nazi Germany and the United States*. Springfield, MA: Psychiatric Genocide Research Institute.

Lee Godie, Chicago's French Impressionist—a movie by Tom Palazzolo and Kapra Fleming. leegodie.com, Chicago, IL. www.leegodiemovie.com [Accessed 18th November 2021].

Levine, P. A. (2015). *Interoception, Contemplative Practice, and Health*. Vol 6. Article 93. pp. 259. Frontiers Media SA. www.frontiersin.org [Accessed November 2021].

Lilleleht, E. (1997). Discipline and the mad self: Psychiatric rehabilitation, moral treatment, and the chronically mentally ill (Doctoral dissertation, Rutgers University, 1997), *Philosophy, Psychiatry, and Psychology*, 9(2).

Marks, J. D. (1979). *The Search for the "Manchurian Candidate": The CIA and Mind Control, The Secret History of the Behavioral Sciences*. New York: Norton.

Metzger, D. (1993) *Writing for Your Life: A Guide and Companion to the Inner Worlds*. San Francisco, CA: HarperOne.

Murray W.H. (2020). *The Evidence of Things Not Seen: A Mountaineer's Tale*

References

Paperback. Sheffield: Vertebrate Publishing.

Neruda, P. (1988). "If each day falls." In: W. O'Daly (trans.), *The Sea and the Bells* (p. 83). Port Townsend, WA: Copper Canyon Press.

New York Times, December 22, 1995. Available at: https://www.nytimes.com/1995/12/22/us/court-ordered-study-condemns-illinois-s-psychiatric-hospitals.html [Accessed 18th November 2021].

Nin, A. (1966). *The Diary of Anais Nin, 1955-1966,* Edited by Gunther Stuhlmann. New York: Harcourt Brace Jovanovich.

Packard, E. P. W. (1868). *The Prisoners' Hidden Life, or Insane Asylums Unveiled.* Chicago: Published by the author. London: Forgotten Books.

Plummer, W. in *People Magazine,* April 22, 1985, "Baglady artist Lee Godie is a wacky success—her paintings are off the wall and in demand."

Prichard, R. W. (1999). *A History of the Episcopal Church - Revised Edition.* New York: Church Publishing Incorporated.

Rainer, M. R. (1993) *Letters to a Young Poet.* Revised edition. New York: W. W. Norton & Company.

Reiland, R. (2004). *Get Me Out Of Here: My Recovery from Borderline Personality Disorder.* Centre City, MN: Hazelden Publishing

Rilke, R. M. (1957). *Rilke's Book of Hours: Love Poems to God.* London: Vision Press.

Robson, D. (2020) 'Spider smarts, The Intelligence Trap: Revolutionise your thinking and make wiser decisions'. New Scientist, Volume 245, Issue 3268, pages 42-45.

Ross, C. A. (2006). *The CIA Doctors: Human Rights Violations by American Psychiatrists.* Richardson, TX: Manitou Communications.

Skidmore, D. "Sweeping revisions in clergy discipline canons prompt mixed reactions," The Archives of the Episcopal Church Episcopal Press and News https://episcopalarchives.org/cgi-bin/ENS/ENSpress_release.pl?pr_number=96-1386 [Accessed 18th November 2021].

Smith, L. E. (1954). *The Journey.* New York: W. W. Norton & Company.

Stassinopoulos, A. (2013). *Unbinding the Heart.* Carlsbad, CA: Hay House, Inc.

Tick, E. (2005). *War and the Soul.* New York: Quest Books

Tick, E. (2014). *Warrior's Return: Restoring the Soul After Trauma.* Boulder, CO: Sounds True.

Tolkien, J.R.R. (1954) *The Fellowship of the Ring.* London: HarperCollins.

Ulanov, A. B. (2005). *Spirit in Jung.* Einsiedeln: Daimon.

Welty, E. (1971). *One Time, One Place: Mississippi in the Depression.* 2nd edition. Jackson, MS: University Press of Mississippi.

Whitaker, R. (2002). *Mad in America: Bad Science, Bad Medicine, and the Enduring Mistreatment of the Mentally Ill.* New York: Perseus.

Whyte, D. (1992). *Fire in the Earth.* Langley, WA: Many Rivers Press.

Wooden, K. (1976). *Weeping in the Playtime of Others: America's Incarcerated Children.* New York: McGraw-Hill.